T. Usproni   1955

DAUGHTER OF FRANCE

La Grande Mademoiselle, by Pierre Bourguignon. The portrait she holds in a frame is her father, Gaston d'Orléans. The two female figures under the portrait of Gaston represent Mme de Frontenac and Mme de Fiesque

Daughter of France

The life of Anne Marie Louise d'Orléans
duchesse de Montpensier

1627-1693

LA GRANDE MADEMOISELLE

by

V. SACKVILLE-WEST

London
MICHAEL JOSEPH

First published by
MICHAEL JOSEPH LTD
26 Bloomsbury Street
London, W.C.1
APRIL 1959
SECOND IMPRESSION MAY 1959

© *copyright* 1959 *by V. Sackville-West*

Set and printed in Great Britain by Tonbridge Printers Ltd, Peach
Hall Works, Tonbridge, Kent, in Bembo twelve on thirteen point, on
paper made by Henry Bruce at Currie, Midlothian, and bound by
James Burn at Esher, Surrey

FOREWORD

I have many people to thank in connexion with this book, apart from the illustrations which I acknowledge separately.

I should like to thank the late marquis d'Ormesson and Mme d'Ormesson for their warm hospitality at St Fargeau; my friend the vicomte Charles de Noailles for endless help and patience, perpetually pestered by my enquiries; Mlle Cécile de Rothschild who gave me Chéruel's edition of the *Mémoires* of Mlle de Montpensier; Mr G. Heywood Hill who out of his conjurer's hat produced a lot of books I might never otherwise have obtained; Miss Ursula Codrington who so admirably coped with my manuscript and, in the process of typing it, indicated with the utmost tact and delicacy the howlers I had made, the dates I had got wrong, the words I had misspelt, and the repetitions I had inadvertently inserted.

Finally, Raymond Mortimer who said to me many years ago in a French vineyard, 'Why don't you write the life of the Big Miss?'

*　　*　　*　　*

The question of translation has worried me not a little. I deprecate the present-day fashion for rendering the style of a bygone age and a foreign language into colloquial English, still more into colloquial American. It does not seem to me that the rather splendid phrase *prendre les sentiments d'une mauvaise gloire* is in any way faithfully reproduced by *horribly puffed-up*, to take an example at random from a recent biography of la Grande Mademoiselle. Yet at times Mademoiselle and her contemporaries wrote so racily in their own idiom that we must perforce transpose it into our own. How could I translate *gage que non* otherwise than *bet you don't* (page 195 of this book) although *bet you don't* sounds more like an English schoolboy than like Louis XIV.

*   *   *   *

I have therefore adopted two methods. I have translated as close as I could the French of Mademoiselle and her contemporaries, for the benefit of English readers unconversant with the French language. On the other hand I have assumed that the majority of readers will have a working knowledge of French and will appreciate an occasional corroboration in the original words. E.g. I do not see how I could translate *assez vertement* except as *pretty tartly*, which, unsupported, might strike a wrong slangy note.

*   *   *   *

For easy reference and clarification, some brief biographical notes will be found on pages 363-371.

ACKNOWLEDGMENTS FOR ILLUSTRATIONS

My acknowledgments are due to:

HER MAJESTY THE QUEEN, for gracious permission to reproduce the Vandyck portrait of Queen Henrietta Maria, and the drawing of Louis XIV as Apollo.

To the marquis de Ganay for a hitherto unpublished portrait of Mlle de Montpensier. It occurs as the frontispiece in a book once the property of la Grande Mademoiselle, now in his possession.

To the late marquis d'Ormesson and Mme d'Ormesson for the portrait of Mlle de Montpensier with her dogs.

To the Duke of Buccleuch, for the miniature of Mme de Montespan which was stolen from an exhibition in London. Its present whereabouts is now unknown.

To the Director of the Prado, Madrid, for the portraits of Louis XIV as a child; Philippe, duc d'Orléans; Mlle de Montpensier; Maria Teresa and the Dauphin.

To the Musée des Beaux-arts, Orléans, for the picture of the duchesse de Lorraine at the hunt.

To the British Museum, for the print of Mlle de Montpensier and the facsimile of a letter from Charles II.

To the Museum of Fine Arts, Boston, for the portrait of Maria Teresa.

To the Musée de Versailles for the portrait of Mlle de Montpensier (frontispiece).

To the Trustees of the National Gallery for the triple portrait of Cardinal Richelieu.

CONTENTS

Foreword   5

Acknowledgments for Illustrations   7

List of Illustrations   11

    I   Childhood   13

   II Adolescence   43

  III The Regency   63

  IV The Parliamentary Fronde   86

   V The Fronde of the Princes   108

  VI Mademoiselle in Exile   152

 VII Mademoiselle Reinstated   189

VIII Interlude   220

  IX M. de Lauzun   228

   X M. de Lauzun and Mademoiselle   277

  XI Lauzun at Pignerol   298

 XII The End   322

      Epilogue   336

Appendices

      The Baptism of Royal Children   345

      The Designations *Monsieur, Madame,*
        Mademoiselle, etc.   346

      Mademoiselle at the Bastille   347

      St Fargeau   349

      Mademoiselle's Letter to the King   350

      Mme de Sévigné's Letter   351

Translation of Louis XIV's Letter to his
    Representatives at Foreign Courts   352
The Death of Anne of Austria   355
Did Lauzun ever marry Mademoiselle?   357
The Half-Sisters of Mademoiselle   359
Biographical Notes   363
Index   373

ILLUSTRATIONS

La Grande Mademoiselle, by Pierre Bourguignon *frontispiece*

Cardinal Richelieu, by Philippe de Champaigne *page* 32

The Duchess of Lorraine at the Hunt, by Claude Deruet 33

La Grande Mademoiselle. An imaginary reconstruction 64

Louis XIV, King of France, by an anonymous painter 65

Louis XIV as Apollo, by Henri Gissey 128

Queen Henrietta Maria, by Sir Anthony Van Dyck 129

La Grande Mademoiselle, by Jean Nocret 160

The château de St Fargeau 161

The château de St Fargeau 192

La Grande Mademoiselle. An unpublished portrait 193

La Grande Mademoiselle, by Henri de Beaubrun 224

Philippe, duc d'Orléans, by Jean Nocret 225

Maria Teresa, Infanta of Spain, School of Velasquez 256

Maria Teresa and le Grand Dauphin, by Pierre Mignard 257

Charles II to Henrietta 288

Madame de Montespan, by Louis de Châtillon 289

CHAPTER I

Childhood
[1627—1637]

DURING the course of the evening of August the fifth, 1626, in the Chapelle de l'Oratoire at Nantes in Brittany, Cardinal Richelieu solemnised a marriage of grave potential importance to the royal house of France and to France herself. All princely marriages carried a certain weight and portent, particularly when they had been arranged, as was customary, to promote some political purpose or to facilitate an alliance with some foreign Power; but this marriage was exceptional in that it held, as it were, an internally domestic interest for the French. It was a family affair, affecting not only the members of the royal family in their high and separate remoteness, but the entire nation in anticipation of their future ruler. It held this particular interest because the bridegroom, brother of the still childless King, Louis XIII, was Heir-Presumptive to the Throne, and any son begotten of the marriage might in his turn be expected to follow naturally in the succession.

The eighteen-year-old bridegroom was Gaston, duc d'Orléans, commonly known as Monsieur. The twenty-year-old bride was Marie de Bourbon, duchesse de Montpensier in her own right, and the richest heiress in France. The youthful duke and his duchess might therefore appear to be embarking jointly upon the sunlit sea of a golden future, in which gaiety, romance, and power should be nicely blended, but under the outward semblance the facts were very different.

The wedding ceremony itself, for some reason, does not

seem to have been celebrated with the splendour exacted by so portentous an occasion. Certainly, the King and the Queen were present, also the Queen-Mother, surrounded by the entire Court; and that must have meant something, in purely decorative terms, at a date when the men of such a company rivalled the women in the finery of their apparel. The formidable Cardinal-dictator was there, presiding in the sumptuous fuchsia-coloured robes of a Prince of the Church over the nuptial rites of a Prince of the Blood. We may set aside for the moment the question whether he was or was not the lover of the Queen-Mother, that foolish and voluptuous Florentine, Marie de' Medici. The meek bride herself, suitably attired in white satin, had been bedecked in addition to her own pearls with further rows of pearls lent to her for the occasion by the two Queens, so without any unnecessary exercise of the imagination it may be assumed that a certain magnificence pervaded the scene in the small chapel. No music sounded, however; and the bridegroom had even omitted to equip himself with a new suit of clothes. According to a member of Monsieur's household, a sadder wedding never was seen. Even such dignity as the proceedings possessed was marred by a most unseemly incident, when two of the Court ladies, bearers of historic names, the duchesse de Rohan and the duchesse d'Halluin, came to blows over a question of precedence in the procession, Mme de Rohan being determined to thrust her way in front and Mme d'Halluin equally determined to frustrate any such intention. The argument quickly developed into a free fight; both duchesses pushed and scratched (*elles en vinrent aux poussades et aux égratignures*), until someone intervened with the decision that the Duchy of Halluin enjoyed the older date of creation. Order was restored, allowing the ceremony to proceed and ending a ridiculous episode only too typical in its vulgarity and frivolity of the curiously contradictory standards of behaviour of those times.

Behind these absurdities lay a deeper tragedy, bloodstained and inauspicious, which made the background of the marriage and took its origin in the deplorable character of the bride-groom. Gaston d'Orléans comes down into history as a weak, treacherous figure, ready to enter into intrigues and equally ready to betray his accomplices whenever it suited him to do so. The first of many betrayals had taken place during the spring preceding the marriage (May 1626) and may briefly be related here as illustrative of the storm growling always beneath the outward glitter and amorous gaiety of the Court, and also of Monsieur's irresponsible, unreliable nature.

The plot which had originated amongst some of the princes and nobles, resentful of the supremacy of Richelieu, had for its object the assassination of the Cardinal. Monsieur was not slow in becoming involved; his own tutor, the maréchal d'Ornano, passionately in love with Marie de Montpensier, was one of the leading spirits; and another conspirator, the duc de Vendôme, Gaston's own illegitimate half-brother, went so far as to write that 'the Crown would sit well on Monsieur's head.' There is no evidence to suggest that Gaston seriously entertained any desire to overthrow the King, but after all he *was* Monsieur, Heir-Presumptive to a very sickly monarch, and it required far less shrewdness than he possessed to perceive the advantages of putting a preponderant prelate out of the way. The Throne, if he ever came to occupy it, would be a more comfortable and roomy place, unshared by the invisible but very real presence of so intransigeant an authority. Gaston, in his light-hearted way, was tempted into allowing his name to be mentioned as the titular ringleader, supported by d'Ornano, the two brothers Vendôme, the prince de Condé,[1] the duc de Longueville, the duc d'Épernon, the comte de Soissons, and a romantic young man of twenty-seven, Henri de Talleyrand, marquis de Chalais, foolish enough to join the conspirators in order to please his mistress the duchesse de Chevreuse, that beautiful, adventurous and dazzling woman of whom it was said that her ideas were 'so brilliant they seemed like flashes of lightning, yet so saga-cious that no great man in any century would have disavowed

[1] Henri de Bourbon, father of le Grand Condé.

them.' She was, moreover, the most intimate friend of the Queen, Anne of Austria; and the Queen, as Richelieu's sworn enemy, could not fail to be implicated in the plot. The Queen's motives were further complicated by her desire to prevent the marriage between Marie de Montpensier and Monsieur, fearing that her own position might suffer from the introduction of a young princess likely to bear children, whereas she herself had remained barren for over ten years. This was on her own frank admission, but in an age of superstition and of complete cynicism as to worldly self-interest other rumours were naturally current. It was said that certain astrologers had foretold the early death of the King, and from there was but a step to the conclusion that the Queen would then retain her crown by the simple expedient of marrying Monsieur. One might add in, for good value, that the Queen-Mother ardently favoured the Montpensier alliance, in itself almost sufficient reason for her daughter-in-law to oppose it.

The group of high personages, working in the dark, either took insufficient precautions or else underestimated the efficiency of Richelieu's secret service. Rumours reached the ears of the Cardinal, who without troubling to institute even the shadow of an enquiry, flung d'Ornano into the fortress of Vincennes. At this, Chalais took fright; went in person to seek Richelieu; revealed the whole story; offered to turn spy; and warned the Cardinal that on the following day he was destined to lose his life at a banquet in the presence of Monsieur. Richelieu retaliated by throwing the two Vendôme brothers into prison,[1] and by confronting Monsieur with the King.

The collapse of Monsieur was complete. A fortnight later he was to be found at the Cardinal's own house at Limours, appending his signature to the following document: 'I, Gaston, brother of the King, recognise the evil intentions of those who, in my name, have desired to trouble the State. I declare that I

---

[1] César duc de Vendôme remained in prison for four years, and was deprived for ever of his governorship of Brittany. We mention this detail only as an instance of the high-handed way in which Richelieu proceeded against the ambitious nobility when opportunity offered.

promise to die sooner than to follow their counsels and at the same time to reveal all facts which come to my knowledge, calculated to disturb the peace of the State. In addition, I will entertain a sincere affection for all those whom His Majesty may honour with his confidence.' That meant Richelieu. As a reward for this humiliating declaration, Gaston received the Duchies of Orléans[1] and of Chartres, the County of Blois, an income of a hundred thousand *livres*, a pension of five hundred and sixty thousand *livres*, and (as a sop to his somewhat childish vanity) an escort of eighty guards in velvet liveries embroidered with his initials in gold. The Cardinal had triumphed, but Monsieur had also known very well what he was about.

Unfortunately for his accomplices, or at least for those who were still at liberty, they were determined not to lie down under this reverse. Mme de Chevreuse was far too mettlesome and meddlesome a woman to accept defeat. Exploiting her influence over young Chalais, she induced him to approach Gaston in the course of nocturnal meetings with the suggestion that Gaston should hurry to La Rochelle or possibly to Metz, putting himself at the head of the Huguenots, and claiming the Throne. It is difficult to understand the folly of Gaston in lending himself for a second time to such reckless and ill-considered proposals, after his recent lesson and after the prodigious benefits that he, as an unimpeachable prince, had managed to secure as the price of his loyalty from the King and the Cardinal. He was risking everything; and one wonders why. Perhaps biographers and historians are too much inclined to attribute rational reasons to the conduct of the dead and gone, who are no longer there to be questioned and cross-examined, and must be judged on the insufficient and probably misrepresenting evidence of contemporary documents. Human motives and impulses being erratic and unanalysable in the extreme, even in ourselves and in those we profess to know

---

[1] Gaston had become duc d'Orléans on the death of an elder brother fifteen years previously, in 1611, but was not confirmed in the title until his marriage.

best, how shall we arbitrate at several centuries' remove, when, furthermore, the whole mental and ethical climate differs so totally from our own?

When Richelieu received information of this new development, Chalais was promptly placed under arrest and Gaston as promptly reappeared with fresh revelations and fresh concessions. He now declared his willingness to marry Mlle de Montpensier, an alliance he had previously resisted, provided he might retain his fiefs, his augmented revenues, and his position of restored favour at Court. It was a bargain. The fate of his friends was, as always, of the utmost indifference to him. Mme de Chevreuse was only sent into exile, but Chalais was brought to trial on a charge of high treason, a trial which was still in progress at the time of Gaston's marriage and which culminated in an execution of the most bungling ferocity. True, the King, less callous than his brother, had placed his veto on the application of torture, and on the authority of his doctor we are informed that he lay shuddering through a sleepless night, nor was he or Richelieu to blame if everything went wrong at the end for the miserable victim. When the time came for Chalais to mount the scaffold, it was found that the professional executioner had disappeared. Two common prisoners were produced and bribed with the promise of liberation if they would fulfil the headsman's duty. Not being experienced swordsmen, they were provided with a cooper's axe in place of a sword, but even with this clumsy weapon it was only at the thirty-fourth stroke that they managed to sever the mangled head from the shoulders.

As an additional touch of horror, the young man's mother attended him upon the scaffold.

Meanwhile it was observed that Monsieur excelled himself in his usual light-hearted gaiety during the fêtes and parties which inevitably followed his wedding. The wedded pair had been escorted to their rooms according to custom, the King

handing a night-shirt to his brother and then leading him into
the nuptial chamber where the Queen and the Queen-Mother
had been occupied in putting the bride to bed. Quiet descended
upon the house; Their Majesties had retired to rest, the ladies
and gentlemen of the Court likewise, when it is legitimate to
suppose that some whisperings and suppressed laughter took
place in many darkened bedrooms over the chances of a future
King of France being conceived that night. The age was not
notable for its prudery or delicacy. The propitious quiet was
suddenly interrupted: this marriage which had been celebrated
without joy, enthusiasm or music, between a reluctant bridegroom and a bride 'with a sheep-like face and a character to
match,' was destined in its earliest hours of consummation to
be farcically frustrated, when the bride's mother irrupted without warning in pursuit of a little yapping dog which had got
shut in by mistake.

This was just the kind of jest best calculated to please the
coarse and not very witty taste of the Court. Monsieur himself
can hardly have failed to appreciate it, whatever his bride may
have thought or may have said to her mother next day. 'Very
amenable and well-behaved (*très douce et très sage*),' it seems
unlikely that she had the spirit to say much. Perhaps she aimed
a surreptitious kick at the dog.

Little dog notwithstanding, a child was born at the Louvre
nine months and fourteen days later (May 29, 1627). The baby
who then entered this world of intrigue, violence and treachery
disappointed her parents and the whole realm of France by
being a daughter instead of a son, and moreover cost her
mother her life. Anne Marie Louise d'Orléans, officially known
as Mademoiselle, was only a week old when the dim and docile
sheep-faced Madame passed for ever away.[1]

A brief little entry in the journal of the King's physician

[1] She never had very much choice in life. At the age of two, she had been betrothed
to an elder brother of Gaston's; and when he died aged four, her hand was transferred
to Gaston, then aged three.

records: 'He [the King] went to the Louvre to see Madame die.'
('*Voir expirer Madame.*')[1].

Nicolas Goulas, gentleman-in-waiting to Monsieur, thought
the new-born princess so red in the face and ugly that he could
scarcely bear to look at her, but the duc de Bellegarde tried to
flatter her father by telling him that she was the most charming
thing in the world and much resembled him. Gaston had the
good sense and wit to reply, 'Do not say that, for if my
daughter were to resemble me she would go straight to the
ramparts.' This was a colloquial expression meaning the dis-
reputable haunts with which Gaston was only too familiar,
thanks to his nocturnal escapades, often in disguise, with a few
wrongly-chosen companions.

He little knew, then, how truly he spoke, in quite another
sense, of his daughter going to the ramparts, as little as any
parent can foresee the future of the new, mysterious, precarious
entity 'whose only language is a cry.'

Mademoiselle was carried from the Louvre to the Tuileries
and installed under the central dome with its view over the
garden, and the view across the uncultivated waste then known
as the Rabbit-warren (now the Place de la Concorde). Although
of the wrong sex and thus not in line of succession to the
Throne, since the Salic law forbade a woman to succeed,
Mademoiselle was nevertheless a very important baby, the most
important in France, as she was also the richest. Her hand
would, in future, hold great value for bargaining, and her
monogram which presently appeared carved in stucco on the
four little towers flanking her nursery, proclaimed the bearer of
the longest string of titles ever to burden so tiny a female
creature in its cot. Mademoiselle, in her own right, as her
mother's sole heiress, was duchesse de Montpensier, Châtellerault, and St Fargeau, souveraine de Dombes, princesse de
Joinville and Laroche-sur-Yon, and dauphine d'Auvergne.
But perhaps the proudest title she ever claimed was *Fille de*

---

[1] *Journal de Jean Hérouard*, Vol. II, p. 310.

France. It was the privilege of the Princes and Princesses of the Blood to be known as *Enfants de France*, and of the younger generation of the daughters of France Mademoiselle occupied the first rank. Strictly speaking, she was really a *Petite-fille*, i.e. the grand-daughter not the daughter of a king, but as she herself usually elected to ignore the distinction I have thought it forgivable, although inaccurate, posthumously to indulge her in this little weakness. Intensely French, and intensely conscious of her royal birth, nothing could have been better designed to give her satisfaction.

Unaware of all this for the moment, she was also unaware that she was immensely rich (in fact the greatest heiress in France if not in Europe), and that the household provided for her must in all ways be worthy of her wealth and rank. In later years, she remarked with complacency that no other Daughter of France had ever been so lavishly treated, not even her own aunts the Queens of Spain and England and the duchesse de Savoie. At the head of this household stood *ma gouvernante*, Jeanne de Harlay, marquise de St Georges. Below Mme de St Georges in the hierarchy of the nursery came Mlle Sauvat the *sous-gouvernante*; then a certain Dame Simonne whose duty was to rock the cradle and attend to Mademoiselle's natural functions; a wet-nurse; seven personal maids to look after Mademoiselle's clothes and linen; and a dressmaker. All this feminine cohort must have servitors to wait upon them: Mme de St Georges had two personal maids and two footmen; the *sous-gouvernante* had one personal maid and one footman; Mademoiselle's seven personal maids had two footmen in addition to a man to wait at their table; and the wet-nurse had someone who is described as *maréchal de la nourrice*. There was also a *huissier de chambre* to whom was entrusted the responsible task of carrying Mademoiselle about. If he had dropped her, this biography might never have been written.

In the kitchens were five cooks and scullions, which does not sound excessive for so large an establishment, but to them we must add bakers, cellarers, and three men in charge of the fruit.

One laundry-maid does not sound excessive either, and perhaps throws a light on the small demand of cleanliness exacted by our forbears in the seventeenth century.

There was an almoner, a clerk of the chapel, a doctor, pages and footmen, a porter, a footman for the porter, two archers, a coachman and a postillion, eight carriage horses and two saddle horses, and two men charged with the curious duty of impounding lost and strayed animals.

In control of all this rabble, of which the foregoing list is by no means complete, were various officers chiefly concerned with Mademoiselle's finances and the administration of her houses and estates, two secretaries and a treasurer. It was an establishment fit for a princess.

Amongst all these functionaries the one who naturally exercised the greatest influence on Mademoiselle's development was the *gouvernante* Mme de St Georges. This kindly and well-meaning lady may be described as one of those personages always to be found on the fringes of any Court. She seemed destined to inherit the function of a royal governess almost by hereditary right. Her mother, the marquise de Montglat, had been governess to all the royal children of the previous generation, that is to say the children of Henri IV and Marie de' Medici: *Nos Seigneurs et Dames les Enfants de France*: Louis XIII himself, whose nickname for her was Mamanga (Maman Montglat), a brother who died when he was only four, Gaston d'Orléans, and the three princesses, one of whom, Henrietta Maria, Mme de St Georges had accompanied to England as a lady-in-waiting on her marriage to Charles I. The appointment in Mademoiselle's household waited as a ripe plum for Mme de St Georges.

To do Mme de St Georges justice, she succeeded in winning the affection of her small charge as thoroughly as her mother had won the affections of Mademoiselle's uncles, father, and aunts. Unfortunately, as a mentor she failed to win her respect. Mademoiselle, who Heaven knows was foolish enough in many ways, and who Heaven knows was exaggeratedly imbued with a sense of her own importance, nevertheless retained sufficient shrewdness to perceive that a little more severity and a good deal less flattery in early youth would have done her a world of good. Mme de St Georges, with her courtly outlook, was not the woman wisely to counterbalance the adulation crawling like treacle round the little girl. Somewhat smugly, but also very sensibly, Mademoiselle later remarked that if she could lay claim to any good qualities, they must be in-born, in no way due to her upbringing, for she had never had occasion to apprehend the slightest reproof. In retrospect she could see clearly that sycophants had conspired to pour a continuous flow of honeyed words into her ears, but what chance had she, as a child growing up in circumstances of such luxury and grandeur, herself the centre of her miniature Court, to preserve any reasonable balance or sense of proportion? It must be difficult enough, even in our democratic days, to safeguard the princeling from the consequences of his birth. No one tried to safeguard Mademoiselle. On the contrary, everyone and every-thing encouraged her toddling footsteps along the path of the highest snobbish level. How could she fail to respond? If any-one talked to her about her maternal grandmother, the duchesse de Guise, she would disdainfully reply, 'She is only remotely my grandmother: she is not a Queen.'

The King and Queen, that sad couple, manifested a genuine affection for their small niece, and came frequently to visit her down the long gallery which united the Tuileries to the Louvre. Mademoiselle called them *mon petit papa* and *ma petite maman*, pathetically persuading herself that the Queen really was her mother, though as she also called Mme de St Georges *maman* some confusion must have resulted in that searching little brain. She knew very well that the King was not her father, since she had a real father, an unworthy object on which she lavished all her adoration. Her natural craving for affection fastened indes-tructibly upon Gaston. She was of no age to judge his true character—that was a revelation to come painfully with advancing years—but knew him only as a blithe play-fellow, always ready for a game with her in the atmosphere of frivolity he created around him. Possibly his somewhat feline evasiveness held an unconscious attraction for her. Some people prefer cats and their slinky undevoted ways, to the solid reliability of dogs. Charming when he was there, you could not be certain of finding him again on the morrow. Mademoiselle, although she might also sense his fundamental instability, was aware that his sudden disappearances were sometimes involuntary, and in her childish mind the blame rested, not on *mon bon Papa*, or on his own feckless, conspiratorial behaviour, but on that sinister figure in red, that ogre, Cardinal Richelieu.

Thus, after a certain November day in 1630 (November 11th, *la journée des Dupes*) she noticed that Monsieur had vanished from Paris and the Court. She was not yet four, and scarcely noticed the simultaneous departure of her grandmother the Queen-Mother, even though that lady had owned a parrot and a dwarf to look after it,[1] but the eclipse of the gay Gaston made so profound an impression that she cast about for some explanation and eventually found it, though by what agency it entered her head she does not relate. Perhaps one of her numerous attendants, perhaps Mme de St Georges herself, let fall some injudicious remarks in her presence; perhaps the whispering gallery of a palace sufficed to sink a sediment of truth on to the floor of that devoted small heart. What Mademoiselle did not know was that not only had Gaston and his mother conspired to overthrow the Cardinal, but that Gaston, frustrated, was now guilty of the even more heinous crime of treachery towards his own country. He had taken refuge with the duc de Lorraine, an ally of France's enemy the House of Hapsburg, and was now inciting him to give all the support in his power to the cause of Spain and the Holy Roman

---

[1] Marie de' Medici never returned to France; she fled to Brussels, England, and Antwerp, and died destitute in July 1642 at Cologne, in a house which Peter Paul Rubens had lent her. Rubens had done much work for her when she was Queen of France; in her old age he was not ungrateful.

Empire. What Mademoiselle did know, as a plain immediate fact, was that the Cardinal had sent her father away, was keeping him away, and was even objecting to his recent marriage (January 1632) with the sister of the duc de Lorraine, Marguerite, because the Cardinal wanted to marry his own niece, Mlle de Combalet, to Gaston. That was how Mademoiselle saw it. This interference with her father's private affairs added to her indignation. Nothing if not loyal, she wept whenever she heard the subject mentioned, and, far from resenting the introduction of an unknown stepmother, was constantly begging people to tell her something more about her.

Gaston could have had no more faithful adherent nor the Cardinal a more implacable enemy. Mademoiselle savagely took her revenge in the only way she could think of, by learning anti-Cardinal street-songs and lampoons by heart, and singing them in a shrill childish voice, probably excruciatingly out of tune, up and down the corridors of the Tuileries and the Louvre. These lampoons and street-songs, in the first decades of seventeenth-century France, when no newspapers existed, took the place of what we should now call the gutter press. Their frankness of expression is the more remarkable when we consider the awe in which the King (symbol of Monarchy) and his First Minister (symbol of delegated authority) were held. It would be putting it mildly to describe them as malapert. The citizens of Paris, always irreverent even towards the objects of their adoration, picked them up as they streamed from the facile pens of the gutter poets. Mademoiselle, that little Parisian-born princess, picked them up also and sang them with real venom. Whether or not Richelieu's attention was ever drawn to these gadfly activities, he held his hand for the moment: the time had not yet come for him to summon Mademoiselle to a full-dress scolding.

In spite of her cares and sorrows, Mademoiselle who was sociable by nature contrived to enjoy herself in the company of her numerous young friends. These *filles de qualité* were all much of an age: mesdemoiselles de Longueville, d'Épernon, de Brissac, de Jarnac, de Brianne, du Lude; the daughters of the duc de Gramont, and many others. Mme de St Georges evidently believed more in encouraging the sound of their laughter in the Tuileries, now for the first time occupied by a royal child, than in supervising the education of her pupil. She believed, with Richelieu, that the art of women should consist of modesty and reserve. Mademoiselle learned to read and write—very badly—and that was about all. Some early letters of hers are still in existence in the *Bibliothèque nationale*; they are short, imperative, polite and to the point. 'Monsieur Goulas, please send my watches soon and believe me always your best friend. D'Orléans.'[1]

Mme de St Georges ignored, or pretended to ignore, the close proximity of the hôtel de Rambouillet and of its famous *salon* created by the social genius of its owner the incomparable Arthénice, in her celebrated blue drawing-room, *la chambre bleue*. No one had thought of painting a room blue before—the orthodox colours were red or brown—no one had thought of mixing high society with eminent men of letters and even with the poverty-stricken riff-raff of their less successful brethren.[2] To be given the *entrée* of the blue drawing-room it was necessary only to be very amusing or very distinguished, preferably the former, and, if possible, both. The poet Malherbe, for instance, one of the earliest feathers in Mme de Rambouillet's cap, was tolerated for his verses and for his pointful comments, but was thought 'boorish and uncivil,' and abrupt in conversation. The great Corneille himself, who came to read his latest plays to an attentive circle, felt himself to be a failure: he read badly, could not decipher his own writing, and possessed no wit to compensate for his deficiencies. On the other hand, they endured Ménage for the sake of his vast if pedantic knowledge

[1] It may puzzle English readers to find Mademoiselle signing her letter 'D'Orléans' as though she were an English peer. Why not by her Christian name, Anne Marie Louise? The explanation is too long to put into a footnote, so I refer the interested reader to Appendix I on pp. 345-346.

[2] We should perhaps remember two precursors, the maréchale de Retz in the sixteenth century, and Marguerite de Valois, *la reine Margot*, who died in 1615.

(he is the original of Vadius in Molière's *Femmes Savantes*) in spite of his conceit and his disgusting habit of cleaning his teeth with a dirty handkerchief; and the pygmy little Voiture, vain and irrepressible, who amused them all with his disrespectful sallies, until one day he went too far and arrived accompanied by a couple of bears. Not that Mme de Rambouillet and her contemporaries objected to practical jokes of the crudest description; they did not seem in the least incompatible with scintillating discussions on subjects ranging from literature, love, and war, to the recently discovered spots on the sun. Solemnity was not allowed to govern the meetings at the hôtel de Rambouillet; music, dancing, and fancy-dress were encouraged; Mlle d'Argennes was not above arranging a booby-trap on top of a door to pour water on Voiture's head, and when the comte de Guiche was observed to over-eat himself at dinner at a country house party, they amused themselves by putting a tuck in his clothes during the night, so that he was unable to fasten them round his waist in the morning.

Mme de Rambouillet herself, the presiding genius, that remarkable woman, spoke both Spanish and Italian, learnt Latin in order to read Virgil in the original, had seven children, and, although no prude, imposed a certain discipline upon her guests: her disapproval of coarse words, current in the speech of the time, was known and respected, also her dislike of noise and of any rough manners which might impair the climate of exquisite courtesy and intellectual distinction she desired in the *chambre bleue*. Physically delicate, she could not endure the heat of a fire, which made her faint, so in order to protect herself and yet not to deprive her guests of comfort, she evolved an arrangement which was to have a surprising effect upon the habits of aristocratic France for at least a hundred and fifty years. This was a kind of day-bed in an alcove, where she could nestle under a bearskin, and either take part in the general conversation or summon a favoured visitor to her side. Here, in her richly-furnished drawing-room, hung with brocade, the floor spread with Oriental rugs, lit by a fifteen-branched silver

chandelier with scented candles, she watched the reputations of
Paris being made and un-made, little knowing that her couch
in its alcove would soon be copied in all the ladies' bedrooms
from the Queen's downwards and would become the familiar
receiving-ground where many confidences were exchanged,
many tears shed, and many an intrigue hatched. A name had to
be given to the innovation, and no less a person than Malherbe
provided it: *la ruelle*, or little street.[1]

Had Mme de St Georges come under the influence of Mme
de Rambouillet and her heterogenous circle, the education of
Mademoiselle might have been conducted along very different
lines. As it was, she grew up knowing no more of intellectual
life and learning than she knew of the stinking, narrow streets
of Paris within its sixteen guarded gates. Only four years
before Mademoiselle's birth an English poet, Sir John Suckling,
had thus described it:

> I came to Paris on the Seine;
> 'Twas wondrous fair, but little clean;
> 'Tis Europe's greatest town.
> How strange it is, I need not tell it,
> For all the world may easily smell it
> As they pass up and down.

But the Tuileries where Mademoiselle lived stood practically
on the edge of the country; she could drive out towards the
Bois de Boulogne without seeing anything of that swarming
labyrinth where the tall houses almost met overhead and where
even such residential streets as the rue de Venise did not exceed
a metre and half in width.[2] Here the population of some five

---

[1] This, at least, is the currently accepted attribution. I doubt its accuracy. The
expression was already in use before Mme de Rambouillet established her famous
couch. See, for instance, a letter from Louis XIII (then the Dauphin) to his father,
April 1606: *Ils étaient tous en un tas dans la ruelle de maman. Je les ai bien éveillés avec
mon tambour.'*

[2] The main thoroughfares, leading to the gates, were wider, five to eight metres,
but these were few in comparison with the six hundred streets estimated in a survey
of Paris, 1639.

hundred thousand, miserably housed, overcrowded, jostled amongst the stream of horses, mules, donkeys, and even pigs, shoved aside to make way for a carrying-chair or, worse still, a coach, with all the accompaniment of collisions, shouts of abuse, and the splashing of the unspeakable mud over the passers-by.

The mud of these unpaved streets, familiarly known as *la crotte*, incessantly churned up by wheels, feet and hooves, received lavish contributions from the droppings of innumerable animals, also from the slops emptied from upper windows, and was never cleared away. Various attempts were made by Louis XIII to institute a public service of cleaners, but either the task was beyond human power or his orders were disregarded: the *crotte* remained, and with the *crotte* remained the stench. How could it be otherwise, when to ordinary mud you added animal and human excrement, heaps of decaying vegetables, entrails thrown out of the butchers' shops, rivulets and gutters running with animal and human urine? Louis XIII, as a little boy of three, returning from St Cloud to Paris, carried in his litter into the faubourg St Honoré, had been so overcome by the smell of the ditch (*la puanteur du ruisseau*) that they had to hold a handkerchief soaked in vinegar under his nose. 'Mamanga,' he had said to Mme de Montglat, 'I smell something nasty.'[1]

It may seem incredible that such a state of affairs should be tolerated in a Paris where gentlemen and ladies went dressed in silks and satins and the observance of courtly manners was so highly esteemed, but what else could be expected when people thought nothing of relieving themselves on the staircases and in the corridors of the Louvre itself, and even the Queen's own gentleman-in-waiting, the comte de Brancas, could drop the Queen's hand *pour aller pisser contre la tapisserie*?

Mademoiselle was growing up: she was seven. Fair-haired, fair-skinned, with blue eyes, her big Bourbon nose not yet

[1] *Journal de Jean Hérouard*, Vol. I, p. 81.

over-emphasised, high-spirited, full of fun, she was naturally
the centre of the privileged children at the Tuileries, wildly
playing their games of hide-and-seek or blind-man's buff, but,
she tells us, never so entirely taken up with the game as not to
listen whenever she overheard her father's affairs being discussed. At last the longed-for day arrived when Monsieur
having made his peace with the King and the Cardinal by his
usual method of renouncing and denouncing his friends,
promising 'to take no further interest in his former associates . . .
or to advance any cause for complaint should they suffer
according to their deserts at the King's hands,' crept back to
France, after some delay, fully reinstated in possession of all his
titles and estates. Mademoiselle trundled off in her big coach to
meet him at Limours (October 1634) and leaves a charming
description of their reunion. Gaston could not believe that
after so long an absence she would recognise him, so, having
removed his blue ribbon of the St Esprit, he mingled with the
crowd of his courtiers. Mademoiselle was brought in and they
asked her which was Monsieur. 'Without hesitating a moment,
I flung myself into his arms.'

Gaston spared no pains to entertain his small daughter. He
could lightly shake off all recollection of the humiliations to
which he had been exposed, he could forget his exiled mother
and his new wife whom he had temporarily left behind him, he
could shut his eyes to the fate of his supporters and confederates,
and could enter with zest into the pleasures of civilised life with
Mademoiselle tripping beside him. She says herself that at that
age she could put everyone into a good humour. She has many
stories to tell of the next three or four years when she was on
and off in his company; how, on learning that she loved dancing,
he organised a ballet of little girls (*princesses et autres de qualité*)
with the gentlemen of his court for partners; birds were released
into the ballroom, when one of them became entangled in the
fluting of Mlle de Maillé-Brézé's ruff, and she screamed and
cried so loudly that the laughter redoubled. 'You may judge
thereby,' says Mademoiselle, 'the age of these ladies of the

ballet.' Poor Mlle de Brézé, she seemed destined to figure as a butt and buffoon at any party she attended. Tiny of stature, with the smallest waist in the world, they mounted her on such high heels that she fell, in the presence of the King, the Queen, and the whole Court, while dancing a *coranto* at a ball given in honour of her own engagement:[1] more laughter, in which her fiancé joined; and so childish was she that two years after her marriage she was still playing with dolls, and had to be sent to a convent to learn to read and write. In such contempt was she held by the strange and merciless Condé family, that Mademoiselle took pity on her and endured her devotion and her visits, 'although for my part I got no pleasure from them.' This was all the kinder of her, because Mlle de Brézé was a niece of the hated Cardinal, and goes to show how warm-hearted and compassionate Mademoiselle could be.

The ballet of the little girls, which Mademoiselle called the dance of the pygmies, by no means exhausted the round of amusements which her father's return had brought into her life. She always loved travelling about (*la joie que j'avais à me promener*), and since Monsieur was now living principally at his château of Blois Mademoiselle accompanied by Mme de St Georges was able to make a kind of triumphal progress through France towards the Loire, fêted in every house she stopped at, attending the marriage of a gardener at Montglat, paying her respects to the King and Queen at Chantilly on the way, then passing through Fontainebleau, received by officers at Pithiviers, the first town on her father's estates, and met by her father himself at his other château of Chambord. They were no museums then, those famous châteaux of the Loire, but full of life and movement, to which Mademoiselle and Monsieur added their own. Mademoiselle had been overjoyed by the summons to rejoin her father, and had written to say so. '*Mon bon papa*, I am dying of joy to obey your command, and will start on Monday, *mon bon papa*.' (August 29, 1637.) She was

[1] To the duc d'Enghien, later the Grand Condé.

much struck by Chambord. 'There is a staircase, so constructed that one person may go up while another comes down, without meeting although they can see one another. Monsieur amused himself by playing a trick on me. He was at the top when I arrived; he came down as I went up, and laughed heartily to see me running as I tried to catch him.'

From Chambord they drove together in his coach to Blois. The château of Blois, not ancient enough to be regarded as an antiquity but just old enough to be considered old-fashioned, had narrowly escaped destruction at Gaston's hands. Someone had suggested to him that he might pull down all the part built by Charles d'Orléans and François I, and replace it by something more up to date. Fortunately, he got no further than pulling down what remained of the wing erected by Charles d'Orléans. Mademoiselle was very happy at Blois. She had friends to play with, her cousins the young ducs de Mercœur and de Beaufort and their sister Mlle de Vendôme,[1] but above all she had her father, who entered into all her amusements, playing battledore-and-shuttlecock with her and always contriving to let her win. Mademoiselle saw through this little deception more readily than she saw through some of his major deceptions, but made no bones about accepting her prize of a watch or some jewel from the shops in the town. He was indeed a kind father. When Mademoiselle was put to bed at seven, which she evidently resented but conceded as reasonable at her age, he would come to her room and tell her stories of his past adventures (one wonders how much he left out) 'with all the grace and natural facility he possessed in expressing himself,' and would talk to her about her unknown stepmother, with whom Mademoiselle was now exchanging letters, and would even allow himself to be persuaded to describe how he had fallen in love. (Here one must wonder again how much he drew upon his imagination, for Gaston's tastes, like his brother the King's, were more apt to turn towards persons of his own sex.) His

---

[1] Sons and daughter of César, duc de Vendôme, an illegitimate son of Henri IV and Gabrielle d'Estrées, and consequently a half-brother of Gaston d'Orléans.

Cardinal Richelieu, by Philippe de Champaigne

The Duchess of Lorraine at the Hunt, by Claude Deruet (1588–1660). Painted for the Cabinet de la Reine in the château de Richelieu, c. 1641–42

affection for his second wife, however, appears to have been genuine. And when he was away from Blois he would arrange expeditions for Mademoiselle; he took her to Amboise himself, for the feast of St Hubert, and to Chenonceaux which belonged to the duc de Vendôme and which she thought most extraordinary, standing as it did partly surrounded by the waters of the River Cher, impressive in its way, and containing a very curious room all painted black, with bones, tombs, and tears for decoration; but in Mademoiselle's opinion some of the rooms needed a little money spent on them for repainting and regilding. She went twice to Chenonceaux, once with Monsieur and once without him, but this was not the limit of her travels; escorted by Mme de St Georges and other ladies, also by a suitable posse of horsemen, she went to the abbey of Fontevrault, where she was received by her aunt the Abbess, an illegitimate daughter of Henri IV and Charlotte des Essarts, saw a naked mad-woman, which entranced her, had a nasty supper which annoyed her, discovered that by virtue of her birth she had the right to be followed into the abbey by all the men of her suite, which gratified her, and insisted on leaving because she was bored when she found that the supply of mad women had run out.

She went also to Richelieu, that wood-ash coloured village in Poitou, where the visitor may still see the remains of the noble park but nothing save the entrance-lodge of the palace and pavilions the Cardinal had built in the place from which he took the title of his dukedom. Mademoiselle, clearly an observant child, noted the beautiful street, *une fort belle rue*, with its houses all of the same design, of recent construction to her eyes though not to ours. In her honour every window in the little town and in the château showed a coloured light from paper lanterns; she must have been becoming accustomed to the demonstrations made everywhere for her reception, but they never seem to have palled on her. Although she leaves a long and detailed description of the magnificent monument Richelieu had raised to his own glory, she refrains with unaccustomed restraint from any back-handed comment on its creator, save to call him the most ambitious and proudest man in the world.

There must, all the same, in the midst of this delightful life have been moments when doubts crossed Mademoiselle's innocent mind. There was, for instance, the episode of Louison Roger, who lived at Tours and for whom Monsieur had what Mademoiselle calls an inclination. How was she to reconcile this with the romance that she had woven round her father's bride, the absent stepmother? It was very agreeable to drift down the great slow Loire from Blois to Tours in Monsieur's galley 'which lacked nothing proper to a real boat at sea,' but what was she to do about Louison when she got there, Louison, that strong brown girl of sixteen, who was intelligent enough, certainly, considering that she had never been at Court? Never to have been at Court amounted to social condemnation in Mademoiselle's eyes. Monsieur could not say enough in her praise, and wished his daughter to accept her as a play-fellow. Mademoiselle, who was then ten and had probably overheard in Paris more than was intended for her ears, was deeply troubled. 'Maman,' she said to Mme de St Georges, 'if Louison is not a good girl, I don't want to see her, even if my papa does love her; and if he insists on my seeing her, I shall not make her welcome.' Reassured, she yielded, and even became quite fond of Louison. So fond did Monsieur become, that Louison in due course presented Mademoiselle with a little half-brother.

So much for Louison, but there had been other incidents of an even more disquieting nature. There had been M. de Puylaurens, whom Mademoiselle accepted as a *favori* of her father, the only one she had ever liked, though what she exactly meant by a *favori* it would be hard to tell. M. de Puylaurens had returned to France with Monsieur, and won his way into her favour by bringing her sweetmeats, asking her to sing him her little songs—probably the ones abusing Richelieu—and treating her in every way as though she were grown-up. Then one day he suddenly disappeared, arrested at the Louvre during the rehearsal of a ballet, mysteriously dying a few months later in prison. Of course, the Cardinal was blamed, probably with justice, and of course, Mademoiselle heard of it. These acts of treachery and vengeance were only to be expected of the wicked Cardinal—Richelieu seen through the eyes of a passionate child—but what rôle had her beloved father played in the betrayal? This seems to be the first time that a suspicion of his true nature crossed her mind. She writes sadly, 'I leave it to others better informed to speak of what happened at Court and of what Monsieur did after the imprisonment of Puylaurens.'

There had been other incidents which Mademoiselle did not pretend to understand even in retrospect—dark intrigues involving the Queen in terrible scenes of discovery and humiliation. Inconceivable though it may appear to our ideas that a queen-consort should traffic with the enemies of her adopted country, it must be remembered that Anne was a Spaniard by birth, had remained a Spaniard in outlook and nature, and lived in an age when secret correspondence and double dealing were a commonplace of the day. Susceptible to the admiration of men, she was neither a particularly indecorous woman nor a particularly virtuous one in spite of her exaggerated addiction to pious observances, which irritated the French; she was neither outstandingly foolish nor outstandingly wise, though capable of sudden decisions surprising in so apparently easy-going and malleable a character. On the whole she deserved what the people said of her, 'The Queen is so kind' (*la reine est si bonne*), although when contradicted or opposed her Spanish arrogance would assert itself and her voice would rise to a most unpleasing angry falsetto (*un fausset aigre*). Cardinal de Retz probably summed her up accurately in saying that she possessed just the right kind of wits not to appear stupid to people who did not know her well. In appearance she looked what she was, a queen, dignified in her bearing, rather plumply settled into her ruff and voluminous skirts, with fine dark eyes, luxuriant curls, and hands so beautiful that they aroused general admiration. For the rest, one must make allowance for her shortcomings: entirely uneducated (she could read and write), she had been married at the age of fifteen to a neurotic boy of the same age, reluctant to consummate his marriage,[1] completely under the domination of his falconer, Charles de Luynes, whose name he would call out in his sleep. Childless; ignored by a husband with whom she shared little more than a belief in the supremacy of monarchy, mistrustful of Richelieu whose advances she is said to have repulsed but whom yet she had the sense to recognise as necessary to the support of the Throne, Anne had led a lonely, cautious life amongst the external splendours of a foreign Court. She had preserved the dignity of her position; it was a pity that she should not have pushed her discretion a little further but should have succumbed to the temptation of carrying on a clandestine correspondence with her friends in Spain.

Richelieu, who had spies everywhere, found her out. There ensued a degrading interrogation of the Queen by the chancellor Séguier at the convent of the Val-de-Grâce where, with her natural piety, she was in retreat, followed by an even more agonising interview with Richelieu at Chantilly, in the presence of two Jesuit priests when, crushed and broken, she was obliged to sign a complete confession and also to accept a written pardon from the King. Spanish and regal pride could not have been more thoroughly humbled. There had even been talk of repudiating her and of sending her back to her own country.

---

[1] It has been said that he did not consummate it for four years, when Luynes pushed him by force into the Queen's bedroom. On the other hand, his physician who kept an almost daily record of his royal patient's doings, gives the following account of what took place on the wedding night. It has the ring of authenticity, knowing what we do of the King's nature and of his abnormal qualms before the act of love: 'He took the Queen to her room; tired, he went to his own room, lay down, and had his supper in bed at 6.45. M. de Gramont and other young noblemen told him bawdy stories in order to give him courage; he was full of shame and apprehension; at long last they reassured him. He asked for his slippers and his dressing-gown, and went to the Queen's room at 8, where he was put into bed with the Queen his wife, in the presence of the Queen his mother; at 10.15 he returned, having slept for about an hour, and having done it twice, as he told us; one could see the signs; his g—— was red.' *Journal de Jean Hérouard*, Vol. II, p. 186.

It was at this juncture that Mademoiselle arrived at Chantilly to take her farewell of Their Majesties before rejoining her father at Chambord. She says with her usual complacence that she restored the Court to good humour, and indeed the excited ebullience of a ten-year-old may well have acted as a tonic on a shattered company. She found the King very sad (*en grand chagrin*), and the Queen ill in bed after the fright she had had and the insult she had received. Mademoiselle was now involuntarily placed in a position to hear more about the whole affair than most of her elders, for Mme de St Georges was the Queen's confidante, not to say confederate, and in order to divert suspicion Mademoiselle was made to stay in the room while the Queen poured out the whole story into sympathetic ears. They flattered her by telling her that she must repeat nothing of what she might overhear, whereupon the honest little creature decided that her best course was either not to listen or to forget everything immediately, in which she succeeded so well that in later years she found herself unable to remember a word, much to her regret, 'as I might now be able to report things doubtless unknown to anybody else.' As it was, the only effect of this side-light on the *affaire du Val-de-Grâce* can have been to increase the vague surmises dawning on a trustful young mind. Her father's exile, the Cardinal's machinations, Louison, M. de Puylaurens, and now this inexplicable trouble between those idols the King and Queen . . .

Mademoiselle was mistaken in supposing that she might have been able to report things unknown to anybody else, for the full details of the affair are perfectly revealed to us today. Sorry though we may feel for Anne of Austria and grievous as may be the spectacle of a proud woman mortified, of her guilt there can be no question. All the associated documents contained in Richelieu's coffer were reassembled after the French Revolution by a private individual and eventually found their way in 1847 into the safe keeping of the national library, where the whole story lies for anybody to read.

This is no place to relate it, though an outline may not be irrelevant as an indication of the world into which Mademoiselle was growing up. It reads more like pseudo-historical fiction, with none of the ingredients missing, than a factual record of real life. There are the secret letters passing between the Queen of France, the King of Spain and the duc de Lorraine; there is the absurdly romantic figure of the duchesse de Chevreuse as the go-between; there is the faithful gentleman La Porte, bearer of letters ostensibly innocent but with the true message written in invisible ink between the lines; or letters written by the Queen in Spanish, surreptitiously passed by her under cover of conversation to La Porte for him to transcribe into cipher; there is the interception of letters by Richelieu's secret police; and finally there is the wildly picaresque episode of Mme de Chevreuse's galloping escape towards the Spanish frontier disguised as a young man (challenged as to her identity, she had the impudence to reply that she was the duc d'Enghien travelling on the King's business) and her near detection when her sex nearly betrayed her, her saddle being found soaked in blood and she had to pretend that she had been wounded by a sword thrust in the thigh. She borrowed two shirts from a man and tore them up into strips to bandage, as she said, her wound.[1]

Such were the adventures that befell the contemporaries of Mademoiselle, and which she was later to emulate in her own clumsy, bungling way.

These accounts of a Queen of France carrying on a secret correspondence with the enemies of her adopted country may seem shocking and incredible to our ears. Unthinkable, we say; and so it is. We take loyalty for granted. Only by turning our accepted notions completely back-to-front can we arrive at any understanding of the situation in France in the first half of the seventeenth century.

[1] See the *Mémoires Particuliers* of Pierre de La Porte; also *Mme de Chevreuse*, by Victor Cousin, Chapter III and Appendices.

For one thing, the frontiers of France had not yet cohered into their natural geographical boundaries. On the east, Lorraine under its own Duke was still an independent state with inclinations towards an Austro-Spanish alliance. On the south, the duc de Savoie, also with Austro-Spanish inclinations, controlled his large territory from Nice on the Mediterranean coast right up past Chambéry to Genoa. On the south-west, the Spaniards included Perpignan, which geographically ought to have been a French city, in their province of Catalonia. On the north-east of France, the Spanish Netherlands stretched from Dunkirk to the Rhine. The greater part of Europe had been involved since 1618 in that peculiarly confused and indeterminate mess of internecine embroilment which we know as the Thirty Years War. It was not a comfortable position for France, and it was further complicated, inside France herself, by the fact that no spirit of national patriotism existed amongst her own great feudal nobles.

Take for example the duc de Lorraine. Half of his Duchy came under the Holy Roman Empire, but outlying bits of it came under the King of France. How could he be loyal to either? The duc de Bouillon had his capital at Sedan, just inside the Holy Roman Empire; but was at the same time one of the great vassals of France. It is thus not surprising to find these apparent treacheries and betrayals going on, where no cohesive patriotism bound people together in the sense that a nation is bound within its tight frontiers and a common interest.

One thing might have strengthened the French in their resistance against the Austro-Spanish enemy, pressing on their frontiers from the Spanish Netherlands, the Rhine, Savoy, and the Pyrenees. That would have been a determined concentration of forces to smash once and for ever the power of the already deteriorating Hapsburg dynasty. Unfortunately for the French, they had no general idea of resistance or of national unity. Even within France herself, the provinces retained their separate character, and came under the governorship of various great lords: Normandy, Brittany, Gascony, Languedoc,

Guienne, all were distinct and capable of rebellion against the central government; we shall see, for example, that the princesse de Condé could shut herself up inside Bordeaux and withstand a siege in defiance of the royal army. The Huguenots of La Rochelle, going even further, did not hesitate to summon the English fleet to their assistance against their lawful sovereign. The cannons of the King of Spain rolled by invitation of French princes through the streets of Paris during the Fronde. The King's own mother, wife, and brother trafficked whenever it suited them with the enemies of France. The princely houses of Orléans, Bourbon, Vendôme, all played for their own hand against one another, now falling into this pattern of alliance or rivalry, now into that. Unless we grasp this chaotic state of affairs, the kaleidoscope of events becomes even more unintelligible than it must already appear, nor shall we so readily understand why the keystone to the arch of Richelieu's internal policy was his determination to break the power of the territorial aristocracy. This he did partly by the wise but bitterly resented destruction of their fortified castles (edict of 1626), partly by declaring the practice of duelling illegal—which to our ears may sound an unimportant measure but which was in fact regarded as an insolent infringement of prerogative—and partly by instituting a system of frequent shifts in provincial governorship, for one reason or another, or, when it suited the Cardinal, for no ostensible reason at all.

Supposing we in England in 1959 translate the position into something like the following terms:

The Duke of Edinburgh is in secret correspondence with Marshal Khrushchev and the Russian Praesidium.

Queen Elizabeth the Queen-Mother with the Dukes of Athol, Montrose, and Argyle is conspiring with Sir Oswald Mosley to restore Scottish independence.

The Duke of Gloucester is busy making arrangements to get the Duke of Edinburgh (or, alternately, the Prime Minister) assassinated.

The Princess Royal, up at Harewood, aunt of the Sovereign,

but entirely under the domination of her father confessor, allows herself to be directed into political intrigues which she scarcely understands but which involve charming the Archbishop of Canterbury into a blind subservience.

The Duke of Norfolk, controlling the whole of Sussex and East Anglia, with all the Howards supporting him, has put Arundel Castle into a state of siege.

The Duke of Devonshire, with all the Cavendishes behind him, has likewise put Chatsworth into a state of siege against the Queen's Household Brigade.

The Duke of Northumberland, backed by all the Percies, is stirring up the Border and is prepared to defend Hadrian's Wall against all comers, be they the Queen's troops or otherwise.

Lord Salisbury, at Hatfield, is plotting the betrayal of Great Britain to an unspecified foreign power.

Lord Anglesey, on his eponymous island, has laid his plans to rouse Wales at any moment and to import mercenary troops—German, Spanish, Austrian, no matter what they are, friends or enemies—so long as he can sustain his governorship over the Principality . . .

This is putting the situation very flippantly. But the analogy is not wholly false. We have criticised Mademoiselle for not taking stock of the enormously important events taking place in the formation of her country. Would our Princess Anne, at the same age, have been any more aware?

Another fundamental weakness, as we should see it, was the absence of a central representative body such as we, despite our grumbles, regard our own Parliament. A miserable peasantry, preoccupied only by scraping a living from the land, reluctantly paying the taxes of the *taille* and the *gabelle*, had of course no voice at all in the management of their country. There were no fewer than six provinces, known as the Pays d'États (Normandy, Brittany, Burgundy, Dauphiné, Languedoc, and Provence) with the right of summoning their own Estates and imposing their own local system of taxation over and above the small contribution they had to make to the national budget. This independence could not make for solidarity. True, there was the main Parlement having its seat in Paris, but its powers and functions were very different from those accredited to the English House of Commons, as can be estimated by the most superficial consideration of contemporary events in England culminating in the execution of Charles I.

The importance of not identifying or even comparing the French Parlement with the English Parliament thus becomes evident. The French Parlement was in no sense an elective body. How could it be, since there was no electorate? It could therefore not be regarded in any way as representative of any section of the population. It was composed mostly of lawyers, *gens de robe*, who considered themselves as guardians of the fundamental laws of France and often claimed that in addition to their judicial functions they had the right to register and even to amend laws passed by the Executive.

This claim could be opposed by the King, who could always override the Parlement by holding a *lit de justice*, at which he himself presided and when the Parlement could do no more than register his decisions.

Richelieu was fully aware of the flimsy construction, and, with his determination to make the Monarchy paramount, was prepared to take every advantage of it. If there was to be a supreme authority in France, capable of cementing all the disparate elements while at the same time depriving them of all real potency, it should be the King's. By an edict of 1641 he struck an astonishing blow at the Parlements, prohibiting them from interference in public affairs and reducing them to the position of mere mouthpieces humbly to approve the decisions of the Crown. That this edict should have been accepted without protest goes far to prove the absence of any organised resistance or even of any reasonable awareness of a fundamental assault on the few existent rights of legislature. The path was laid for the absolute dictatorship of Louis XIV, still a very long way ahead.

CHAPTER II

Adolescence
[1637 – 1643]

MADEMOISELLE was back in Paris after her happy time with her father in Touraine. She did not fail to go out to St Germain to pay her respects to Their Majesties who received her warmly (*qui me firent de grandes caresses*) and to each of whom she presented a little enamelled watch from Blois, perhaps two of those she had won playing battledore-and-shuttlecock with Monsieur. In Paris, she threw herself with zest into every kind of amusement: parties, dances, comedies, and even gave a grand entertainment at the Tuileries on her own account. The recently instituted *Gazette*,[1] the first newspaper ever to appear in France, recorded that 'Mademoiselle offered a ball and a play (*comédie*) to the Queen, when the gracious charm of that princess, now at the dawn of her life, showed what must be expected from the meridian of her days.' Mademoiselle herself was not so sure. Nothing if not candid in self-examination, she evidently realised that spoilt little girls pass through a detestable stage. One of her intimates was Mlle de Longueville. Mademoiselle was rising ten, and Mlle de Longueville twelve. 'She and I were in the habit of making fun of everybody, although it would have been easy to turn the tables on us, for we wore the most ridiculous clothes and made every sort of grimace, in spite of all the

---

[1] *The Gazette de France*, founded in 1631 by Dr Théophraste Renaudot, was a weekly to which Richelieu and even the King contributed political articles. It was Richelieu's brilliant anticipation of the suggestive power of the Press, at a date when no Press, either popular or responsible, existed. The only other publication, the *Mercure de France*, founded in 1605, could scarcely be considered as a newspaper, since it appeared only once a year.

scoldings we got from her governess and mine. The only way of stopping us was to forbid us to see one another, which they knew would be a hard privation on account of the great friendship between us.'

But towards the end of 1637 a most unexpected announcement put an end to these schoolgirlish frivolities, and removed Mademoiselle to St Germain: the Queen was with child and wanted her favourite niece to keep her company.

The Queen's condition was surprising in manifold ways. She was already a woman of thirty-six, and had been married for twenty-one years. She had lately passed through a crisis in her relations with her husband, as a consequence of the affair of Val-de-Grâce, which, one would have thought, could not serve to bring them any closer together. (Still, reconciliations may work wonders.) Furthermore, the King, as a change from his more habitual preferences, had lately fallen in love with Marie de Hautefort, one of the Queen's ladies, to the extent of losing his head and behaving in a manner reckless of either discretion or dignity. Mademoiselle, a chaperone not yet eleven years old, observed all this going-on, without seeming to offer any criticism; probably she was beginning to take such things for granted. 'The Court was most enjoyable at that time,' she writes; 'the King's love for Mme de Hautefort,[1] and his efforts to keep her constantly entertained, added greatly to our fun. We often went out hunting with him, all the ladies dressed in bright colours, on splendid palfreys (*haquenées*) richly caparisoned, and, as a protection against the sun, we all wore hats trimmed with many feathers. Coming home, the King used to sit in my coach between Mme de Hautefort and me, entertaining us most agreeably on many subjects.' There was another side to this idyllic picture: 'If they had had a quarrel, all amusements were suspended, and if at those times the King

---

[1] She was, in fact, unmarried, but her position as *dame d'atour* to the Queen gave her the right to be called Madame. The *dame d'atour*, which could be translated as tirewoman, was responsible for the *toilette* of her mistress, and in particular for the dressing of her hair.

came into the Queen's rooms, he would speak to no one and no one dared speak to him; he would sit in a corner, often yawning and falling asleep. Then he would spend the greater part of the day writing down what he had said to Mme de Hautefort and what she had said to him . . . His melancholy cast a chill over everybody.'

Mademoiselle adds an observation which we may find endearing, although in her eyes it naturally appeared unworthy of a King: 'He became bewildered whenever he saw somebody he was not used to, like a simple gentleman coming from the provinces to the Court.' It throws a light on that unhappy misfit known as Louis XIII. Never was there a monarch less suited by temperament to the position his birth had imposed upon him or more conscious of his obligations and his responsibilities. How far happier he would have been as the simple gentleman to whom his niece had compared him.

The character of Louis XIII deserves and demands a long and sympathetic study, a task which should tempt any young historian on the look-out for a subject.

It is possible to present a not unpleasant evocation of life in the lovely surroundings of Fontainebleau in the earliest years of Louis XIII as the Dauphin. The little boy adored his father, the gay, boisterous Henri Quatre, le Vert Galant. Jean Hérouard, the Dauphin's physician, writes in his journal: 'He cannot be parted from the King, nor the King from him.' (*Ne peut laisser le roi, ni le roi lui.*) The Dauphin trotted after the King, going for a walk to see the swans or the hounds, or sitting beside him to watch a company of English players in a performance of *Henry IV, part II.* The little prince was so much amused by Falstaff's 'My lord, tap for tap' that for days afterwards he strutted about saying in as deep a voice as he could put on, 'Tiph, toph, milord.'

Henri IV, however, was not always there, and an essentially lonely little boy ran wild. We might expect to find the King's eldest son, heir to the Throne, spoilt, flattered, cossetted. It was far otherwise. Hérouard's diary reveals that he was whipped nearly every day, sometimes over his clothes, but sometimes on the bare flesh, for such tiny offences as not eating his supper or in an attempt to correct his alarming temper. This was something more serious than childish tantrums—'he wanted to thrash everybody, screaming frenziedly'—but it was not the way to set about dealing with a difficult, passionately jealous child. Henri IV himself, that rough, jolly, soldierly Béarnais, believed in this form of correction, and would beat him with his own hands, when the Dauphin retaliated by pulling his father's beard. That word whipped (*fouetté*) recurs so often that one is relieved to read for once a more humane entry, 'He tried to hit and scratch the Queen but she pacified him by giving him some jam.' How right she was. Jam, when one is only three years old, is a far more appeasing corrective than repeated birchings.

And we know for certain that he liked it. 'Papa,' he wrote, 'all the apothecaries of Provins have come to me to ask you, very humbly, to give my company a different garrison-post, because my *gendarmes* like the rose-jam (*conserve de roses*) and I am afraid they will eat it all and I shall have none left. I eat some every night when I go to bed.'

Alternately petted and frightened by his father, rather neglected by his mother who does not seem to have meant much to him in childhood, left very much in the hands of servants who did nothing by their conversation or habits to discourage the incredible coarseness of the royal nursery, it should early have become apparent that the future Louis XIII was afflicted with a strangely unmanageable nature. Hérouard, in constant attendance, a kindly man, was more concerned with his patient's physical troubles than with the problems of his psychology. The child was delicate, and he stammered. The doctor examined his mouth to see if an operation was indicated; he would have done better to reflect that a little more affection and gentleness would not come amiss. Even the *gouvernante*, Mme de Montglat, the *Mamanga* of babyish speech, who retained the Dauphin's love simply because he needed to bestow it on somebody, appears as a somewhat harsh, dry woman, worthy and conscientious but lacking the warmth he undoubtedly needed.[1] The day might have been foreseen when he would turn with all his latent cravings towards the first person to give him true companionship in all the pursuits he most enjoyed: his hunting, his dogs, his horses, his hawks, his gallops across country, his escape into the woods. That person was not a woman. It was Charles d'Albert de Luynes, the keeper of the royal falcons, a young man of so pleasing a personality that 'if you want to dislike him you must keep out of his way.' (*Pour le haïr il fallait ne pas le voir.*) He was thirty-three; Louis XIII was ten, and had just had to sustain the shock of his father's assassination.

Like others of his race, Louis XIII was not exclusively homosexual. He was capable of falling in love with women—there was Mme de Hautefort, and there would be Louise de La Fayette—and a very strange pattern these abortive love-affairs followed. It has been contended, probably with truth, that Louis XIII, twisted, masochistic, warped, suffered from an inverted chastity and that his passions were cerebral rather than physical. He shrank, in other words, from the natural fulfilment of his desires. On the other hand he took an almost hysterical pleasure in emotional scenes, loudly complaining of ill-treatment at the hands of the love of the moment, whether it be Marie de Hautefort or the marquis de Cinq-Mars, and keeping a written record (as Mademoiselle had noticed) of the recriminations that had passed on either side. The more unhappy they made him—and he seems to have called out all the cruellest instincts of the contemptuous bully, whether feminine or masculine—the more he revelled in exposing his

[1] In fairness to Mme de Montglat, of whose severity the rather sentimental Hérouard clearly disapproved, it must be stated that her orders came direct from Henri IV: 'I regret not having heard from you that you had whipped my son, for I wish and command that you should whip him whenever he turns obstinate or does anything wrong, knowing by my own experience how much good it did me, having been thoroughly whipped at his age.'

own humiliation. Mme de Motteville said with truth that the only tender spot in his embittered soul was the capacity for appreciating his own sufferings.

Yet strange quirks were related of him, strange little inconsistent freakish cruelties towards creatures even more defenceless than he. It was said that he took pleasure in squashing the heads of sparrows between his fingers.

He was happy only, in the simple sense of the word, out hunting when his skill and intrepidity were notable, or busy with his hands at some craft, it might be cooking or it might be shoeing a horse or labouring at his forge where he made ironwork, and above all in the retreat of a little hunting-box he had acquired not far from Paris, a *chétif château* in a wooded district near a village called Versailles. Not, you would say, a character fit to bear the burden of kingship, as pitiable a spectacle as an ordinary man invited to heave up the weights that only a Sandow with bulging biceps could have lifted. Yet Louis XIII—and here, I think, we must accord him all the respect he has sometimes been denied—never shirked his unwelcome responsibility. As was natural to one of his birth and epoch, he had a profound sense of the duty which then comprised the Divine Right of a King. He had, moreover— and this is perhaps his supreme achievement—the intelligence to realise that Richelieu was a greater man than he. Detractors of Louis XIII may argue that it was only too easy for so shy, eccentric and reluctant a monarch to resign his problems of government into other hands. The proposition is tenable, but it would perhaps be putting the case more fairly to say that he had the good sense to know when authority can and should be delegated and left for its execution to a stronger control. That control he found in his First Minister, the gaunt, ill, indomitable prelate borne in his huge litter along the roads of France, more ostentatious in his way of life than the Sovereign himself, riddled by the most painful diseases, unable to sit upright because of the haemorrhoids and anal ulcers that obliged him to lie on his side; and, what must have been almost as distressing as the physical suffering to a man of his fastidious nature, enduring the stench that came from his tortured body. In vain did Richelieu try to disguise this, scenting his room with musk and amber and sending to Meaux for the relics of that obscure saint whose name might now be forgotten were it not commemorated as the patron saint of the cab-drivers of Paris— Saint Fiacre.[1] St Fiacre unfortunately had no effect upon the ills of the greatest statesman that France has ever produced, whom Louis XIII could recognise as the bulwark to his throne, but whom Mademoiselle with her limited personal vision could only dislike.

It is to be hoped that Mademoiselle, singing her little streetsongs, never came across some of the unrepeatably coarse, mean and cruel attacks on a sick man who, to the very end, worked for what he believed to be the salvation of France.

On September 5th, 1638, the Queen gave birth at St Germain to a son. Richelieu, absent with the army near St Omer, rejoiced at the news which meant that Monsieur was now no longer Heir-Presumptive to the throne. Inspired by a spirit of prophecy, he expressed to the King his belief that in the future Louis XIV God had given the world someone destined for great things. Monsieur, stunned, had to be given ocular proof that the new arrival was indeed a boy, and was reported as saying that though he was very well satisfied that the child came out of the Queen's body, he did not know who the Devil had put it in. Mademoiselle, on the other hand, failed to put two and two together or to realise the change in her father's situation: instead of thinking that he would now never be King of France, she made up her mind that she would be its Queen. Her aunt Anne had been partly to blame for putting this idea into the child's head, laughingly saying to her, 'You shall be my daughter-in-law,' never foreseeing that she might be taken seriously. Mademoiselle was now seldom

---

[1] For an account of St Fiacre, an Irish-born saint, see the Rev. Alban Butler's *Lives of the Saints*, Vol. VIII, pp. 386–387, August 30th.

out of the nursery, watching the baby and calling him her little husband. The King was amused, and made no objection; Richelieu was not amused, and ordered Mademoiselle back to Paris. Screaming and protesting (*ce ne furent que pleurs et que cris*), she was taken away, not even straight back to her own Tuileries but to Rueil near by, where the Cardinal was awaiting her.[1] The helplessness of childhood, even of royal childhood!

Richelieu had never been tactful in his dealings with Mademoiselle. He was probably quite unaware that he left her in a rage every time he encountered her by chance, and told her that as her godfather he felt responsible for her, 'repeating the same thing incessantly,' she says, 'as one does to children.' Imbued with an, I fear, egregious sense of her own dignity, there was nothing she resented more than being treated as a child; the grievance is so recurrent that it must have been constantly in her mind. Richelieu is scarcely to blame: he had other things to think of than the susceptibilities of a small princess who did everything she could imagine to irritate him and whose father was perpetually endeavouring to get him assassinated. Besides, the ordinary human gift of getting on to easy terms with people seems to have been left out of this great but lonely and unlovable man. 'He was a good friend; he would even have liked to be popular (*aimé du public*), but although he possessed many qualities necessary to that effect, he never had the *je ne sais quoi* (*sic*) which is more essential than anything else.' This is Cardinal de Retz summing up, and it rings true. One is strangely reminded of General de Gaulle. Richelieu could make himself feared but not loved. He could alarm; he could not charm. He was not at all the right person to tackle Mlle de Montpensier.

Now he had sent for her, to receive a formal scolding, and she confronted this tall, pale, terrible priest looking down on her from a towering height with his hooded eyes, above his knife-bone nose between his sunken temples. She was not to

[1] There is a description of Rueil by John Evelyn, *In Praise of Gardens*.

call the Dauphin her little husband, he said; she was old enough to know better; her conduct had been most unbecoming. He spoke so seriously and clearly frightened her so much, that she made the only reply she could: she burst into tears. The Cardinal, disconcerted, in the attempt to pacify her, and doubtless inspired by a vague recollection that the young could always be appeased by being given something to eat, could think of nothing better than to offer her luncheon. In spite of this, it was a very angry Mademoiselle (*fort en colère*) who drove away to Paris.

The next five years, as Mademoiselle rose gradually from the age of eleven to the age of sixteen, brought few real changes into her life and did very little to enlarge the periphery of her interests. Her heart might be deep, but her intellect was shallow as a saucer. External events might just as well not have existed for all the notice she took of them; it meant nothing to her that a war, in which her own country was involved, should have been devastating most of Europe for some twenty years and showed no sign of coming to an end. Admittedly, she was still young, but young people matured earlier in those days, even marrying at fourteen and fifteen, and after all Mademoiselle was living in the midst of people closely concerned with public affairs: she should have kept her ears open. It may, perhaps, have been puzzling to know, however dimly, that France was fighting Spain when one of one's aunts was Queen of France and a Spaniard, and another aunt Queen of Spain and a Frenchwoman; puzzling, also, to know that her father wished her to marry M. de Soissons, who had taken up arms against the King. She made no attempt to sort out these dynastic complications, nor, more surprisingly, was she interested in projects of marriage for herself. The rivalry between the 'set' that frequented the hôtel de Créqui and the 'set' that frequented the hôtel de Ventadour bulked with far more immediate importance. Whenever young men attached to the hôtel de Ventadour drifted over to the hôtel de Créqui, Mademoiselle and her friends, amongst whom Mlle de Longueville reappears, with 'inconceivable intrigues' established a secret compact to avoid dancing with them. Mademoiselle had her own reasons for disliking the hôtel de Ventadour, which belonged to the Condés: 'I never knew what to talk about, and therefore very few people talked to me; I saw them whispering amongst themselves, and I was treated so much as a little girl, although that is in fact what I was, that I always came away with a mortal resentment within my heart.' This absurd feud, as Mademoiselle acknowledges, was the cause of the aversion she long maintained for the young duc d'Enghien (the *Grand Condé*) and for all members of his house. She had the grace later on to see these puerilities in their true perspective: 'Such were our Affairs of State and our preoccupations; thanks be to God that time has dissolved our hatreds.'

In justice to Mlle de Longueville, who hitherto has been presented only in her teens as an empty-headed giggling girl, it should be said that she grew up into being a serious, courageous and well-balanced person, keeping her head far more steadily than most of her contemporaries when the troubles of the Fronde came upon them. At the advanced age of thirty-two, she married the duc de Nemours, and it is as the duchesse de Nemours, author of *Mémoires*, that we remember her—a cold little obituary notice to set in memory of one of the most sensible women of her day.

These great private houses were the social centres of aristo-cratic Paris given up to the pursuit of pleasure: balls, ballets, theatrical representations, fêtes to celebrate a marriage. In contemporary memoirs they succeed each other in dazzling profusion, leaving our eyes blinded by the illumination of a million candles. Richelieu himself figured as a princely host; at the Palais-Cardinal or hôtel de Richelieu as it was currently called,[1] his private theatre could seat three thousand spectators. Music played a prominent part; the King had an orchestra of

[1] Now the Palais-Royal. Richelieu bequeathed it at his death to Louis XIII.

twenty-four violins, *les vingt-quatre violons*, which could some-times be hired or borrowed by a favoured few to play during supper-parties. But it was not only indoors that the gallant company enjoyed itself. No less than today, much of the life of Paris went on in the open air; true, there were then no boule-vards where the Parisian might indulge his predilection for strolling, but there were the gardens of the Tuileries where courtier and citizen alike could admire the aviaries where the King kept his falcons, and the swans floating upon *l'étang aux cygnes*. The public, however, was excluded from the part previously known as the *Jardin Neuf*, renamed *Parterres de Mademoiselle*; this was reserved for the royal family and their friends. Then there was the five-acre *Jardin de Renard*, with a restaurant close at hand, on a terrace overlooking the Seine, rendezvous of all the nobility, where you could dine, gossip, flirt, listen to the band, or watch the fireworks sizzling down into the river. Above all, there was the Cours-la-Reine, laid out in 1628 by Marie de' Medici, and planted with those unfamiliar trees introduced into France from India by Richelieu, known then in his honour as *cardinals*, but to us as horse-chestnuts—that leafy and ambrosial feature of spring-time Paris. Marie de' Medici had introduced the Florentine custom of driving out in the cool of the evening, and here you could watch the procession of 'coaches, liveries, coats-of-arms, nothing escaped the eye, everything was inquisitively and maliciously observed, and, according to the splendour or otherwise of their equipage, people were either admired or disdained.'[1] No better or more authentic description could be given of this famous four-fold avenue than that of Mlle de Scudéry writing in *Le Grand Cyrus*: 'the wide alleys full of little painted and gilded carriages, occupied by the most beautiful women, followed by an infinite number of men of quality, admirably mounted and magnificently dressed, coming and going and saluting them as they passed.'

*　　　*　　　*

[1] La Bruyère, *Caractères*.

When we look at the portraits of these eminent personages of the reign of Louis XIII, it may seem to us that fashion varied very little from decade to decade, but in point of fact the tyranny of fashion was quite as operative and quite as costly in those days as in our own, and far more so for the men. Women, on the whole, adhered fairly faithfully to the tight, whale-boned bodice, not always designed with a due regard for modesty, and ample skirts not exaggerated into the Spanish fashion of ballooning over the framework of the farthingale (*vertugadin*). Men, on the other hand, whether in the gratifi-cation of their own vanity, or under the necessity of keeping up to date, or indulging for the sake of their ladies in the display instinct of certain birds, diversified their attire fre-quently and in a variety of ways; trimmings might be different, cloaks longer or shorter, trunks close-fitting or puffed, doublets pointed or rounded. The material itself might change its character. Then for the real dandy his accessories could add a large item of expenditure: gloves with red velvet or green satin revers at the wrist, or reaching to the elbow and fringed with gold, sometimes so strongly scented as to make the unwary sneeze and Mademoiselle herself step backwards hold-ing her nose for fear of being overcome; hats flat, hats tall and pointed, hats trimmed with heron's plumes, hats called by the irreverent '*chapeaux de cocu.*' Stockings could be obtained in fifty different colours under fantastic names, some of which have become familiar to us through *Cyrano de Bergerac.* Here are a few more which Rostand did not mention: dying monkey, rejoicing widow, lost time, resuscitated corpse, amorous desire, she-monkey's smile, sad friend, mortal sin, dying Spaniard, and several others too squalid for polite pages.

To all these accessories, not forgetting the knot of ribbon at the sword-hilt, was given the odd name of *petite oie*—little goose. Molière did not fail to make fun of it in *Les Précieuses Ridicules.* 'What do you think of my *petite oie*? Do you think it goes well with my costume?'

The true dandy's hair was a worry to him. All right if it was naturally curly, but what if it turned into rat's-tails in the rain? The heavy wig had not yet come into being, although the word *perruque* begins to appear, and also some bits of false hair known as *coins*. Curling irons were in use, but their effect could not stand up to damp weather: the curl they put in rapidly came out, and so for his lanky locks the gallant carried a pocket-comb, constantly in use, '*indispensable à un élégant.*' He had need of all the artificial aids at his command, including cosmetics, for it must be remembered that the faces of the majority of people, men and women alike, were marked and pitted by smallpox. We tend to forget this, and should be greatly startled should we encounter their ghosts as they really were.

Thus equipped, the gallant could offer entertainment to his ladies. They, sumptuous in their vast skirts, the hand-mirror dangling from the waist, their hair scented with orris, *chypre*, amber, or *poudre d'Espagne*, seductive with their low *décolletage*, the provocative *mouche* placed near the eye or the mouth and variously named the impassioned, the kiss, or the assassin, would stroll with him under the trees, when suddenly they would come on a supper-table all ready-set but which must be greeted with cries of surprise: this was known as a present (*un cadeau*). To the sound of hidden violins, laughter, and exquisite compliments, they would then dine as the lights began to twinkle in the Seine.

All this cost a great deal of money, and it was not every courtier who could afford the expense. Many of them lived on credit rather than on payment in cash. It is amusing to find that clothes could be hired for a special occasion, from a kind of Moss Bros. of the day, and that some tailors, for a consideration, would consent to take back worn or out-moded garments or to remake them according to the latest fashion. At all costs a brave front must be maintained, or the pitiless derision of friends and enemies be endured.

Nor was it sufficient to be fashionably dressed: the courtier's speech must conform also to the ruling of the hour. The Parisian populace, irreverent, born to mockery, thought the catch-phrases and distortions of the French language extremely funny, also the deliberate mispronunciation of certain words, *amirable* for *admirable, chouse* for *chose, Roume* for *Rome, Roussie* for *Russie, souleil* for *soleil, paresse* for *paroisse.*

The one place where prince and courtier alike could escape from the curiosity of the crowd, from the importunities of his creditors, from the suspicions of his wife or mistress, or merely from the strain which life in the glare of criticism imposed, was in the establishments known as the *maisons des baigneurs.* In these so-called baths he could drop his public personality, his rank, and even his name. 'Here one was tended and cherished, and could indulge oneself in all the pleasures offered by the luxury and depravity of a great city. The proprietor and all his employés guessed from a glance or a gesture if you wished to preserve your incognito, and all those who served you knowing perfectly well who you were assumed ignorance of everything about you, even to your name.'[1] For those who thought that sort of game worth the candle, Paris was indubitably well organised.

If these were the outward shows that marked the man of fashion, it was just as necessary to conform to the principles laid down for the *honnête homme.*[2] This curious expression has nothing to do with our associations with the word honesty. The nearest translation is perhaps man of the world, but in the eyes of the seventeenth century there was more to it than that, for it implied also a generous measure of amorous gallantry: 'One cannot be an *honnête homme,*' writes Bussy-Rabutin to Mme de Sévigné, 'unless one is permanently in love,' and in *Le Grand Cyrus* Mlle de Scudéry stated that no one could achieve a consummate *honnêteté* without having the desire to please. The frequency with which the expression occurs in letters and memoirs proves the importance attached by Mademoiselle's contemporaries to a quality social rather than moral.

---

[1] Waelckenaër, *Mémoires sur Mme de Sévigné.*

[2] An illuminating use of the adjective is shown by Mademoiselle, when she writes that it was indicated to the Queen of Sweden that she was outstaying her welcome at the French Court, *mais fort honnêtement.* This might be rendered as *tactfully.*

The more women you could seduce the better; well and good; that was part of it; but it was also essential to possess perfect politeness (by which they did not mean refinement, for their conversation and their habits were often anything but refined), a quick wit, an elegance of bearing, compared with which 'their private lives, the decency of their morals, and the intrinsic value of their souls, were of little account.'[1] Mme de Motteville, in some ways an innocent but in other ways a surprisingly sagacious woman, saw the matter very clearly. She calls it 'that apparent civility practised in society in the midst of hatred and envy.'

It was to Mademoiselle's credit that, brought up in so cynical a world, she should have preserved the virginity of her spirit for as long as she preserved the virginity of her heart and her body.

As well as her pleasures, Mademoiselle also had her sorrows, amongst them her first real disillusion concerning her father. It is sad to see that bright trust beginning to chip and tarnish. The story of Cinq-Mars is perhaps too well known to bear repetition in detail.[2] This handsome, dissolute young man, *Grand Ecuyer de France,* commonly called M. le Grand, had been insinuated into the service of Louis XIII by Richelieu, partly as a spy, partly as a 'toy,' in the Cardinal's phrase, who might deflect the King's affections from Mme de Hautefort. The scheme succeeded only too well. Louis conceived for this youth of nineteen a passion which gave Richelieu far more trouble than he had bargained for. The King was furiously jealous— with good reason—and a stream of letters, nauseating in their self-abasement, pursued the Cardinal who was expected to act as a go-between and peace-maker. 'M. le Grand cold-shoulders me, I do not know why ... Although I went twice to his room to beg him to forget anything I might have said or done to anger him, he says I do not love him . . .' Richelieu,

---

[1] M. Majendie, *La politesse mondaine et les théories de l'honnêteté en France au XVII siècle de 1600 à 1660.* Vol. II, p. 892.
[2] He is the hero of Alfred de Vigny's novel, *Cinq-Mars* (1827).

exasperated by the endless storms, quarrels, reconciliations, promises no sooner made than broken, at last spoke sharply to Cinq-Mars, threatening to put him down lower than where he had found him. Stung in his pride, Cinq-Mars turned against his former protector. He entered into an agreement with Spain, and once again the Cardinal was in danger of assassination.

Once again, also, Gaston d'Orléans, who had been involved, played his usual part of saving his own skin by revealing the names of his confederates. It was the sixth time that Louis XIII officially pardoned him. Cinq-Mars and his friend de Thou were arrested and executed, but this time Mademoiselle was better informed. 'Monsieur was unfortunately mixed up in the affair, and it was even believed that the deposition he made against them to the Chancellor (Séguier) was what really lost them and was the cause of their death . . . He came to supper with me; he was as gay as though M.M. de Cinq-Mars and de Thou had not fallen by the way. I confess that I could not see him without thinking of them, and in my joy (at seeing him) I felt that his own joy made me sorrowful.' She had travelled that far along the road of understanding her father's character. She was beginning to put the pieces of the puzzle together and to see the pattern of the picture. Fortunately for her, she could not then read, as we can now read, some of the things that Gaston was capable of saying when cornered. Never was there anyone so eel-like and undependable. Biographers must not be prejudiced, so let a contemporary note speak for itself: 'When the Queen told Monsieur that he had failed to observe a solemn undertaking which he had signed, he replied that he had signed it indeed, but had not confirmed his promise verbally. The King and the Queen then reminded him that he had often sworn solemnly not to contemplate any action which would tend to cause a rupture between him and the King; he replied that when taking an oath he always made some mental reservation.'[1] Ingenious duplicity could scarcely go further.

*   *   *

[1] V. Cousin, *Mme de Chevreuse*, p. 367.

Three deaths came within six months of each other, all affecting Mademoiselle in varying degrees. The first gave her nothing but a pleasure she did not attempt to conceal: Richelieu died at the Palais-Cardinal on December 4, 1642. He had been to Lyon, to attend the trial of Cinq-Mars and de Thou; and the state of his health, as of his determination to carry on his work to the end, may be gauged from an eye-witness's description of his journey:

'On the twenty-fourth of August 1642, Monseigneur the Cardinal de Richelieu slept at Viviers. He was travelling down the River Rhône, in a boat which had been fitted with a wooden apartment upholstered with scarlet velvet flowered in crimson, the ground-work being of gold. In the same boat there was an antechamber furnished in the same fashion; at the prow and at the stern of the boat were some soldiers of his guard wearing scarlet coats . . .

'His Eminence was in a bed adorned with purple taffeta.

'Monseigneur the Cardinal of Bichi, and Messieurs the Bishops of Nantes and Chartres were there with a large number of abbés and gentlemen, in other boats; in front of them there was an advance-guard frigate, and behind came another boat filled with musketeers and their officers. When they came alongside some isle, soldiers were sent ashore to see if there were any suspected persons to be found, and, not discovering any, they guarded the banks until two boats following had passed. These were filled with nobles and soldiers, well armed. Then came the boat of His Eminence, to the stern of which was attached a small covered boat containing M. de Thou, a prisoner guarded by an adjutant from the royal guards, and a dozen of His Eminence's guards.

'Behind the boats came three barges containing the wearing apparel and the silver vessels of His Eminence.

'On the banks of the Rhône, in Dauphiné, rode two companies of light horse, and as many on the borders of Languedoc and Vivarais. There was a very fine regiment of foot that went into the towns where His Eminence intended to enter or to sleep.

'When his boat came alongside the shore, a wooden bridge was fixed, stretching from the boat to the shore. After this was made secure, the bed on which the said lord lay was carried ashore, for he was ill with a sore or ulcer on the arm. Six strong men carried the bed by means of two bars, padded and provided with straps on the places where the men gripped them.

'On their shoulders and round their necks were certain trappings lined with cotton and covered with buff-leather, so that the straps or webbings around their necks were like stoles, which descended to the bars under which they were passed. Thus these men carried the bed and the said lord into the towns or into the houses where he intended to lodge.

'But what astonished everybody was the fact that he entered the houses by means of the windows; for before his arrival, masons were brought who broke down the windows of the houses, or made holes in the walls of the rooms where he intended to lodge, and then a wooden bridge was constructed stretching from the street to the windows or holes of his lodging. Thus, in his portable bed, he passed through the streets, and was carried up the bridge and placed into another bed prepared for him in his room, that his officers had adorned with rose and violet damask and very costly furniture.

'His chamber was guarded on all sides, also the vaults and the roof of the building where he slept.

'I saw him in his room; his aspect was very colourless on account of his sickness.'

The second death touched Mademoiselle more closely. Mme de St Georges had served her faithfully if injudiciously for many years, and as Mademoiselle knelt in tears by her bedside to receive the last farewell of a dying woman, she recalled many kindnesses, was deeply moved, and could only be persuaded away at Mme de St Georges' own request. (February 1643.) It now became necessary to nominate a successor, Mademoiselle being still unmarried although of marriageable age at fifteen. Her own choice would have fallen on Mme de St Georges' sister, Mme de Vitry, but her father decided otherwise. Monsieur's first wife, Mademoiselle's mother, had had a Mme de Fiesque in her household; Monsieur, who had mistrusted her as an intriguer and was now afraid that she would expect to receive the same appointment when his second wife should arrive in France, took the opportunity of assigning her to his daughter. Mademoiselle, not without humour, wondered whether the lady's health would be equal to so exhausting a charge.

Mme de Fiesque was a widow of a certain age. For the first few days all went well while she entertained her pupil with stories of her youth, but it very soon became apparent that she intended to hold the reins of control far tighter than her predecessor. She began by making an inventory of all Mademoiselle's jewels, in order to prevent her from giving them away to her friends, more especially to a young Mme de Montglat for whom Mademoiselle had one of her particular affections. Next, she took away the key of Mademoiselle's writing-desk, saying that it was not desirable for Mademoiselle to have it in her keeping, and that she must be shown all Mademoiselle's letters and be told to whom they were written. Worst of all, she took to supervising the conversation of Mademoiselle and her young friends, telling them (as was no doubt true) that they chattered only of *bagatelles* and that at their age they ought to be conversing on serious subjects. She also drew up a memorandum for Monsieur, embodying the rules of conduct she thought Mademoiselle ought to observe: she must make the sign of the cross on waking, and a great deal more concerning 'everything that one would prescribe for a child, although I was already sixteen'—the old familiar grievance. Nor would she allow Mademoiselle to spend the evening in that delightful Cours-la-Reine without first obtaining permission from Monsieur. As Monsieur was now living at the hôtel de Guise, at some distance from the Tuileries, it often happened that the reply was not received in time, or Monsieur not to be found, when Mademoiselle, bored and sulky, had perforce to stay at home. She saw through the reason for this prohibition: Mme de Fiesque at her advanced age had no taste for late hours.

It was not to be expected that a spoilt and high-spirited princess would submit meekly to such a change of treatment. 'There was no maliciousness I would not employ to be revenged upon her.' The doctor having ordered a remedy for a slight cold, Mademoiselle refused to take it; Mme de Fiesque ('thinking that I should be handled like a child') shut her into her room and forbade all visitors. Mademoiselle escaped, went to Mme de Fiesque's door, turned the key on her, and carried it off. No locksmith being available, Mme de Fiesque remained for several hours imprisoned, her vexation not diminished by hearing the shrieks of her grandson whom Mademoiselle had locked into another room.

The third death occurred at St Germain on May 14, 1643. Louis XIII had not long survived his great Minister, and after weeks of suffering he succumbed to his old enemy, intestinal tuberculosis. The little Dauphin, who had just been christened, was brought in to visit his father. 'And what is your name now?' he was asked.

'Louis XIV, papa!'

'Not yet,' murmured the dying man.

CHAPTER III

The Regency
[1643 – 1648]

THE new King was not yet five years old. When the duc de Chevreuse lifted him on to his throne to be presented to the Parlement, he appeared to be neither surprised nor perturbed, but when his mother and his governess, Mme de Lansac, stood him on his feet and tried to persuade him to speak he sat down again quite calmly without saying a word.[1] The Chancellor Séguier then, after kneeling to the King, announced that the Queen, whose piety and virtue he so much esteemed, had been appointed Regent with *full, entire, and absolute authority*, a startling change from the tone he had used to her at the interrogation of the Val-de-Grâce, when he had attempted to tear a compromising letter from her breast.

Paris burst into the wildest rejoicings, due not only to the natural fickleness of people always ready to acclaim novelty, but to a genuine affection for Anne, 'adored more for her misfortunes than for her merits,' whose unhappy married life had somehow touched their hearts and whose advent to power seemed to promise a bright future for all. Poets announced an age of gold; people danced in the streets. Nothing was heard on all sides but a repetition of the old cry, 'The Queen is so good.'

[1] *Journal d'Olivier d'Ormesson.*

Le temps de la bonne régence,
Temps où régnait une heureuse abondance,
Temps où la ville aussi bien que la cour
Ne respiraient que la joie et l'amour.[1]

The very fact that she removed herself and her two little boys[2] from the old, gloomy Louvre to the far more modern and cheerful Palais-Royal, now no longer the Palais-Cardinal, seemed significant of the truth that Richelieu was soundly and safely dead. Here she could enjoy the amenities of a gilded bath-room and of an oratory decorated by Philippe de Champaigne and other painters with scenes from the life of the Blessed Virgin. All the exiles returned, Mme de Chevreuse amongst them. Prison doors flew open; debts were remitted. The Queen-Regent had suffered enough from that crushing tyranny; she was not likely to impose a second Richelieu; France and the Regent could look forward to an era of freedom such as they had never known.

There was a further cause for rejoicing, better founded, as it turned out. Five days after the death of Louis XIII, the young duc d'Enghien, then only twenty-one, had by the sheer brilliance of his tactics inflicted upon the Spanish army at Rocroi (May 19, 1643) a disaster from which it never recovered. Of eighteen thousand Spanish infantry, it was said, seven thousand were prisoners and eight thousand dead. Well might the Cardinal de Retz say of him, 'He was born a captain.' The war between France and Spain might drag on for another five years, but the day was in sight when France and not Spain should become the dominant power in Europe.

The nobility of France had rejoiced in particular over the disappearance of Richelieu. He had devoted much of his

---

[1] The days of the good Regency,
Days of a happy abundance,
Days when the city as well as the Court
Breathed nothing but blitheness and love.
[2] Philippe, duc d'Anjou, had been born in September 1640.

La Grande Mademoiselle. This is obviously an imaginary reconstruction, but probably very much what she looked like

Louis XIV, King of France, by an anonymous painter

energy to their abasement. The princes hated him, and the territorial aristocracy had ill-endured the demolition of their feudal fortresses at his command. Furthermore, with a woman now nominally at the head of affairs, they could reasonably hope to recover their privileges and to regain control. What did the Queen-Regent know of government, she who had always been kept in the background, she who might be good and kind but was abysmally ignorant, who might have a taste for underground intrigue but who had never displayed any of the Amazonian vigour of a Mme de Chevreuse or a princesse Palatine? Sudden authority, however, may give self-confidence with startling results. To the general consternation the Regent immediately announced the appointment of Cardinal Mazarin as her Prime Minister.

After one Cardinal, another. Richelieu had at least been French, of good birth even though provincial. Of this Sicilian *Mazarini* little was known save that he had been Papal Nuncio in Paris for two years (1634–1636), had returned to Paris in 1640 without any ostensible reason, had been employed both by Richelieu and Louis XIII though without any very definite function, and had lived so quietly and obscurely that at the time of the King's death he was generally believed to have returned to Italy. An almost unknown quantity, he was observed, when he took his place at the head of the Council table, to have no cognizance of procedure, failing to recognise his colleagues by name, and nervously taking off his hat to all and sundry.[1] In his favour he was said to be tall, handsome, with bright eyes and a certain gentleness of expression, attractive to women and per-haps only too attractive to the widowed Queen. Mademoiselle went even more wrong than usual in her estimate of his ability, dismissing him as 'unskilful and unworthy.' That had not been the opinion of Richelieu, a better judge, who on his death-bed had written to Mazarin saying, 'I leave my work in your hands, to carry it on to completion.'

Unskilful Mazarin certainly was not. Great he might not be,

---

[1] *Journal d'Olivier d'Ormesson.*

nor by nature foresighted or strong and determined as Richelieu
had been in his domestic and foreign policy; not of the calibre
to inaugurate schemes such as Richelieu's for the strengthening
of the Monarchy and the reduction of the enemies of France
upon her frontiers, but of sufficient ability to execute, like a
practised lawyer, the provisions drawn up in his master's last
will and testament. A minor little man, a very clever little man,
executor to a great man, a diplomatic manipulator rather than
a creative statesman, must be Mazarin's final though not
damnably pejorative epitaph.

It was not long before the inevitable cabal started against
Mazarin, and a party was formed, called *Les Importants*, including amongst others the duc de Beaufort, the duc de Vendôme,
the duc de Mercœur, and Mme de Chevreuse, who always
brought trouble wherever she went. For once, Gaston d'Orléans
was not implicated; it was in fact he who unwittingly saved
Mazarin's life by taking him in his own coach to a dinner
at Maisons-Laffitte, on the evening when the duc de Beaufort
and his accomplices had arranged to despatch Mazarin should
he be on his way alone. The plot was revealed; the Regent
openly blamed M. de Beaufort who by now was in prison at
Vincennes while his friends took the road of banishment. We
should not dwell so long on this abortive and short-lived
affair of the *Importants* did it not contain the germ of an
uprising which sundered France into civil war and had
a particular repercussion upon the fortunes of la Grande
Mademoiselle.

She, meanwhile, silly empty-head, was far more interested
in a typically fantastic quarrel between Mme de Longueville
and Mme de Montbazon,[1] rightly dismissed by Mme de
Motteville as *ces importantes niaiseries*, and also, more under-
standably, in the arrival of her unknown stepmother. Louis XIII

[1] For details of this affair, known as *les lettres tombées*, see *La jeunesse de Mme de
Longueville*, by Victor Cousin, Chapter III; also *Mme de Chevreuse*, by the same author,
pp. 242–244; also *Mémoires de Mme de Motteville*, Vol. I, pp. 136–144.

shortly before his death had authorised Gaston to send for his wife, on the curious condition that they should be remarried in France. Marguerite de Lorraine, now known as Madame, was preceded by precisely the kind of legend best suited to appeal to the picaresque ideas of Mademoiselle: abandoned by Gaston at Nancy, she had disguised herself as a man, darkened her face with soot, borrowed the coach of a Cardinal in which she successfully passed through the lines of the French army, exchanged the coach for a horse, and rode to rejoin her husband in Flanders. It recalled the exploits of Mme de Chevreuse; a Corneille heroine could not have done better. But when Mademoiselle and Monsieur met her at Meudon (May 26, 1643) a disillusion of all romance was in store: Monsieur and Madame did not appear in the least pleased to see one another. Contrary to expectation after all their separations and tribulations, they met coldly, in the courtyard of the château of Meudon; Madame then went upstairs, and reappeared only when Monsieur called her to the chapel where the Archbishop of Paris awaited them to receive the declaration of the validity of their marriage. Madame, with tears in her eyes, protested that it was quite unnecessary, after which they all bowed and curtsied and retired. Mademoiselle was bitterly disappointed. Madame retained no trace of that beauty she had heard so highly praised; she was badly dressed; when she got to Paris she knew no one at Court, and had to be instructed by Mademoiselle in the niceties of the French way of life. I suspect that Mademoiselle enjoyed that job.

Monsieur and Madame took up their residence in the palais d'Orléans, which Marie de' Medici had given to Monsieur and which was sometimes called, as it still is, the Luxembourg.[1]

The war with Spain still trailed on although negotiations for peace were already in progress; Monsieur went to take command of the army in Flanders, with some success at the siege of Gravelines, occasioning his daughter 'an inconceivable joy,

---

[1] They called it Luxembourg, not le Luxembourg.

because I always felt all possible tenderness towards him, even when I thought he did not treat me very well.' Always true to herself, she took far less interest in the continued triumphs of the duc d'Enghien, 'because owing to the dislike I felt for him I did not trouble to find out what he was doing.' Mademoiselle had never liked her Condé cousins, and indeed they constituted a very peculiar clan which would have taken a far larger measure of intelligent and closely affectionate understanding than Mademoiselle had ever been willing or qualified to accord. The Condés were a little closed rather mad world in themselves. There seems to have been, to say the least of it, a strain of hereditary eccentricity in the family; Condé's father had ridden stark naked in broad daylight through the streets of Sens, surely an odd thing to do. Mme de Rambouillet said of Condé's father that he had given his wife only two days of happiness: the first when by marrying her he raised her to so high a rank, and the second when by dying he set her free. Horrifying reports were later to be spread about Condé's only son: he was said to suffer from lycanthropy, a form of delusion which persuades the victim into the belief that he is an animal. So far as I know, Condé's son never aspired to the high legendary distinction of being a werewolf (*loup-garou*) but he did sometimes think he was a dog and must restrain himself from barking in the presence of the King; at other times he thought he was a bat in danger of bumping into the wainscot (*lambris*) of his rooms, or even that he might be a drooping plant that his servants ought to water. More excitingly alarming to his poor distorted mind, and also more comical to his contemporaries (the French not being endowed with the blessed gift of compassion) was his conviction that he might be a partridge in danger of being shot, or other variations on the same theme. 'I apologise for the gate having been opened to you by my wife,' said the gatekeeper to a M. Etternot who had been given a pass into the garden of the Luxembourg by the duchesse de Guise; 'if I had been there, I should not have opened it. My wife did not know what was taking place. They were chasing the duc d'Enghien,[1] who imagined himself to be a rabbit.' (*On y pursuit à la chasse M. le duc d'Enghien qui s'imagine qu'il est lapin.*)

Condé himself was by general consent the most insufferably overbearing of men, no truckler making concessions to gain favour—'M. le Prince would rather win battles than hearts'— and even in boyhood had been subject to such terrible attacks of temper that fears were entertained for his sanity. His brother Armand de Conti was physically malformed, almost a hunchback. Their sister Anne, duchesse de Longueville, *superbe et fort hautaine*, languid in manner but capable of suddenly dazzling flashes of mental agility, her beauty damaged by smallpox, not too clean in her person (*elle était malpropre et sentait mauvais*) commanded the devotion of that not inconsiderable personage the duc de La Rochefoucauld (author of the *Maximes*) and played her part amongst all the other intriguing ladies during the Fronde. She had been born in prison, through no fault of her own: it just happened that her father had been thrust into Vincennes for three years and that her mother had voluntarily though perhaps reluctantly shared his incarceration, and having presumably nothing else to do had given birth to four children, three of them stillborn including a pair of twins, and a fourth, this girl who survived to become the elder sister of Condé and of Armand prince de Conti.

The three of them, the sister and the two brothers, were closely united; it might be said, unnaturally as well as naturally united. It was not only Retz, with his wicked pen, who hinted at an almost incestuous bond between them (*un certain air d'inceste*). Mme de Longueville said outright that simple pleasures had no appeal for her (*Je n'aime pas les plaisirs innocents*). How can one judge these obscure complications of the human heart from the few indications left by contemporary memorialists? It might be just gossip and current scandal, yet it does seem that some strange, love-hate, quarrelsome, inescapable

---

[1] The title borne by the prince de Condé's eldest son and heir, as Condé himself had borne it until the death of his father.

link existed between the trio. 'The passionate devotion' (*amour passionné*), noted by Retz, of the prince de Conti for his sister de Longueville, drew from Mme de Nemours the remark that a proposed marriage between Conti and Mlle de Chevreuse greatly disturbed Mme de Longueville with the fear that she might lose something of her hold over her brother—and also, adds Mme de Nemours with a shrewd feminine touch, she did not welcome the idea of a younger and more beautiful woman being imported into the family circle. The relationship between Conti and his sister drew also from Mme de Motteville, not usually a scandalously-minded person, the comment that Conti who 'perhaps because he loved her too much, hated her at moments because, desirous that she should prefer him above all others, could not bear to think that he did not share all her secrets.' Poor Conti, who must have been remarkably innocent, remained for a long time unaware of the relationship between his sister and the duc de La Rochefoucauld. 'He and she (Mme de Longueville and La Rochefoucauld), acting in concert together, blinded him to such an extent that even after four years he had no idea at all of what was going on.' Conti was the least considerable member of this trio of siblings: he tagged along in their wake. 'I very nearly forgot to mention him,' says Retz; 'he was a zero, only to be multiplied because he happened to be a Prince of the Blood.'

One cannot help feeling sorry also for M. de Longueville, overwhelmed by his brothers-in-law (*accablé de ses beaux-frères*), informed by his wife that if he ventured to disapprove of her behaviour she would make him the unhappiest of men, and doubtless worried also by the dislike entertained by his daughter by his first marriage for his second wife.

Not an easy family to marry into.

They seem to have enjoyed annoying people unnecessarily, when Mme de Longueville was not engaged in fatally charming them. Their *hauteurs et bizarreries* gave offence to everyone from the Queen-Regent downwards: Mme de Longueville, having asked for an appointment with Anne, kept her waiting two or three hours, an unheard-of piece of impertinence. Even Condé was shocked.

Eccentricity, madness, and genius in the loose sense of the word were all mixed up in the Bourbons. How can genius in kingship be denied to Louis XIV, however much we may deprecate his European policy? He did deservedly give his name to his own splendid century. Genius in generalship in war is by common consent of historians accorded to Condé. As for Mademoiselle, also a Bourbon, we have already said enough and shall have more to say in proof of her aberrant conduct. She was no genius, neither was she mad. She might have entertained foolish ideas about marriages with kings and emperors, but never had she imagined herself a bat bumping against a wall. All the same no one could deny her a share in the intransigent Bourbon humour.

A very strange and interesting clan, the Bourbons. A study of their heredity should be most repaying. Why should some of them (Louis XIV and Condé) emerge as such dominating characters each in their own way, and why should others (Louis XIII and Gaston d'Orléans and presently Philippe duc d'Anjou) remain as such weak, evasive figures, sometimes pitiable and sometimes merely contemptible?

Mademoiselle had plenty of things to occupy her mind. Her own aunt, Henrietta-Maria, was being driven away from that inexplicable island where rebellious factions were daring to challenge the Divine Right of their Sovereign Lord and King. The troubles of England were about to cross the Channel, in the person of Charles I's unhappy wife, *la malheureuse reine* as she sometimes signed her letters. We tend perhaps, in reading history backwards and posthumously, to overlook the human and personal element. We think of Henrietta Maria as Queen of England, dressed in all the stiffness of courtly portraiture; we forget the woman of flesh, feelings, and beating heart.[1]

[1] This is why I have chosen as an illustration (Plate opposite p. 129) the Van Dyck profile which to my mind shows the soft, young, vulnerable character, stripped of its formal trappings.

Henrietta Maria had had her fair share of troubles. After the first misunderstandings of their married life, when, a bride fifteen years old, she had made her mistakes and he had made his and it had taken some years before their very different temperaments could become adjusted, she and her husband had achieved a true union of love, and it was with anguish that she now left him to the dangers she could no longer share. He mattered to her more than her children, but these also she had to abandon—her three sons, Charles, James, and Henry, and the baby Henrietta born June 1644 at Exeter to a fugitive mother 'reduced to a small corner of her realm for her last confinement.' Childbirth had always been difficult, perhaps because she was slightly deformed with a crooked spine; but on this occasion the poor Queen, recently recovered from rheumatic fever, was desperately ill. 'Mayerne, for love of me, go to my wife,' wrote Charles I to Sir Theodore de Mayerne, his own physician. She was given no time for a reasonable recovery. The baby was not a fortnight old when Lord Essex in command of the Parliamentary troops threatened to invest Exeter and refused to grant a safe-conduct to the Queen, rudely replying that if he escorted her Majesty anywhere it would be to London to answer to Parliament for the war. Such inhumanity towards a sick woman fills one with shame. Flight was the only possible answer. Entrusting the baby to the care of Lady Dalkeith and Sir John Berkeley (I confess I have never been able to understand why she did not tuck the baby under her arm and take it with her), Henrietta Maria started off in a litter for Pennycomequick (Falmouth) and embarked for her native France in a Dutch ship from Falmouth bay. She may have felt that she was at last to reach sanctuary, but, weak and ill and deeply sorrowful though she was,[1] she still had much to go through before she could sink into the hospitable arms of

---

[1] The day before she left Exeter, she had written to Charles I: 'I will show you by this last action that there is nothing which lies so close to my heart as your safety. My life is but a small thing compared with that. For in the present state of affairs your condition would be in great peril if you came to my relief, and I know that your affection would make you risk all for my sake . . . My dear heart, farewell.'

her French relations. Never a good sailor—'Mam's bad fortune at sea' was her son Charles' breezy way of putting it in a letter to his sister, or, as the *Mercure de France* delicately suggested on the occasion of her first arrival as a bride in England, '*elle était un peu ébranlé des vagues de la mer*'—after being chased to the Channel Islands by a rebel English cruiser, her Dutch ship fired on, struck by a shell, and nearly captured, the Queen of England was eventually driven by a gale on to rocks off the coast of Brittany and landed in a small boat in a fishing village. Here, at least, she must have been greeted with the reassuring music of her own language. Or did the speech of Breton fishermen sound as uncouth in her ears as the speech of her husband's subjects, which she had never been able wholly to master?

Paris! Paris, where she had been born, at the Louvre. She came back to the Louvre now (November 1644) as a guest received with all the honour due to a queen and a *Fille de France*. The entire royal family met her; there were exchanges of '*ma soeur*' and '*ma tante*'; clattering cavalcades of musketeers, *chevau-légers*, and many noblemen and gentlemen riding around the coaches; everything possible was done to make the traveller feel that she had indeed come home. She was given lodgings in the Louvre, the use of St Germain, and an allowance of 10,000 crowns a month, but we may wonder nevertheless how much she enjoyed being the poor relation, dependant upon the charity of France. 'She was in such a lamentable state that everyone pitied her,' wrote Mademoiselle; and Mme de Motteville, after commenting on the loss of her beauty—she had grown terribly thin—charitably added that constant suffering had perhaps added a gravity to her bearing which might have been lacking had she never known anything but happiness.

At first, the relief of safety was something to be thankful for. She had her own little Court. English royalists attended it, and a sprinkling of the Cavalier poets too—Edmund Waller, Sir William D'Avenant, whom she greatly favoured in spite of his having lost his nose, Sir John Denham who for a time was in attendance upon her and was presently joined by Abraham Cowley as an assistant secretary in dealing with the nine ciphers she used in her correspondence with her husband—a complicated task which kept Cowley busy all day and up all night two or three times a week. To these was presently added Richard Crashaw, discovered in great poverty, 'being a mere scholar, and very shiftless,' by Cowley who impressed him into Henrietta Maria's service. She was thus closely in touch with England; messengers went backwards and forwards; she even sent King Charles such money as she could raise to help his depleted funds. But gradually she found herself coming to the end of her resources. The French allowance was not enough, and after the first few months she could no longer afford the coaches or the ladies and maids of honour, the escort, the footmen, with whom she had arrived. They began gradually to disappear, until she was reduced to selling her jewels and her silver to pay the wages of her servants and the bills of her tradesmen. Mme de Motteville, coming to offer her respects, found her alone, writing letters, when Henrietta Maria showed her a little golden cup, saying that this was all the gold she had left, and that her servants had come asking her for money and threatening to leave her if she did not pay them, which she was unable to do. Mazarin, perhaps unjustly, ended by getting the blame:

> Des Anglais qui n'ont pas de pain
> Que tu laisses mourir de faim
> Et de leur reine desolée
> De ses bagues par toi volées . . .[1]

One consolation, after two years of this deteriorating existence, was the arrival of her little daughter Henrietta (July 1646) whose journey from England caused the English ambassador in Paris to describe it as 'a pretty romance.' Lady Dalkeith, her

[1] The English who lack bread,
Left by you to die of starvation;
And their Queen despoiled
Of her rings by you stolen.

devoted governess, in fact kidnapped the child, 'disguised herself in a shabby cloak and gown, placed a hump of old rags on one shoulder to conceal her graceful figure, and, dressing the little princess in a ragged suit of boy's clothes, walked to Dover with the child on her back ... The only risk of detection lay in the angry exclamations of the little princess herself, who resented the shabby dress she wore as much as the name of Pierre which had been given her for the time being, and told everyone they met on the road that she was not Pierre but the Princess, and that these rags were not her real clothes.'[1]

Henrietta Maria was naturally overjoyed, but, unable to afford the luxury of a fire, was obliged to keep the baby in bed for warmth. Retz found her without a log of wood in the house. What more natural than that she should refer to Cromwell as *ce scélerat* or that the Montpensier fortune should glitter before her eyes?

The Prince of Wales arrived at Fontainebleau in September 1646. A swarthy boy, his dark complexion showed traces of the Medici blood that he and Mademoiselle had both inherited through their common grandmother; yet she, the French girl, was fair, and he, the English boy, was dark. Very odd. She evokes a pretty picture of his meeting at Fontainebleau with his mother and his French relations. The Queen of England, the Queen-Regent, the little King of France, the princesse de Condé, and Mademoiselle herself went out to greet him in that lovely autumnal forest; the Queen-Regent kissed him, and there were presentations all round. On this first occasion he did not make too bad an impression on Mademoiselle: 'He was only sixteen or seventeen,' she says, with all the superiority of nineteen, 'rather tall for his age, a fine head, black hair, a brown complexion, and passably agreeable in his person. But what was extremely inconvenient, was that he neither spoke nor understood a word of French.'

*   *   *

Madame, by Julia Cartwright, p. 12.

Everything possible was done for the entertainment of the young English prince. At Fontainebleau he went out hunting; in Paris he attended a party given by Mme de Choisy in honour of Mademoiselle. Down the long gallery which Louis XIII and Anne had so often traversed to visit Mademoiselle in her nursery, now came Henrietta Maria herself from the Louvre to the Tuileries, to dress her niece with her own hands, accompanied by Charles who held up a torch to throw light on the proceedings. A charming family picture! and one which must have encouraged the hopes of the Queen of England. Prince and princess, by her desire, wore the same colouring: Charles' *petite oie* (see page 54) was of red, black, and white, Mademoiselle's plume and the ribbons securing her jewels repeated the scheme.

On arrival at Mme de Choisy's, she found him waiting to assist her from her coach, and when she paused before a mirror to adjust her coiffure he again held up a torch for her convenience. He followed her everywhere, their cousin Rupert of Bavaria acting as interpreter between them. His manner towards her was certainly irreproachable; it was more; it was so marked that it began to attract attention. The Queen of England missed no opportunity of telling her how greatly she had taken the Prince of Wales' fancy: he could speak of nothing else, she said. But for her restraining hand he would have come to Mademoiselle's room at all hours; he was in despair on hearing of the Empress's death for he dreaded seeing a marriage arranged between Mademoiselle and the Emperor. Mademoiselle listened dutifully, without believing everything that she was told.

It is clear, however, that she was pathetically pleased at finding herself the centre of attention. The festivities and Mademoiselle's triumph reached their peak at a great party given at the Palais-Royal; it took three days to prepare her dress, all plastered over with diamonds. The tufts were of red, black, and white. Of her gems, we know only that she possessed a great diamond which had been given to her great-grandfather the duc de Joyeuse by Henri III, worth, according to Mademoiselle, over two hundred thousand *livres*.[1]

In addition she wore the Crown jewels and also such jewels as were still left to poor Henrietta Maria, who must have sighed over the pouring out of so much wealth. Mademoiselle was satisfied with her appearance. 'No one could have been more magnificently arrayed than I that day, and many people told me that my fine figure, my look of health, my white skin and the sheen of my fair hair became me no less well than the riches scintillating upon my person.'

In the ballroom, lit by torches, a throne under a canopy had been raised on three steps. Both royal boys, the King of France and the Prince of Wales, having refused to use it, Mademoiselle seated herself 'with these two princes at my feet. I did not feel in the least embarrassed at finding myself there. Everyone told me that I had never looked less embarrassed than on that throne, and that I should occupy it longer when once I was in possession of one.'

Mademoiselle looked down on the dark head of the Prince of Wales and thought of the Emperor. *Je ne regardais plus le prince de Galles, que comme un objet de pitié.*

It may seem strange that Mademoiselle with her vast fortune and her royal birth should not by now (1646) have been married off to some foreign prince or even to some French Prince of the Blood. She was nineteen. Already at the tender age of nine her father without her knowledge had promised her to the comte de Soissons, an elderly Bourbon cousin who had once aspired to the hand of Mademoiselle's own mother; and to console her for her disappointment in not being allowed to call the infant Dauphin her little husband, also to soothe her feelings after the scolding from Richelieu, her kind Aunt Anne had said to her, 'It is true that my son is too young; you shall

---

[1] One would like to know what has become of this diamond. Mademoiselle, who later gave it up to the King to help towards the payment of his troops, says that Cardinal Mazarin got hold of it and gave it to the Italian commissariat.

marry my brother instead.'[1] Apart from these two, neither of whom could be regarded as suitable or serious suitors, no attempt had been made either to woo Mademoiselle or to make use of her value as a bargain in the European marriage-market. She herself had never betrayed the slightest inclination for any young man, yet these gallants of the French Court cannot have lacked personal charm: they were decorative, brave, gay, and in the most favourable of circumstances were constantly in her company: balls, hunting-parties, and the beautiful surroundings of St Germain or Fontainebleau should surely have added a romantic service to the advantages of propinquity. All around her Mademoiselle saw her friends marrying, generally for position but surprisingly often accompanied by love. It was even possible, though rare, for a girl of exalted birth to marry a man very much her inferior; thus, Marguerite de Rohan, daughter and heiress of the duc de Rohan, after considering such eligible bridegrooms as the Duke of Weimar, Prince Rupert son of the Elector Palatine, and the duc de Nemours, set her heart on a simple gentleman named Henri Chabot who was so poor that he would gratefully accept the offer of a meal. The dismay of the proud Rohans may be imagined, 'Roi ne puis, prince ne daigne, Rohan suis.' The duchess tried to kidnap her own daughter who had gone into hiding; thwarted, she passed a warning round to all the priests she could think of; Chabot and Mlle de Rohan escaped to the Loire where they were duly married by a priest who had been summoned from Rome. Mademoiselle remarks—was it with surprise?—that their love for one another lasted several years. We may at least deduce that she had small sympathy with marriages made for love alone, since on one occasion she dismissed one of her women for having entered into such a union.

Adulterous love, of course, seemed more usual than conjugal. Mademoiselle took it for granted, and, living as she did in the midst of highly emotional people, knew what passions it could arouse in the human breast: the duc d'Enghien, that national

[1] Ferdinand, son of Philip III of Spain, Cardinal-Archbishop of Toledo, 1609-1641.

hero, himself a married man, was known to have fainted when saying good-bye to Marthe du Vigean on leaving for the wars. It may be doubted, however, whether Mademoiselle with her forthrightness and honourable principles would have indulged herself as a married woman in the accepted round of successive lovers, as complicated and interchangeable as the formations of a quadrille. Speaking of herself at the age of ten, she says, 'I already had such a horror of vice . . .' We have no reason to suppose that she altered her opinion in later years.

It may be noticed also, without wishing to press the point too far, that her friendships were always with women rather than with men, and that those friendships were apt to be deeper and more violent than is customary. There was Mlle d'Épernon, whose marriage was proposed with Casimir Vasa, King of Poland; Mademoiselle took it into her head that she herself might marry the King of Hungary; thus, she and her friend would spend the rest of their days together, thought Mademoiselle whose geography might be a trifle imprecise but who did at least know that a proximity existed between the two countries. When Mlle d'Épernon 'preferred the crown of thorns to the crown of Poland,' and decided to enter a convent, Mademoiselle's despair knew no bounds; she felt like a person 'carried beyond reason into violent grief.' 'All the same,' she added, 'the friendship I feel for her will last as long as my life.'

She was intensely sensitive to feminine beauty, censorious when a woman was dowdily dressed, appreciative of grace and wit in their most feminine expression. Yet she was no believer in a docile submission to man. 'Let us escape from slavery,' she wrote to Mme de Motteville; 'let there be one corner in the world where women can be their own mistresses.'

Sour grapes may have entered into Mademoiselle's indifference to the opposite sex. We must—and why shouldn't we? —admit that she was very ugly, uncouth, hoydenish, and devoid of charm for men. We know that her normally fair complexion could become blotched with red when she lost her temper. She strode where she should have tripped, swore where

79

she should have coaxed, was haughty where she should have been affable, frank where she should have been dissembling, rough where she should have been gentle. It was discouraging to hear her boast, 'Mine is no tender soul.' Was she herself aware that she was missing something other women enjoyed? 'I do not know what sweet sayings are,' she wrote, 'for no one has ever dared to address any to me, not on account of my birth, since some queens we know of have heard them,[1] but on account of my humour which is known to be far removed from coquetry.'

All this may be true. It will lead us nowhere to say that Mademoiselle had a complicated character. We have by now been taught to believe that we all have complicated characters, with depths and contradictions unrealised by ourselves. Mme de Motteville, lacking the benefit of our Freudian outlook, probably hit off Mademoiselle's waverings with sufficient truth in remarking that she never knew when it would be to her advantage to say a definite Yes. The things she really desired (by which Mme de Motteville means the Crown of France) were always overlaid by fleeting caprices, and that which she most wanted she could never grasp at the right moment.

Nevertheless, it was inevitable that the question of her marriage should crop up from time to time. Mademoiselle, whatever her personal feelings, was not averse from the thought of a crown. The notion that she might become Queen of Spain on the death of her Aunt Elisabeth[2] probably existed only in her own imagination, although she contends that both the Queen-Regent and Mazarin encouraged it; it seems unlikely in the extreme that either of them would have contemplated handing Mademoiselle, her fortune, and her fine French territories over to the enemy in the midst of a mortal war. Her plan

[1] This remark has been interpreted as an obvious dig at the reputed amours between Anne of Austria and the Duke of Buckingham. It seems to me far more likely that Mademoiselle was alluding to the suspected liaison between Anne and Cardinal Mazarin.

[2] Elisabeth de France, daughter of Henri IV and Marie de' Medici, 1602–1644, married Philip IV of Spain, 1615.

of marrying the Emperor[1] or at any rate his brother the Archduke Leopold ('I should have preferred the Emperor') met with no better reception, and indeed involved her in a most unpleasant scene with the Queen-Regent, while Mazarin without contributing any remarks sniggered at all Mademoiselle's replies. No doubt he, astute diplomatist and manipulator that he was, would gladly have juggled with the tempting possibility of breaking the Austro-Spanish alliance by such a marriage, but Mademoiselle had not played according to the rules of the game. She had been indiscreet; she had talked; she had listened to the unwise counsels of a certain abbé de la Rivière and of a certain Saujon who now found himself imprisoned in the Bastille. So beguiled had she become by this Imperial vision that, having heard that the Emperor was extremely pious, she determined to emulate his devotion, and so well did she succeed (for she never did anything by halves) that for a whole week she forgot all about the Empire and thought only of taking her vows as a Carmelite. Even when this whim had passed, she continued for a while in the ways of austerity, denying herself the pleasure of going to the Cours-la-Reine, and reading the works of Saint Teresa instead. She ceased to put on a *mouche*, that piquante beauty patch recently come into fashion (one is slightly surprised to find that she made use of them at all); omitted to powder her hair; neglected it so much that it grew long and dirty, she who always set great store by personal cleanliness; muffled her throat with three scarves which suffocated her in hot weather; and gave up wearing coloured ribbons, as though she were forty years old.

Mademoiselle, in fact, had succeeded in making a thorough fool of herself. Reading her account of the interview with the Queen-Regent one does not feel that, for all her defiance, she came out of it very well. 'The conversation seemed very long-drawn to me; disagreeable recapitulations always do seem long; I became bored, and seeing that it would never come to an end if I did not take my leave, I said I did not think Her Majesty

[1] Ferdinand III.

had anything further to say to me, made my curtsy, and came away fairly victorious from this contest, but very angry indeed.'

The other marriage project is of more immediate interest to us. What if Mademoiselle had become Queen of England? What kind of a figure would she have cut at the Court of Charles II? We may feel sure that, one way or another, she would not have remained a cipher like poor Catherine of Braganza, whose projecting rabbit-teeth did not escape Mademoiselle's reporters.

This time it was other people who were genuinely anxious for the match, and Mademoiselle herself who would not entertain the idea. It had long since occurred to Henrietta Maria that her niece's immense wealth would come as a very welcome contribution to the impoverished royal exchequer. Henrietta Maria, now widowed, and entirely dependent on charity, did everything in her power to force the marriage upon two reluctant young people. Charles' first visit to Paris had not gone badly; his second visit (here to take a liberty with chronology, for it occurred three years later, in 1649) was far less successful. Charles, now King of England[1] in name though not in fact, was preceded by Lord Jermyn and Lord Percy, both of whom paid assiduous court to Mademoiselle, and the whole question of marriage was reopened. The Queen-Regent and Mazarin both advised it; Gaston admitted that Henrietta Maria had formally asked for her hand, but although Mademoiselle as a dutiful daughter replied that she would obey him in all things, he told her only, in his usual evasive way, that she must do as she pleased. Mademoiselle was in a dilemma (*je fus fort en inquiétude et j'avais l'esprit bien embarrassé*). On the one hand the abbé de la Rivière pointed out the prevalent dearth of eligible princes—the Emperor and the King of Spain were both married, the King of Hungary was betrothed to a Spanish infanta, the Archduke Leopold would now never become King of the

---

[1] The execution of Charles I took place on February 9th, 1649.

Netherlands, the King of France was too young, and M. le Prince (Condé) was already married and his wife in excellent health. All these were cogent arguments. On the other hand, Mademoiselle, shrewd enough when her belongings were concerned, realised that if she married Charles she would have to sell all her possessions and risk the whole of her fortune to help him regain his kingdom. This idea did not appeal to her. 'Having always been happy and brought up in luxury, these considerations alarmed me greatly.' Nevertheless, she said, thus revealing her generous nature, if she had to marry him at all, she would rather marry him while he was in adversity, as when he recovered his throne he would feel himself under an obligation to her.

Lord Jermyn pressed her; he was diplomatic enough to tell her that the Queen-Regent and Monsieur had said, 'She is a creature who must be cajoled; she does only what she wants to do, and we have no power over her,' which naturally gratified Mademoiselle, as just the reverse of that old grievance of being treated as a child. But when they passed on to the subject of religion Lord Jermyn came up against a stumbling-block. Mademoiselle seemed to take it quite for granted that Charles would become a Catholic; he could surely do that for her, who on her part would have done so much for him? Lord Jermyn, whose insular feelings may be imagined, explained patiently that the King of England neither could nor should embrace the Church of Rome; to do so, would be to renounce for ever the hope of regaining his dominions.

It is clear from Mademoiselle's writings that at this stage she did briefly contemplate marrying Charles II. The day she drove out towards Compiègne to meet him, she had taken the trouble to curl her hair, which was not her usual practice. No sooner had she entered the royal coach than the Queen-Regent in her teasing way exclaimed, 'One readily recognises people who expect their admirers; see how tidy she is!' Mademoiselle wanted to reply that her motive was the honourable one of marriage, but did not dare. In this well-disposed frame of mind, she began by thinking that Charles had improved in looks since she had last seen him ('he might perhaps have won my favour at that time'), but this propitious impression did not last for long. Once in the coach, Louis XIV, boy-like, began asking his cousin Charles about the dogs and horses of the Prince of Orange and about hunting in the Netherlands; Charles answered him in French. But when the Queen-Regent asked him for news of his own affairs, he at first would not answer, and, on being pressed, excused himself by saying that he could not speak the language.

Mademoiselle was shocked, so much shocked that from that moment she decided against the marriage. To be a King, and unable to speak of his own situation, at his age! She proceeds to give us a very unexpected portrait of our Charles II: 'At dinner, he would not eat any ortolans but threw himself on an enormous piece of beef and on a shoulder of mutton, as though he had never been accustomed to anything else. After dinner, the Queen amused herself by leaving me with him; it was a quarter of an hour before he addressed a word to me. I should like to believe that his silence was due to respect rather than to a lack of passion, and to tell the truth I could have wished that he had shown me less (respect). As I was getting bored, I called M. de Comminges to come and make him talk. M. de la Rivière said, "He looked at you all through dinner and is still looking." I replied, "It is all very well for him to look without trying to please; he does not utter." M. de la Rivière said, "You are being coy about the soft nothings he has been saying to you." "Not at all," said I; "come near us, when he returns, and you will see how he sets about it." I went up to him, and, for something to say, asked him for news of certain common acquaintances; he answered, but no soft nothings. The hour of his departure having arrived, we accompanied him into the forest. He took leave of the King, and came to me, saying, "I think Lord Jermyn, who is more eloquent than I, has explained my intentions and my desire; I am your very obedient servant." I replied that I also was his very obedient servant; Jermyn paid

me a great many compliments; the King (Charles) bowed to
me, and went.'

It is not very difficult to read between Mademoiselle's naïf
lines. Charles might be trying to behave according to his
mother's schemes and instructions, and furthermore could not
fail to perceive the advantages both financial and political of a
union with a fabulously wealthy French princess, but he had
long since developed far too pretty a taste in women to be in
the least allured by a large-limbed, large-nosed, ruggèd, unfeminine creature with doubtless many virtues but lacking the
divine gift of charm. Mademoiselle might be rich, she might be
worthy, but she was not *coucheable*. Charles did as he was told;
kings had to put up with arranged marriages to brides they had
never even seen; but his courtship was dutiful rather than
enthusiastic. Mademoiselle says she was bored; Charles must
have been even more bored than she. He must have longed to
get away to the enchanting duchesse de Châtillon, the Bablon
of his nickname for her, and perhaps he also tossed a thought
back to Lucy Walter, 'brown, beautiful, and bold,' on whom
he had recently begotten his much-loved son James, Duke of
Monmouth.

CHAPTER IV

The Parliamentary Fronde
[1648 – 1649]

THE biography of a decorative but secondary figure such as Mademoiselle, important only in her own eyes, and so easily led astray on chases after the wildest of geese, is no place for a detailed history of the Fronde; yet in so far as she played something of a buffoon's part in it and in so far as her own reckless behaviour on one dramatic occasion brought about a radical change for several years in her personal existence, the Fronde cannot be passed over without a few pages of comment and exposition.

The Fronde amounted only to a civil war on a miniature scale. Anomalous and amorphous, it could take no recognisable shape. Condé, one of the principal actors, remarked that it deserved only to be recorded in burlesque verse. Its symbols of straw and paper, worn in hats or carried on fans, were only too indicative of its character as a tragi-comic farce. Its duration of four years, 1648–1652, was interrupted half-way through by a compromise treaty. Its military operations were negligible. Some heads were broken in the streets of Paris, and some scuffles took place in the provinces, but in no sense could it be regarded as a major conflict between the Monarchy and the nation. In this respect it differed greatly and in every important respect from the Civil War waged in the neighbouring kingdom of England, and about to culminate there in the unprecedented condemnation of an anointed Sovereign. Rulers had been murdered wholesale before then; kings and emperors, princes, dictators, tyrants, all had perished in their scores by the poisoned cup or the dagger of revenge; usurpers had died upon the battlefield; but never until Charles I emerged, pale in his white shirt, upon the balcony of Whitehall on a January day, had such a sight been seen as a King formally condemned to the stroke of the executioner's axe by his own Parliament, representatives of his own subjects.

Nothing of this kind happened during the Fronde. No attempt was made to depose the King of France or to over-throw the Monarchy. Condé himself, who eventually un-sheathed his glittering sword on behalf of the Parliamentary party, spoke these proud words: 'My name is Louis de Bourbon, and I have no intention of shaking (*ébranler*) the Crown.' The Fronde, began, none the less, as a democratic movement in the best sense of the word, since it originated, not in popular and ill-organised riots, but in the determination of the Parlement to improve the lot of the people by resistance to the increasing burden of taxation. An extract from the speech of the Advocate-General, Omer Talon, at a *lit de justice* in January 1648, is worth recording here, since it will give some idea of the condition of the poor hind in his province:

'For ten years the country has been ruined, the peasants reduced to sleeping on straw, their furniture sold to pay the taxes, so that to maintain luxury in Paris millions of innocent persons are forced to live on bread made of bran and oats . . . owning nothing but their souls, because no means has been found of putting them up to auction.'

These brave and bitter words were reinforced by a denial of the King's absolute right to impose his will upon the Parlement at a *lit de justice*. That practice, the Advocate-General said, had never been established until 1563 when a national emergency concerned with the wars of religion had rendered the novelty tolerable. It was strange, he continued, that a thing done once without precedent, a thing he could show to be contrary to its origin, should now pass as ordinary usage in the *true or feigned* necessities of the State. All this was very much in the nature of a constitutional protest; an attitude which, if only it could have been sustained, might have gone far towards altering the reign of *le Roi Soleil* and even of more distant and dire events in the history of France.

Unfortunately the issues remained neither so simple nor so worthy. It was not for Omer Talon, considerable orator though he was, to play the part of a Pym or a Cromwell. The conflict which had begun as a justifiable controversy between Crown and Parlement, continued as a feud between the faction of a haughty aristocracy and the now insufferable favourite of the Queen-Regent, Cardinal Mazarin.

Richelieu had broken the power of the nobles, leaving angry and frustrated men, with every intention of recovering the position they had lost. The unpopularity of Mazarin offered the obvious opportunity: once rid the country of the foreigner, and the French princes would have things all their own way. This is reducing the matter to its most elementary terms, to clarify the puzzling situation where Princes of the Blood are found taking arms against the forces of a Crown which by their birth, their natural instincts, and their worldly interests they were surely bound to uphold and support.

Popular indignation against Mazarin had been growing. The prophesied Age of Gold, far from materialising, had been replaced by fresh taxation, fresh oppression, until 'the people of France saw themselves treated as veritable galley-slaves.'[1] There was destitution in the provinces, but it was naturally in the capital that the growls of discontent made themselves most threateningly heard. Richelieu, who knew his Paris, had always said: 'Do not awaken that great beast.'

If the conflict between Parlement and the Crown had first found its official expression at the *lit de justice* in January 1648, the first demonstration by the citizens occurred in August of

[1] Omer Talon.

the same year. Condé[1] had achieved another of his shattering victories against the Spanish army under the Archduke Leopold at Lens. (August 20th.) So notorious was Mademoiselle's dislike of Condé that no one dared tell her the news, but left it written on a piece of paper for her to find on her table when she got up in the morning. This may seem cowardly of them but just goes to show how Mademoiselle's household had learnt to avoid provoking Mademoiselle's temper. With her usual candour, for she is always ready to record and to acknowledge her mistakes, she was at a loss to disentangle her personal feelings from what was obviously a great gain for the State: 'In this dilemma I was less a good Frenchwoman than I was a good enemy . . . I ought not to have been resentful of the victories of M. le Prince; he carried them off so often that I ought to have got used to them, but one does not accustom oneself to things one does not like.' Much against her will, she was obliged to attend the *Te Deum* celebration at Notre Dame carpeted with seventy-three tattered banners of Spain and the Empire, on a day (August 26th) which she notes as being 'rather remarkable.'

It was remarkable indeed, for Mazarin had taken advantage of the general rejoicings to arrest two members of the Parlement, Blancmesnil and the septuagenarian Pierre Broussel, whom the populace called their father. This was the signal for an outburst of fury; Mademoiselle, trying to make her way to the Luxembourg, found the Pont-Neuf barred with chains, but the quarrel of the citizens was not with her, and as soon as her liveries were recognised the chains were unhooked to allow her passage. 'The people of Paris,' she remarked with her usual boastful satisfaction, 'had always loved me because I was born and brought up there; they felt more respect and goodwill towards me than they usually felt towards persons of my standing.' Shallow-pated as ever, she could not take the affair seriously, but beguiled herself by noticing the lack of grace of men unaccustomed to wearing swords, 'that was how I amused

[1] By the death of his father in December 1646, the duc d'Enghien had become prince de Condé, commonly known as M. le Prince.

myself, while all France trembled.' She did, however, come to her senses when, next morning on hearing the roll of drums, she sprang from her bed and looked down from her window on the bloody spectacle of wounded men.

The *journée des barricades* (August 27th, 1648) was the true beginning of the Fronde. The Regent and Mazarin were compelled to give way and order the release of Broussel. It was the first victory of the people. The very name of Fronde had its origin in the sling or catapult dear to the gutter-snipes of Paris; it caught on so well that before long the haberdashers were trimming gloves, fans and handkerchiefs with the emblem, and bakers were twisting their rolls into the shape of a sling. Street-songs took it up:

> 'Un vent de fronde
> S'est levé ce matin;
> Je crois qu'il gronde
> Contre le Mazarin.'

So intense, so blinkered was the feeling against Mazarin that the triumph of his diplomacy abroad in concluding the Peace of Westphalia (October 1648) which brought the Thirty Years War to an end, passed unnoticed and unrecognised in the tumult of home affairs. Public abuse was now undisguised; Mazarinism, a word invented by Cardinal de Retz, took its place in the language; all the lampoonists of Paris were busy turning out scurrilous verse and prose known as Mazarinades. The ballad-mongers, voicing the sentiments of the people, became more and more outspoken:

> 'Pestons contre cet animal
> Qu'on appelle le Cardinal . . .
> Ce Zany, ce Pantalon,
> Ce Jongleur qu'on déguise en prêtre . . .
> Ce détestable Cardinal . . .
> Adieu, cause de nos ruines . . .
> Par la cherté de la farine,

Par la crainte de la famine,
Enfin par toutes nos misères
Dont nous gardons le souvenir
Allez sans jamais revenir.'[1]

There were said to be over two thousand of these Mazarinades,
and some did not stop short of proclaiming that the Queen-
Regent was Mazarin's mistress.[2] The whole situation seemed
so inflammable and unsafe, that Anne took the extraordinary
step of secretly removing the King and his brother at three
o'clock in the morning to St Germain. It was Twelfth Night
(January 6th, 1649), moonlit and cold; Mademoiselle, aroused
from sleep with a summons to join the royal family in the
Cours-la-Reine, was in the worst of tempers, not improved on
finding that she was expected to yield the warmest place in the
coach to the old princesse de Condé. Eight of them packed into
the enormous coach: the Queen-Regent, the two sleepy little
boys, Louis the King and Philippe duc d'Anjou, the old
princesse de Condé, her son the prince de Conti, Mademoiselle,
the young princesse de Condé with her baby still in his
swaddling-clothes, and the marquise de Senneçy, a lady-in-
waiting to the Regent. Anne, unexpectedly, was in high
spirits; 'I never saw so gay a creature,' according to Mademoiselle; 'she could not have been more so, had she just won
a battle, taken Paris, and hanged all her enemies.'

This strange assortment of a royal family had need of all
their good humour, for on arrival at St Germain they found
not even the barest comforts of life for their reception. The

[1] Let us rail against that beast
Called the Cardinal . . .
That Merry-Andrew, that Pantaloon,
That trickster disguised as a priest . . .
That detestable Cardinal . . .
Good-bye, cause of all our ruin . . .
By the high cost of flour,
By the dread of famine,
And by all our miseries
Which we shall never forget,
Go! and never return.
[2] It seems likely that she was; some historians have believed her to be his wife.

palace was echoing and empty; everything that had not been carted back to Paris had been put away for the winter. The Regent could get nothing sent out from Paris, because everything was stopped at the gates lest it might be the property of Mazarin; a wagon loaded with the King's baggage had been ordered back to the Palais-Royal; the King and his mother had to make shift with borrowed furniture. Monsieur managed to borrow a bed from Condé. 'Those who had beds had no hangings, and those who had hangings had no clothes.' Mademoiselle, who at first had only two chemises, one of which was washed during the day and the other during the night, was more fortunately placed, for the gates were opened to allow her coach free passage (was she not the darling of the Parisians, and had not the chains across the Pont-Neuf fallen before her?) She received not only a mattress and some linen from Mme de Fiesque, but to her supreme satisfaction was able to gratify the Queen-Regent's humble request for a few of her things (*ses hardes*) to be sent under the protection of Mademoiselle's charmed name. 'The King and the Queen lacked everything, but I could get whatever I wanted.' Even so, she had to put her mattress on the floor, in an attic beautifully decorated and gilded, but with only a very small fire and no glass in the windows, and had to share the mattress with her little sister[1] who had no bed. Mademoiselle sang her to sleep, but the child fidgeted, woke, cried, and had to be sung to sleep again. It was altogether a strange experience for Louis XIV and his Court, perhaps especially for Louis. He was said to have conceived a dislike for Paris which led later on to the transference of the seat of government to Versailles.

Meanwhile Condé with an army of eight thousand men was laying siege to Paris. It was not a very serious siege so far as fighting went, but it did leave the capital short of food and it did have the effect of splitting the princes into two opposite

[1] She does not say which of her three half-sisters: Marguerite Louise, known as Mlle d'Orléans, 1645–1721; Elisabeth, known as Mlle d'Alençon, 1646–1691; Françoise Madeleine, known as Mlle de Valois, 1648–1664. See appendix X, 359–362

camps. Condé's brother the prince de Conti, and their brother-in-law, the duc de Longueville, presented themselves at the Porte St Honoré at two in the morning (January 10th, 1649), were refused admittance, sent word to Retz, obtained an interview with M. de Blancmesnil and M. de Broussel, the two counsellors whom Mazarin had arrested, and sent through Blancmesnil a formal declaration to the Parlement that they desired to support its interests without condition or reserve. Their example was rapidly followed by a score of noblemen, bearers of the greatest names in France: the duc de Beaufort, known as *le roi des Halles*,[1] coarse of speech, as handsome as he was stupid, of whom it was said that any woman in Paris from the highest to the lowest would give anything to sleep with him; the prince de Marsillac, besotted by Mme de Longueville; the duc d'Elbeuf; the maréchal de La Motte; the duc de Bouillon. It must not be supposed that these gentlemen were wholly disinterested. They all wanted something for themselves, for their wives, mistresses, friends, or mistresses of friends. A very much abbreviated list may give some idea. The prince de Conti wanted Mme de Chevreuse to be recalled; he wanted a *tabouret* for the princesse de Marsillac, and a *place forte* for himself in Champagne; the duc de Longueville wanted money, and several other favours; the duc de Beaufort wanted the governorship of Brittany for his father, the old duc de Vendôme, and compensation for all his houses and castles destroyed in Brittany during the reign of the late King (see page 40); the duc d'Elbeuf wanted Montreuil, the payment of monies due to his wife, and 100,000 francs for his younger son; the duc de Bouillon wanted Sedan or the equivalent in cash, the governorship of Auvergne, which already belonged to somebody else, the royal domains in Alsace, and the recognition as princes of France for himself and all members of his house; the maréchal de La Motte wanted money; the duc de La Trémouille wanted the Roussillon and Amboise; the marquis de Vitry wanted to

---

[1] King of the Markets. This would correspond to our saying King of Billingsgate, or Smithfield.

be made duc and the *tabouret* granted to his wife; the duc de Luynes wanted money and the recall of Mme de Chevreuse; the comte de Fiesque wanted the *tabouret* for his wife, and so it goes on. A most illuminating document, though not very edifying.[1]

A spider in the centre of the web, which is where he liked being, Paul de Gondi, then Co-adjutor to the Bishop of Paris, spun his threads and persuaded himself that he played a more influential part than was in fact the case. An ambiguous figure, Italian by origin, sensual (*je ne me pouver passer de galanterie*), lazy by nature but rendered active by ambition, the Cardinal de Retz is one of the interesting characters of the time. Physically his insignificant stature, his bandy legs, his peering myopic eyes, his over-dark complexion, his taste for flashy clothes and baubles, his prinking ways, might all have rendered him slightly and meanly ridiculous, but with his wit and gallantry he contrived to be not unattractive to women. Mentally he was agile, subtle; a born though not very successful intriguer, endowed with a most remarkable memory. But as Mazarin was inferior to Richelieu, so was Retz with all his intelligence inferior to Mazarin. A monstrous huge sturgeon caught in the river near his home on the day of his birth, perhaps symbolically set the key to his inflated sense of his own importance.

Mme de Longueville and Mme de Bouillon in a fine histrionic gesture offered themselves as hostages for the good faith of their husbands. 'I ask you to conjure up the picture,' says Retz, with his keen eye for any dramatic occasion, 'of these two, standing on the steps of the Hôtel de Ville, looking all the more beautiful for the apparent carelessness of their dress (*plus belles en ce qu'elles paraissaient negligées, quoiqu'elles ne le fussent point*), and each carrying in her arms a child as beautiful as its mother. The place de Grève was crowded even up to the roof-tops, men shouted, and women wept with

[1] *Demande des princes et seigneurs qui ont pris les armes avec le Parlement et peuple de Paris*, 15 mars, 1649. Given in *Choix des Mazarinades*, Vol. I, pp. 431–436, by C. Moreau.

emotion on seeing grand ladies with their babies in the crook of their arm.' Amid these public rejoicings the two ladies were given rooms in the Hôtel de Ville where they lost no time in establishing a political and social salon, and where, to the music of violins, the princely party of *frondeurs* was formed. Retz describes how the marquis de Noirmoutier with three other men, still in their steel cuirasses and accoutrements of war, trampled into Mme de Longueville's room, crowded with feminine grace (*toute pleine de dames*). 'That medley of blue scarves, steel breast-plates, violins in the *salon* upstairs, and trumpets sounding in the Grève below, gave an impression of something in fiction rather than in real life.'

Retz was a born journalist.

Condé alone, outside the ramparts, remained temporarily faithful to the royal cause.

The Peace of Rueil, signed on April 1st, 1649, concluded the first Fronde, or *fronde parlementaire*. The Court returned to Paris (August 18th, 1649) amid what Mademoiselle describes as an unparalleled confusion of people. The citizens in their thousands packed the streets on the route of the royal procession, incessantly shouting *Vive le roi*! It was very hot, Mademoiselle had a headache, she was crowded with seven other people into the Queen's coach, and it took them from three in the afternoon till eight o'clock at night to drive from Le Bourget into Paris. No wonder that she remarked she had never been so bored. She never liked not being the centre of attention.

She had her compensation when, much admired by all, the eleven-year-old King, dressed all in gold, led her out to dance the first *courante* at a ball offered by the city of Paris at the Hôtel de Ville in honour of his return. He performed this task with 'so much seemliness and delicacy (*mignardise*) that he might have been mistaken for Cupid dancing with one of the Graces.'[1] This was not subservient flattery; Louis XIV loved dancing, and danced very well.

[1] *Registres de l'Hôtel de Ville pendant la fronde.*

Mademoiselle, however, was destined to suffer a temporary eclipse which removed her from the fêtes and celebrations: she fell ill with smallpox. She never liked being out of the great world, but in this case she had to admit that her retirement brought her certain advantages. 'Although I am no beauty,' she writes, 'this illness did not leave me red in the face; previously, my complexion used to be very blotchy, but the smallpox took it all away. The whole Court,' she goes on, 'sent to enquire after me with every imaginable care, even people I did not know; at a loss how to pass the time, I used to read all the notes people had brought or had sent to my door.' There was one exception: Condé omitted to enquire, 'which increased my dislike of him.' The first time she met him, after her recovery, at the confirmation of the King and his brother, he teased her by saying that he did not believe she had been ill at all, but had only been pretending: *je ne reçus pas bien cette plaisanterie et il s'en aperçut.*

Condé's arrogance had by now gone far beyond the bounds of a mere discourtesy to Mademoiselle. Intransigent by nature, he considered himself the saviour of the royal cause and assumed all the airs of a dictator at Court. He lost no opportunity of offending Mazarin and even the Queen-Regent, taking under his protection a certain marquis de Jarzé whom she had banished from her sight for impertinence; Condé made a point of appearing with him everywhere, in the Cours-la-Reine, in the Renard gardens. The *ruelles* of all the Court ladies echoed with this scandal.[1] Far more serious were the differences between Condé and Mazarin, which, petty enough to begin with in themselves, in fact represented the overture to a duel between the two men for the mastery of France. The occasions might be insignificant, the cause was profound. It was intolerable to a man of Condé's birth, position and temperament to ask favours from the Italian favourite of the Queen-Regent. Condé demanded the governorship of Pont de l'Arche

[1] *Journal Inédit*, Dubuisson-Aubenay.

for the duc de Longueville, who already had the whole of Normandy under his control; Mazarin, true to Richelieu's policy of diminishing the territorial power of the nobility, refused it. Condé quite unjustifiably stipulated that Mazarin's nieces should marry only men of his, Condé's, choice; Mazarin, fully aware of the rivalry between the house of Condé and the house of Vendôme, retaliated by saying that his niece Laura was already sought in marriage by the duc de Mercœur, son of the duc de Vendôme. Condé's manner towards Mazarin, always mocking, scornful and contemptuous, became personally insolent. Tweaking the Cardinal by the chin, he exclaimed, 'Good-bye, Mars!' in allusion to Mazarin's well-known cowardice in the face of danger. There could be only one end to such a ferment: Condé, with his brother Conti and the duc de Longueville were arrested and thrown into prison at Vincennes (January 1649).

Mazarin had gone too far, Princes of the Blood were not so lightly to be clapped into prison. Nothing but high treason to the State could have warranted so rash and ill-considered a step. It was the signal for an outburst of resentment and indignation, in which the great ladies played a spectacular part. Mme de Longueville, ordered to present herself at the Palais-Royal, refused, and fled to Dieppe in her husband's province of Normandy, whence, having tried in vain to raise the population, she escaped on horseback to Pourville; here, in attempting to board a vessel in a gale of wind, she was flung into the sea and was rescued unconscious. No sooner re-covered, than she started to wander along the shore, where after several days she embarked on a boat for Rotterdam. Lovely, mischievous, and foolish, fatally seductive to men, with her blue eyes, her air of languor, and her sudden flashes of wit, Mme de Longueville could not be accused of lacking courage.

Left behind in Paris, Mme de Chevreuse, the princesse

Palatine, Mme de Montbazon and Mme de Châtillon continued their good work of stirring up trouble in the *ruelles* and the *salons* which were their domain. The political influence of these women must not be underrated; their intelligence might be too highly esteemed—Cardinal de Retz said in absurd serious-ness that the princesse Palatine had as great a capacity for conducting the affairs of State as Queen Elizabeth of England herself—but in this extraordinary society where love counted so much and stability so little, the underground craftiness of women and their romanesque desire to steer and interfere as much as possible came as a very potent factor in the affairs of troubled France. Mme de Motteville, usually wise, must have lost her head and her sense of proportion when she remarked that *les dames* were ordinarily the chief cause of disorders in States, and that the wars which brought ruin on to Kingdoms and Empires seldom arose unless provoked by the beauty or the malice of women. That she could even allow so wildly foolish an opinion to flow off her pen shows the awe and mistrust these ladies were able to impose.

A real surprise, however, with startling consequences, was provided by the tiny princesse de Condé—that seemingly silly Claire-Clémence de Brézé, who had still played with dolls two years after her marriage and whom Mademoiselle had be-friended when she saw her despised by her husband's strange, closely-bound, and cruel family. Ordered to leave Paris after Condé's arrest, she obeyed the injunction to such good purpose that she was next heard of in Bordeaux, where, aided by the duc de La Rochefoucauld and the duc de Bouillon, she put the city into a state of defence against Mazarin. On hearing of this exploit in his prison, Condé exclaimed, 'What! my wife makes war while I cultivate carnations?' His wife was indeed making war, and in July 1650 the entire Court accompanied the army to lay siege to the rebel town. Mademoiselle, very much against her will, had to go too. How leisurely things moved in those days! They stayed a month at Libourne on the way; Mademoiselle complained of the heat (*il faisait une chaleur horrible*). The Queen-Regent remained all day lying on her bed, seeing nobody, and dressing only in the evening; Mademoiselle had to sit with her, with nothing to do except write letters to distant Paris, or, when they removed to Bourg, to watch from the window the boats on the Dordogne, when she was not stitching at an embroidery.

This was not at all in accordance with Mademoiselle's idea of war, nor was the siege of Bordeaux when they finally arrived there. She calls it, rather rightly, an imaginary siege; Mazarin climbed into a belfry to see what was going on; the maréchal de la Meilleraye was incapacitated by gout; and within less than three weeks (September 5th to October 1st, 1650) an amnesty was concluded. Mademoiselle took some credit to herself for insisting that the terms of the peace should be observed and all promises kept, and was not displeased when the Queen-Regent said, 'Mademoiselle is becoming furiously *frondeuse*.'

On the way back to Paris (November 1650) they learnt that the citizens, enraged by a rumour that their *roi des Halles* the duc de Beaufort had narrowly escaped assassination by orders of Mazarin, had hung effigies of the Cardinal dressed in all his robes at all the cross-roads and on the Pont-Neuf, accompanied by posters setting out the various crimes for which he deserved to die. Paris was in effervescence; it was becoming obvious that a crisis was at hand. Bands of horsemen patrolled the streets at night. The Parlement renewed its petitions to the Queen for the release of Condé and the other princes. Here, if ever, was an occasion when Gaston should have weighed in with the double authority of his consanguinity as a senior member of the royal family and in his official capacity as *lieutenant-général de l'État*; but Monsieur never liked being stirred into positive action. It was easier to slide away: *Monsieur levait les épaules*— Monsieur shrugged his shoulders and procrastinated from the morning to the afternoon, from the afternoon to the evening. His own wife said he laboured more in coming to a decision than she had ever laboured in giving birth to her children. It took Retz three days of expostulation and exhortation to persuade him that the hour for evasion was past. At last Monsieur, who for some time back had refused to speak either to the Queen-Regent or to Mazarin, emerged from his retirement. He went to the Palais-Royal, had an angry scene with the Queen-Regent after hearing Mazarin declare that the duc de Beaufort and the Cardinal de Retz were no better than Fairfax and Cromwell; that the Parlement was coming to resemble the English Parliament, and would soon be behaving in France as the House of Commons had behaved in England. Monsieur swore that he would never set foot in the Palais-Royal again until Mazarin was out of it, and left the room without bidding anybody farewell.[1] It might appear as though Monsieur had for once been badgered into taking a strong line. He had lost his temper, stalking out of the Palais-Royal like that, but Monsieur's losses of temper are not impressive. They represent only the irascibility of a weak man forced by the circumstances of his birth into taking a reluctant part. He lost his temper because he was scared: 'He (Mazarin) frightened Monsieur' (*fit peur à Monsieur*), who was so much relieved at getting himself intact (*sain et sauf*) out of the palace that on regaining his coach he declared he would never again entrust himself into the hands of that madman and that fury—a most undeserved epithet to apply to the puzzled, worried, indolent, ignorant, gentle, pious, and foreign princess, Anne of Austria, who hated to be bothered with public affairs and who could so pathetically say she wished it were always night-time because although she could not sleep, she welcomed the silence and the solitude instead of the day-time when she saw only people who betrayed her.

Six days later, after nightfall (6th-7th February, 1651) Mazarin crept out of Paris by the Porte Richelieu, draped in a red cloak and wearing a plumed hat. He had taken the precaution of sending five other men, similarly attired, to five

[1] *Mémoires de la duchesse de Nemours.*

other gates.[1] Next day the Parlement resolved to banish him from France.

The disappearance of Mazarin was immediately followed by the reappearance of the three princes.[2] All the way from St Denis, where Gaston d'Orléans, the duc de Beaufort, Retz and five thousand gentlemen on horseback had ridden out to meet them, the roads were lined with crowds and coaches and the acclamations of the people for M. le Prince surpassed all expectations. They appeared to have forgotten that he had laid siege to Paris; they saw in him only the triumphant enemy of Mazarin. The Queen-Regent in the Palais-Royal awaited him with very different feelings: she complained of the heat in the room, but everybody knew that the true reason of her complaints sprang from quite another cause. She could not foresee how Condé would comport himself. If he had been arrogant and masterful before, what would he be now, with the desire for revenge burning in his heart, the people of Paris at his feet, Mazarin out of the way, and a powerful phalanx of the nobility ready to support him? How was she to interpret the oracular words he was known to have uttered, 'I entered prison the most innocent of men, I come out as the most guilty'? What had he been hatching during the long days of his captivity? Deprived of the guiding counsels of Mazarin, importuned by the Parlement, suspicious of all, especially of Gaston d'Orléans, opposed by Retz with his influence over the clergy, Anne found herself alone to confront the return of this dangerous, incalculable man with unknown designs upon the ultimate authority.

Anne received the princes as she lay in her bed. The *ruelle*, that informal meeting-place, that recognised gathering-place for social intercourse, where friends could sit and gossip, was just the place for Anne to receive Condé and the others in that

[1] Morosini, Venetian Ambassador.
[2] Mazarin went round by le Havre, where they had been transferred, to set them personally at liberty, February 13, 1651.

easy-going way. They did not stay very long; a quarter of an hour in the *ruelle* sufficed for the exchange of conventional civilities; the dreaded meeting had superficially passed off without incident, as it should between civilised people, and the princes went off to dine with Gaston and Mademoiselle. What a change had taken place in Mademoiselle's feelings! Far from regarding herself as a weathercock, she patted herself on the back for her self-command in switching over from hatred to friendship. The reconciliation between her and Condé was complete, and seems to have satisfied them however peculiar the form of its expression may appear to us. Certainly they did not mince their words. They both began by admitting the extreme dislike they had had for one another. Condé informed Mademoiselle of his delight on hearing that she had got small-pox; of his ardent wish that she might be permanently marked and disfigured; nothing, in fact, he said, could have excelled the hatred he felt towards her. Mademoiselle retaliated by telling him that never had she been better pleased than by the news of his recent imprisonment; that she had always prayed for it; and that she could not think of him without wishing him ill. After this cousinly interchange of candour (the word Mademoiselle uses is *éclaircissement*), they concluded with many assurances of mutual friendship, to the satisfaction of the assembled company. Condé's younger brother, the prince de Conti, then approached Mademoiselle in his turn and was assured by her that she had taken no pleasure in his imprison-ment; on the contrary, she had been sorry to hear of it. He thanked her warmly for her kind words. Perhaps, as a robust young woman herself, she felt some pity for the poor envious hunchback.

The reconciliation nearly had a most surprising sequel: the princesse de Condé fell critically ill with erysipelas in the head and for three days her life was despaired of. If Mme la Princesse were to depart this world, as seemed likely, no time should be lost in arranging a second marriage for M. le Prince. A bride was ready to hand: M. le Prince should marry Mlle de Montpensier.

Mademoiselle took this suggestion quite seriously. She discussed it with her faithful secretary Préfontaine, saying that the thing was feasible, considering the close friendship which now existed between M. le Prince and Monsieur, and the dislike of the Queen-Regent for Monsieur, which rendered any marriage between her (Mademoiselle) and the King out of the question. She did, however, have the sense to see that an alliance between the Houses of Orléans and Condé would be strongly resisted at Court; an increase in Monsieur's preponderance, backed by so redoubtable a son-in-law as Condé, would never be tolerated. Fortunately, the recovery of Mme la Princesse put an end to the matter.

It will have been observed that Mademoiselle had alluded to the unlikelihood of a marriage between herself and the King. This did not mean that she had ever quite given up the idea of obtaining the *couronne fermée*, for at the back of her mind lurked always the possibility that her *petit mari* might become her *grand mari*. It is not easy to determine how seriously she entertained this crazy ambition. The possibility certainly did not exist only in her imagination, for Mme de Motteville relates that one of the Queen-Regent's maids of honour once went on Mazarin's instruction to offer the King's hand to Mademoiselle, on condition that she should prevent her father from allying himself with Condé. 'Make yourself Queen, Mademoiselle,' she said, 'and then you will be able to banish the princes.' With the sensible side of herself she must have known that such a match was impossible of realisation. Apart from the discrepancy in their ages, a boy of thirteen and a woman of twenty-four, there existed, as Mademoiselle recognised, the dislike and mistrust which the Queen-Regent not unnaturally felt for Gaston, sufficiently active to deter her from the thought of a union between her son and his daughter. Even Mazarin, in command of the Queen's heart as a woman and her political adviser as Regent—even Mazarin who at that one moment had considered an alliance between the senior and the junior branches of the royal house in no unfavourable light, and had tentatively written to the Queen-Regent to that effect, wisely dropped the subject in anticipation of the resistance it was likely to arouse. Mademoiselle should likewise have laughed the idea away. She cannot wholly be blamed. Nobody played fair by her, in that world where nobody played fair by anybody else and the whole intricate mesh was, and is, as difficult to unravel as a skein of wool tangled by a kitten. The Queen-Regent, for instance, would promise the hand of the King her son to Mademoiselle, probably out of sheer mischief, and then would make fun, saying, 'Not that it would be for the sake of her nose, though that is big enough.' (*Ce n'est pas pour son nez, quoiqu'il soit bien grand.*)[1] Mademoiselle of course could not know, though she might well have suspected, being versed in the cruel and crooked usage of her equals, that Anne might say one thing to her face and quite a different and far less kindly thing behind her back.

We may recall by contrast, the eager generosity with which Mademoiselle, then aged fifteen, and pleasure-loving as was natural to her years, had endeavoured to assuage the grief she imagined would be felt by the Queen-Regent in the first year of her widowhood. 'I followed her everywhere; I deprived myself of pastimes which I should have enjoyed, in order to give her my company everywhere she went; and although she took very little notice of my care, and never told me anything about anything, I did it ungrudgingly and the affection I felt for her made me bear it all.'

There may be two sides to this picture. Anne of Austria may not have at all welcomed the presence of an adolescent Mademoiselle, blundering like a clumsy though well-meaning puppy, perpetually at her heels.

Mademoiselle was a simpleton in many ways. She was easily

[1] *Mémoires de Pierre de La Porte.*

self-deceived. The glamour of the Throne was potent, and busy-bodies were not lacking to keep the spark alive.

That beautiful and dissolute intriguer, the princesse Palatine, who was equally at home travelling the roads of France on horseback disguised as a man or on foot disguised as a monk, or astonishing a not easily astonished Court by her gallantries, and by passing herself off for five years as Mme de Guise, which she had never been, took a hand in the game. She capriciously abandoned her friendship with Condé, and sent an emissary, Mme de Choisy, to inform Mademoiselle that a scheme was afoot to make her the Queen of France. 'If you do that,' said Mademoiselle, 'I will give you Bois-le-Vicomte.'

Was Mademoiselle being sarcastic? Bois-le-Vicomte was one of her minor estates, a poor offer in return for the Crown. Sarcasm was not her habit: she was too blunt and direct to indulge in its subtleties. But on this occasion we may assume that Mademoiselle saw through Mme de Choisy, that small toady and parasite, running backwards and forwards like a mischievous weasel between the ankles and under the petticoats of the great.

A few days later Mme de Choisy reappeared. 'La princesse Palatine is interested in your affair, but she is a rogue (*gueuse*) and you must promise her 300,000 *écus* if she is successful. As for me, I want my husband to become your Chancellor. We shall have a very good time, because you will make la Palatine your *surintendante* with a remuneration of 20,000 *écus;* we will have a *comédie* every day at the Louvre.' Mademoiselle was not sure how to take these childish proposals, nor did she relish the idea of being so completely dependent upon la Palatine, but when Mme de Choisy went on to say that she and the King would be married within a week after he had reached his majority,[1] she admits to having been shaken. 'Although I am not particularly gullible, I did not know what to believe.'

Whatever she might say, she was, in fact, very particularly gullible, which is one of the reasons for which one likes her.

---

[1] On September 7th, 1651.

Never was there a person more given to wishful thinking. The King having gone out riding seven or eight times with Mademoiselle and Mme de Frontenac, the Queen-Regent decided that he must be falling in love with Mme de Frontenac and forbade any further excursions. The King, aged twelve, and speaking for the first time with the authentic accents of Louis XIV, angrily exclaimed, 'When I am the master, as I soon shall be, I shall go wherever I choose.' Mademoiselle would have none of the Queen-Regent's explanation. She preferred to believe that Anne feared he would grow too well accustomed to her, Mademoiselle's, company, and growing accustomed, would come to love her, and loving her, would realise that she was the best match for him, failing the Infanta of Spain.

At this juncture Charles II reappeared upon the scene, with shaven head and a big beard, having escaped from his lost island after the Battle of Worcester. (September 3rd, 1651.) He regaled Mademoiselle with stories of his sojourn in Scotland; how there were no women there; how the Scottish people thought it wrong to listen to violins (would Mademoiselle allow her violins to play for him? he asked), and how bored he had been, longing only to return to France, and a dozen other civilities which disposed her greatly in his favour. After that, he came every other day to visit her; they danced; once he came unexpectedly to supper with his mother and his brother the Duke of York; they played little games afterwards, but Mademoiselle felt vexed because, unprepared, she had not given them a good enough dinner. Charles' French had improved, but not much; it was only in paying court to Mademoiselle that, according to her, he became really eloquent, forgot his own language, lost his English accent, and drove her to the conclusion that 'Love was more French than of any other nation.' Innocent vanity! for once not mistaken. Charles formally asked her to marry him. He must have been surprised by the reply he got. Mademoiselle told him that if he did not go back soon to England he would find it difficult to recapture his Throne, and that if he remained in Paris she would sadly watch him enjoying himself, dancing the *tricotet*[1] when he ought to be elsewhere, either getting his head broken or else replacing the Crown on it, which he would be unworthy to wear unless he had gone to fetch it at the point of his sword and at the peril of his life.

Mademoiselle, perhaps unfortunately for the Stuarts, was never destined to become Queen of England.

[1] A particularly lively dance.

CHAPTER V

The Fronde of the Princes
[1652]

ON the 30th of January, 1652, Cardinal Mazarin rejoined the King, the Queen-Regent, and the Court at Poitiers. He had not come alone, and he had not come unopposed. He had brought with him an army of four thousand Germans under the command of the maréchal d'Hocquincourt, one of Condé's most determined enemies. At first, the campaign did not go at all well for the *frondeurs*. Gaston d'Orléans, now lieutenant-general of France although openly allied with the princes, withdrew his own troops from the royal army and sent them to block Mazarin's passage over the rivers, but the hundred musketeers from Languedoc[1] were overcome on the Yonne and Mazarin passed the Loire at Gien without meeting any resistance. Condé, who had rushed into Saintonge, received a check on the Dordogne. In great alarm, the Parlement as soon as Mazarin's entry into France became known, had renewed the edict of banishment and had set upon his head a price of fifty thousand *écus*, speedily elaborated by the wags of Paris into a kind of tariff: so much for the Cardinal's ears, so much for his nose. He was officially declared a disturber of the peace, guilty of high treason; his library and all his furniture should be sold, fifty thousand *livres* bestowed on anyone who should bring him to justice alive or dead, and the duc d'Orléans should be requested to use all his authority in the execution of the decree. The Fronde of the princes, united with the Parlement, was now seriously engaged. There were three armies in France,

[1] Gaston was governor of Languedoc.

108

each distinguished by a differently coloured scarf: a green scarf for Mazarin, a white scarf for the King's troops, a biscuit-coloured scarf for Condé.

The incorrigible frivolity of the French could not be better demonstrated than by the attraction which Paris and its pleasures continued to exercise upon them. *Carnaval* came, and the duc de Nemours, instead of following up his success in crossing the Seine at Nantes with the mercenary troops he had collected in Flanders, arrived in Paris on some flimsy excuse to participate in the festivities. Mademoiselle, now an avowed *frondeuse*, gave a great party for the *mi-carême*, and meanwhile the twelve thousand mercenaries (no mean army) melted away for lack of pay. The parties were duly reported to Mazarin: 'It would be idle to regale Your Eminence with an account of the carnival fêtes; they were all due to the inconstancy and levity of Mademoiselle . . . She had marionettes to act the part of Your Eminence . . .'

It was all very well for Mademoiselle to play the hostess. Compared with the exploits of Mme de Condé and Mme de Longueville her rôle had so far been too tame for her romantic spirit. But, as we shall see, her opportunity was at hand. The town of Angers had capitulated, it was said, through the treachery of the duc de Rohan. The King's troops had advanced from Saumur on the road to Tours, and were already at Blois where the Court had joined them. Before long, they might be in a position to threaten Paris. Mazarin now sent a message to the magistrates of Orléans, the capital of Gaston's duchy, requesting them to open their gates to himself and the King. Gaston, meanwhile, had sent the comte de Fiesque requesting them to admit the ducs de Nemours and de Beaufort. The citizens of Orléans, small blame to them, had only one desire: to remain neutral. They had seen what war had done to Gaston's neighbouring territory of the Blaisois, laid waste by M. d'Hocquincourt and the King's army, and feared that a similar fate might befall their own region and that the provision of corn which they had taken the precaution of bringing into safety within their walls might be pillaged. They therefore sent M. de Fiesque post-haste 'hot, agitated, and muddy,' back to Paris to beg his Royal Highness to come immediately to Orléans where his presence was necessary if that great and important city were to be preserved. Gaston could not make up his mind; first he said he would go, then he said he would not, with so many changes that Mademoiselle wagered with Préfontaine that in the end it would be she who went to Orléans.

So it turned out. 'On Monday 25 (March 1652) Mademoiselle's coaches waited in the courtyard of the palais d'Orléans (the Luxembourg) and she in a grey habit all covered in gold to go to Orléans.'[1]

Gaston was at a window to watch her departure. She was accompanied by the duc de Rohan, two members of the Parlement, Préfontaine, the marquise de Bréauté, and Mmes de Fiesque and de Frontenac. Crowds saw her off and lined the streets, blessing her as she went. On the way, the duc de Beaufort met her, riding on beside the door of her coach, also a mounted escort of five hundred which surrounded her, and a little farther on they were joined by the duc de Nemours. Mademoiselle was beginning to enjoy herself; the day was fine; she abandoned her coach for a horse, and rode across the plain of la Beauce with all her cavalry jingling around her. 'I began, from then onwards, to give orders.' Nemours told her that she must hold a council of war, which made her laugh at the novelty of the idea, but he said seriously that she must grow accustomed to war-talk and that nothing would be done without her authority. Nothing could have been more to her taste; she, who had always affected to despise love, now saw herself in her true function as a heroine, a commander.

It was perhaps as well that she could neither hear nor read some of the comments on her expedition. A current joke in Paris said, 'As the walls of Jericho fell to the sound of trumpets,

[1] *Journal*, Dubuisson-Aubenay.

so will those of Orléans fall to the sound of violins.' A letter to Mazarin said, 'Mademoiselle took the road to Orléans determined to put on an act *à la Jeanne d'Arc.'*

Dear Mademoiselle. She took herself so seriously; she saw herself so heroically.

Arrived at Artenay, she was met by a firm though civil message from the magistrates of Orléans to the effect that they could not receive her. It would be most embarrassing for them, they said, she being on one side and the King on the other. They begged her to take a lodging in some near-by house pretending to be ill; in return, they would promise not to admit the King and to welcome her as soon as he should have passed by. Mademoiselle refused to listen to prudent counsels. Getting back into her coach, she drove off almost unattended, leaving her officers and troops to follow as best they pleased. She can seldom have been in higher spirits. Had she not got in her pocket the prediction of an astrologer: 'You will succeed in everything that you undertake between midday, Wednesday, March 27th, and Friday, and during that time, you will even do extraordinary things'? And was not this precisely the 27th of March, eleven o'clock in the morning, as her coach came to a halt before the Porte Banier?

The gate was locked and barricaded; the governor of the city declined to open it, and sent Mademoiselle a present of confectionery instead. Thereupon, despite the protests of her gentlemen (who appear to have rejoined her) she started to walk up and down the moat, attracting a great concourse of people looking down upon her from the ramparts and shouting *'Vive le roi, les princes, et point de Mazarin!'* Mademoiselle shouted back, 'Go to the hôtel de ville and tell them to open the gate,' but they made no move to do so, any more than did a captain whose men presented arms but who replied by gestures that he had not got the keys and in response to Mademoiselle's threats would only continue to bow. Finally some boatmen appeared, offering their services; could they row her to the

Porte de la Faux, she asked, which opened on to the water? but they answered it would be easier to force the Porte Brûlée, which they would do if she so desired. Mademoiselle scrambled up on to a high piece of ground to watch their operations; 'I climbed like a cat,' she says, 'catching my clothes on all the thorns and brambles, and jumping over hedges without hurting myself.' Mme de Bréauté screamed out in fright.

As the door showed signs of yielding, Mademoiselle came down from her post of vantage and they placed two boats as a bridge for her to cross the river, propping a tall ladder in the farther boat. Mademoiselle was too much excited to count the number of rungs. She remembered only that one was missing, inconveniently to her in her long skirts. Still, there she was, alone—for she had forbidden any armed guards to follow her, wishing to prove her trust in the goodwill of the citizens—the great wooden door was cracking under the blows of the boatmen, assisted now by willing hands on the other side; two planks were torn away; not more than two because of the strong iron bars across; a hole appeared; a footman lifted Mademoiselle over the mud and pushed her through the hole, when, no sooner had her head appeared, than drums began to beat, the shouts of '*Vive le roi, les princes, et point de Mazarin!*' revived, and Mademoiselle found herself being carried shoulder-high on a wooden chair through the streets of Orléans. 'I do not know if I was sitting in the chair on on one of its arms; my joy had made me feel quite beside myself; everyone was kissing my hands, and I was in fits of laughter at seeing myself in so entrancing a situation.'

Here, for five weeks, we must leave her, happy in her complete command, referring to Orléans as *ma ville*, flattering herself that she could manage those two quarrelsome brothers-in-law Nemours and Beaufort, receiving the wife of the governor, whom she thought very ugly, intercepting couriers and reading the private letters they carried, trying (to do her justice) to re-establish some kind of order in the province, 'even to the restitution of a chicken,' and in general behaving as a beloved but incontrovertible autocrat. (*J'agissait avec une puissance absolue.*) She had received letters from both her father and Condé. Gaston wrote, 'My daughter, you may imagine my delight at your deed; you have saved Orléans for me and assured Paris; everyone says that your action was worthy of the grand-daughter of Henry the Great.' (Henri IV.) Condé wrote, 'It is a blow which only you could have struck.' In the streets people were singing:

> Or, écoutez, peuple de France,
> Comme en la ville d'Orléans
> Mademoiselle en assurance
> A dit: Je suis maître céans.
>
> On lui voulut fermer la porte,
> Mais elle passa par un trou,
> S'écriant souvent de la sorte
> Il ne m'importe pas par où.[1]

No wonder that her head was slightly turned. All the same, with endearing diffidence, there were moments when she mistrusted her own adroitness. She was filled with alarm when she found herself called upon to address the Assembly which she herself had summoned at the hôtel de ville. She instructed her friends to stand behind her: 'I have never spoken in public and am very ignorant, and if I see you looking at me I shall lose my head.'

Once again, it was perhaps as well that she did not know of certain things which had been arranged behind her back. She did not know that the boatmen had been bribed; she did not know that the applause at the hôtel de ville had been led by

---

[1] Listen you French people:
How Mademoiselle in the town of Orléans
Said with authority
I am the master here.

They wanted to shut the door against her,
But she got through a hole
Saying that so long as she got in
She did not care where or how.

an organised *claque*. It might have leavened her confidence and
her swagger.

On the fourth of May Mademoiselle returned to Paris, met
at Bourg-la-Reine by Condé and the duc de Beaufort. There
were the usual rejoicings, the usual visit to the Cours-la-Reine,
the usual press of courtiers in Mademoiselle's rooms, so that
she remarked she was 'like the Queen of Paris.'[1] With her
customary lack of judgement, and still intoxicated by her own
success, it appeared to her that all was going well for the
frondeurs, and she was greatly astonished when M. de Nemours
said to her in private, 'Things have changed very much since I
last had the honour of seeing you; at that time, if we had
considered making peace, it would have amounted to cutting
our own throats; but now, if peace is not made, we are lost.'
Mademoiselle exclaimed. She could not see that their affairs
were in a bad state, she said; she had taken Orléans, M. le
Prince had won a victory at Bléneau,[2] the troops were in the
best possible condition, and the *frondeurs* were masters of Paris.
But Nemours said she did not know what was good for her: if
peace were incontinently made, she would be Queen of
France, whereas if they delayed she would be nothing, any
more than any of the others.

Here was the old dream revived. Condé threw tinder on the
flame; the thing he desired most passionately in the world, he
said, was to see her Queen of France. What was Mademoiselle
to make of all this? Hers was not the head to cope with such
dizzy chimeras.

It seemed, however, as though M. de Nemours' cautious
outlook had some foundation. On that very day the maréchal
de Turenne in command of the royal army inflicted a heavy
defeat in a suburb of Étampes on the troops of the Fronde, some
of whom had formed part of Mademoiselle's escort at Orléans.
(She was not best pleased on hearing that an officer had said,

[1] The real Court was with the King, at St Germain.
[2] Condé had defeated the royal army at Bléneau on April 6th, but had failed to
follow up his success.

'Thanks be that to God Mademoiselle was not there, or the disorder would have been even greater.') Six days later, on May 11th, Condé captured St Denis, only to lose it again on the 13th. On June 1st the duc de Lorraine arrived in Paris, as Gaston and Condé had long been urging him to do, but his troops were so unpopular in Paris that no man amongst them dared acknowledge his nationality for fear of being thrown into the river, moreover the influence of the princesse de Guémené prevented Lorraine from marching to the relief of Etampes, now besieged by Turenne. Worst of all for the *frondeurs*, Paris itself, weary of war, was rapidly dividing into two camps, one of which, led by the princes and by the more extreme members of the Parlement, wished to continue the struggle; the other, while still determined to rid the country for ever of Mazarin, openly designated itself as the Party of Peace. Mademoiselle must have been blind indeed if she remained unaware of all these indications.

The first inkling she had that matters might be coming to a head, was one night when, leaning at her window in the Tuileries till two o'clock in the morning, she heard the march of armed men passing all along the banks of the Seine. They were Condé's men, whom he had ordered to retire to Charenton, there to take up a stronger position against the rapid advance of Turenne upon St Cloud. Mademoiselle, saddened, and realising that a big encounter was now inevitable, characteristically conceived the idea that she would be able to help them in their plight. She told Préfontaine that she would not take any medicine that evening—even heroines are human— for she believed that on the morrow she would do something as unforeseen as she had done at Orléans. She little knew how true a word she spoke.

In the morning (July 2nd) she was aroused at six by a knocking on her door; it was the comte de Fiesque, come to tell her that Condé had been attacked at daybreak near Montmartre, had been refused admittance at the Porte St Denis, begged Monsieur to come as soon as possible, and trusted that Made-

moiselle would not abandon him. He, Fiesque, had already
been to see Monsieur, who had replied merely that he was not
feeling well. Gaston never felt well when any decision had to
be taken. He preferred to roll away into escape from responsibility. The street-songs as usual sized up his character:

Je veux dormir.
Je naquis en dormant. J'y veux passer ma vie.
Jamais de m'éveiller il ne me prit envie.
Toi, ma femme et ma fille, y perdez vos efforts.[1]

Mademoiselle rushed to the Luxembourg, where she found
Monsieur standing at the top of the staircase. Surprised, she
said she had expected to find him ill in bed. Gaston surpassed
himself by his answer: 'I am not ill enough to be in bed, but
too ill to go out.' Mademoiselle implored him, even with tears,
to take horse and to go to Condé's rescue; seeing that no
supplications would move him, she said he should at least go
to bed and play the invalid if he would not take action. Gaston
walked up and down, pursued by Mademoiselle asking him if
he intended to sacrifice Condé to Mazarin. The duc de Rohan
and the comte de Chavigny came, and although they failed to
budge Gaston they did end by inducing him to send Mademoiselle as his proxy to the Hôtel de Ville.

She met with a far greater success there than she had had
with her father, in fact it seems to have been one of the few
occasions when that hare-brained princess conducted herself
with some sense and power of persuasion. She spoke in her
father's name. Would they mobilise men in all quarters of the
city? Yes, it had already been done. Would they send two
thousand men to the relief of M. le Prince? This was promised.
Would they station four hundred men in the Place Royale?[2]
This also was promised. She kept her main request for the end:
Would they allow free passage into Paris for the princes' army?

[1] I want to go to sleep.
I was born asleep. That is how I want to spend my life.
I never had any desire to wake up.
You, my wife and my daughter, are wasting your time trying to make me.
[2] She wanted these as a reserve for Condé in case of need.

At this, they all looked at each other, and the maréchal de l'Hôpital said, 'You know very well, Mademoiselle, that if your army had not come so close to the city, the King's army would not have come either.' At this point, apparently, Mademoiselle rounded on the maréchal with the threat that if he refused to sign the order she would pull out his beard, and that he should meet his death at her own hands (*elle lui arracherait la barbe, et qu'il ne mourrait jamais que de sa main*), which frightened him so much (*l'intimidait de telle sorte*[1]) that after retiring for deliberation, during which time Mademoiselle alternately prayed to God and worried *ces messieurs* with messages urging them to hasten, they came back with the required permission. As Mademoiselle, triumphant, came out into la Grève,[2] escorted by the maréchal de l'Hôpital, the surging crowd offered to drown him if he had not given her satisfaction. With her touching faith in her power over the people of Paris, she told him to go quickly back into the Hôtel de Ville before her coach should have driven off.

On her way, she had her first real taste of what war could mean. In the rue de la Tixanderie[3] she met 'the most horrifying sight,' the duc de La Rochefoucauld riding, supported on either side by his son and by another man, having received a musket-ball through his eyes and nose, so that his eyes seemed to be falling out, and he kept blowing the blood away as though he feared one of his eyes might fall into his mouth; his face pouring with blood, down on to his white doublet. Mademoiselle's pen could become quite eloquent when she was deeply moved. A little farther on, in the rue St Antoine, she met the sieur de Guitaut, hatless, with his clothes all unbuttoned, as pale as death, with a great wound in the body. 'Are you

---

[1] Majendie, op. cit., p. 524, Vol. II, quoting Conrart.

[2] The present *place de Grève* has been given that name only since 1806. In Mademoiselle's day it was the place de l'Hôtel de Ville. The reason she called it *la Grève* was because *la grève* meant an open space beside the Seine where discontented workmen assembled and complained. Hence the derivation of the French word for strike—*se mettre en grève*—a thing that Mademoiselle would never have tolerated for one moment.

[3] Now merged into the rue de Rivoli.

dying?' she called out to him, but he shook his head. M. de Roche-Giffard passed unconscious on a ladder, like a corpse. All down the rue St Antoine she saw nothing but wounded men, on horseback, on foot, or being carried on planks, ladders, and litters, and many dead.

She was approaching the Bastille, and entered a house with windows giving on the street. Here she was immediately joined by Condé, 'in the most pitiable state, his face dusty, his hair tangled, his collar and shirt all bloody, his cuirass dented with blows, his naked sword in his hand, having lost its sheath.' He had, in fact, been in the thick of the fighting under the ramparts, called superhuman by his partisans and a demon by his adversaries. At one moment, pouring with sweat and suffocating on that hot July day under the weight of his armour, he had gone to roll naked in the grass of a meadow, like a horse wanting to relax.[1] 'You behold a man in despair,' he said to Mademoiselle; 'I have lost all my friends.' He flung himself into a chair, wept, and said she must forgive his grief.

Monsieur came, and embraced Condé as though he had never been guilty of failing him; between them they decided that the princes' army should enter Paris that evening, which was in accordance with the promise Mademoiselle had extracted at the Hôtel de Ville. Mademoiselle was anxious and 'furiously troubled,' but could still think herself back in Orléans, as she saw that she could give orders and be obeyed. She knew that Condé had been fighting all morning in the faubourg St Antoine with five thousand men against Turenne's twelve thousand; the battle had not gone too well in the princes' favour, their cavalry regiments had fled, and there still remained the hazardous operation of leading the remainder into the safety of the city. Mademoiselle left the house and went to the Bastille. Here she mounted on to the towers, whence with a telescope she could see the heights of Charonne and a great number of people and coaches, from which she rightly assumed

[1] Conrart, *Mémoires*.

the presence of the King. She could also see the enemy and their cavalry, massing with the obvious intention of cutting off the retreat through the Porte St Antoine. The 'unforeseen something' she had to do that day was now imminent. The cannons of the Bastille were all directed on to Paris; at Mademoiselle's command they were reversed and trained on the royal army far below. She sent a page galloping to inform Condé, but he had already seen what she had done, and gave an immediate order for his troops to retire into Paris through the Porte St Antoine.

Turenne advanced in pursuit, and it was then that the cannons of the Bastille let fly, causing such unexpected havoc that the advance was arrested. On the heights of Charonne, the royal party could not make out what was happening. Mazarin said, 'Good, they are firing on the enemy.' But as the firing continued, someone else said, 'I am afraid it is against *us*.' Someone else said, 'It may be Mademoiselle who has gone to the Bastille.'[1] The maréchal de Villeroy said, 'If it is Mademoiselle, then it is she who has made them fire on us.' Mazarin is reported to have exclaimed, 'That cannon-shot has killed her husband.'[2]

It did not occur to Mademoiselle, at what was perhaps the most dramatic moment of her life, that she had lost Louis XIV and the Crown of France for ever. All she knew was that she had made a big gesture and had saved Condé.[3]

After her long day—and it had been terribly hot—Mademoiselle could not sleep. She lay awake thinking of all the poor dead men she had seen. She had even seen a dead man still riding his horse, which struck her as particularly pitiable. All day long she had seen nothing but death and wounds. After all, Orléans had been taken without bloodshed; she was not yet broken to such sights. But she was philosophical: 'I

[1] A more histrionic, but inaccurate, version is *Ce doit être Mademoiselle!*
[2] His contemporaries reproduced it in Mazarin's Italian accent: *elle a toué son mari.*
[3] See Appendix III, p. 347. Mademoiselle at the Bastille.

ended by perceiving that what soldiers say is true, one sees such a quantity that one becomes accustomed and feels less pity for the last than for the first, especially for those one does not know.'

The next day passed peacefully enough, if anything can be called peaceful in a capital city crowded with drunken soldiers, many Spaniards and Germans amongst them, adding their noise and their numbers to the population in the narrow, stinking streets. Everyone now was wearing a twist of straw in his hat, in imitation of Condé's men who had adopted this symbol for easy recognition at the battle of the faubourg St Antoine. Even the monks and the horses sported their wisp; not to do so was to risk being taken for a pro-Mazarin. Mademoiselle fastened hers to her fan, tied with a blue ribbon. Paris, always ready to be amused by a new fashion, threw itself with delight upon this one, yet, before it had time to lick its wounds and to recover a little from the events of July 2nd, a fresh danger threatened which came not from without, but from within.

'Monseigneur, the Hôtel de Ville is besieged; they are burning the door, all the companies on guard have fired into the windows of the great hall. All is lost without your help. I assure you that there is not a moment to be lost.'

This letter was brought to Gaston d'Orléans, who was just changing his shirt after a hot afternoon at the Hôtel de Ville and who was so much astonished by the news that he came out of his room half-dressed in the presence of Mademoiselle and three other ladies. He should not have been so much surprised, for the session had been a stormy one. To put it briefly, Gaston and Condé had both declared that they would lay down their arms only when the King had consented to banish Mazarin; the members of Parlement present, who presumably belonged to the Party of Peace, received this declaration in silence, whereupon the princes left the hall, flourishing their bunches of straw 'in a gesture that promised nothing good.' It was even reported that Condé went out on to the steps and shouted to the crowd, 'Those people will do nothing for us; they are *mazarins*; do whatever you please.'[1]

Gaston tried to send Condé back to the Hôtel de Ville, but he would not go, saying that he was not a man to abet sedition. In the end, it was Mademoiselle who volunteered to go, but this time she could not get there, by reason of the fighting in the streets and the inability of her messengers, at that late hour, to obtain any reply. Coming back to the Luxembourg, she had an unpleasant experience: her coach caught on a cart full of dead bodies, so that she had to change over to the window on the other side 'for fear some overhanging feet or hands might hit me on the nose.'

It was now midnight, but Gaston was not satisfied and Mademoiselle set off once more upon her errand. It must have been a curious expedition, Mademoiselle's coach preceded by torches and rolling along streets now empty of people save for the military pickets, to the trot of horses and her guards; the day had been very hot and the night was 'the finest ever seen'. No one was about, save for Mme Riche, a vendor of ribbons, with the beadle of St Jacques de la Boucherie, both of whom had come out to take the air, she in her chemise, he in his under-drawers; they entertained Mademoiselle for a moment with their rough Parisian speech (*patois de francs badauds*) and made her laugh in spite of the plight everybody was in. In the place de Grève her coach was stopped; a man came to the window asking if M. le Prince were there, and by the light of the torches she saw that he had a weapon under his arm. He had moved away before she realised that he had probably intended to assassinate Condé.

The duc de Beaufort now came forward to meet her and took her into the Hôtel de Ville. This had been the scene of horrible massacres during the day. A sinister silence reigned, as

[1] Conrart, Memoirs.

Mademoiselle and Beaufort clambered over the floor-joists still smoking and smouldering from the fire; they looked into the great hall where the Assembly had gathered, but not a soul was to be seen; she thought she had never seen so solitary a place. The only person they eventually found was a M. le Fèvre, unrecognisable in somebody else's borrowed wig, who told them that the maréchal de l'Hôpital had escaped through a window.

It was now four o'clock in the morning, day was beginning to dawn, the place de Grève was filling up, a musket-shot passed between Mme de Fiesque and Mme de Sully, frightening them both. Mademoiselle decided to go home. She slept through the whole of the day.

For once, Mademoiselle showed some sound judgement when she remarked that the affair at the Hôtel de Ville had dealt a bludgeon-blow to the *frondeurs*. 'It took away the confidence of the best-intentioned people,' she writes; 'it intimidated the boldest, and diminished the zeal of others; in short, it had the worst possible effect.' The Party of Peace was daily gaining ground. Paris had been shocked by the death of some of its most eminent civilians; people were beginning to realise that a capital city cannot live divided within itself, with no central government, no lawful authority, and no cohesion amongst its self-appointed leaders. Condé mistrusted the duc de Lorraine; Beaufort mistrusted Nemours; the Co-adjutor Retz mistrusted Beaufort, from whom top-secrets had to be kept lest he betray them to women; everybody mistrusted Gaston. The armies of Turenne were not far off, at Villeneuve St Georges; at any moment the attack might be renewed and the streets again be wet with blood. The King, titular head of the State, was absent in the safety of St Germain; true, although he had constitutionally attained his majority, he was only a boy of thirteen, kept fretting in immature idleness by Mazarin, whom he sulkily resented, muttering, 'There goes the Grand Turk,' as he watched the Cardinal pass by. His absence could make no realistic difference to the Paris of the Fronde, still, he was the King, representative of the Throne, the Crown, the symbol of the homogeneity of France, a name to hold them all together. The demand for his return became more and more insistent.

Meanwhile, Conde was to all appearances master in Paris. He had the semblance of power and employed it with the support of a battered Parlement to set up a government having, of all people, Gaston d'Orléans at its head. This might have worked as a provisional measure, for Gaston was, after all, the uncle of the King, had Gaston's own reputation and character not rendered such an appointment preposterous in the extreme. Moreover, Gaston had forfeited all remnants of such popularity as he might have enjoyed, by his indifference to the bloody events at the Hôtel de Ville where the resplendent and romantic figure of Condé himself had deservedly suffered a fall from the favour of the people. Even so, during the four months which followed, a curious interlude characteristic of this confusing civil war, Condé and Gaston between them managed to preserve some semblance of authority. Paris returned outwardly to the aspect of normal life; the walks and gatherings in the Cours-la-Reine and the Renard gardens were resumed. Mademoiselle went riding in the Bois de Boulogne, the weather was perfect, the mud in the streets had dried up, the resilience of the French reasserted itself. They did so well, that the Court might almost have been in residence; as it was, they established what was called the black Court:

> Messieurs de la noire cour,
> Rendez-grâces à la guerre;
> Vous êtes Dieu dessus terre
> Et dansez à Luxembourg.
>
> Petites gens de chicane,
>   Canne
> Tombera sur vous,

Et l'on verra madame Anne
Vous faire rouer de coups.[1]

There came a rude shock in high quarters when, at the end of July the duc de Beaufort killed the duc de Nemours in a duel. Brothers-in-law,[2] they had never been on good terms since Orléans and now they fell out over some petty quarrel about rank. The duel took place in the horse-market behind the hôtel de Vendôme; each of the principals was accompanied by four friends, who in turn fell upon one another; two were killed, one seriously wounded, the others all slightly wounded. Mme de Nemours, devoted to her husband in spite of his attachment to Mme de Châtillon, fainted away on hearing cries of 'He is dead!' The heart of Mademoiselle, who had rushed to her bedside, was wrung with pity.

Mademoiselle herself at this time experienced a personal sorrow in the death of her little half-brother. She had greatly rejoiced over his birth, had celebrated it by a display of fireworks, and had written to his father and mother 'in transports of joy enough to soften rocks for ever.' Monseigneur le duc de Valois can never have figured as a very promising scion of the royal house of France: he could neither speak nor walk; and, had he lived to grow up, would have been afflicted by a crooked leg, attributed by the doctors to the fact that Madame, his mother, had held herself sideways during the whole of her pregnancy. Mademoiselle records this medical opinion with, I think, some satisfaction though without comment. Her relationship with her father's second wife had begun well

[1] Gentlemen of the black Court
Be thankful to the war.
You think yourselves God above the world
And you dance at Luxembourg.

Pettifogging little creatures,
A whip will descend on you;
Madame Anne
Will soon be seen thrashing you.
[2] Mme de Nemours was Beaufort's sister.

enough, but had deteriorated. How could it be otherwise? Stepmothers are never in an easy position, and Mademoiselle herself was not cut out by nature to be a stepdaughter. She was recalcitrant enough as a daughter.

The death of her little brother upset Mademoiselle considerably. She was strolling according to her custom in the Renard gardens when word was brought to her, 'Your brother is very ill.' She went at once to the Luxembourg; reassured on being told that the child was sleeping, she went home for the night; was up very early next morning and went straight into the nursery sick-room where she found M. de Valois being carried in arms 'for he was only two'; was reassured again by the doctors; went away; met Condé; told him her brother was dying—she seems to have had more sense than the doctors—sent for news again that evening; was told that the child was better; and was awakened in the morning with the news that he was dead. She went immediately to the Luxembourg, where she found her father greatly distressed and her stepmother drinking soup, since, as she explained to Mademoiselle, she was again with child and must look after herself.

Mademoiselle was deeply moved. Although in those days they must have been well accustomed to the death of small children, the sight of her brother lying dead in his cot was too much for her; he looked as beautiful as a little angel; priests were praying around him; she broke into such a passion of weeping and sobbing, that she had to be led away. These intimate glimpses into their family life are most revealing of the characters concerned, the warm-hearted Mademoiselle rushing backwards and forwards to the nursery, her constant messages of enquiry, her obvious contempt for Madame, who had always been something of a hypochondriac; Gaston in a softened mood, displaying for once a more attractive side of himself, arousing his daughter's ready sympathy. It must be admitted that, her emotional crisis past, Mademoiselle soon returned to her daily preoccupations. She received many expressions of condolence, which pleased and gratified her, and everybody went into the deepest possible mourning, Condé himself affecting a cloak long enough to trail on the ground. All this was the tribute conventionally paid on the death of a royal prince, however tiny the shoulders that had borne the weight of so great a title. Mademoiselle would have expected no less; would indeed have been astonished and indignant at any infringement of the customary observance; yet we may read between the lines that after her sorrow had subsided and after all the compliments had been paid, she soon became somewhat bored and restive. Court mourning put an end to entertainments; and although she could still go and walk every evening in the Renard gardens, the disturbed condition of the country outside Paris forbade her even to find some relaxation in her favourite pastime of riding. 'I was in despair,' but she worried her father into giving her permission provided she went with an escort, an injunction she largely disregarded. She was no coward, frightened though she might be of water and of ghosts.

She very soon had other matters to occupy her mind. It is impossible to resist the suspicion that, during the four months of this short and farcical period of the Fronde, July to October, Condé and Charles de Lorraine amused themselves by making fun of and a fool of Mademoiselle. Her head, never screwed on very tight, had swivelled so far sideways as to point her big nose in a martial direction, until she now saw herself as a commanding officer in the field, the natural sequel to her exploits at Orléans and the Bastille. A princess by birth, she fancied herself an Amazon by nature. Perhaps she would gladly have cut off her breasts, had she been aware of the legend. Yet perhaps not. *Une belle gorge* was an asset and a feature; it bulged, it ballooned, it even emerged sometimes from the restraining bodice, when a transparent veiling revealed rather than concealed the charms it professed to shroud.

The princes of Condé and Lorraine, with a psychological

insight far in advance of their time, clearly amused themselves by exploiting the Amazonian side of Mademoiselle. They were French; they were malicious; they were young in spirit if not in years—Condé was thirty-one and Charles de Lorraine forty-eight. They were, for the time being, triumphant. Some of their triumph they owed to Mademoiselle, but that did not deter them from regarding her as fair game to tease and to use as a popular asset.

Having put up Gaston as a figurehead of government, Condé now enticed his daughter into the rôle of a captain of cavalry. This would suit her taste. She was easily at home in the saddle, and she loved the tossing plumes and the clatter of accoutrements and the thunder of galloping hooves and the spectacle of brave men riding to death or glory. She should be encouraged to raise a regiment of her own—and she should pay for it out of her own pocket. She could well afford the expense involved. Extra troops were needed, but owing to the usual rivalries and jealousies amongst the nobility, all vying with each other for the various commands, matters had come to a standstill for fear of offending one or the other. Condé was struck by the bright idea that this difficulty should be overcome by putting some of the new troops under his own name and that of his brother the prince de Conti and that of Gaston d'Orléans. Then, says Mademoiselle, the fancy took him to add, 'We must create one in the name of Mademoiselle; she has done so many extraordinary things during this war, that we must do one extraordinary thing which shall be entirely for herself.'

She was delighted. 'For the next week, nobody talked about anything but my regiment.' The command was given to the comte de Brancas, but as there were many other commissions to be bestowed among the twelve companies composing it, and the applications for the command of a company were manifold, Mademoiselle and M. de Brancas spent every day seeking how they could please everybody and offend no one. In spite of these precautions, the inevitable disputes ensued. Gaston turned irritable and complained that all his officers were deserting him in order to serve under his daughter, a complaint which doubtless flattered his daughter not a little. She even had a little scrap, not the first one, with Condé himself in the Renard gardens, when they both lost their tempers and parted with bitter words. Mademoiselle stalked away, but Condé in a more conciliatory mood ran after her and they made it up as he began to laugh saying, 'Even if one does sometimes forget oneself, do believe that you are always the mistress and that one is very sorry.'

M. le Prince had learnt how to manage Mademoiselle. For all her storms and indignations, she cannot really have been very difficult to manage. A little bit of flattery went a long way; and as they were both Bourbons, with the same violent blood running in their veins, they could afford to quarrel without lasting resentment. A family quarrel; almost a nursery wrangle between children who have grown up together and squabbled over their toys.

Only, unfortunately for France, they were no longer children, but adults handling the dangerous explosive elements destined to go up nearly 150 years later in the taking of the Bastille, no longer crackers and harmless fireworks. As history comes gradually into perspective, we can now see the Fronde as a first small begetter of the Revolution, but how could Louis de Bourbon or Anne de Montpensier foresee such mighty consequences for their sputtering squib?

Monsieur le Prince; Mademoiselle; secure in the arrogance of their abbreviated titles. *Enfants de France*, they were less son and daughter of the true France than the poorest peasant on their neglected estates.

Mademoiselle found her regiment rather expensive. '*La somme était un peu forte.*' It is to her credit, and characteristic, that she insisted on keeping her financial support secret. 'I did not want anyone to know that it was I who paid'; and she adds with a touch of acerbity shooting out like a lizard's tongue—no

APOLLON. LE ROY.

Louis XIV as Apollo in the Noces de Thétis et de Pélée performed
at the PalaisBourbon. By Henri Gissey (1621?–1672)

Queen Henrietta Maria, by Sir Anthony Van Dyck

viper's tongue, no viper she—that this small deception easily got past His Royal Highness her father 'since it cost him nothing.' She was not close-fisted; on the contrary, she liked spending her enormous fortune and, in her later years, as will presently be seen, handed it most lavishly away. Yet there was a curiously cautious streak in her nature; it was not for nothing she came of a nation with a notoriously acute sense of the value of money; besides, great wealth begets suspicion, and like most very rich people she probably resented the idea that she might be taken advantage of. Anything but cynical, in fact far too naïve for the society in which her lot was cast, it seems to have occurred to her from time to time that she would not allow herself to be treated as a haystack with a herd of cattle tugging mouthfuls out of it all round until nothing was left.

Still, her regiment rewarded her. She loved her regiment. It came trotting on parade before her in squadrons, led by the officers with drawn swords; and then arranged itself around her coach, some in front and some behind, escorting her as the coach trundled along—'I must confess,' she says, 'I did think they looked very fine; never were troops better attired than mine.' And then with her ever endearing simplicity she adds, 'I must confess that I went a bit childish (*je fus un peu enfant*) and that I felt much pleasure and rejoiced in the sound of the trumpets.'

Her regiment gave her something to think about, so that she was not unoccupied. She also busied herself by interfering between Condé and his officers, remarking rather smugly that they were lucky to have her at hand since she was often able to put matters right. She then reminded Condé that after the battle of the Porte St Antoine it was she who had sent messages in his name to enquire after the wounded, for neither he, nor her father, she told him, would have thought of doing such a thing, yet that was the way to win the hearts of the people, to retain the affection they felt for their superiors, and to turn them into good and friendly servants. Whatever we may think of Mademoiselle's social philosophy, the tempestuous Condé accepted her scolding with the meekness he habitually displayed in his dealings with his cousin after their first wrath had subsided. As already indicated, le Grand Condé knew how to manage la Grande Mademoiselle.

It was especially fortunate, on this occasion, that they should again happily have composed their differences, for a situation arose on the very same day which might otherwise have caused them an extreme mutual embarrassment. News arrived from Bordeaux that Mme la Princesse, eight months gone with child, was on her death-bed suffering from a continuous fever. This was rightly considered a poor outlook for the lady by her friends in Paris, who instantly started arranging the next marriage for her widower.

In her saner moments it must by now have become apparent to Mademoiselle that the Crown of France, *la couronne fermée*, was indeed shut, and closely shut, away from her grasp for ever. Later on she suffered a small, mean pang of jealousy and envy on hearing of a marriage suggested between the King and her own younger half-sister: 'I should not have liked to see her put above me.' Sisters are sisters all the world over, whether in the bourgeois nursery or in the Court of seventeenth-century France.

Having, then, renounced her dream of marrying the King, Mademoiselle allowed herself to be tempted towards the next best thing. She had long since begun to find it convenient to refer to Condé's great qualities and to the merit he had acquired by his great actions; she even called him the most reasonable man she knew, a curious and quite undeserved compliment. The recovery of Mme la Princesse had put a stop to the first bout of gossip, but the seed had been sown, and on the occasion of the princess' second illness the attitude of Mademoiselle can only be described as coy. 'M. de Chavigny was talking to Mme de Frontenac on the terrace of the Luxembourg; I went up to them and asked what they were talking about, as is my wont. They said they were talking about poor Mme la

Princesse and remarrying M. le Prince. I blushed and went away.'

Presently, she went to the Renard gardens, where she met Condé. They paced up and down the avenue together twice, without speaking a word to one another; Mademoiselle thought he believed that everyone was staring at them; they were both much embarrassed, which in the circumstances was perhaps not surprising. When, a day or two later, Gaston sent one of his gentlemen to summon her, saying that she was to come accompanied only by Mme de Frontenac and Mme de Fiesque, her anticipations rose to a peak, especially when Mme de Frontenac said, 'I believe Mme la Princesse is dead and that they want to expedite the marriage before news of it can reach the Court.' 'What do they want of me?' she asked the baron de Clinchamp, who came to meet her as she alighted from her coach. 'One may imagine how his reply, "You will know when you get inside," increased my curiosity.'

Gaston and Condé left the gaming-table and came towards her as she entered. 'Guess what we want of you?' Mademoiselle pretends that she was baffled, though we may reasonably assume the answer that was in her mind. 'I did not understand and I never can guess anything.' (*Je ne devine jamais rien.*)

Anticlimax followed: it was only a letter from the duc de Lorraine, of whose dealings with Spain she rightly disapproved, begging her forgiveness and asking her to receive him. No mention of any marriage or of the death of Mme la Princesse, who in fact managed to survive for another forty years.

Mademoiselle always betrays a weakness for Charles de Lorraine. Their relationship might be somewhat involved, since he was brother to Madame, Mademoiselle's stepmother, for whom she had no love, a family complication as potent in those days and in that exalted society as it might be today on any humbler level whether in France or elsewhere. The disadvantage was outweighed by her personal liking and admiration for him, also by the extreme courtesy with which he always treated her, for she was far from indifferent to such punctilious observances. Others had noticed that even in the open air, as it might be in the Tuileries or the Renard garden, he invariably kept his head uncovered in her presence. Sometimes he even overdid his politeness, helping her into her coach, which was natural enough, but then walking beside it through the streets of Paris, resting his hand on the door and proposing to escort her all the way back to her lodging. When out of favour with her, and desirous of gaining her pardon, he sprang on to the first horse he could find at the Porte de Luxembourg, and, meeting Mademoiselle's coach near the Porte St Germain, flung himself from the saddle to go down on his knees in the street, refusing to rise until she had forgiven him. Mademoiselle raised him up, embraced him, and took him into the coach with her. A strange little scene, Lorraine kneeling in the mud, Mademoiselle grandly alighting, Condé arriving in the middle, and unquestionably a rabble of the Parisian populace gleefully goggling in the background, with cat-calls and appropriate raffish remarks—for despite the exalted condition of royalty and the aristocracy, and the inflated estimate they held of their own importance in the hierarchy of the State, the mob, which was nothing if not ribald and irreverent, often treated them with a healthy disrespect.

Subsequently Lorraine came to kneel in her *ruelle*, telling her that although he had often joked with her and had not treated her seriously, he did in fact realise her worth and desired only to be her servant. Mademoiselle found all this extravagant conduct highly acceptable. She liked hearing from him that the Spaniards revered her for her exploit at Orléans. It is most pleasing, she said, to listen to one's own praises, and in addition to that she found him most agreeable in all his discourse.

Blandishments apart, he possessed other qualities calculated to appeal to her romantic nature. He was a soldier; and although Mademoiselle (perhaps unconsciously) evinces a weakness for attractive women, she also liked mettlesome men and was only too apt to exalt them into the stature of Corneilleian heroes. The age of Corneille was still in full swing; the age of Racine had not yet arrived. Condé, plainly, was just such a hero and Charles de Lorraine another one, with Mademoiselle playing the heroine between the pair of them, excessive, over-sized characters, irresponsible in many ways but vital, and as garish as a cock-bird in display. Not that either Condé or the duc de Lorraine was noticeable for elegance in his person; they were both slovenly and even dirty; contemporary comments on their lack of care and spruceness abound, even in that age when cleanliness was not considered among the outstanding personal virtues. Mademoiselle herself remarks that Condé was the dirtiest of men. (*C'est l'homme du monde le plus malpropre.*)

M. de Lorraine was, from this point of view, not much better. Mademoiselle thought him so ill-dressed and uncouth, that all the Court wanted to laugh at him; but even as Condé, a captain richly plumed and armoured, had his resplendent reputation for ever hanging as a tapestry behind him, with the smoke of the cannons of Rocroi blowing across the scene, so had M. de Lorraine a charm all of his own for Mademoiselle.

She seems very soon to have forgotten his really outrageous action in allying himself with Spain the traditional enemy of France, and to have remembered only that he was *fort honnête homme*. In addition—and this again formed part of being an *honnête homme*—he could take teasing in good part. *Il entend raillerie* is the current phrase. Mademoiselle could appreciate Charles de Lorraine, and she who loved enjoying herself could always be made to laugh by him. His rollicking high spirits easily won her over. He must, indeed, have been a gay madcap full of fun; a joker clever enough to twist himself out of any awkward situation. An adept at evading questions he did not want to answer, he would respond up to a point, but when pressed too hard he would either seize a guitar and cry, 'Let us dance, ladies!' or else would begin to sing and dance himself, so drolly that nobody could help laughing. Mademoiselle comments that if people had not known him for a very able man, they would have thought him crazy. He amused her very much during the week he spent in Paris.

That week was the culmination of Mademoiselle's good time. She made the most of it, and the princes played up to her; putting it more colloquially, one might say that they played her up. M. de Lorraine tried to revive her idea of marrying the Archduke Leopold, by suggesting that the King of Spain would then give him the Netherlands. 'You would be the happiest of people; he would interfere in nothing, he would spend all his time with the Jesuits, and you would be the ruler.' Mademoiselle had no intention of marrying the Archduke, but these little intrigues and insinuations added spice to life.

Then there were fêtes and parties, a last flare-up for the *frondeurs* before the royal vengeance descended upon them, and above all there was an excursion of a nature best designed to appeal to Mademoiselle's taste, for it combined both a social and a military occasion. The princes invited her to accompany her father on a day's visit to their camp outside Paris. Doubtless Mademoiselle would have preferred to go independently, not overshadowed by her father, but when she got there she managed to take the centre of the stage. The expedition nearly started with a solecism, for Mme de Châtillon and the duchesse de Montbazon both asked for seats in Mademoiselle's coach, and that would not have done at all, for, although the French officers would have been merely amused, the Germans in M. de Lorraine's army would certainly have exclaimed, 'What! here comes Mademoiselle bringing the mistresses of M. le Prince and M. de Beaufort with her!' Mademoiselle, who had a great respect for appearances, was fortunately able to refuse these two inconvenient applications on the plea that the nine available seats in the coach were already bespoken.

As it turned out, two of her guests failed at the last moment, so they were only seven as they set off in fine style at half-past eleven on a September morning, picking up M. de Lorraine at the hôtel de Chavigny on the way. He kept them waiting, and apologised saying that he had been to Mass; but when he eventually took his place in the coach he found himself the only man among six ladies, and knowing his waggish humour it seems permissible to suppose that many jokes were cracked at the expense of Mme de Châtillon and Mme de Montbazon as the coach lumbered on its way towards Charenton. Here they were met by Condé with three squadrons of cavalry, all in gleaming breast-plates. Mademoiselle thought it a fine sight, and noted also with approval that Condé was far cleaner than usual; he had shaved, he had had his hair powdered, he had encircled his throat with a white scarf, presumably well laundered for the occasion, and across his breast, under a loose jacket of buffalo-hide he wore his blue ribbon. As he joined Mademoiselle in her coach, everybody paid him compliments on his smart appearance. Condé laughed their compliments off, as though he had somehow been false to himself (*il en fit des excuses comme d'un grand crime*). Such frivolities were not for him, a serious soldier and a great commander, but as no man or woman is made wholly of one piece in one consistent character, and as they were all evidently very gay and in high good humour, he fell in with their mood. He and M. de Lorraine even said that a truce must be called and no shot fired so long as Mademoiselle was amongst them; she protested a little, but they said it was due to the respect in which they held her. 'I gave way to this argument,' she wrote afterwards; 'I do like to be respected.'

Condé might be in fine plumage; Mademoiselle herself was all in black, being still in mourning for her little brother, M. de Valois. She had, however, tied a blue scarf round her arm out of compliment to Condé, and into the middle of the bow she had stuck a yellow ribbon, the colour of Lorraine. After all, she was only twenty-five, still a young woman, with the natural taste of her sex and years for felicitous clothes and pretty colours; she was terribly plain; her great nose and Condé's great nose, the Bourbon noses, must almost have filled the coach between them, protuberant, cousinly, inherited; but still it would please her to tie the blue and yellow round her arm, and to encourage her ladies to follow her example.

Arrived at Grosbois, Condé gave them a fine feast. Kneeling, they toasted Mademoiselle, bugles were sounded, and a courteous message was received from M.M. de Turenne and de la Ferté, to the effect that their army also was hers to command. Mademoiselle, clumsy and tactless, nearly upset the conviviality by remarking that Mme de Châtillon and Mme de Montbazon had asked to come with her; Condé scowled (*M. le Prince fit là-dessus une terrible mine*), but M. de Beaufort saved the situation by taking it in good part. Mademoiselle was perhaps not on her best behaviour: troops and trumpets, cavalry and accoutrements, always went to her head. After inspecting the army of the princes, she suddenly set off at full gallop for the enemy camp and was stopped only by Condé seizing her reins and forcibly turning her horse back towards the quarters of Lorraine. M. de Turenne, he said, would be put into a very difficult position if she were to appear in their midst. Thwarted, she did not agree at the time, but generously admitted later on that M. le Prince had been right.

M. le Prince constantly gives proof of a long-suffering patience with his blundering and impetuous cousin. He might scowl, he might be on the point of losing his temper, but in the end he always comes back to his attitude of affectionate indulgence. No small element of teasing entered into it. Mademoiselle's little escapade in the direction of the enemy camp had carried her so far forward that the moon had risen before she could complete her inspection of the Lorraine troops, and could be put safely back into her coach and sent back to Paris. Condé must have longed to be rid of her. Yet, at the end of a long day, he could still joke. 'Give us the order of the day,' he said, meaning the password, and she gave them *Saint-Louis et Paris*. Condé pounced on her, saying, 'That is exactly the same as you gave me the day you went to Orléans; give me one for tomorrow.' She gave them *Sainte-Anne et Orléans*. This amused Condé. 'I should have guessed,' he said, 'what saint amongst all the saints of Paradise you would choose;[1] and what city amongst all the cities of France, Orléans; so, if ever I should make a two-days' war against you I shall know how to pass everywhere without let or hindrance.'

It was at this time that Mademoiselle sat for her portrait, the plumed helmet proudly set on her fair curls.

They might jest, but the preposterous state of affairs could not continue indefinitely. Already negotiations for peace were on foot between Mazarin and Gaston; Condé protested that it was without his consent, Gaston declared that Condé had been similarly occupied, which, in the light of subsequent events, seems improbable. Wherever the truth may lie, it is certain that an envoy of Mazarin's, the abbé Fouquet,[2] had called on Gaston at the Luxembourg and after some discussion about the terms of a truce received an assurance from M. de Chavigny that Monsieur would co-operate even if M. le Prince would not.[3]

The two parties in Paris were now more sharply and visibly divided than ever. On the 24th September, in opposition to the straw of the *frondeurs*, an assembly of leading citizens at the Palais-Royal ordained that a piece of paper or a white ribbon worn in the hat should be adopted as the symbol of the Party of Peace, which henceforth became known as the *têtes de papier*. Straw and paper! appropriate emblems for such a civil war.

Mademoiselle, loyal but misguided, in a last flare-up of her combative spirit would have none of this. It was said that she marched up and down in front of the Palais-Royal shouting 'Vive la paille! Point de papier!' She does not mention this

---

[1] Mademoiselle's baptismal name was Anne.
[2] Brother of Nicolas Fouquet, Louis XIV's *surintendant des finances*.
[3] Mazarin wrote to l'abbé Fouquet:
'It is easy to see that M. le Prince is making fun of us and has no wish to conclude (peace) . . . You acted very well with His Royal Highness (Gaston) and brought things to the point we desired . . . I hope you will lose no opportunity of getting M. de Chavigny to press H.R.H. not to bargain any longer (with us) but to break with M. le Prince, who shows clearly that he wishes only to continue the war.'

demonstration herself, but she does record that she asked her father's permission to go to the Palais-Royal, arrest the principals, hang some of them, and send the officers to the Bastille. Gaston had the sense to refuse.

It was becoming obvious that the Fronde of the Princes was at an end. Mazarin, to facilitate matters, had once more removed himself from France to Bouillon just across the Luxembourg frontier, a diplomatic exile as some illnesses are diplomatic illnesses. Already the populace had started to shout, 'Long live the King! Down with the princes!' On the evening of the 12th October, Condé and Lorraine came together to say good-bye to Mademoiselle; the imminent return of the King made it prudent, indeed imperative, for them to take their departure from Paris.

Mademoiselle wept, and had good cause to do so. She confided her feeling of desolation to the pages of her memoirs: it had been so fine to see the great alley-way of the Tuileries full of well-dressed people, M. le Prince had worn a beautiful costume of flame colour, with gold and silver and black on grey, and his blue scarf under his open surcoat, and now everyone was gone. The place was empty. 'One felt oneself so alone,' she wrote; 'one was so surprised not to see anybody any more. It was most worrying, and to make matters worse a rumour spread that the King was coming back and that we should all be driven out.'

This rumour was fully and rapidly justified. The princes had gone on October 13th, 1652; on October 21st the King, preceded by troops under the command of Turenne, rode his horse in triumph into Paris. He was accompanied by the King of England and a cavalcade of peers and marshals of France. The Queen-Regent followed in her coach with her twelve-year-old son, Philippe, duc d'Anjou, beside her. The entire Court clattered in the wake.

Vengeance fell very quickly, if not from the skies then from the Throne. Any decree authorised by the King would be irresistible. There was no limit to what he might ordain: he could make, or he could destroy. He could order anybody into exile on their own estates, even the haughty members of his own family. The most intransigent scion of the Blood Royal, the most intractable and intemperate of them, son or daughter of France, le Grand Condé or Mlle de Montpensier, must shrink in obedience to his decree. The very day of his return, letters-patent banished from Paris the ducs de Beaufort, Rohan and La Rochefoucauld, with many other noblemen and counsellors; all the households of Condé and his brother Conti and their sister Mme de Longueville; Mme de Châtillon and Mme de Montbazon. Guards were set over Mme de Fiesque; Mme de Frontenac went into hiding. Shortly afterwards, a royal decree deprived Condé, Conti, La Rochefoucauld, Mme de Longueville, and the prince de Tarente of their honours and dignities, and confiscated their possessions. The furniture was all sold from the hôtel de Condé, which then remained empty but for the concierge. The Cardinal de Retz found himself in prison at Vincennes. It was a clean sweep.

La Rochefoucauld, the devoted lover of Mme de Longueville, behaved with unusual nobility. The injuries he had received during the fighting in Paris had left him three-quarters blind in one eye, half-blind in the other, wearing spectacles and smothering his head 'with more shawls and bonnets than any old woman'; he begged for leave to remain in Paris to continue the treatment for his eyes. Sooner than obtain this favour by signing an amnesty which would have amounted to an act of submission and renunciation of his friends, he escaped from Paris after one night in concealment, and after hiding in the fields, a half-blinded man, eventually succeeded in gaining Brussels.

Gaston d'Orléans, as might be expected, behaved with no nobility or dignity at all. If the Cardinal de Retz is to be believed, and his report is so circumstantial as to be convincing, he found Monsieur in a state of panic. Madame his wife was with him, exhorting him to control himself, for his fright was taking the form of a violent rage (*un emportement inconcevable*), so that you might have believed him to be on a charger, armed from head to foot, and ready to drench whole countrysides in blood. Madame, who, to make matters worse, was huge with child,[1] was terrified, and Retz himself, well accustomed though he was to Gaston's querulous and unmanageable moods, saw that he was even more agitated than usual. 'Well, what then?' he said to Retz. 'Is there any hope of safety in making one's peace with the Court? Did you not tell me that the King would never return to Paris without first coming to terms with me?' 'Sir, I told you that the Queen had given me that assurance, but I also warned Your Royal Highness against placing any trust in it.' 'That is true,' said Madame, 'he told you so over and over again, but you would not believe him.' 'I am not complaining of *him*,' said Monsieur; 'it is of that damned Spaniard (*cette maudite espagnole*) that I am complaining.' 'This is no time to complain of anybody,' said Madame; 'it is time to act one way or the other. You wanted peace when it only depended upon you to make war, and now you want war when you can no longer make either war or peace.' 'I could make war tomorrow,' cried Monsieur, 'with greater ease than ever—ask M. le Cardinal de Retz.'

His tone was becoming more and more embattled, but Retz saw through his manœuvre: he sought only a pretext for excusing himself afterwards on the plea that he could have done wonders had he not been dissuaded. Retz therefore replied coldly, 'No doubt, sir.' 'And the people are still on my side?' 'Yes, sir.' 'And M. le Prince would return if I were to summon him?' 'I think so, sir.' 'And the Spanish army would advance if I wished it?' 'It seems highly probable, sir.' This absurd dialogue appears to have satisfied Monsieur for the moment; he left the room, when Madame, between tears and

---

[1] The child, a fourth daughter, Anne-Marie d'Orléans, called Mlle de Chartres, was born about three weeks later and died aged three.

laughter, turned to the Cardinal. How much it had resembled a scene from an Italian comedy! How much it had reminded her of Trivelin's remark to Scaramouche: 'What fine phrases I should have made, had you not had the sense not to contradict me!'

Retz had been right in his diagnosis. Monsieur rejoined them, having come to the conclusion that although it was most annoying of the King to come to Paris without a ratified truce with the Parlement and without a previous agreement with him, his uncle, it was nevertheless not his duty to oppose the return. Everybody knew that he could if he would, and everybody would do him the justice to recognise that nothing but his regard for the good of the State had persuaded him to adopt a line of conduct which must, to him, be particularly painful. Doubtless his little summary had given him considerable satisfaction now that the roars of frightened defiance had subsided, but Madame, whom Mademoiselle is apt to dismiss as a hypochondriac and a poor thing, had given proof throughout of far better sense and spirit than her husband. She may, as Retz suspected, have been at heart in favour of a sustained resistance to the King and to a continuation of the Fronde, but now that the game was manifestly lost she saw more clearly than Gaston and would not suffer his pitiful compromises to pass unchallenged. She turned on him, says Retz, firmly and even angrily. 'That bit of reasoning, Monsieur,' she said, 'might do for M. le Cardinal de Retz, but not for a Son of France. Since it is no longer a question of war, the only thing you can do is to go and meet the King with good grace.'

Monsieur gave a shriek as though she had suggested his throwing himself into the river. The 'Allez-vous-en donc, Monsieur, tout à cette heure,' with which she stung him, might be freely rendered in English as, 'Get yourself out of here, then, and as quick as maybe, while the going is good.' 'But where the devil am I to go?' he said, rather piteously and, we may suppose, rather crossly with the irascibility of a weak, scared man. Always reluctant to face a difficult issue, he solved the immediate problem by retiring into his own room, ordering Retz to follow him. Retz would naturally have expected Monsieur to pursue their conversation and to come to some conclusion as to the line of action he should follow, but all that Monsieur had to enquire was whether he had received any word from la princesse Palatine about the King's return to Paris.

He was a very poor weak thing, was Monsieur, lacking the calibre to stand up against the opposing and complicated demands that the collapse of the Fronde exacted from him. His friends were not much help to him. Retz was half convinced that he might carry out his wild threat of going to the Halles, throwing barricades across the streets, marching on the Louvre and driving out the King. M. de Rohan went so far as to send horses to await him at the Tuileries, but Monsieur only got into a terrible state (*il était dans une agitation inconcevable*), made a lot of noise, and did nothing. M. de Beaufort openly advised him to chase all Mazarin's adherents to the devil. Monsieur, frightened and bewildered, did not know what to do; one moment he was embracing Retz and asking him with tears in his eyes if he might really hope to capture the person of the King; next moment he was running to the window to listen for the beating of drums, and whenever a musket shot went off he thought that a regiment was on its way to arrest him. The one thing he flatly refused was the wiser counsel of going in person to meet the King and to make his peace.

Paris, an enormous disturbed beehive, buzzed with rumours. Amongst other speculations of more serious import—for instance, was the return of the hated Mazarin soon to be anticipated?—was a personal one which, knowing the callous instability of the mob, we may assume to have been tinged with a malicious rather than a benevolent interest: what fate was in reserve for Mlle de Montpensier? She had enjoyed her hour of popularity; she had figured, briefly, as the reckless heroine, almost as a leader, regardless of consequences; she had let off that unfortunate cannon at the Bastille; she had crawled through a muddy hole into Orléans. There was a touch of the clown about Mademoiselle, something unwise and ill-advised, something rash and silly, something half-comic, half-heroic, something which endeared her to a populace always more prompt to acclaim a figure they could laugh at than a figure they must solemnly admire. And she had, after all, been on their side. She had risked everything she valued, her position, her property, her great fortune, her favour at Court, all the things that meant most to her mundane mind, in support of the people with bits of straw in their hats.

That populace, however, volatile and fickle and forgetful, was already avid to learn what price she must now pay for her indiscretions. The French character is neither indulgent nor compassionate: success is acclaimed, failure is derided; the wolfish pack descends upon the fallen in a herd-instinct of destruction wholly unworthy of so highly civilised a race. It was now the turn of Mademoiselle to suffer such a reversal of popular fortune. Sarcastic broad-sheets began to appear about her; the broad-sheets that always represented the barometer of the popular temper.

Mademoiselle herself, during those agitating days of the King's re-entry into Paris, had behaved with her usual foolishness and impetuosity. She had gone to watch his arrival from the windows of Mme de Choisy in the hôtel de Blainville, which gave on to the place du Louvre, and had observed, down in the street, a man peddling lanterns to hang in windows as a sign of rejoicing. '*Lanternes à la royale!*' he called out, '*Lanternes à la royale!*' Mademoiselle shouted back at him, 'Have you none *à la fronde?*' 'God Almighty!' said poor Mme de Choisy to her dangerous firebrand guest, 'do you want to get me assassinated?'

Mme de Choisy, with nothing of the heroine in her make-up, could not understand Mademoiselle who in those dire days never failed to have her hair dressed in case she might suddenly be summoned by the Queen, and who continued to dine to the accompaniment of music. 'What,' said Mme de Choisy, coming in as she sat at dinner, 'have you the heart to listen to violins, when we are all about to be driven out?' Mademoiselle's answer was worthy of her. 'We must expect anything and make up our minds to it.' There are moments when one can imagine her in a tumbril.

She was nevertheless very uneasy. She had already refused to go out riding with her father, saying that evil stories were current and that she had been told she would be sent away to Dombes, one of her territories in the neighbourhood of Lyon. Was she afraid of being kidnapped? Her father assured her that there was no question of her being relegated to Dombes; but, perhaps sagely, she put little faith in his assurances.

Then the evil stories began to take more concrete shape. Condé and Lorraine had been gone a week all but a day, when the first definite blows began to fall. She was having her hair dressed as usual one morning when an official of the Court entered her room bearing a letter he must deliver to her by command of the King, a mean and petty letter, desiring her to quit her apartments in the Tuileries by noon next day, as he could dispose of no other lodging to offer his brother. Until she could find alternative accommodation, he added, she could go and stay with the duc de Damville at the hôtel de Ventadour.

This request naturally upset Mademoiselle very much indeed; she was fond of the Tuileries (*que j'aimais fort*) which had been her home ever since she was a week old, and moreover the order presaged nothing good for the future. She went off to the Luxembourg to consult her father, who showed himself in a most unhelpful mood, expressing a surprise which can scarcely have been anything but hypocritical and merely advising her to obey the royal mandate. Mademoiselle was hurt, though with her usual generosity it appears that she did not realise at the time how scurvily he was behaving towards her. 'He saw me without a roof over my head and not knowing where to find one, yet did not offer me a room in the Luxembourg. I was so unaccustomed not to receive some little sign of friendliness from him, that I did not then notice that he ought to have offered me a lodging. I went to stay the night with Mme de Fiesque, rather dazed by everything that I was seeing.'

Worse was to come. On the day of the King's return she got word that her father had been ordered away from Paris. She had heard rumours that he was playing a double game, trying to make his peace with both the King and the Parlement, and she had even gone so far as to say to Viole, the president of the Parlement, in her frank, indiscreet way, 'You know my father; I would not answer for him.' Yet her personal loyalty remained unimpaired. No sooner had she heard of his threatened exile than she sent him a little note by a page who brought back only a verbal answer, 'Tell my daughter that she doesn't know what she is talking about' (*Dites à ma fille qu'elle ne sait pas ce qu'elle dit*). This highly discourteous message should have given her some indication of Gaston's state of mind, even if she knew nothing of the scene that had recently passed between him and Retz and Madame in the privacy of Madame's apartments. Gaston might be treacherous, but whatever their moral character people usually remain true to their upbringing. It was not in conformity with Gaston's birth and training to ignore the prevalent rules of etiquette. He should not have said '*ma fille*' to a page; he should have said *Mademoiselle* or *Son Altesse Royale*. These things mattered to those people. Yet, when on receiving confirmation of the order, she hurried in person to the Luxembourg she was naïvely surprised to find him in such ill-humour. What else could she expect? Mademoiselle herself was in no very calm mood; she had been turned out of the Tuileries; she was temporarily homeless, a refugee, seeking hospitality from her friends; and she was worried, in her silly loyal way, about the princes, a lost cause if ever there was one. She flew at M. de Rohan, whom she encountered on arrival at the

Luxembourg, reproached him with trying to make his peace at Court, with betraying the interests of M. le Prince, and gave him her opinion pretty tartly (*assez vertement*). Then she went into Madame's room, where she found her father and asked him if it were true that he had been ordered away. Gaston replied that he was not answerable to her for his actions. 'What!' said she, 'are you going to abandon M. le Prince and M. de Lorraine?' but he would not return any other reply. She begged him to tell her if she also would be driven away, when he fairly rounded on her and a lamentable scene ensued between them.

He refused, he said, to intervene in her affairs; she had conducted herself so injudiciously towards the Court that he would have nothing to do with her concerns. She had never listened to his advice . . .

She retaliated. Was it not on his instructions that she had gone to Orléans? She had not got it in writing, because he had given her his commands verbally, but she had got other orders from him in writing about what she was to do when she got there; also letters so full of loving-kindness and affection, she could not believe that he would go back on them as he was now doing.

Gaston, cornered, swivelled quickly to a different line of attack. 'And what about the St Antoine affair?' he said; 'don't you think, Mademoiselle, that it did you a lot of harm at Court? You enjoyed yourself so much playing the heroine and being told that you were on our side and had saved it twice, that, whatever happens to you in future, you will find consolation in the remembrance of all the praise that was lavished on you.'

Gaston, with all his faults, must be given credit for some insight. It was clever of him to foresee that Mademoiselle could live on her exploits for some years to come, as a camel on its hump. She would find consolation in remembrance and recollection. Gaston was far from being a stupid man.

Meanwhile he was a badgered and worried man, and his

daughter's reply cannot have pleased him. 'I don't think I served you any worse at the Porte St Antoine than at Orléans,' she said; 'I did both these things, with which you are now reproaching me, by your order, and if I had to do it all over again I should do it, because it was my duty to obey you. If you are in disgrace with fortune now, it would be only fair that I should share your ill-fortune, and if I had not served you I should share it just the same. I know nothing about being a heroine; my birth obliges me to act grandly and proudly in all my doing; you can give it whatever name you choose. For my part, I should describe it as following my own inclinations and my own path; I was not born to do otherwise.'

She then renewed her request that he would allow her to remain at the Luxembourg. He replied that he had no room. Mademoiselle said she thought she had as good a right to lodge there as anybody. Gaston said sourly that everyone living in the palace was necessary to him, and that they were not going to turn out. 'Since Your Royal Highness is unwilling,' said Mademoiselle, 'I shall go to the hôtel de Condé, which is empty.' 'I do not wish you to.' 'Well then, Monsieur, where *do* you wish me to go?' 'Wherever you like,' he said, and went away.

It had not been an edifying interview.

Mademoiselle was left knowing no better than the people of Paris what was coming to her. She had only one advantage over them: she did at least know where she, physically, was and where she laid her head each night, though even that pillow was becoming less and less predictable. Fortunately she had good friends in Mme de Fiesque, Mme de Montmort, Mme de Frontenac and the faithful Préfontaine. Her idea was to conceal herself within one of their houses, leaving one house by the back door in order secretly to gain another. In this manner she spent the first evening under the roof of Mme de Montmort who, although flattered by the trust placed in her by her illustrious guest, was overcome by the housewifely worry of having nothing worthy to offer for her supper. Mademoiselle's tribulations had not caused her to lose her appetite, and she dined well off an excellent fricassée, some cold meat, and some delicious stewed fruit. Her tribulations had not broken her spirit either, for she called for paper and ink and wrote long letters to M. le Prince and M. de Lorraine, begging them to do something so amazing as to bring peace about; she could not contemplate, she said, spending a whole winter in the country; she could not understand how people could bear to do such a thing: how much more agreeable it would be if they could all spend *Carnaval* in Paris again together. Such frivolity, at such a juncture, was truly incomprehensible. Préfontaine, to whom she showed her letters, was appalled, and said so. 'It throws me into despair,' he said, 'that Your Royal Highness who has so much good sense should entertain such fantastic ideas.' Mademoiselle would not listen to him. 'Be silent,' she said, 'you don't know what you are saying,' and sent her letters to an officer of Condé's with orders to leave at dawn.

Préfontaine had more sense than Mademoiselle. He saw clearly that she could not remain indefinitely in hiding, but instead of encouraging her pride and, with it, her resistance, he went ingeniously about the task of persuading her to take a voluntary departure. 'You are forgetting, Mademoiselle,' he said, 'that a sedentary life is inimical to your health and that it would be very bad for you never to move out of the room into the fresh air; besides, this is the time of year when you nearly always get your sore throats. If you fell ill, you would have to reveal your presence. You are not the mistress of your health as you are of your person.' Mme de Frontenac weighed in: 'If you would like to go to Pont,[1] Mme Bouthillier would be delighted to receive you; the air is salubrious; you could be there in secret and could move about as freely as you chose.'

Mademoiselle capitulated; they must have breathed a sigh

[1] Pont-sur-Seine, Aube.

of relief. Préfontaine was to have everything ready by the following day.

Before he could begin making his dispositions, however, he received the news that Monsieur had left for Limours; Mademoiselle sent him in pursuit. He caught up with Monsieur at Berny, a short way out of Paris. Monsieur got out of his coach, which we may take as an indication that he was in one of his rages or panics; normally, he would have beckoned Préfontaine to speak with him at the window; instead, he stood in the road saying, 'You are to tell my daughter, from me, that she is to go to Bois-le-Vicomte and that she is not to play about with all the false hopes she may be given by M. de Beaufort, Mme de Montbazon and Mme de Bonnelle, of helping M. le Prince and of doing something remarkable, for there is no longer anything to be done. You know that I am better loved and more highly esteemed than she, yet no protest has been made against my departure.' (Presumably, he meant by the people in the streets, seeing his coach go past.) 'So she has nothing to hope for, and must go away.'

Préfontaine pleaded on Mademoiselle's behalf. Bois-le-Vicomte was not a suitable retreat, he said; in the goodness of her heart she had given it over, during the recent war, to many unfortunate people, some of them very ill persons; it would take a long time to purge it of infectious diseases. All that Mademoiselle desired, he said, was to follow His Royal Highness her father, or else to live with Madame. 'I don't want her to come with me,' said Gaston, 'nor to go with Madame, who is on the eve of her confinement; my daughter would be a nuisance to her. If she does not want to go to Bois-le-Vicomte, then let her go to one of her other houses.'

Préfontaine insisted; Gaston lost his temper and said, 'No, I don't want her; if she comes, I shall chase her away.' Préfontaine turned for support to the duc de Rohan, but, Gaston remaining obdurate, he had no choice but to go back to Paris with the message. Mademoiselle, deeply hurt, permitted herself a bitter little reflection, 'I remembered then how I had been refused lodging (at the Luxembourg) and I have never forgotten it since.'

The day, which had begun thus badly, did not improve as the hours went by. At least twenty people wrote notes to Mme de Fiesque saying that Mademoiselle was about to be arrested. Préfontaine tried to persuade her to go to Bois-le-Vicomte instead of to Pont, but she turned on him saying that if he did not wish to leave Paris he might remain there: she could get on very well without him. He answered that he would say no more and would follow her to the ends of the earth if she would allow him to accompany her. Later on, Mademoiselle repented of her injustice: 'He had only said what he deemed his duty, as a good and faithful servant, but sometimes it is those whom one believes the least.'

His troubles were not yet over. Mademoiselle was now thoroughly frightened and thought only of escaping from Paris as soon as possible. She woke early; Préfontaine kept her waiting, and when he arrived Mademoiselle was very angry. 'I scolded him violently (*je le grondai horriblement*).' Devoted though he was, he cannot always have found her service very easy; besides, he had spent a busy and worrying morning: he had been to fetch money, he had given the necessary orders for the flitting of Mademoiselle's household, and he had been to see Mme de Fiesque who had been rude to him. 'After all that, Mademoiselle, I cannot feel that I deserve to be scolded for being a quarter of an hour later than you expected me.' Finally, he had the satisfaction of seeing her climb into a borrowed coach, with no armorial bearings, a coachman and footman with no livery, and only two horses.

Mademoiselle was gone at last; Paris had lost her. No one knew where she was, nor where she was likely to be found next, nor in what circumstances of disgrace or safety. The mystery added zest to the interest. As usual, the topic of the hour found expression in a street-song: Monsieur, they sang, had hurried away before dawn, and:

Mademoiselle son aînée
Disparut la même journée,
Mais où cette princesse alla
Fort peu de gens savent cela.[1]

[1] Mademoiselle his eldest daughter
Disappeared the same day,
But where that princess went to
Very few people know.

CHAPTER VI

Mademoiselle in Exile
[1652—1657]

MADEMOISELLE'S spirits and natural courage could never remain repressed for very long. By the time she had put the River Marne between herself and Paris she had dismissed Paris from her mind and felt resolved to accept anything that her destiny might send her. With her love of fun and adventure, she even began to enjoy what was surely the oddest party she had ever given. Its oddness consisted largely in her own anonymity. For the first time in her life she was no longer Mademoiselle, she was 'Madame Dupré,' as we might say Mrs Smith, travelling with five friends[1] in a coach, and a couple of friends on horseback.[2] For security, it was necessary that they should treat her in public as one of the company. She took it all in wildly good part; it was a new game to play, and she played it with all the zest of any gay young creature escaping from her own personality behind the mask and domino at a masked ball. It is an exciting, rare experience to escape from oneself; especially, perhaps, when one is born a public not a private figure. Mademoiselle was a fugitive not only from Paris but from her own rank.

They spent the first night at a moated house called l'Épine, belonging to Mme de Frontenac's aunt, Mme Bouthillier, where they passed a most hilarious evening. Mme Bouthillier, who was awaiting them a little farther on, at Pont, was not the

[1] They were: Mme de Frontenac, Préfontaine, two of Mademoiselle's women, and a maid belonging to Mme de Frontenac.
[2] These were La Guérinière, Mademoiselle's *maître d'hôtel;* and an anonymous *gentilhomme* attached to the Frontenac household.

widow of a *surintendent des finances* for nothing, and could afford to keep her many houses always fully equipped in readiness for any chance arrival. Mme de Frontenac had only to knock on the door and give her orders to the concierge, 'Please prepare a room for this lady, a friend of mine who is travelling with me.' Then they all sat down to an excellent grilled supper, including cheeses so delicious that Mademoiselle, who seems to have had a taste for cheese, ate more than she had ever eaten in her life. (As they were now in the heart of the Brie country, having passed through Brie-Comte-Robert earlier in the day, it is not difficult to guess the cheese which found such favour, and we may hope that it was sufficiently *coulant*.)

Mademoiselle's companions were so much astonished to find themselves sitting at table with her, that Mme Bouthillier's servants, waiting on them, would surely have seen through the prank had they only been more quick-witted. So says Mademoiselle, who thought it deliriously funny—she, who was accustomed to eating alone, or with her equals, or with a few privileged friends, and who was certainly not accustomed to see anyone seat themselves unbidden in her presence. With good humour and gaiety she turned an embarrassing situation into a spree: they all called each other my brother, my sister, my cousin . . . It must have required a considerable effort before Mademoiselle's serving-women could bring themselves to address her as '*ma cousine*'; or did they, also, enjoy the escape from their normal personalities? Did Préfontaine feel that he was paying her something back as he called her '*ma sœur*'? We shall never know, but we do know from Mademoiselle's pen that the drollery kept them laughing for days.

All that night long, Mme Bouthillier's servants roasted chickens and pigeons, so the coach was well-provisioned when it set off in the morning on its way south.

Mademoiselle, in spite of occasional alarms, now began to enjoy the novelty of casual encounters on the road. She had covered many leagues of the roads of France during her short life, but always travelling as a great lady, either in company of the Court on its progresses or with her own retinue in her own right. She had never enjoyed the freedom of entering a village inn, as she now did at Sourdun while the horses were fed and watered, and of finding a monk eating his meal in the kitchen. She was masked; she was unrecognisable; her anonymity was complete. She immediately engaged the monk in conversation: to what order did he belong, she asked? for he had discarded his cowl and mantle and was sitting there dressed only in a white habit.

She has recorded their dialogue.

'You are very inquisitive,' he said—which, in itself, was not the sort of reply Her Royal Highness was accustomed to receive.

'My curiosity is surely reasonable?'

'I am a Jacobin,' he said then, meaning a Dominican.

'Where have you come from?'

'From Nancy; and you, where do you come from?'

'From Paris,' said Mademoiselle, who, seizing this unexpected opportunity, asked him what was thought of M. de Lorraine in his own country; was he much beloved?[1]

'Yes,' said the monk, 'he is a good prince. But is it true,' he added, 'what I was told at Troyes, that the King was going back to Paris?'

Mademoiselle told him that it was quite true; the King had in fact returned two days ago; and then she added, with an effrontery born of her new independence, that M. le duc d'Orléans and Mademoiselle had both quitted the capital.

'I am sorry to hear that,' said the monk; 'he is a good fellow (*c'est un bonhomme*). As for Mademoiselle, she is a grand lass (*c'est une brave fille*). A pike would suit her as well as a mask; she is courageous. Do you not know her at all?'

Mademoiselle said no, she was not acquainted with her.

'What!' said the monk, 'don't you know that she jumped

[1] Nancy was the capital of Lorraine.

over the walls of Orléans to get into the town, and that she saved the life of M. le Prince at the Porte St Antoine?'

Mademoiselle said that she had heard something about it.

The monk pressed his questions.

'Have you never seen her?'

Mademoiselle said no, she had never seen her, whereupon the monk began to depict Mademoiselle to herself:

'She is a fine young woman,' he said, 'as tall as you are; quite handsome, with a long face and a big nose. I cannot tell whether you resemble her in your features as much as you resemble her in her general build. If you would take your mask off, I could tell you.'

Mademoiselle excused herself; she could not remove her mask, she mendaciously said, because a recent attack of small-pox had left her face still very red. Had he ever spoken with Mademoiselle, she asked?

'A thousand times!' he replied. 'I should recognise her amongst a hundred persons. I often went to the Tuileries where she lived. I know her Almoner, and she used to come most first Sundays in every month to the house of our foundation, St Honoré, with the Queen.'

'Is she a good Catholic?'

'No,' said the monk; 'the fancy took her once, but she got bored with it and it passed off; she took to it too violently for it to last.'

'And what about her stepmother?' said Mademoiselle. 'Do you know her?'

'Yes, indeed,' said the monk, and his reply throws a light on the much-maligned personality of Madame. 'She is one of those saints whose feast-day is never celebrated. She keeps to her chair and never walks a step; she is slow and indolent, always half-asleep. There is all the difference between her and Made-moiselle, who is lively and moves quickly. But who are you, madame, questioning me so closely?'

Mademoiselle drew lavishly on her inventiveness for her reply. She was a widow, she said; her husband had been a gentleman of Sologne; their house had been pillaged by some army or other, passing that way; she herself had taken refuge in Orléans, which she had unfortunately left the very day that Mademoiselle arrived there; she was now on her way to Champagne to stay with her brother and her sister-in-law. Really, Mademoiselle had mistaken her vocation; she should have been a novelist.

The monk, whom we may suspect of having a very shrewd idea of the identity of the masked lady, then invited her to visit the monastery of St Honoré, should she ever find herself in Paris. Mademoiselle teased him, saying that she was a Protestant; he then tried to convert her, but she turned his arguments aside by saying that it was too serious a subject to discuss in so light a way; she hoped to spend a little time in Paris during the winter, when they might renew the argument.

He told her his name, which she forgot; he told her also that he was very tired. Did the Jacobins never travel by *coche*,[1] she asked? Yes, he said; he had tried to get a seat in the *coche* at Troyes, but it was too expensive, so he had set off on foot. He had been overtaken on the road by the *coche* devoid of passengers. The driver had pulled up to offer him a free lift (*l'avait prié de s'y mettre pour rien*), which he refused: too proud. 'The habit I wear,' he said, 'does not prevent us from distinguishing between right and wrong.' It is difficult to see what the monk meant by this: what harm could have come to him, spiritually, by taking advantage of a friendly offer?

Mademoiselle can never have had any knowledge of such bottom-of-the-purse poverty and pride. Pride she knew, a different sort of pride, the pride of arrogance, not of humility. She was learning something; something of the reality of life; or at any rate she ought to have been learning something, but we may wonder how much she learnt. I fear that Mademoiselle, for all her high spirit and sense of fun, and courage in adversity, had been endowed by Nature with a very shallow little bowl of understanding. Her horizon was limited: the unimportant

---

[1] The *coche* was a sort of public bus, or *diligence*.

things were important to her and would always remain so. She possessed neither the intellectual power nor the capacity to lever herself out of the groove into whose deep furrow she had been born. However much it might amuse her to travel as Mme Dupré, masked, sitting at a kitchen table with a monk eating his dinner, she derived no more from their encounter than, 'I was much entertained by this adventure, and thought it augured well for the rest of my journey.'

It would be wearisome to follow her journey in detail. She stayed for two days with the ever-obliging Mme Bouthillier at Pont; Mme Bouthillier had a good cook, so 'Mme Dupré' ate well, which she much appreciated, and furthermore had the treat of visiting the local fair, still behind the disguise of her sobriquet and her mask. She was not inactive; she continued to write letters and to receive news: Paris was still wondering where she had gone; at Blois, also, her disappearance was much discussed; Mme de Fiesque had spread a story that she had gone to Flanders; she corresponded with M. le Prince and M. de Lorraine; officers and messengers galloped backwards and forwards; M. St Mars, bringing her a letter from M. le Prince, was so much surprised to find himself sitting at dinner with her that he lost his head and started talking to her about the princes' army instead of keeping up the fiction that he had just arrived from Paris. Mme Bouthillier, tactful hostess, pretended not to hear.

St Mars, primed by M. le Prince, was full of proposals when Mademoiselle retired with him into an inner room after dinner. They had a long confabulation. Where should Mademoiselle go? M. le Prince thought she might go to Honfleur, a port in Normandy which belonged to her. If she went to Honfleur, he said, she could get help from Ostend; and in the last resort she could make her escape by sea. 'No, thank you,' said Mademoiselle in effect; 'I dread the sea, and if only M. le Prince realised to what extent I dread it, he would not advise me to embark upon it.'

She was neither the first nor the last French passenger to fight shy of a Channel crossing; she would not go to Honfleur; she did not like the Normans; the aristocracy of Normandy was a feeble lot (*un faible secours*), who for the last three days had stayed safely at home (*les Normands ne découchent pas de chez eux*), besides, she would have no means of defending herself, were Honfleur to be attacked; she could not count on the support of M. de Longueville;[1] no, she would keep to her intention of seeking a refuge in her own château of St Fargeau. She had made up her mind, which after a period of indecision is always a comforting thing to do.

There were alarms, of course. Mademoiselle had not entirely dismissed the fearful thought that she might at any moment be pursued and arrested. Mme Bouthillier did what she could: she offered a little moated château as a refuge, she offered accommodation in two farm-houses. Préfontaine, with the good sense that even Mademoiselle periodically acknowledges, discouraged these suggestions. 'However fast you may run,' he said, 'they will catch you if they mean to, and you will get Mme Bouthillier into terrible trouble with the Court if she says that she does not know where you are. It would be taking advantage of the kindness she is showing Your Royal Highness. You had much better wait patiently until you see what is going to happen.'

Poor Préfontaine. He, also, had his troubles arising from his devotion to his royal mistress. His coach was attacked on the road, his horses stolen, and all his money, clothes, and linen. Mademoiselle was most unsympathetic. All she cared about was the loss of a story she had written, some verses by Mme de Frontenac, and something entitled *Royaume de la lune*, which sounds very like the world of unreality which Mademoiselle inhabited. Préfontaine, a practical man, and, as I see him, a very long-suffering man, was more concerned with the loss of his own goods and of certain important documents belonging

[1] Governor of Normandy.

to Mademoiselle, left in his charge, than with the loss of a few manuscripts. He became really cross with Mademoiselle when she threatened to send a messenger to M. de Turenne, asking him to return them. 'Préfontaine was very angry with me, seeing that that was the only thing I cared about. I hardly minded at all about his money, his clothes, or his linen (*dont je ne me souciais guère*), so long as I could recover the papers I wanted. He took things more seriously than I did, and was worried about his money . . .'

One cannot blame Préfontaine for showing some irascibility.

The arrival at St Fargeau was most unpropitious. With the extraordinary lack of foresight habitually displayed by these grand people on their journeyings, Mademoiselle contrived to arrive at two o'clock in the morning; no preparations had been made to receive her; the bridge was broken down, so that the coach could not be driven into the courtyard and Mademoiselle had to alight and scramble in as best she could on foot, through grass knee-high, in pitch darkness. Surely it would have been simple to despatch a groom on horseback in advance? Apparently not. It is, of course, conceivable that Mademoiselle was keeping her destination secret; she had had a fright on the road, getting word of a posse of soldiers whom she was convinced were on the look-out for her, and it is clear from her own statement that she regarded St Fargeau as a remote hiding-place, 'in a great desert, and so little known that I might be believed to be in a different world'; but these miserable arrivals, with no comfort and not even a bed to sleep in, were of too frequent occurrence to be explained by anything but sheer incompetence.

Here, then, were Mademoiselle, Mme de Frontenac, Préfontaine, La Guérinière her *maître d'hôtel*, and a rabble of servants, confronting a vast and ruinous building in the middle of the night. Mademoiselle had never been there before, and did not know in the least what to expect. She could probably discern the outline of the six massive circular towers, which must have looked forbidding enough, but what she actually saw is best described in her own words, 'an old house with neither doors nor windows; it filled me with dismay. They took me into a dreadful room, with an upright beam in the centre. Fear, horror, and grief took possession of me to such an extent that I began to cry; I thought myself most unhappy, being exiled from the Court, not having a better residence, and thinking that *this* was the finest of all my châteaux.'

Her attendants realised that she could not remain there that night. Tired though she was, she mounted a horse and rode off to a small house called Dannery, at two leagues of distance, where she was welcomed by the bailiff of her estates, and given a room to share with Mme de Frontenac. 'Do not wake me in the morning,' she said, 'I intend to sleep all day.' But she was not to find rest even there. The place appeared to be haunted. The curtains of Mme de Frontenac's bed opened and closed twice; Mademoiselle, who was frightened of ghosts, called out to her. 'It is the wind,' said the lady, but there was no wind. Mademoiselle, alarmed, asked her to come into her bed, which Mme de Frontenac did with alacrity, confessing that that had been her first impulse and that nothing but her respect for Mademoiselle and the fear of startling her had restrained her. Some days later, Mademoiselle learnt that her foster-brother had been killed, and decided that it was he who had been trying to bid her farewell.

Nevertheless, they had some trouble in persuading her to return to St Fargeau. La Guérinière rode over to inspect it, and came back with the information that it was strong enough to resist an assault, and that even if the attackers managed to enter by one door, she could get out by another. Two days passed before she would make up her mind; nocturnal scares not-withstanding, she had taken a fancy to the little house at Dannery: there were plenty of books, she could go for walks, she could please herself, she could go to bed early and get up late. Her fear of being followed, attacked, and arrested seems to have been entirely without foundation; she always enjoyed

La Grande Mademoiselle, by Jean Nocret, 1615–1672

dramatising any situation; so long as she remained far enough away in the country, the King and his advisers were content to leave her in peace. They knew quite well where she was, even if the Paris versifier had forgotten the exact name of her retreat:

> J'ai su d'un bourgeois
> Qu'elle était dans le Bourbonnais,
> En un sien logis fort antique
> Composé de pierre et de brique,
> J'ai mis en oubli le château,
> Mais je sais bien qu'il rime en *geau* . . .[1]

Finally she consented to go back. The morning was fine, and the impression much more favourable. They led her into a room which pleased her so much that with her habitual resilience she instantly began to make plans for improvement by altering the doors and the chimney-piece and forming an alcove. Was there a local architect? she asked, having decided that provincial workmen would be better than Parisians, an opinion she later reversed. There were certain drawbacks to making the alterations, as they naturally rendered the room temporarily uninhabitable and obliged her to move into an attic overhead; moreover, ten days elapsed before her bed arrived from Paris, a difficulty she overcame by commandeering the brand-new bed of the St Fargeau steward, who, hapless man, had just got married.

The Paris versifier was not quite correct in placing St Fargeau in the Bourbonnais; it was near to the confines of Burgundy, not many miles from Auxerre and Avallon, in a district known as la Puisaye, a curious name which is said to

[1] I was told by a citizen
That she was in the Bourbonnais
At a very ancient house of hers
Built of stone and of brick.
I have forgotten the (name of the) château
But I know it rhymes with *geau*.

The château de St Fargeau

derive from *puits* and *haies*, wells and hedges, or else from two Celtic words, *poel*, a lake, swamp, or pool, and *say*, a forest. Whichever derivation we may accept, the name is sufficiently descriptive of a well-watered, well-wooded country, abounding in little rivers, the Loing, the Vrin, the Ouanne, the Branlin, the Orcière, the Agréau, the Bourdon, flowing between those vast woods which are one of the beauties of France, and abounding also in game, St Fargeau itself having originally been a hunting-box. To this day one has a sense of deep country, as one gazes down the perspective of apparently interminable rides cut through the forest, but in Mademoiselle's day it must indeed have been dense and trackless, and so obscure that the village of St Fargeau is not even marked on a map dated as late as 1753, a century after her sojourn.

Mademoiselle, with her avowed and very French dislike of rural life, had expressed dismay at the prospect of spending a winter at St Fargeau, little knowing that she was destined to remain there for four years. Paris was everything, its attractions irresistible, apart from the fact that anybody who wished to cut anything of a figure in the world must hover continually within the circle of the Court. An absentee courtier was far worse than an absentee landlord; Louis XIV had a habit of saying acidly, 'I don't see him,' which was to be taken in the sense of a dangerous rebuke. Richelieu's policy of discouraging the nobility from living too influentially on their estates, had succeeded only too well, as they were to find to their cost, urban-minded people that they were, allured by the glitter of the Crown and its rewards. Paris was the lovely mistress, the province the dull wife. Even in our own times, as, motoring, we pass the shuttered châteaux, we may reflect on the two-months of villegiature unwillingly undertaken in the interests of economy by their owners accompanied by far, far too many members of their tribe.

Not that the courts of Louis XIII and Louis XIV did not enjoy the pleasures of hunting, or of picnics, or of *promenades*, provided these excursions could be made to resemble parties

as much as possible. It was simply that their interest lay in
people rather than in a contemplation of the beauties of Nature.
French literature of the middle and late seventeenth century
reflects something of the indifference with which the works of
God were regarded. In the days of the Pléiade French poetry
had much kinship with the English attitude towards woods and
meadows, flowers and streams; the smoke rises blue from
cottage chimneys, and the heart of the exile in a city yearns for
the gentle familiarity of the country home.

> Quand reverrai-je, hélas, de mon petit village
> Fumer la cheminée; et en quelle saison
> Reverrai-je le clos de ma pauvre maison,
> Qui m'est une province, et beaucoup d'avantage?
>
> Plus me plaît le séjour qu'ont bâti mes aieux,
> Que des palais Romains le front audacieux;
> Plus que le marbre dur me plaît l'ardoise fine,
>
> Plus mon Loire gaulois, que le Tibre latin,
> Plus mon petit Lyré que le mont Palatin,
> Et plus que l'air marin la douceur Angevine.

The poets of the Pléiade could be as tender as Suckling, as
green-minded as Marvell. That school, which represented
indeed a most uncharacteristic facet of the French genius had
long since expired *sine prole*. We may look in vain through the
pages of Corneille, Racine, Molière, Boileau, for any interest
save in human beings under various aspects, sometimes out-
rageously heroic, sometimes presented in the classical trappings
of a sublime artificiality, sometimes grotesquely caricatured,
but always men and women moving against the background
of the palace, the Doric temple, or the elegant *salon*. There is
no breeze to blow, no leaves to stir. Even the grasshoppers, the
frogs, and the foxes of the delicious La Fontaine are not
of the animal creation as we understand it: they are purely
anthropomorphic.

*　　　*　　　*

163

In spite of her disgrace, her banishment, and her disinclination for rusticity, Mademoiselle contrived to be very happy at St Fargeau. I think she was right in saying, 'No one is less easily bored than I; I can always find some occupation, and can even amuse myself by day-dreaming. I am only bored when I am with people I don't like, or when I am contradicted.' The winter was a hard one, even in the favoured Burgundian climate; there were some days when she could not go out, but at the first sign of good weather she went out riding, or, if the frost were too severe, walking. It is diverting to see the Court lady turning into a squire and a gardener. 'First of all I made a mall; trees had been planted, but there were so many brambles and holes that one could never have believed it possible to make an alley. But as the scrub was cut away, and soil brought in, we found a fine alley; only, as I judged it not long enough for a mall, I had it lengthened by a hundred paces on a terrace. It looks very well, for from this terrace one can see the château, the woods, the vineyards, and a meadow crossed by a river, which in summer becomes a pool: this landscape is quite pleasing. St Fargeau was a wild place when I came there, one could not find a herb to put in the pot.'

As time goes on, she becomes quite attached to her retreat. She begins to refer to it as *my* St Fargeau, and refuses to leave it for a grander house at Châtellerault where she owned the castle,[1] or for Blois where she probably rightly suspected her father of wanting to keep her closer under his eye. They told her St Fargeau was ugly, and the *Muse historique* took it up:

Mademoiselle est à Blois
Dont Monsieur, son père, est fort aise;
Et je maintiens (ne lui déplaise)
Blois étant un séjour fort beau,
Qu'elle est mieux là qu'à St Fargeau.[2]

[1] She was duchesse de Châtellerault.
[2] Mademoiselle is at Blois
  Which is a great relief to Monsieur her father,
  And I suggest, with all due respect,
  Blois being a lovely place for a sojourn,
  That she would be better advised to stay there than at St Fargeau.

Mademoiselle thought otherwise. *Je n'avais nulle envie de changer de demeure.* She had made herself very comfortable by now, with her own room, an ante-room, and a gallery where she hung the portraits of all her relations, including, we notice, Charles, King of England. She put a billiard-table in the gallery. Her own room, she says, was very pretty, with a *garde-robe* and a little cabinet where there was no space for anyone but herself. Here she hung more portraits, and some mirrors. 'I was delighted (*j'étais ravie*) and thought I had made the loveliest thing on earth. I showed my apartments to all my visitors, with as much complacence in my work as the Queen, my grandmother, when she showed off her Luxembourg.'

Encouraged by her initial success, she ended by writing to Paris for an architect and began her work of reconstruction in good earnest. Fortunately for her and for St Fargeau, the architect she employed was François Le Vau, a younger brother of the better-known Louis Le Vau, the architect of Versailles and Vaux-le-Vicomte. Anyone seeing St Fargeau today, damaged though it has been by fire, will think that Mademoiselle expressed herself too modestly in saying that she had done no more than repair an old house, 'which nevertheless had a certain grandeur about it.' She wished she could have spent more on it than 200,000 francs. She had, in fact, found it in a state of complete dereliction, and had transformed it into the thing of rather original magnificence it still is.[1]

It must not be supposed that Mademoiselle spent those years without stirring from St Fargeau. Paris might be forbidden her, but she was free to roam elsewhere, and, a restless person *qui aimait fort à me promener,* she undertook numerous little journeys, either to take the waters at Forges, or to visit her father at Blois or her friends in their various châteaux. From her earliest childhood she had enjoyed seeing other people's houses, one of the more amiable tastes she shared with her father. She never fails to comment; sometimes a house is only *assez jolie,* but

[1] For a short history of St Fargeau, see Appendix on page 349.

sometimes, as at beautiful Valençay, where she arrived by torch-light, she thought she had come into a magical place. She went for a few days to the hospitable Mme Bouthillier at Pont, to watch the vintage. She went to Villandry, where she must have seen the amazing 'knot' parterres in their original con-dition (now happily restored), and here she found a pretty little boy who was no other than her own half-brother, son of Gaston and of that Louison Roger of whom Mademoiselle had been so wary at Tours[1] (page 34). Mademoiselle had always been fond of children, who, oddly enough, considering her alarming stature and rough striding ways, liked her in return—two little girls, clustering against her, once asked her to put them in her pockets, and the duc d'Anjou, aged eight, came running to throw his arms round her knees saying that he had always taken her side against everybody. She now resolved to take her half-brother into her own household, without, however, asking their father's permission lest it might be refused. He had never been given any name, being known only as *le mignon*. Mademoiselle cast about for a suitable title to bestow on him, but found herself in a difficulty, as all her estates were large and considerable, and their names had been borne by many princes of the royal house; this would never do, she thought, but after casting round for some time she remem-bered a small place near St Fargeau called Charny. *C'était un beau nom;* she called her brother chevalier de Charny.

But when she did not want to go, nothing would budge her. She records with an almost audible chuckle the *invention admirable* she hit on once when her father summoned her to Blois: she returned the answer that all her horses were out at grass. Gaston saw through this. He sent her others; she held them back for two months.

Nor must it be supposed that she lacked company, for her memoirs are full of visitors coming and going. In addition to the visitors, she had her permanent attendants, Préfontaine, Mme de Frontenac, the younger Mme de Fiesque, and presently

[1] Louison had gone into a convent.

the old *gouvernante*, Mme de Fiesque, who belatedly arrived from Paris to be sarcastically greeted by Mademoiselle, 'Ah! madame, and how comes it that you are here, you who believed me to be in Flanders?' Although on this occasion Mme de Fiesque answered so humbly that Mademoiselle's heart was touched and she treated her 'with more kindness than she deserved', neither of the Mmes de Fiesque ever succeeded in winning her affection. (I have often wondered why she put up with them for so long, or, indeed, why they put up with her.) In fact, Mademoiselle's little Court was no more immune from internal jealousies, squabbles, and partisanships than its greater prototype. The younger Mme de Fiesque and Mme de Frontenac were more closely allied than Mademoiselle at first suspected, calling one another *mon camarade*; old Mme de Fiesque hated Préfontaine because he would not repeat everything Mademoiselle had told him. Mademoiselle uses an odd little word, *micmac*, to describe the situation; translated, it means petty little intrigues. Some people might be well advised to adopt it into their vocabulary. Mademoiselle herself had a healthy contempt for that sort of thing (though I must regretfully acknowledge that when she found Mme de Fiesque's writing-desk open she read the letters), but her own treatment of Préfontaine might well have alienated a less devoted man. She scolded him incessantly; he even left St Fargeau once, to spend the night at the neighbouring house of a friend, seeing her in such ill-humour; the Fiesque ladies seized the opportunity to malign him; this enraged Mademoiselle, who sent a groom at full gallop after him, late though the hour was and the rain pouring down; Préfontaine returned at midnight, soaked to the skin, to find Mademoiselle saying, 'The best way of reconciling me with people, is for others to insult them.'

Ségrais, who never really understood her and misjudged her to the extent of saying that she never had any true love for Lauzun, hits off certain aspects of her character, very obvious and not at all subtle. 'She hated any form of control. One had to go a long way round when one wanted her to take one's advice, and to induce her to believe that she had arrived at the decision for herself. Even then, as she could never come to any conclusion straightaway, she would return to it later on and present it back to one as though it had been her own idea.' A maddening employer to work for. Yet even the exasperated Ségrais adds: 'She knew what she was like, and sometimes said, "My God, why did you make me in this mould? (*Pourquoi m'avez-vous faite de l'humeur dont je suis?*)".'

On the whole, she found life peaceful and free from worry (*douce et exempte d'ennui*). Very methodical in her new rôle of squire and châtelaine, she put all her affairs in order twice a week, after which she felt free to enjoy herself. Letters arrived regularly by courier from Paris. She had her greyhounds, *la Reine* and *Madame Souris*, as pets; after hunting the hare with some neighbours, she sent to England for a pack,[1] also for horses, as she never did things by halves, and took to hunting three times a week, which she much enjoyed. 'There is splendid hunting country round St Fargeau,' she says, 'and very well adapted to English hounds which usually go too fast for women to follow, but as it is well-wooded I was able to follow them everywhere.' She was also very much pleased by a team of cream-coloured ponies with black manes and a black stripe down the back which M. de Hollac sent her from Germany.

She played at battledore-and-shuttlecock, as she had played with her father many years ago at Blois, two hours every morning and also after luncheon, for she liked taking a lot of exercise; furthermore, she could now play at mall with Mme de Frontenac. For her evening entertainments, she had arranged a little theatre, well lit and prettily decorated—how could one exist without *la comédie*! Three winters running, she engaged a troupe from Lyon, who subsequently became known as *les comédiens de Mademoiselle*. How could one exist without music either? The picnics she gave in the forests were sweetened by the sound of violins. It would be pleasing to visualise amongst

[1] Presumably harriers, not beagles.

the musicians a Florentine boy whom her uncle the chevalier
de Guise had brought her on her request from Malta at a time
when she wanted to learn Italian in order to read Tasso in the
original. Unfortunately, not relishing a rural life, he asked for
his dismissal. Several years later, Mademoiselle recognised him
acting as a mime in the King's ballet. She remembered him as
Baptiste; she seems to have forgotten or more likely had never
known his surname, which was Lulli, or, as the French wrote
it, Lully.

This does not exhaust the list of Mademoiselle's interests,
diversions, and activities. She who had never liked reading,
now took a taste for it and caused herself to be read aloud to
while she stitched (most clumsily, I suspect) at her embroidery.
Nor was this all. She began to fancy herself as an author. She
remembered her unfinished story, *La vie de Mme de Fouquerolles*,
happily retrieved from the raid on Préfontaine's coach with
his linen and money; completed it; and, impatient to see it in
print, sent to Auxerre for a printer and set up a hand-press in
a room at St Fargeau. This was only the first step, and there is
one thing we owe to Mademoiselle's enforced villégiature, we
who live almost to the exact year three centuries later: we owe
her Memoirs.[2] It was at St Fargeau that she started writing
them, urged, as she says, by some people she was fond of (*à la
prière de quelques personnes que j'aime*). We know who they
were: M. and Mme de Frontenac, and Préfontaine. They must
all have been in favour that day. True, Mme de Fiesque, of
whom Mademoiselle was anything but fond, added her voice
to their persuasions, but far from this turning her perversely
against the suggestion as we might expect, she agreed readily
enough. It was a brilliant idea (*une idée géniale*) on the part of
those four, whose joint task of keeping a restive princess quiet
and occupied can have been no sinecure. There was a good
reason why she should have taken so kindly to the idea: she

[1] She broke off in 1660, resumed them in 1677 and kept them up until 1688, five
years before her death.

had already tried her hand at authorship; furthermore, had been reading the memoirs of *la reine Margot*,[1] and was inspired by the thought of emulation. Her attempt at authorship in that very indifferent little work *Mme de Fouquerolles* is greatly excelled by her autobiography, but is autobiography not the easiest of all forms of literature, where the amateur may rival and sometimes surpass the professional? A degree of shapeliness is imposed by chronology, and for the rest a certain confusion matters not, may indeed give a greater impression of reality than the more orderly narrative of a practised pen. Life is not to be recorded in perfectly composed phrases; life escapes, bursts out, erupts, and is suddenly seen to be more important and interesting and vigorous to the people living it than to the people who read about it. Men and women open the door, enter the room; they may be in a rage, in tears, or shouting with laughter; we cannot tell in advance, nor can we anticipate who will enter next. It might be a child, a dwarf, a Cardinal, a prince, or a monkey. There is an ingenuous veracity in the very roughness of the record; in the absence of polish; a day-by-day vitality in the quick scribbling never intended for the eyes of posterity. Mademoiselle, writing in a brick tower in la Puisaye in 1652, can never have supposed that an English-woman, reading her words in another brick tower in Kent in 1952, would have found such life and liveliness in her chronicle.

Mademoiselle was no trained writer. Her grammar and her syntax were alike deplorable (*d'une incorrection choquante*), some-times resulting in such ambiguity that it is difficult to disentangle to whom she is referring or what she means. As for her spelling, it was so phonetic as to be non-existent. She was not alone in this. We are well aware that our predecessors, whether in France or England, observed a glorious disregard for orthography, even in the variation of their own signatures, but Mademoiselle went beyond all limits. For d'Haucourt she wrote Docour; for Beaufort, Bofor. She wrote *cand* for *quand*, which is under-

[1] Marguerite de Valois, the first wife of Mademoiselle's grandfather, Henri IV.

standable. One smiles, as at the efforts of a child. But it is vastly
endearing to find that when, with her customary magnanimity
she sometimes has to admit that she has been to blame or in the
wrong, she simply writes *Jay utor*.

I leave it to French-speaking readers to appreciate what she
meant by that.

Her calligraphy was no better. Even her father, well broken
in to it, could not always decipher those warm-hearted little
notes she used to send round by hand to the Luxembourg,
those protesting letters she wrote to him in Blois or those
urgent reports from Orléans. 'In future,' he says, 'get your
secretary to write the important parts. You know why.' She
knew why. 'It is because I write so badly that it gives people
so much trouble to read my writing.'

There must have been moments when Préfontaine regretted
the encouragement that he had given to Mademoiselle. 'So
badly do I write,' she says, 'that I handed it all over to Préfontaine to put in order,' and as she wrote with reckless rapidity
the long-suffering man must have been showered with constant
snow-storms of illegible script, when, doubtless, he had plenty
of other business to fill his days. There was much to be done at
St Fargeau, that derelict property, and Mademoiselle with her
active mind was not the type of employer to leave her retinue
much leisure. She must have kept them on the trot all the time.

She had no notes or diary to assist her in the compilation of
her Memoirs, so must rely upon her memory, which, as she
boasts, was God-given and good. She plunges straight into the
job she has accepted. It was what we should expect of her, and
the first paragraph gives a clear picture of her then state of
mind and of her intentions:

'There was a time when I should have found it difficult to imagine
any form of diversion for a person who, like myself, was accustomed
to living at Court with the rank to which my birth entitled me,
when reduced to dwelling in the country; for I had always thought
that nothing could offer any amusement in a compulsory banishment,
and that absence from the Court must, for persons of high rank,

represent complete isolation despite the number of their domestics and the company of visitors. Nevertheless, since I came into retirement, in my own house, I have found with a quiet satisfaction that in the recollection of the events of one's life Time passes agreeably enough . . . so as I am aware of some facility in remembering everything that I have witnessed and even those things which have happened to me personally, I am today setting myself a task at the request of some people I am fond of, which I should never have believed myself capable of undertaking. I shall therefore narrate here everything that I have noticed from my childhood up to the present hour, without observing any rule except the dates, as scrupulously as I can. Thanks to the serviceable memory which God gave me, and to my native curiosity which has made me discover many rather peculiar things, I hope that nothing will escape me and that the recital will not prove tedious (*que la lecture n'en sera pas ennuyeuse*).'

Nothing did escape her, except the important things. There can be no better summing-up than Voltaire's in two lines: 'Her Memoirs are those of a woman absorbed in herself, rather than of a princess, witness of great events. (*Ses mémoires sont plus d'une femme occupée d'elle, que d'une princesse témoin de grands évènements*.)' How right Voltaire was, as usual. She had failed to perceive any historical significance in the Fronde; to her it had meant excitement, it had meant the plumed and armoured emergence of great captains such as Condé in the familiar streets of Paris, it had meant meeting M. de La Rochefoucauld covered in blood, it had meant firing off that disastrous shot from the Bastille, it had meant that she got herself painted with a plumed helmet on her blonde curls, it had meant that she herself played a pseudo-heroic part in the whole absurd and abortive affair. It was perhaps symbolic of the Fronde that Mademoiselle should have played any part in it at all. Slings and catapults, not heavy artillery, were her weapons. The Fronde and Mademoiselle were, in a way, made for one another.

Yet shall we blame her for her failure to discern that the Fronde had any historical significance? It is seldom that any save the few prophetic spirits can discern the trends of the future, and when they do so they are usually discredited and discounted by their contemporaries. It is very much easier to see history in perspective, than to see all round the periphery when you yourself are living at the centre. Mademoiselle, it must be admitted, even by me, her biographer though by no means her apologist, was endowed with none of the qualifications necessary to statesmanship. She had not been born with a masculine mind, which is, perhaps, the deepest failure of her life if only she had known it. Had she been born a thoroughly feminine woman she could have found her fulfilment in a dozen normal ways, but Nature had endowed her with many of the attributes usually ascribed to the male, as her contemporaries were not slow to recognise. 'She is better adapted to handling a weapon than a spindle,' says an anonymous author, 'she is proud, enterprising, and free in her speech, unwilling to tolerate contradiction, impatient, active, and ardent, incapable of dissimulation, and says what she thinks without heed.' Rough and forthright, honest and spacious, her nature in many ways matched her physique. She must have appeared very large and hoydenish in a Court peopled by soft, perfidious, intriguing, and amorous women.

It was true that many of the ladies of France interfered in politics. Both the *salon* and the *ruelle*, humming with wit and spitting with spite, aspired to the making or undoing of ministers. Mme de Chevreuse, Mme de Longueville, the princesse Palatine, Mme de Montbazon, Mme de Châtillon, in varying degrees were real forces in the seething world of intrigue. Nor did the women always rest content with the work of their tongues; they were also prepared to engage in escapades involving real physical hardihood; Mme de Chevreuse (who startled London by swimming the Thames) and la Palatine both fled from trouble on horseback dressed as men; Mme la Princesse rode into Bordeaux at the head of two thousand troops. Mademoiselle was thus not alone in physical courage, but there is a considerable difference between her and those other women. They achieved, for the most part, their influence on public affairs by the woman's traditional weapons of influence over men: beauty, charm, and passion unscrupulously turned to account. Mademoiselle had none of the feminine advantages, and perhaps would have scorned to employ them had she been better endowed. It is a striking fact that she would never marry, nor, in that dissolute Court where you could never be sure what man you would find in what woman's bed, did she ever take a lover.

Yet, in spite of what one of her biographers calls *une mine et des inclinations un peu trop mâles*, her Memoirs reflect nothing of a detached masculine intellect. She saw the events of her day smally, in terms of personalities. Like any maiden aunt, she delighted in genealogies and liked working out the exact relationship between herself and her family. In St Simon's expressive word, '*elle cousinait*,' meaning that she went back deep in her ancestry and wore mourning for distant cousins even when she had no need to. Gossip and scandal delighted her, intrigue fascinated her for all her protests that she disdained it, though being no St Simon or Mme de Sévigné her endless weaving and unweaving of petty situations lack the tang which alone can redeem so empty a monotony. She was not malicious enough to be amusing, seldom clever enough to draw the outline of a character in a few strong strokes. One is left with the impression of an overcrowded stage where the actors move rapidly backwards and forwards, some of them larger than others, but most of them distinguishable only by labels, pinned on to their backs, bearing their resounding names.

It is sad to have to register that the latter half of Mademoiselle's sojourn at St Fargeau was taken up with a sordid and painful wrangle with her father over money, *mes misérables affaires*, as she called it. Her account of it is long and wearisome to read; it can be abridged by saying merely that during her minority Gaston had been responsible for the management of her fortune and estates, and that on information supplied by her advisers (including Mazarin himself, so far back as the siege of Bordeaux) she had been forced to the conclusion that his stewardship had not been honestly conducted.[1] Not only had he ceded one of her properties (Champigny, near Chinon) to Richelieu,[2] but he was now found to be personally in debt to her to the tune of 800,000 francs, euphemistically called the mistake in the reckoning (*erreur de calcul*). Even this vast sum does not appear to have covered the whole truth. The discrepancy must have been fairly obvious, for she says, 'In order to make out that Monsieur owed me only 800,000 francs, it had been necessary to hide a thousand things, and the calculation had been so heavily mishandled that it was necessary only to know how to read to discover so visible a mistake, *and I had noticed it*.' Mademoiselle was rendered very unhappy indeed by all the proceedings, especially when her grandmother the duchesse de Guise took a hand and in collusion with Gaston tricked her into signing a falsified document without reading it first. She ought, of course, to have known better, but, too proud and perhaps also too nice in her sentiments, had refused, saying that it was only the ratification of a transaction already agreed by the lawyers. Far from this being the fact, the net result of the document she had signed blind was to remit the whole of the debt. What people!

One's feelings, as one reads through all these dead yet so living pages, stained by Mademoiselle's frequent tears, embittered by her disillusion, are very mixed; at moments even tinged with compassionate amusement. Mademoiselle declares that she hates litigation and we believe her, yet at the same time we know that her Montpensier possessions are very dear to her and that she has not been born a Frenchwoman without having a very sharp sense of business. We watch her trying to behave generously, yet determined to pursue the matter to its

[1] She attained her majority on reaching the age of twenty-five, i.e. in 1652.

[2] To her great satisfaction, she recovered this property, with a heavy compensation for deterioration, from Richelieu's heir the duc de Richelieu. She set great store by it partly because of its intrinsic value and partly because she resented having been despoiled of it. One of her gentlemen, La Guérinière, told Gaston that she would never relinquish Champigny, not even if he put her on to a pillar like St Simeon Stylites.

rightful end. We would perhaps prefer to see her grandly abandoning all her claims, yet we remember affectionately her anxiety to spend every available penny on the improvement of her new toy, St Fargeau. We wince on seeing her duped. We suffer with her on following the gradual change in her attitude towards a father she had once trusted so implicitly and loved so dearly. She can now write, 'He received me in a friendly manner, for he is never stingy (*chiche*) in giving outward demonstrations.' She can now say, weeping over a letter from him, 'This is a very different letter from the one he wrote me at Orléans; I was necessary to him then, but now I am useless.'

There were moments when she went so far as to fear physical violence. She knew that someone (Goulas, described as *secrétaire des commandements de Monsieur*) had reminded him that the Romans had power of life and death over their children, and had suggested that so great a prince might behave as he pleased towards his own daughter.[1] Gaston, instead of throwing the man out of the window, as in Mademoiselle's opinion it behoved him to do, made no reply. There ensues a very curious passage which reveals the depths of depression to which Mademoiselle, for all her valour and gaiety, could descend, and also throws a light on what she thought of her own character. 'In my melancholy reveries I reflected that His Royal Highness was the son of a Medici. Although the Queen, my grandmother, was a very good woman without the faults of her race or her nation' (we must remember that Mademoiselle was only three when Marie de' Medici went into exile, and had thus had little opportunity of judging that sensual, ignorant and irresponsible woman) 'illnesses sometimes skip a genera-tion. In short, the slightest thing frightens people in the state of mind I was then in . . . and I even thought to myself that the poison of the Medicis might have descended to me, for me to entertain such ideas. But then, as though to reassure me, my

[1] In this connexion, we may recall that, on receiving a letter from Goulas, Mademoiselle first held it over the fire, lest some subtle poison might escape on opening it. From the first, Goulas had never taken kindly to Mademoiselle (see p. 20).

misfortunes revived the weakness of the Bourbons and I flattered myself that their goodness (*bonté*) might have prevailed in me ... I admired the Providence of God and the grace He had given me to retain my health and balance, for with my temperament, sanguine and melancholy, I should have died, or at any rate gone mad.'

Gaston, throughout, had been in his most evasive mood, as was to be expected from an uneasy conscience. His daughter could not pin him down; it rings very true when she writes, 'H.R.H. at a loss to know what to say, stroked my dogs' (*la Reine* and *Mme Souris*) 'otherwise not a word would be spoken,' and then he would say, 'Let us go and see Madame,' or else, 'It is getting late, and tomorrow is Easter; don't let us talk any more about it.' At moments he became quite hysterical, cursing everything he heard about the Court; saying that the King had fallen in love with Marie Mancini, Cardinal Mazarin's niece,[1] and would marry her. Gaston declared that he would never return to Court, and that if all his money were taken from him in an attempt to starve him out, he would retire with his family to Chambord where there was enough game to last for a long time, and would eat even to the last deer sooner than go to Court. 'As I knew him well,' says Mademoiselle, 'I found it hard to believe that he would long continue in that determination.'

He ended by taking the mean revenge of a small man. The most unhappy sequel to their disputes was the dismissal of Préfontaine on Gaston's order, despite all his assurances to the contrary. I confess that I am unable to see by what right Gaston could thus dispose of Mademoiselle's private secretary, now that she was of age and her own mistress, but neither she nor Préfontaine, heart-broken though they were, seem to have considered resistance possible. She did, indeed, think of appealing to her kind Aunt Anne, and she did think, in a fit of despair,

[1] It would appear true that Louis XIV, enamoured of Marie Mancini, seriously considered making her his wife.

of retiring to a convent, but in the end she and Préfontaine contented themselves as best they might with gaining ten days for Préfontaine to wind up outstanding affairs at St Fargeau and to put all Mademoiselle's papers in order for her future use. Thus the most loyal and upright servant she ever had, left her. He had not had an easy time. He said sadly to Mme de Puisieux, 'You know Mademoiselle well enough, madame, to know that she accepts advice from nobody, and that when she does seek it, it is for the pleasure of disregarding it.' As her treasurer, he had had to cope with her headstrong extravagance when she first gained control over her fortune, overspending her income during the first twelve months by 300,000 francs and would not retrench during subsequent years, yet so ably had he contrived that when the time came for him to quit she was not in debt. She had often treated him harshly and unjustly, but now, bereft of him, she began to realise his worth. Even now, in absence, he kept an eye on her concerns, for, when she sent him a *blanc-seing*, what we should now call an open cheque, in the desire to give him 20,000 *écus*, he returned it torn across, saying that in her present state of affairs he knew she would have need of her money, and begging her never to give *blancs-seings* lest they might be abused. One can well imagine Préfontaine's fatherly panic at the prospect of Mademoiselle distributing *blancs-seings* to all and sundry. She had the grace to resolve that she never would, and to remark that he was both disinterested and grateful. Nor did she immediately seek to replace him. 'I dealt with all letters from the officials on my territories and from the farmers; I answered them; I despatched them by the first hand I could find; I wrote to my lawyers in Paris about all my business. How surprised I should have been, when I was at Court, if anyone had told me that I should come to know the price of bricks, of lime, of plaster, of cartage, of workmen's time-sheets, in short, all the details of the building trade, and that every Saturday I should check their accounts! and yet I have been on that job (*j'ai fait ce métier-là*) for over a year.' She felt very lonely without anyone she could trust; Mme de

Fiesque and Mme de Frontenac had, of course, rejoiced over Préfontaine's departure; she avoided them as far as possible. Vague thoughts of reconciliation with the Court began to enter her head, and some significant little phrases creep into her pages. 'I scarcely read the gazettes that people sent me; the Court amused itself with balls, *comédies*, and ballets, for the King, who dances very well, likes them extremely. None of this moved me, as I reflected that I should see quite enough of it *on my return*,' unlike Mme de Fiesque and Mme de Frontenac, who never ceased lamenting. Condé wrote to her, offering his help against Monsieur if she could make use of it, but she wrote back saying that although she had held good in his, Condé's, service as long as she could, the time had now come to yield and that, if she could with honour and without stooping to anything contemptible, enter into negotiations with Cardinal Mazarin, she would do so.[1]

Yet, such is the perversity of human nature (and Mademoiselle was always quick to recognise her own perversity) the opening prospect did not enchant her as much as might be expected. She was proud of St Fargeau, which she rightly regarded as her own creation. She had become fond of it. 'I went back to St Fargeau as eagerly as usual, but regretting the certainty of leaving it before long; really, I did not feel as happy as you might think. I repined over the thousand things I might have done, relearning Italian for instance, in order to read Tasso. Few people would willingly exchange Paris for Tasso. But when one emerges from an infelicity like mine, one remembers it for so long that sorrow makes too hard a callus for happiness to soften or penetrate.'

The obvious answer is, why not renounce the Court, then, become a private person, and stay where you are? We do not doubt the sincerity of Mademoiselle's sentiments. But the grasp of her birth and upbringing, of her outlook and convention, was too imperative; a permanent breach with her family too unthinkable—and we must remember that her family was the

[1] Mazarin had returned to France 3rd February, 1653.

royal family, its head the King, almost a sacred personage in her eyes.

In August, 1656, Gaston had made his peace with the King, at the price of renouncing all his friends, the duc de Beaufort, the duchesse de Montbazon, M. de Louvière, and others who had gone into exile on his account. Mademoiselle admits to being very much annoyed by this piece of news, all the more so that Mme de Fiesque and Mme de Frontenac went into transports of joy, taunting her with being on bad terms with her father and saying that she would never return to Paris. With many tears, she decided on a great gesture (*un grand dessein . . . fort beau*). By the hand of a notary who had to be kept waiting till her tears were dried, she wrote to Gaston that she would remit his debts. Her life at this time went in alternate ups and downs; the discussions with Gaston trailed miserably on and on, he would dictate letters to her saying that once their differences were composed he hoped she would come to receive the caresses of a loving father, sickening her to such an extent that she exclaimed, 'All these reminders cut one's throat (she is referring to Orléans); one would be thankful to have no memory.' Then her prospects would seem to brighten a little: the King sent her word that he would be willing to intervene in her affairs, and this, at least, put her once more into touch with him. 'I thought over what I had better do, and took my decision all by myself, for I had no one to consult. I did the best I could . . . and wrote humbly thanking him, and saying that I should long since have approached him with the prayer that he would do what he was now doing, but that my respect for him restrained me.' This exchange of letters cheered her, and compensated in some measure for another mortification she had to endure when on the death of Mme de Guise she found herself entirely cut out of her grandmother's will. She had not expected this, after the shabby treatment accorded her in the dealings with her father. Nor did she relish having to answer so many letters of condolence on the death of Mme de Guise and to tell so many lies. 'For I had to allude to my affliction and I felt it but little, her conduct not having imposed it on me.' Mademoiselle did not like telling lies; it had never been her habit. 'All the same I wore mourning as austerely as though I had worn it in my heart, for, in this world, one must always preserve appearances as far as possible.' She was not a princess of France for nothing.

Some little pleasures she had. Her wealth enabled her to send her half-brother, the chevalier de Charny, to an *Académie* where young gentlemen learnt the arts of horsemanship and other matters necessary to a military career. He left her with regret, but comforted himself with the reflection that he would now become an *honnête homme* worthy to serve her. Two of Mademoiselle's excursions must also be recorded. The first was to Chilly, near Corbeil, where, in the great château built in the previous reign by the marquis d'Effiat,[1] she splendidly entertained the Queen of England, her son the Duke of York, and her daughters the recently widowed Princess of Orange and the twelve-year-old Henrietta, once the infant that had to be kept warm in bed all day because her mother could not afford a fire. Henrietta Maria seemed more prosperous now; she came surrounded by a vast court of English and Dutch, and, says Mademoiselle, all the princesses and duchesses of Paris came to swell her circle. Her daughter the Princess of Orange, although in deep mourning, was hung with the most superb ear-rings Mademoiselle had ever seen, ropes of pearls, diamond bracelets and diamond rings. It was said that her mother had brought her to France with the scheme of marrying her to Louis XIV. Henrietta Maria, who never tired of impressing her own penury on Mademoiselle and had not yet given up the idea of marrying her to Charles II, said, 'My daughter is not like me; she is magnificent, she has jewels and money; she loves extravagance. I am always telling her that one must be thrifty; that I once was like her and even better, and that she

---

[1] *Surintendant des finances* under Louis XIII. The château de Chilly belonged to Mademoiselle; I have been unable to ascertain how it came into her possession.

can see for herself the condition I am now in.' Is it legitimate to suppose that adversity, which Mme de Motteville had regarded as an enobling influence on Henrietta Maria, had on the contrary turned her into a self-pitying, rather whiney schemer?

The Princess of Orange, no doubt primed by her mother, embraced Mademoiselle most warmly, said how much she had wanted to meet her; how much she had loved her even beforehand, the King her brother having professed such feelings of friendship; how happy she was to be in France; how much she had disliked Holland; and how, once her brother had regained his throne, she would go back to England to live with him. Henrietta Maria exclaimed, 'I have never known my daughter talk so much; you have a great power over her, and I see that you would govern her completely if you were to be long together.' We do not know whether Mademoiselle was taken in by these flatteries, nor whether she was taken in when Henrietta Maria returned in private to the old charge, first saying how much she deplored the troubles with Gaston, and then going on to say, 'And that poor King of England! you are ungrateful not to ask after him. Alas! he is so silly as still to love you. Think! if you had married him you would not now stand as you do with your father; you would be your own mistress; for I am convinced that the poor wretch (*ce pauvre misérable*) will never be happy without you.'

The poor wretch was himself absent from this family reunion, for France had concluded an alliance (2nd November, 1655) with the Protector, and it had been hinted to Charles that he would not care to find himself in Paris with the ambassador of Cromwell.

On her way home from Chilly, Mademoiselle had a curious little experience. She slept at Poissy, reflecting on the strangeness of having been visited by so many people, so near Paris, and she an exile. From Poissy she could see the lights of Paris itself, from Verrières to Rueil, without any regret at not being able to go there and glad to find that she possessed so much self-command. I think that after the resplendent party she had just given, a salutary change from the chicaneries of St Fargeau and from the very real worry over the disputes with her father, Mademoiselle found herself invigorated and even in an exalted mood, for she puts in one of those little paragraphs of description which makes one think of her as a potential romantic novelist. 'I found M. de Guise waiting for me in the forest of St Germain. As I had left Chilly late, it was bright moonlight; I saw from afar the most beautiful horses, as though they had escaped into the woods, and men lying on the ground beneath the trees.'

Her other excursion has become somewhat famous in history, for its vivid picture of that singularly eccentric queen, Christina of Sweden. Christina had abdicated two years previously (June 1654) and after sojourning for some time at Antwerp, Brussels, and Rome, arrived in France in July 1656. Mademoiselle, full of curiosity, went to see her at Essonne, first taking the precaution to enquire how the queen proposed to receive her. She must insist upon being given an armchair.[1] The comte de Béthune exclaimed that she must be joking, but Mademoiselle replied that it was better to ask too much than too little. Christina, who had not been brought up in the strict etiquette of the French Court, and who in any case was the most unconventional of people, was clearly much amused when M. de Guise brought the message. 'Anything she likes!' she replied, 'and would she like to precede me? From what I have heard, it is as well to know, for, if she found herself in a doorway she would not give way.'

Thus reassured, Mademoiselle went off. She found Christina in a fine Italianate room, about to watch a ballet, and surrounded

---

[1] The question of what people sat in, or on, in the presence of royalty, was of the highest importance. Princesses might lean on the back of a chair, duchesses were entitled to a stool (le tabouret), the others had to stand or sit on the floor. In demanding an armchair (le fauteuil) Mademoiselle implied that a princess of France was the equal in rank of a crowned sovereign.

by a crowd of people. Mademoiselle had heard so much of her odd manner of dressing that she feared she might burst out laughing; Christina surprised her indeed, but not in such a way as to provoke laughter. 'She wore a grey silk skirt trimmed with gold and silver lace, a doublet of flame-coloured camelot trimmed with the same lace and a little plait of gold, silver, and black; on her skirt a knotted handkerchief in Genoese lace, with a flame-coloured ribbon; a blonde wig with a bun at the back, as women wear; a hat with black feathers, which she was holding in her hand.

'She is fair; her blue eyes are at times gentle, at other times very stern; a fairly good mouth, though large; beautiful teeth; the nose big and aquiline. A very small woman, her doublet disguises her bad figure.[1] Taken all in all, she looked to me like a pretty little boy.'

Christina came forward to meet Mademoiselle—what disparity there must have been in their size!—embraced her, said that she had been passionately desiring to make her acquaintance, gave her a hand to help her over a bench, but tactfully said, 'You would be quite able to jump over it.' Mademoiselle's armchair had duly been placed in readiness.

They watched the ballet, Christina plying Mademoiselle with questions—how was her father? where was he? to what House did her stepmother belong?—until, perceiving that Mademoiselle was not paying much attention to the ballet, she exclaimed, 'What! you take so little notice, after being so long without seeing one! You do surprise me.' Mme de Fiesque arrived, and was presented; Christina saying just the right thing to please Mademoiselle, commented, 'But she is not at all beautiful, to have got herself so much talked about. Is the chevalier de Gramont still in love with her?' Mademoiselle thought she was anxious to show that she knew everybody and all about them.

After the ballet, a comedy. Here the Queen of Sweden really began to astonish her guest: she swore hearty oaths over the

---

[1] One shoulder was higher than the other.

passages that pleased her; she lay back in her chair, flinging her legs first on one side and then on the other, throwing them over the chair-arms, 'in short, taking up attitudes that I had never seen, save in Trivelin and Jodelet, two buffoons, one French and the other Italian.' Christina repeated the verses that caught her fancy, and also continued to pour out conversation. From time to time she would fall into a reverie, heaving deep sighs, then all of a sudden she would return like a person awakening with a start. 'She is,' Mademoiselle concluded, 'quite extraordinary.'

After the play they went out to watch fireworks. Christina was holding her guest's hand by now, and as some fuses fell near them, alarming Mademoiselle, she teased her, saying, 'How now! a *demoiselle* who has seen incidents and has done such fine and great things, frightened?' Mademoiselle replied that she was only brave sometimes, and that had sufficed her.

Christina then told her that her greatest desire was to take part in a battle, that she would never rest content until it had happened, and that she was furiously envious of the prince de Condé, 'the greatest man in the world. Your very good friend?' 'Yes, madame, and my close relation.'

The fireworks over, Christina led her into a little gallery and shut the door. They were alone. Now Christina's loquacity redoubled. She made Mademoiselle tell her all about her quarrel with Monsieur, an unfortunate topic which produced a torrent of sympathy: Mademoiselle was quite right and Monsieur quite wrong; she would go to see him, as she wished to reconcile them; it was most unjust to deprive her of people who had served her well (Mademoiselle had evidently told her about Préfontaine); she would do everything in her power to have them restored, and to bring about a reconciliation between Mademoiselle, the Court, and her father; she, Mademoiselle, was not born to live in the provinces; she was born to be a queen, Queen of France; she was the most beautiful, amiable, richest and greatest princess in Europe, and she the Queen of

Sweden would talk to M. le Cardinal about it. Appalled, Mademoiselle begged her to do nothing of the sort.

This was not the only time this queerly assorted pair met. The next time, Mademoiselle, arriving late at Montargis (she seems always to have timed her journeys for the most inconvenient hours), was told that the Queen had gone to bed. She must have been pretty certain of her welcome, for she pretended not to understand the Italian of Christina's servants and went upstairs alone. She found Christina in bed, a lighted candle beside her and a napkin twisted into a night-cap round her scalp, not a hair showing for she had recently shaved her head; a collarless nightgown, with a huge flame-coloured bow; sheets that came only half-way up the bed, and an ugly green counterpane. Mademoiselle, who as we have had occasion to note was sensitive to the appearance of women, remarks drily, 'She did not look pretty like that.' (*Elle ne me parut pas jolie en cet état.*)

Things do not seem to have gone quite so cordially; Christina was probably tired, and Mademoiselle ended by feeling that her visit had been too far prolonged. I suspect that Mademoiselle's friends frequently found her visits much too far prolonged. They talked about the King; Mademoiselle knew that Christina had not been favourably looked on at Court, because she had told the King and Olympe Mancini that they ought to get married and that she would be their confidante. 'If I were you, I should marry the person I loved.' That might be a humanly sage counsel, but scarcely acceptable to the King's entourage. Yet on the following morning when Mademoiselle went to see her off, she decried marriage, advising her against it and saying how abominable it was to have children. She looked pretty again, in a radiant humour, her wig powdered, wearing a new doublet, and lingering although her gentlemen urged her to start. 'You would do me an ill-turn in separating me from Mademoiselle; perhaps I shall never see her again.' Mademoiselle was puzzled; for one thing, she thought Christina ought to have returned her visit, and for another she was disconcerted when Sentinelli, her captain of guards, and two other men followed Christina into her coach. This was not in accordance with the ideas of Mademoiselle, who would never have dreamt of travelling without her retinue of *dames d'honneur*, much as she disliked them. 'Nothing is more bizarre than to see a queen without any ladies at all ... But,' she concluded philosophically, 'what else can one expect of a Queen of the Goths?'

Nevertheless, the strange little creature continued to exercise a fascination over Mademoiselle. Even the grim event which had just taken place at Fontainebleau could not deter her from going to see Christina for the third and last time. The story of the tragedy is well known. Christina had with her the marquis Monaldeschi, one of her favourites, whom she had convicted of secretly opening her letters; she told him to go into the *Galerie des Cerfs*, where he found Sentinelli awaiting him with a priest to whom he was ordered to make his confession. Sentinelli then fell upon him with his sword; Monaldeschi tried to throw himself out of a window, but they were all shut. As he was wearing a coat of mail, Sentinelli had great difficulty in despatching him, and battered his victim so unmercifully that in spite of repeated washings the floor of the gallery remained stained with blood. It was said by some that Christina stood by to watch the deed.

Although the French were well accustomed to murders, executions, and even to tortures when the terrible 'question' was applied, and would no doubt have regarded it as quite natural for the Queen of Sweden to dispose of a culpable servant by any means she thought best, they considered that she had committed a grave solecism in selecting a room in a royal palace where she was, after all, the guest of the King of France. Mademoiselle was perfectly well informed of what had taken place, 'very cruel and barbarous, especially for a woman,' and was also aware of the disapproval Christina had incurred at Court, but she went to Fontainebleau all the same. Christina

DAUGHTER OF FRANCE

who had dressed hurriedly on hearing of Mademoiselle's arrival, sent for her to her bedroom. This time she thought Christina 'as pretty as the first time I had seen her,' in a black velvet doublet, a flame-coloured skirt, and velvet cap with black feathers and orange ribbons. With unusual slyness, Mademoiselle asked if she intended to return to the Court; Christina replied that she did not know, she was entirely at the King's commands. Then Mademoiselle's eye fell upon Sentinelli's *bâton* in Christina's *ruelle*; she remembered having seen it in his hand, and recalled with horror the abhorrent deed that he had done.

CHAPTER VII

Mademoiselle Reinstated
[1656 – 1660]

IN following Mademoiselle up to the end of her adventure
with Christina of Sweden, our chronology has become
slightly disarranged, for the Fontainebleau visit took place
in November 1657 and we had left Mademoiselle still living
at St Fargeau in 1656. It was an unhappy household. Mme de
Fiesque and Mme de Frontenac, *les comtesses* as she called them,
did not trouble to disguise their satisfaction over that very sore
subject, the split between Mademoiselle and her father. If she
is to be believed, and I see no reason for disbelieving her, the
two ladies were really very disagreeable companions,[1] Fiesque
the worse of the two; some people said she had never grown
older than eighteen; Mademoiselle thought her a little mad,
with what she describes as *un air evaporé*, whereas Frontenac
was only very silly (*fort sotte*). There was a suspicious little
incident one evening when Mademoiselle, in search of Mme
de Fiesque, knocked on Mme de Frontenac's door; was kept
waiting until Mme de Fiesque finally emerged, her eyes even
wilder than usual, so that Mlle de Vandy said, 'I don't know
what is the matter with you today, you are not yourself.' What
M. de Frontenac, who made occasional appearances at St
Fargeau, thought of his wife we are not told; we know only
that she refused to sleep with him and that he once burst into
Mademoiselle's room while she was doing her hair, looking
like a man condemned to death and as thin as though he had

---

[1] Old Mme de Fiesque had died, unregretted, in 1653.

just risen from a serious illness.[1] Well might Mademoiselle write of her 'domestic war' and of her house divided, with herself as the weaker party. She had made one attempt to replace Préfontaine but it had not been a success, in fact it had been a most abortive and comical failure. She had invited a M. le Boultz to undertake the duties of steward and bailiff, a man of recognised integrity but manifestly lacking in the art of managing women, least of all Mademoiselle. With the best of intentions, he began by telling her that she knew far too much about her own affairs: ladies should not interfere in business. Persons in her position should play and amuse themselves, without a word about their concerns ever coming to their ears. For his part, he said, if he had the honour of dealing with hers, he would never mention them, and if she tried to question him he would change the subject. Mademoiselle's indignation bursts out. Had she not been managing everything for herself since Préfontaine left, administering her territories, dealing with lawyers, workmen, and farmers? 'I was not at all pleased, this was not what I wanted, I who like to control my own people and to have everything accounted for.' So M. le Boultz went back to Paris and Mademoiselle continued to fight her battles alone.

Through all her tribulations she retained her sense of humour over the antics of some of her friends. She could be vastly amused by M. de Frontenac, an extremely self-satisfied man who always thought his own possessions superior to anybody else's, even to his clothes, which he claimed to be of his own design and which he would exhibit as a child its toys. He once came into Mademoiselle's bedroom at Chambord and spread his new breeches and doublets all over her dressing-table, greatly to the astonishment of Monsieur who happened to enter.

It is clear that Mademoiselle had a weakness for excessive or

[1] M. de Frontenac seems to have got on better with Red Indians than with his wife. He had been sent as Governor-General to Canada, with such success (*il avait tellement gagné la confiance des sauvages*) that he was recalled to Quebec for a second term of office.

eccentric characters and would forgive much to a person she considered out of the ordinary. She had been delighted at Chilly on renewing her acquaintance with Gabrielle de Morte-mart,[1] now married to a Burgundian neighbour, the marquis de Thianges. Mme de Thianges, small and laughter-loving, had her full share of the Mortemart wit, being 'no more charitable to others than they were to her,' and certainly enlivened existence in the rustication of a country château. With no more inclination than most of her compatriots for life in the provinces, she had refused to follow her husband into Burgundy when he could no longer afford to live in Paris, and only when he threatened to put her into a convent did she compromise by saying that she would go and live with Mademoiselle at St Fargeau.

Mademoiselle liked to go to bed early, Mme de Thianges liked to sit up all night. When Mademoiselle would not keep her company, she would seek out Mme de Fiesque, who slept overhead, and would return in the small hours making the devil of a noise (*faisant un bruit enragé*). When allowed, she would keep Mademoiselle listening to her chatter till two o'clock in the morning, and after that would go to her own room to play games and eat little snacks with her own maids and Mademoiselle's pages and footmen till four or five. In consequence, Mademoiselle had always started her luncheon before Mme de Thianges had begun to get up, when she would have to be summoned several times, and would arrive followed by all the pages and footmen (*tout ce qu'il y avait de pages et de valets de pied dans le logis venaient après elle*), three or four pages carrying her train, half-dressed with her hair in disorder, saying that she did not mind Mademoiselle's guests seeing her in that guise, as sensible people (*honnêtes gens*) would attribute such familiarity to her hostess's indulgence and stupid people would just think her mad, which she would not mind. Some-times Mme de Thianges went rather too far and complicated the already too-complicated assortment at St Fargeau, on one

---

[1] Elder sister of Athénaïs de Mortemart, who became Mme de Montespan.

occasion breaking a glass of wine all over the hair of the chevalier de Béthune who was not only a particularly sober young man but particularly clean in his person. Mademoiselle made her apologise; she agreed to do so as a sacrifice to God, being given to an occasional attack of religion; 'I call it an attack,' says Mademoiselle, 'because it never lasted very long.'

Mme de Thianges provided comic relief amid the stress and tension. She might bicker with Mlle de Vandy, but that only made Mademoiselle laugh. Mlle de Vandy was a born door-mat, whom Mademoiselle seems to have treated kindly but as the fancy took her; 'good and cautious, she was afraid of giving offence to anybody.' (All the more honour to her, that she took Mademoiselle's part *tout doucement* against Mme de Fiesque and Mme de Frontenac.) Vandy, it follows almost without saying, was also something of a prude, sufficiently so for her decorum to creep into the rhymes of the time:

> Brusque Vandy, vous êtes un peu fière
> De vous fâcher pour un madrigalet
> Qui n'a rien dit de votre corselet . . .
> Et qui n'a pas passé votre jarretière.[1]

Scandalised by Mme de Thianges' conduct, she sometimes tried to reform her, which only made Mademoiselle laugh the more.

Better times were coming. Mme de Fiesque left St Fargeau at the beginning of 1657 after a violent scene of her own making when Mademoiselle received her insults with un-wonted calm, and although Mme de Frontenac was inconsolable at the loss of her *camarade* the atmosphere was considerably lightened. Best of all, the reconciliation with the King was rapidly proceeding; Gaston having been taken back into favour, there was now no reason why Mademoiselle should not also

---

[1] One might colloquially translate:

> Off-handed Vandy, is it not rather silly of you
> To be annoyed by a little madrigal
> Which never even mentioned your bodice,
> And went no higher than your garter?

The château de St Fargeau

Le Ciel a pris plaisir de la rendre parfaite
Affin qu Elle seruit aux autres de Leçon
On n'en voit plus de sa façon
La Nature a rompu le moule qui la faite

P. Delaistre

La Grande Mademoiselle. A hitherto unpublished portrait. It occurs as the
frontispiece to a book, once the property of Mademoiselle, now belonging
to the marquis de Ganay

be forgiven, more especially as her generous gesture in remitting Gaston's debt had been properly appreciated. On July 27th, 1657, she set off from St Cloud for Sedan, where the King and all the Court were established. It was a long journey, attended by a certain amount of risk, because on the second day at La Ferté-Milon the large party of persons who had waited to travel under the protection of Mademoiselle's armed escort was joined by Colbert, then in the service of Cardinal Mazarin, with two loads of money for the King's expenses and it was feared that robbers might fall upon them along the road. Nothing, however, occurred to inconvenience Mademoiselle, except that with her nervous fear of water she was terrified while fording the River Aisne; she even contrived to give them all a picnic in a meadow, sitting on the grass beside a little stream, with provisions she had bought at Reims; the horses were taken out of the coaches, the bugles sounded, Mademoiselle thought it just like an army on the march. Mme de Béthune made them all laugh by saying that if they were attacked she would go and sit on the money.

It was nearly five years since Mademoiselle had seen her royal relations. One might have expected the meeting to be a little constrained and embarrassing, but she gives no hint of anything of the kind. This is one of the many occasions when she affords us so valuable and revealing a glimpse of these outwardly stiff, circumscribed personages amongst themselves: they talk and behave as naturally as any family of aunt, niece, and cousins meeting after a long absence. True, few aunts would have cause, after warmly kissing their niece, to say that although they bore her no ill-will for capturing Orléans they would gladly have strangled her for the affair of the Porte St Antoine, but any aunt might have added that everything was now forgotten and that the subject should never be mentioned again, and certainly every aunt would then scrutinise the niece and say, as Anne said, 'I don't see that you have changed at all; you have improved in looks; you are fatter and your complexion is better.' 'But had you not heard tell that my hair had turned grey? I did not want to deceive you, so I used no powder today.' Her aunt peered more closely, and expressed a polite surprise. Even so, after showing her niece some new ear-rings she had had made, she presently took the opportunity to rearrange Mademoiselle's hair, which was not done to her liking, thus making it plain to our minds that she thought her ugly niece incapable of making the best of herself. She asked if Mademoiselle had not been bored at St Fargeau; how had she managed to pass the time? Mademoiselle said no, she had not found the time to hang heavy on her hands and gave an account of her various amusements and occupations. One does not admit to having been bored when one has been sent away in disgrace—the equivalent of being sent to bed early without supper, or stood in the corner.

It is all very convincingly natural, after making due allowance for that chasm of difference in their worldly circumstances.

And so it goes on. Mademoiselle had not yet seen her cousins the King and his brother again. They had been boys of fourteen and twelve when she left Paris for St Fargeau; as rough and coarse and rude as any normal schoolboy. The King of France and the duc d'Anjou, behind the camouflage of their weighty titles, behaved in private very much as we might expect to see our sons behaving if we could demean ourselves to peep through the keyhole. M. de La Porte peeps through it on our behalf:

'The King insisted on sharing a small room with Monsieur.[1] In the morning, when they woke up, the King without thinking what he was doing spat on his brother's bed, when his brother purposely spat back on to the King's bed; and the King, rather cross, spat in his brother's face, and then his brother jumped on to the King's bed and pissed all over it; the King did likewise over his brother's bed; and then, as they both had run out of spit and piss, they began

---

[1] The duc d'Anjou, since the accession of his brother, had been known as Monsieur, or *le petit* Monsieur to distinguish him from his uncle Gaston d'Orléans; so we shall now refer to him as Monsieur and to the duc d'Orléans, Mademoiselle's father, consistently as Gaston, hoping that this will not lead to confusion.

dragging the bed-clothes off each other, and then started to come to blows. I tried to stop the King, but as I could not, I had to send for M. de Villeroi *qui vint mettre les holà* (which we might translate as reading the Riot Act over them). Monsieur had got much crosser than the King, but it was much more difficult to quieten the King than Monsieur.'

A real rough-and-tumble between boys. The last sentence is illuminating: Monsieur had worked himself up into a worse temper, but it took longer to appease the King. The petulant, finicky character of Monsieur, a wind-bag of fuss and irritability, though not lacking in elegance, gaiety, and charm, could not compare with the stronger and more authoritative nature of Louis XIV.

The royal brothers seem to have taken a long time to achieve adult conduct in private, however resplendent a figure the young Louis XIV in white and gold may have cut in public. At home, they continued to behave as schoolboys or under-graduates. Philippe threatened to break his Lenten fast by eating a stew out of a saucepan. Louis told him not to. Philippe said he would. Louis said, 'Bet you don't (*gage que non*).' Philippe insisted; they struggled for the dish; Philippe's hair got splashed, and as he was very proud of his hair (*qui aime extrêmement sa chevelure*) he lost his temper, flung the dish in Louis' face, and shut himself into his own room in sulks for the whole of the next day.

Louis was now a young man of nearly nineteen, Philippe nearly seventeen. Their mother amused herself by facetiously preparing Mademoiselle for the meeting; she would find the King greatly changed, she said: he was so tall now, and fat, and ugly, but he looked healthy all the same; and as for Monsieur, he had scarcely grown at all, but she would think him good-looking; she suddenly discovered a resemblance to Mademoiselle, and exclaimed, 'My niece eats exactly like my son; she does put me in mind of him.' Mme de Beauvais endorsed this opinion. 'Jesus!' she remarked, 'the ideas that occur to me whenever I look at her!' and the Queen laughed.

Nothing more was needed to set Mademoiselle off on one of her wild-goose chases. She decided there and then that a marriage had been resolved between herself and Monsieur.

One wonders exactly how much her friends and relations enjoyed teasing la Grande Mademoiselle, who was so pathetically easily teasable.

I have often suspected that Anne of Austria was not over-fond of Mademoiselle. She had had an affection for her as a small child, and was probably though illogically grateful to her for being a girl not a boy, long before Mademoiselle began to make a violent nuisance of herself during the Fronde. Then she became a worry and an embarrassment, a trampling rogue in the pastures of the royal herd, but that could be dealt with—there were other rogues and rebels, such as Condé who came out into the open, and Gaston who wriggled his serpentine way through the undergrowth—they could all be suppressed in the end by banishment, even as Mademoiselle herself was sent away to St Fargeau and kept quiet there for several years out of mischief. That was a fairly simple problem: a sharp order signed by the King could resolve it. What I really surmise, is that dear Mademoiselle was a bore, and it is worse to be a bore than to be a worry. She talked too much, and at too great length, and expanded too long over her various ambitions or grievances or her wild ideas of marrying an Emperor, a King of France or of England, none of which ever came to anything, or of remaining what she was, the virginal, rough, boyish, generously unsophisticated witling historically known as la Grande Mademoiselle. We know her as that; but to Anne of Austria she was no more than a naughty niece who had to be received back with as much display of affection and forgiveness as possible into the family circle. The boys came, Mademoiselle's first cousins. The King arrived first, at full gallop on horseback, so wet and muddy that his mother who had been watching from a window, wished he would change his clothes before presenting himself. Mademoiselle said that she did not mind however untidy he was; and in came the dirty young man, to whom his mother said, 'Here is a young lady (*demoiselle*) who is very sorry to have behaved so badly (*bien fâchée d'avoir été méchante*) but who will be very good in future.'

The King laughed (*il se mit à rire*); he was young and gay and full of charm in those days before he had grown into the heavy alarming autocrat we associate with the name of Louis XIV. So easy-going were his manners, that Mademoiselle was faintly shocked. Perhaps her ideas were becoming old-fashioned, rather *ancien régime*; it surprised her to see the King take the last seat at the table, saying that since that was the only place left he must perforce take it, and it surprised her even more to see him offering food to other people, insisting that they should eat with him. *Pour moi, qui ai été nourrie dans un grand respect, cela m'étonnait.* But his light-heartedness served her to good purpose: he could laugh, instead of frowning, clearly the best way of passing off an awkward situation, and then his mother as a tactful woman turned the conversation aside by asking what had become of his brother. 'He is following in my coach,' said the King; 'he would not come on horseback, unwilling to present himself in an untidy state of dress; he is as neat as could be. There,' suddenly exclaimed the King, as they heard a coach rumbling in, 'here comes my brother.' In came Monsieur, dressed all in grey with flame-coloured ribbons, very smart and dapper, the young pansy prince who was presently to become the unworthy husband, not of Mademoiselle, whatever her imaginings, but of the adored and adorable Henrietta of England. He greeted his mother, then turned towards Mademoiselle, and drew her aside into the embrasure of a window; they seem always to be getting into the embrasures of windows in summer when they were not leaning up against the fireplace near the fire in winter. He kissed her, and stood chatting with her in a cousinly way, paying her compliments on her appearance (*il me trouvait si embellie*). How easily pleased she was, and how ready to record tributes to her valour and even to the good looks she knew she did not possess! She puts them all down in the Memoirs she never intended anyone but herself to read. I think her boastfulness sprang pathetically from her own sense of failure, and made her want to represent herself to herself as more important and sought-after than she really was. She returned Monsieur's compliments by telling him he had grown since last she saw him—not surprising in boyhood, at his age, after a lapse of five years.

Nothing could have been more friendly, or passed off better. Mademoiselle even had a little formal reconciliation with Mazarin, and subsequently invited him into her coach, when he said, 'If somebody had told you in 1652 that Mazarin would be sitting beside you, you would not have believed it, yet here he is, that Mazarin to whom you attributed such wicked things.' (*Ce Mazarin qui faisait tant de mal.*) A strange pair, Mazarin and Mademoiselle. They had been enemies, and now here they were sitting in a coach side by side, exchanging a falsity of remarks.

Of such was the kingdom of France.

We have now dragged Mademoiselle along up to the year 1657. She is thirty. For many years, and for one reason and another, she has missed or eluded the maiden's conventional goal of matrimony. She might still be dreaming, in her vague silly way, of marrying Philippe, *le petit Monsieur*, thirteen years younger than herself, even as she had once dreamt of marrying his elder brother. 'Monsieur came to say good-bye to me, between seven and eight in the morning, which is remarkable for him since he usually does not get up till eleven.' She flattered herself.[1] It is not difficult to imagine Monsieur's comments on his elderly cousin—Monsieur, that tardy riser, that dandified boy, mischievous of tongue, unkind of character, heartless, and utterly insignificant for all his superficial charm,

[1] St Simon suggests, not without plausibility, that Monsieur had an eye on her vast inheritance, '*Il muguetait sa riche succession.*' St Simon, *Mémoires*, Vol. I, p. 50 of the Pléiade edition, 1953.

who would never be remembered had he not chanced to marry, for her misfortune, one of the most lovable of princesses.

Mademoiselle was well out of that union, if ever it existed save in her imagination. Before very long, she would be called upon to attend two marriages, not her own. I think this (1657–1660) represents rather a dull period in her life, so let us pass over it quickly. It follows the usual trend, reinstated as she now was. It all sounds very familiar: September 1657 she is in Paris, not very well, with a skin infection; she recovers, and buys the château of Eu in Normandy from Mlle de Guise— really, *franchement*, what a passion she had for acquiring properties, when one would have thought she had enough already! We find her also at Champigny,[1] which, as we have already noted (page 175) she had recovered from the duc de Richelieu. She liked Champigny, but I suspect that her liking for it was largely because she had had to fight for it. I cannot make out what Champigny was like, and must just take Mademoiselle's word that she enjoyed returning to this ancient domain of her Montpensier grandfather, was received with delight by all the local gentry, and was welcomed by the canons of the church chanting in her honour, also by a band of oboes and bagpipes (*hautbois et musettes*) which Mademoiselle for once not taking herself too seriously had the grace to think rather funny (*assez comique*).

For some reason, however, she was in a most irritable humour during her sojourn at Champigny. There was a touch of the bully in her, perhaps especially provoked when her feudal feeling for her provincial properties was involved. She had no patience with those servitors who were either busy or indisposed. Off she went, dressed in a tight jerkin, whip in hand (*un fouet à la main*) in pursuit of a certain M. Madeleine, who was much astonished and not a little alarmed to see her burst into his room without warning. 'I ought not to have to do this sort of thing,' she said. 'Nor should you do it,' he replied; 'people of your rank could well dispense with it . . .

---

[1] In the present department of Indre-et-Loire; Touraine in Mademoiselle's time.

You are far more efficient than you ought to be; you know our job as well as we know it ourselves, and you discuss your business like a trained lawyer.' Mademoiselle rather sadly replied that necessity, not choice, had taught her.

'I tried,' she notes rather piteously, 'not to be bored; I often went for walks, and when it rained (as it did frequently) I played battledore-and-shuttlecock and worked at some embroidery.'

She fortunately found some distraction in visits from the princesse de Tarente and her sister-in-law Mlle de la Trémouille. These two ladies arrived from Holland with a new parlour game whose boldness and novelty enchanted Mademoiselle. Mlle de Scudéry had set the fashion of introducing real people into novels under fictitious names; it remained for the princesse de Tarente and Mlle de la Trémouille to carry the idea a little further by writing their own character sketches with the utmost candour as concerned both their physical and moral qualities. These spirited ladies spared themselves nothing. In a society where gallantry was little less than an ever-changing skirmish of amorous rivalry, jealousy and intrigue, and especially, we may add, in a Latin country like France where the relationship of the sexes is palpable in the very air, it is indeed remarkable to find so reckless a disregard of normal feminine vanity. Few women, one would imagine, would go to the length of expressly drawing attention to defects which might otherwise pass unnoticed, not only by society in general but by any actual or potential lover. Yet Mme de Tarente points out that her head is big, her face too long, her complexion coarse and too dark, her forehead too high and too prominent, her teeth ill-arranged and not white enough, her hands too thin, although on the whole she is rather stout. Mlle de la Trémouille is no better pleased with herself. She dances badly, her wit is neither lively nor resourceful, her ignorance is crass, and her memory so unreliable that she forgets the little she has ever been able to learn; her arms are very ugly and much too short, her eyes lack vivacity, her lower lip is prominent, her bosom may be white enough but very ill-formed.

No woman could wish for a better opportunity of describing her dearest enemy.

Mademoiselle, in her odd mixture of boastfulness and humility, took kindly to the idea and instantly sat down to compose her own portrait. A curiously revealing document resulted, a real inconsequent muddle of physical description and an attempt at psychological analysis. It is too long to reproduce here,[1] but I give some irresistible extracts. It is headed: Portrait of Mademoiselle by herself, done at Champigny in the month of November 1657.

'I ask for no pity, for I do not like pitying others . . . I begin with my exterior appearance. I am tall, neither fat nor thin, with a fine figure and very much at my ease. I look healthy; my bosom is fairly well formed; hands and arms not beautiful, but the skin is good, as also on the bosom. My legs are straight, my feet shapely; my hair is fair, and beautifully ashen (*d'un beau cendré*); my face is long, with a fine outline; nose long and aquiline; mouth neither large nor small, but pleasingly shaped; lips bright red; teeth not good, but not horrible either; eyes blue, neither large nor small, but lustrous, soft, and proud as is my whole bearing. I look lofty, though not haughty. I have good manners and am easy-going, but in such a way as to command respect rather than the reverse. I am very careless as to my clothes, though not to the length of being dirty; I hate uncleanliness; I am clean; and everything I put on seems to look well on me, not that I dress well, but negligence sits less badly on me than on others. [If only Mademoiselle had known Herrick's 'sweet disorder in the dress' she might have quoted it.] I talk a lot, without saying anything silly . . . I don't talk about things I don't understand . . . I know I am only too ready to pride myself on some things, on nothing more than in being a good friend, very loyal in my friendships . . . No one could be more discreet than I nor could equal the loyalty and consideration I have for my friends . . . I am a very mischievous enemy, very bad tempered and very apt to get

---

[1] The full text can be found, pp. 127–134, in Vol. VIII of Mademoiselle's *Mémoires* published at Maestricht in 1771, by J. Edme-Dufour and Ph. Roux.

into a rage . . . but at the same time my spirit is honourable and good. (*J'ai l'âme noble et bonne.*) I am incapable of any base or black behaviour; I am far better adapted to dispense mercy than justice. I am melancholy . . . I like people, and the conversation of *honnêtes gens*, . . . but I am never bored by anything, although not everything amuses me . . . I like anyone who has outstanding merit in his own profession. Above all I like soldiers and hearing them speak of their calling, and although I said I never talked about things I don't understand, I confess that I love talking about war; I am very brave; I have great courage and ambition . . . I am prompt in taking my decisions, and tenacious in executing them . . . I am not self-seeking, am incapable of stooping to anything base, and am so indifferent to the things of this world [Oh, Mademoiselle!] so scornful of other people, so pleased with myself, that I would spend my life in solitude rather than check my proud temper in any way . . . I like being alone; I am not tolerant towards others, though I exact a great measure of tolerance for myself . . . I like to give pleasure and to be obliging, but I also like to be provoking and annoying . . . The violin is my favourite instrument; I should like to dance more than I do, and I dance very well; I hate card-games and I love energetic games . . . also hunting and riding. I am much more sensitive to sorrow than to joy, being so much better acquainted with the one than with the other . . . I have a great devotion to my business affairs . . . and am as suspicious there as in everything else. I like order and regulations down to every detail. I do not know if I am generous; I know very well that I like ostentation and glamour, and that I like giving [presents] to people I am fond of, but as I do it as the fancy takes me I don't know if it can be called generosity. When I do good it is with the best possible grace . . . I am neither scandal-mongering nor mocking, although nobody is more aware than I how ridiculous people are . . . I paint badly, but I write well, in a natural style and without difficulty. As for gallantry, I have no leanings that way . . . mine is no tender soul . . . I am the most grateful person in the world . . . I am no intriguer . . . I have a very good memory, and I do not lack judgement . . .'

So now we know what Mademoiselle thought of herself. On the whole it is rather a sad little account, all the sadder when we reflect that the greatest tribulation and sorrow of her life still lurked unsuspected behind the veils of the future.

Meanwhile, one small relief must be recorded: she managed to replace Préfontaine. It may be foolish and sentimental to feel pleased over something which came to comfort so spoilt a creature as Mademoiselle, who from her birth upward had had nothing to complain about in any material way. She had never known hunger or cold, she had never been brought up against the harsher realities of life, she had had a great deal of fun and excitement, and such troubles as she had had to face had mostly been brought upon her by her own fault. The only real grief she had so far experienced lay in her disillusion over her father and the sordid disputes involved; that was very genuine. Still, one cannot estimate one's degree of compassion by rational standards, and when I see Mademoiselle making herself unhappy (she who had so considerable a capacity for that form of self-indulgence) I confess that I desire only to wipe away her large, childish tears.

She had minded the dismissal of Préfontaine. Now, as the outcome of a visit to her father at Blois, she obtained his permission to engage a certain Guilloire in his place. The permission was not very graciously given. Guilloire was a friend of Préfontaine, said Gaston, but no matter: she might engage anyone she liked. Well, then, said Mademoiselle, may I send for him? Gaston told her not to be impatient. Mademoiselle pleaded: her affairs were suffering from lack of assistance; however much trouble she took herself, she could not cope with everything, and that worried her greatly. Still she could get no definite answer out of her father. Returning to the charge, she persuaded him to say that since he had given her his word she could consider the matter settled, but he repeated that she must have patience. She knew Gaston too well by then. 'The first person who speaks to Your Royal Highness will make you change your mind, and I shall be in the same quandary.'

All ended well. She got her Guilloire, and liked him. 'From
the first moment, I felt as though I had known him all my life.
I was very well satisfied with him, and I think he was with me.'
He had indeed many qualities to recommend him to his new
employer, who amused herself by writing his Portrait with the
same candour as she had written her own. From this we learn
that he carried out her orders with alacrity; that he was the
most devoted of friends, cordial and sincere to the last degree;
the most disinterested of men; faithful; always willing to listen
to advice; not vindictive; hating no one; quick to lose his
temper but of short duration; not given to frivolous pleasure;
disliking all games of chance except Tric-trac; and passionately
fond of children and dogs. This tiny little man, no taller than
Mlle de Vandy, tiny herself as a woman—how odd they must
have looked, flanking their outsize princess—was just what
Mademoiselle needed. She and Guilloire spent several days
going through all her papers. 'I had to explain everything to
him, as I had docketed them all with my own hand, and my
writing is not easy when one is not used to it; he would not
have deciphered them in a thousand years. I write badly even
when I am writing my best, but these had been written in
haste, and to tell the truth I had some difficulty in reading them
myself.'

She spent Christmas at St Fargeau, returning to Paris with
a bad cold which kept her in bed but which did not keep
Monsieur away from her *ruelle*. He brought her some Portu-
guese oranges, and expounded to her the mysteries of lotteries,
which had become all the rage in Paris just then. 'A young
prince,' she decided, 'handsome, well-built, brother to the
King, seemed to me a very eligible husband.'

Paris was very gay; there were constant balls and ballets,
sometimes fancy-dress parties where Monsieur masqueraded as
a girl, we may presume not unwillingly. There were the usual
absurd quarrels: Mademoiselle was accused of having tried to
pass in front of Princess Henrietta, and Christina of Sweden

who had reappeared at Court refused to come to a reception at the Louvre unless she could take precedence over the Queen of England; this being declined, she revenged herself on them by coming disguised as a gipsy. She gave further offence by going to talk business with Mazarin, dressed as a Turk. Mazarin himself was suffering terribly from gout, which did not prevent him from giving a supper-party for the King, the Queen, the Queen of England, Princess Henrietta, Mademoiselle, and a concourse of ladies and courtiers. 'He took us into a gallery full of every imaginable kind of precious stones, jewels, furniture, textiles, lovely things from China, crystal chandeliers, mirrors, tables, cabinets, silver plate, scents, gloves, ribbons, fans, as full as the booths at a fair, only there was no junk, everything had been carefully chosen . . . four or five hundred thousand francs worth of goods.' These great Ministers of the Crown certainly knew how to do things on the grand scale. Even Mademoiselle was dazzled, when she and the Queen were invited to draw the tickets for a lottery in which there were no blanks. Everything was distributed; a M. La Salle drew the principal prize, a diamond worth four thousand *écus*, and Mademoiselle got one worth four thousand francs.

Behind all this extravagance and frivolity, the nagging war with Spain continued in the Netherlands. The smoke of battle blows constantly across the background. Condé, still in open rebellion, was with Don John of Austria and the Spanish troops. The King, whose unfortunate taste for conquest had already begun to reveal itself, fostered by this we must admit unavoidable war, went off to Dunkirk to rejoin his army, accompanied by his mother and his brother. The reports which reached Mademoiselle of Monsieur's behaviour were not calculated to increase her esteem of her potential bridegroom. She liked men to be brave and martial; the brothers compared badly, to Monsieur's detriment; the King was day and night in the saddle; Monsieur on the contrary stayed near his mother 'like a child, and he seventeen years of age!' or dallied by the sea-shore with her maids of honour, splashing them and being splashed in return, and amusing himself by buying the ribbons and stuffs that came over from England.

The campaign ended in the celebrated Battle of the Dunes (June 14th, 1658) when Turenne inflicted an overwhelming defeat on Don John and Condé. It nearly saw the end of the King's life also, and the remaining fifty-seven years of the reign of Louis XIV might have been lost to history. The King lay desperately ill of a fever; the most alarming rumours, not without foundation, reached Paris; all Paris for five or six days awaited news which seemed to go from bad to worse; it was said that he had received the last sacraments at midnight. Mademoiselle, who had been on the point of departing for Forges, deferred her journey. She was very much distressed: not only was the King her first cousin, who treated her kindly, but it was dreadful to contemplate the death of a young king, and what about the grief of his mother the Queen, and what about the succession to the Throne? She had the sense to see (not that it required any exceptional degree of perception) that Monsieur would not prove a worthy inheritor. 'I was quite fond of him (*j'aimais bien Monsieur*),' she writes, 'but I thought him too young (*tout enfant*) to govern or even to know what was good for him. Not that he lacks intelligence, but up to the present he possesses no solidity. The people he frequents, and his especial friends are better calculated to do him harm, than to do any good to the State.' Mademoiselle, silly-billy though she was, could exhibit some judgement sometimes, even if it were only in the last resort.

To do her justice, in the extremity of her alarms and agitations she never once refers to the possibility of her own marriage with Monsieur during those five or six days when he stood on the brink of becoming far more eligible than he had ever been. Should Louis die, Monsieur would instantly and automatically succeed as King of France—Philippe VII. Mademoiselle had always dreamt of being Queen of France; in fact I have sometimes been tempted to believe that the failure to perch *la couronne fermée* on top of her blonde head might account for much though not for everything in that muddle of a character which makes up la Grande Mademoiselle. Now, in a real emergency, she could sink her own interests in a consideration for the dignity of the Crown. 'I knew quite well that the King would never marry me and I had every reason to believe that Monsieur would never be altered by any change in his status . . . but I had such love and pride in my dynasty that I wanted all its members to live up to the standard of the King, my grandfather.'

Louis recovered, in spite of the appalling remedies administered in those days. How any of them managed to survive at all remains a mystery; and, of course, only the toughest did. Litters of babies died off, with no more notice taken than if they had been kittens or mice, except that one cannot help wondering what their mothers felt about it, after all that hope, excitement, anticipation, and discomfort culminating in agony and then nothing to show for it. Even if children escaped the perils of infancy, they still had to face unidentifiable perils throughout adolescent and adult life. Louis had youth and a strong constitution on his side, and heaven knows that he must have had need of them. It is said that a quack doctor cured him on this occasion, but what doctors were not then quack? The treatment our forbears were subjected to does not bear thinking about in detail, either in terms of ignorance or of brutality. (No doubt our descendants will be saying the same thing of us, three hundred years hence.) Operations without anaesthetics; purgatives of a violence to exhaust a bull; incessant blood-letting—but perhaps that was good for such choleric people—and all drugs a gamble of hit or miss. They tried antimony on Louis XIV, the miracle drug which was supposed to cure almost anything. Mr Aldous Huxley, with the gusto he habitually brings to such out-of-the-way pieces of information, the queerer and more horrifying the better, succulently describes the various advantages of antimony put up in the form of Perpetual Pills, so called because they acted as a purgative, passed straight through the body, could be recovered, washed, and used again. (One is at least glad to hear that they could be washed.) This appealed to French thriftiness, for they could 'be treated as heirlooms' and after passing through one generation could be handed on, to the next.[1]

We are not told whether such economy was practised in the royal sick-room; we know merely that the King survived not only his malady but his doctors.

Towards the end of the year (1658) the Court departed for Lyon on one of those royal progresses which become so monotonous in descriptions. This time, it was undertaken with the intention of getting the King affianced to a possible bride, Marguerite de Savoie, a proposition which came to nothing, for the proceedings were interrupted by a far more important proposal, nothing less than an offer of his daughter's hand from the King of Spain. The Infanta recounted later that her father on hearing of the Savoy project, had thumped on the table exclaiming, 'Este no puede ser y no sera.' (It cannot and shall not be.)

Completely unexpected, the message threw Anne of Austria into delighted consternation. It meant an invaluable alliance; it meant peace instead of war. But how to dispose politely of the Savoyards, now hopefully assembled in anticipation of a splendid outcome? The young Louis, obedient to his mother's wishes and conscious of his duty towards his country, had begun by showing some alacrity in his courtship of Marguerite (though Mademoiselle relates that he irrupted into the princess's bedroom one morning, in the hope of finding her half-dressed and discovering whether she was really hump-backed as he had been told). Now, under fresh instructions, his ardour visibly cooled off; and we may well believe that it was without reluctance, for he was furiously in love, poor boy, with Marie Mancini, Cardinal Mazarin's niece, a boy-and-girl attachment which seems to have gleamed with utter sincerity in the midst of that artificial life. Anything coming as a reprieve must be welcome

[1] *The Devils of Loudun*, p. 195, by Aldous Huxley.

to two young creatures faced by eventual separation. A suspicion of the true reason for the change in the King's manner towards Marguerite was not slow in dawning upon her mother the duchesse de Savoie; it was even said that in her rage and frustration she beat her head against the wall.

Although the visit to Lyon ended abortively for the princess Marguerite, it afforded Mademoiselle the opportunity for an expedition she much enjoyed. She went to her little principality of Dombes, only five leagues distant.[1] She left Lyon after Christmas in high spirits. 'One would have thought the weather was purposely making my journey pleasant; there was a fine frost and a spring-like sun'; she left her coach and took to horseback. On the way a gentleman in the service of the Archbishop of Lyon put his pack of hounds at her disposal; nothing could have pleased her more, and a hare which started up in just the right place seemed as obliging as the weather. Mademoiselle and her cavalcade, progressively swollen as the local nobility joined her, rode along the banks of the Saône; in that temperate climate the corn was already high enough to turn the countryside green; the surrounding hills were sprinkled with the villas of the merchants of Lyon, 'not as pretty as in the environs of Paris, but very pretty for Dombes.' On the whole, Mademoiselle thought that no painter could have depicted a lovelier landscape. The peasants were handsome, their women nearly all pretty, dressed in the fashion of la Bresse, with the finest teeth in all the world. It was perhaps a pity that they should be so lazy, and it might do them good to pay the *taille* from which they had hitherto been exempt, but Mademoiselle was glad nevertheless to learn that they ate meat four times a day and that there were no beggars.

Clearly, Mademoiselle enjoyed every moment of her visit. Arrived at Trévoux, she was greeted by the local militia ('in fairly good order') and by the municipal magistrates and the

[1] Today, roughly speaking, the département de l'Ain; préfecture Bourg-en-Bresse. Dombes, or La Dombes, was an independent principality with Trévoux for its capital, and was absorbed into France only in March 1762.

governor who harangued her, kneeling, and presented her with the keys of the town. A Te Deum in the church; a salvo of gunfire; acceptable presents of sweet lemons and muscat wine; the Parlement of Trévoux waiting on her attired in scarlet robes ('they knelt before me, as do all Parlements before their Sovereign'); more harangues and speeches, including a reply from Mademoiselle herself ('I spoke as well as I could, and I think I spoke well'); a service in the church where she noted with some satisfaction that they prayed only for her and not for the King—all this was very much to her taste. Even the winter weather held out: 'It is extraordinary that during the last days of the year one should be able to walk abroad by moonlight till six o'clock in the evening.'

All the same, behind this idyllic picture of the gracious princess condescending to appear for the first time amongst subjects who had expressed a desire to see their liege-lady in person, and in spite of her appreciation of the beautiful country, its handsome peasantry and their prosperity, and a loyal Parlement, there darted the sharp mercenary sting never very far below the surface of the French character. Mademoiselle's address to her Parlement was really a masterpiece of urbane hypocrisy. She had pointed out that the first duty of a ruler was to see that justice was administered in his estates, and then had gone on to say that she relied on them, the members of her Parlement, to carry out the things they ought to do, otherwise she would feel herself responsible before God for any lapse in their conduct. This meant something that Cardinal Mazarin skewered instantly on the register of his quick Italian mind. 'Well, Mademoiselle, you *are* rich; you have had a present from your domain; you have imposed fresh charges on your Parlement.' Mademoiselle replied rather tartly that she wished she had property within five leagues of every town where the King chose to sojourn: that would at least defray the expenses of her journey.

*   *   *

Mademoiselle had rejoined the Court at Lyon, and on a cold January day of 1659 the whole cumbersome train set off towards Provence where there had been some troubles, much to the annoyance of everybody who had looked forward to spending the rest of the winter in Paris. The King rode every day with the Court ladies, who suffered very much from the cold in spite of their fur-lined jerkins and their feathered caps of black velvet which did not come low enough down to protect their ears. Mademoiselle, who by now had had considerable experience of spending the winter in the country, remarks that one's curls (*boucles*) do not suffice to keep the wind out of one's ears. The King, however, young, gay, very much in love with Marie Mancini and temporarily released from the obligation of marriage with Marguerite de Savoie, was in far too exuberant a humour to notice the discomfort of the ladies. The Infanta of Spain, an unknown figure stiff in the ceremonial of the Spanish Court, was a long way off, and much negotiation must take place before that marriage could be arranged—meanwhile Marie Mancini was there, very much there, loving, responsive. He talked cheerfully to everybody; took, at Marie's instigation, to reading romances and poetry; and teased his brother about his amorous adventures in both directions to such an extent that finally their mother, observing Monsieur's blushes, crossly intervened.

Mademoiselle left the Court at Cosne and went to spend a week at St Fargeau. (It is a curious experience for someone who has intensively been reading her Memoirs suddenly to come upon that Reckitt's blue signboard saying COSNE and then on the right-hand side of the village street to see a signpost pointing down a small turning, St Fargeau 32 kms.)

Back in Paris, the usual round of festivities began again, before the suspension of Lent. Mademoiselle had crept into the Louvre by a back door, being unsuitably attired in a tight jerkin and wishing to escape notice, but Monsieur met her and took her into his mother's ante-room, where he regaled her with an account of his recent doings: he had been to a party dressed as a girl (*en demoiselle*); a M. de Quevilli[1] had approached him with soft words, which far from displeasing him had pleased him greatly . . . all this he was recounting shamelessly to Mademoiselle when the Queen hearing their voices next door called them into her room where they found her with Mazarin. What a conversation-piece could there have been painted, if only an earlier Zoffany had been looking through a peep-hole!

The Cardinal was in his most amiable mood: he wanted to give Mademoiselle a little dog from Bologna, as pretty as could be, and sent for it there and then. 'I love dogs,' says Mademoiselle, adding frankly that she preferred greyhounds to spaniels, 'but even if it had been a huge mongrel I should not have minded, and next day I showed it to everybody, delighted to be able to say a hundred times over that it was a present from M. le Cardinal.' Having been taken back into favour, she was clearly determined to remain there. The days of the Fronde were best forgotten; it was on the whole advisable to keep on the right side of those in power. Her vicissitudes had temporarily taught her a most uncharacteristic diplomacy, and also inspired her with one of the sharp phrases which occur from time to time in her scribblings. 'In this world,' she says, 'although one knows how to distinguish between that which is permanent (*solide*) and that which is only an empty breeze (*ce qui n'est que du vent*) one must snuff (*humer*) the breeze, for sometimes it is more prudent to do so than to hold it in contempt.'

At the risk of becoming repetitive, we must allude to one particular *Carnaval* party, for here for the first time occurs casually a name to which Mademoiselle did not then attribute any importance in her life. She, and Monsieur, and Mlle de Villeroy and Mlle de Gourdon were all dressed in silver piped with pink, black velvet aprons, and black velvet hats with rose

---

[1] Or Quercilli; the name is difficult to decipher in Mademoiselle's manuscript. Anyhow, it is no great matter.

and white feathers. The whole accoutrement suggested the peasant costume of la Bresse, so obviously Mademoiselle had amused herself by bringing it back as a novelty to Paris after her excursion to Dombes. The ladies of the party had done their hair *à la bressane*; they carried shepherds' crooks, varnished bright red and decorated in silver; they were accompanied by four gentlemen disguised as shepherds: the duc de Roquelaure, the marquis de Villeroy, the comte de Guiche, and a still rather obscure young cousin of M. de Guiche, who having arrived from his province of Gascony had been kindly received into the household of the duc de Gramont, and whom Mademoiselle briefly includes in the list of shepherds as 'Péguilain.' Not even M. de Péguilain.

Shortly after this party, which incidentally was attended by the King and some of his circle, dressed as old men and old women, Mademoiselle gave up writing her Memoirs for seventeen years, when she resumed them as she explicitly says on the eighteenth of August 1677. (I have sometimes wondered how many of us would have the determination to start all over again.) A great deal had happened in the meantime. The year 1659 was largely taken up with negotiations for the Spanish marriage; the Peace of the Pyrenees, Mazarin's crowning triumph, was signed on November 7 after his celebrated conference at Bidassoa with Don Luis de Haro. The Court spent most of the summer at Bordeaux and subsequently at Toulouse, moving into Provence after the New Year. Mademoiselle was greatly impressed by the Pont du Gard, which she walked across, regretting only that she could not ascend to the topmost level because she had hurt her foot. She saw the Rhône by moonlight—a beautiful sight, but which frightened her, she who was always alarmed by water, partly because the Rhône was so swift and wide, partly because the bridge at Avignon was in a bad state of repair. The palace of the Popes she thought very old, very uncouth, and furnished after the Italian style. In an agony of terror, and recommending herself with many prayers to God, she was obliged to entrust herself to a boat in order to rejoin the Court at Arles. Thaw had set in; great lumps of ice bumped about, ice-floes and almost ice-bergs in Mademoiselle's imagination (*des rochers d'une effroyable grosseur*). In spite of all this, she managed to go to sleep on board and was thoroughly chaffed on arrival at Arles: 'What! you came by water? What! you were not frightened?' At Court, as Mademoiselle observes, little suffices for much chatter, so clever and so futile are they at it. The joke about Mademoiselle taking a boat down the Rhône lasted them for a whole evening.

From Arles the Court moved to Aix. Mademoiselle, as we have had frequent occasion to remark, enjoyed seeing new places; she was a born sightseer. Yet she makes no comment on Aix; she was not happy there; she had a presentiment of some-thing that was happening to her, she could not tell what; she wept for two hours and was uneasy for twenty-four; then she shook her apprehensions off and prepared to welcome Condé, who was about to be officially reconciled to the King and restored to favour.

This is one of the occasions when one sees how tiresome she must have been and how often they must have wanted to get her out of the way. She would insist on intruding where she thought she had a right to be, but where other people thought that with her clumsy tactlessness she was better absent. 'I was with the Queen, very eager to see M. le Prince. "Go and spend a little time in your lodgings, my niece," said the Queen, "for M. le Prince has asked me that nobody should be present when I first see him."' Mademoiselle gave her a sour smile (*je me mis à sourire de dépit*). 'But I don't count,' she said, 'and I believe M. le Prince would be very much surprised not to find me here.' The Queen insisted; Mademoiselle had to submit, but she went off in a dudgeon to complain to Mazarin who, with his accustomed urbanity, soothed her down with profuse apologies. She saw Condé next day. 'He resumed his place back at Court as though he had never left it . . . We talked about the war, and teased each other a lot about all the foolish things we had done and the King entered most good-humouredly into our jokes.' How times had changed since Mademoiselle's childish enmity towards Condé, and since the Fronde, and since the days when Mazarin's effigy was hung at the street-corners of Paris!

The year 1660 was full of incident not only for Mademoiselle, but for France as personified in the figurehead of France's youthful King. For Mademoiselle, it brought the death of her father. It seems clear that Gaston died of what we would now call a stroke but which Mademoiselle calls a *transport au cerveau*. She had had her troubles and disagreements with him, also the first disillusionments of her only too-trustful and ingenuous nature, but now when she heard his life was in danger she could not sleep; so many sorrowful recollections passed through her mind that she found herself unable to determine what she was really thinking. (*Il me serait difficile de pouvoir dire véritablement ce que je pensais.*) How well one knows that frame of mind, when one wishes one had been more understanding, more compassionate, and altogether gentler towards someone gone beyond recall.

Mademoiselle spent several sleepless nights wondering whether she had been a sufficiently dutiful daughter. It is difficult, at this interval of time, to sort out what she really felt about her father's death. Probably she could not have explained it to herself, so how much more difficult for us to explain it on her behalf.

However that may be, there was Gaston dead (February 2nd, 1660), leaving Mademoiselle richer than ever. It would be wearisome to go into details of what she financially gained by his death, and as I can never understand my own finances in 1959 I don't see why I should be expected to understand Mademoiselle's in 1660, nearly three hundred years ago. Her income came to something like £330,000 a year, so far as I can make out, and over and above that tidy sum one must remember the far lower cost of living. It would need a statis-

tician or an economist to estimate the equivalent value of that
income today.

Mademoiselle put all her household into coal black, even to
her scullions and the trappings of her mules, her horses, and
her pack-animals. She thought the effect very fine, when all
the great train set off for the first time in this deepest mourning.
The Court was still on the move, gradually working its way
round by Aix, Marseilles, Narbonne, and Perpignan where on
April 10th it rained so hard that the whole convoy was held up
as all the rivers were in flood, and so cold that Mademoiselle
was driven to take refuge in the kitchen, the only room in the
house where she could find a fire to warm herself and to dry
her damp chemise in the kitchen chimney—not, as she remarks,
the most savoury of incense burners.

The culmination and ultimate destination of this royal
progress was St Jean de Luz when the King of France and the
Infanta of Spain were at last to be united as man and wife and
their two countries bound by treaty after years of war. The
King and the Infanta, Louis and Maria Teresa, knew, of course,
nothing of one another, etiquette forbade any personal encounter, everything had to be done by proxy. We know much
of what was going on in the King's heart, and of his rebellious
sorrow at the enforced parting with Marie Mancini. Mazarin
inexorably insisted on it. He wrote to the King in terms which
no subject, however powerful, would have dared to address to
the Louis XIV of later years. The duty of kings, he wrote, was
to consider the good of their people, not to sacrifice that good
to their personal passions. The correspondence between the
King and Marie was becoming a public scandal: it must cease.
If the King would not listen, would not give way, would
persist in his aberration, quite a different sort of scandal would
result: he, the Cardinal, would fetch his nieces from La
Rochelle and embark with them on a ship bound for Italy or
even for a desert island. He would never return. Let the King
answer yes or no.

Louis submitted; he could not well do otherwise, with the Spanish envoy due to arrive any day for the momentous conference with Mazarin. There was a final flare-up, a last pathetic incident when Mazarin's spies caught a messenger carrying a little dog into La Rochelle—Friponne, the King's own dog, wearing a collar engraved 'To Marie Mancini.' There was a letter too, asking her to burn everything she had ever received from him. A few days later Marie wrote to her uncle, the Cardinal, assuring him that nothing further had come from the King and that she heard he thought only of enjoying himself at the theatre in the evenings, and spent half the day trying to learn Spanish.

She would have been gratified to read Voltaire's comment: 'At the time of his attachment to Marie Mancini, he easily learnt Italian from her, but at the time of his marriage his efforts at learning Spanish were less fruitful.'

Of the Infanta's feelings we know less, but may deduce a good deal from various bits of information that have come down. The duc de Gramont, despatched as French ambassador to Madrid with the formal request for her hand, was allowed an audience, and amid the forbidding ceremonial of the Spanish Court endeavoured to extract some message which he might carry back to his master. He could get nothing but the same reply, monotonously repeated 'as a doll which has learned to speak,' '*Diga à la Reina, mi Señora y mi Tía, que yo estare siempre rendida à sus pies.*' (Tell the Queen, my Lady and my Aunt, that I shall always be at her feet.) The vast farthingale, or *guardia-infante*, seemed a symbol of her unapproachability. Mme de Motteville thought it particularly outrageous, 'a monstrous contraption, nearly circular, as it might be a number of barrel hoops sewn inside the skirt, only barrel hoops are round, whereas their *guardia-infante* is flattened at the front and at the back, widening out at the sides.' This much we might have discerned for ourselves from the portraits set on canvas by Velasquez, but those are static representations; they do not move. Mme de Motteville supplies the touch of an eye-witness account: 'When they walked, it went up and down' (*se haussait et se baissait*).

It was known that the Infanta was deeply religious; known also that she was anxious that her confessor should accompany her, for she could not speak a word of French. She also wanted to take her dwarf, a hideous creature who could make chocolate in the Spanish way, presumably flavoured with cinnamon. The confessor and the dwarf were granted, but a difficulty arose when the Infanta asked for her personal maid, known as la Molina, an ugly, dark-skinned woman with long gold ear-drops, the very embodiment of the devoted abigail who might be expected to make mischief. Moreover, it was feared that the constant presence of so ugly a creature might lead to Maria Teresa giving birth to a baby resembling her, and in any case it was not the custom for a new queen to arrive in France with her own attendants: they would be supplied by the country of her adoption. Finally la Molina was conceded, and even supplemented by a young girl whom the Infanta called Philippa. This child was a foundling of the Madrid palace, in whom the Infanta's father, Philip IV, had always taken so much interest that Maria Teresa made no bones, later on, about believing her to be her half-sister. La Molina cooked Spanish dishes for her mistress, who never lost her dislike of French food, and when Molina was sent back to Spain after revealing herself to be the trouble-maker so rightly anticipated, Philippa took over the brewing of soups and chocolate, a little kitchen of Spain in the alien heart of Paris. Maria Teresa 'did not want anyone to know, so drank them in secret, of which everyone was well aware.'

Mademoiselle, on account of her deep mourning, could only on the day of the real marriage, by special dispensation, take an official part in the ceremonies, but she contrived to attend the marriage-by-proxy at Fuenterrabia under an incognito which deceived no one. She was thus enabled to watch the King of Spain and his daughter; to observe the extreme gravity of his demeanour; and to note the dramatic moment when the Infanta without even touching the hand of Don Luis de Haro became Queen of France. They merely held out their arms towards one another in a symbolic gesture not devoid of beauty and dignity and the Infanta spoke a low 'Yes.' The French thought her atrociously badly dressed (*son habit était horrible*) and her hair unbecomingly puffed out with false hair (*monos*) but there was something in her modest virginal bearing which touched even the astringent critical sense of the French. The real marriage would be celebrated a week later (June 9th, 1660) by the Bishop of Bayonne in the church of St Jean de Luz, when Louis strictly speaking should not yet have set eyes upon his bride. Was it curiosity or a natural gallantry which made him circumvent this almost barbarous prohibition? Circumvent it he did, roguishly knocking at the door and presenting himself as a stranger. There were great jokes over this. The Infanta had to pretend not to know who he was, but afterwards confided in la Molina: '*Y como, que me agrada: por cierto qu'es muy lindo mozo.*' (Did he please me? he certainly is a very handsome youth.) Nevertheless, she wept bitterly at the thought of leaving her father: '*Ay, Molina, mi padre! ay, Molina, mi padre!*'

CHAPTER VIII

Interlude
[1660 — 1666]

I SHOULD like to skip rather quickly over the years 1660 to 1666 in so far as they affected public affairs in general and Mademoiselle's personal life in particular. Repetition becomes boring, and in the next chapter I shall have to go backwards in recapitulation, a chronologically confusing method of writing a biography, but as this was never intended to be a scholarly work I hope my sins as a historian may be forgiven me.

I shall therefore enumerate briefly the events of those years which preceded Mademoiselle's greatest and most unexpected adventure.

Mazarin, the true author of that unbelievable reversal of the situation between France and Spain, did not long survive its consummation. A sick man, suffering from a peculiarly painful form of gout, as courageous as his predecessor Richelieu in keeping up his work to the end—it appals one to read the descriptions of what these men endured—he died in the early months of the following year (March 9th, 1661). The King, after somewhat piteously remarking that he felt himself too young to govern and that he wished his First Minister could have lived another four or five years, lost no time, in fact not twenty-four hours, in informing the great Officers of the Crown and other Ministers that in future he intended to keep control of affairs in his own hands; they could continue in their various functions to serve under him; if he wanted their advice, he would ask for it; after which he dismissed them to make what they could of this cursory but epoch-making declaration. With our hindsight we can see that this assumption of autocratic power was the true beginning of *le Grand Siècle* and *le Grand Roi*. We may doubt whether Louis' expressions of regret and diffidence were either very permanent or genuine. He had hitherto always been rather the little boy between his mother and the Cardinal. He had had to obey. Now he would command. I do not think that is putting it too dramatically. One does not wish to exaggerate, but surely that 9th of March, 1661, must be recognised as marking a turning-point in the history of France. The work of two Cardinals, the greater and the lesser, had left the Monarchy paramount internally and France externally the dominant power in Europe. Neither of the Cardinals had been loved: Richelieu had been feared and Mazarin mistrusted. A lampoon on Mazarin's death shows, as always, the barometer of popular feeling:

> Ci-gît l'Eminence deuxième:
> Dieu nous garde de la troisième.[1]

They need not have dreaded the emergence of number three. There was no Eminence number three in the offing. There was only the King now, and the broad highway lying open and empty for the chariot bearing the young Apollo-dictator towards the goal of his vainglorious ambitions.

Small wonder that many accounts should have come down to us of the brilliant frivolity of that young Court, where everyone seemed criss-cross in love with everybody else, and where fêtes and parties, games, dancing, plays, masques and music, flirtations and escapades succeeded each other in Paris, St Germain, and Fontainebleau without pause throughout the spring and summer of 1661. It was a time for youth. Charles II, still in his twenties, had recently and triumphantly been restored

---

[1] Here lies Eminence number two:
God defend us from number three.

to the English Throne. Even marriages were in the air, mostly destined to turn out very unhappily, but providing a further pretext for display. At the beginning of April the Court received its brightest and sweetest ornament when Henrietta, the beloved sister of Charles II, married the lamentable Philippe d'Anjou, now duc d'Orléans—Monsieur. One should perhaps not condemn Monsieur so sweepingly: he had his charm, I suppose, and may hang as one of the more brittle lockets upon the necklace of history, but considered as a human being there is not much to be said for him, and the incivility of his manners towards his wife arouses a storm of uncomprehending indignation in the heart of the most hardened reader. The passion he professed for her just before their marriage, if ever sincere, was of the shortest duration. He was rude and unkind to her beyond belief. How could he treat her so badly? How *could* he? One asks oneself. Here was this little prinking shrimp of a prince married to a rare girl he did not deserve. He should have gone down on his knees in gratitude. For Henrietta, not yet seventeen at the time of her marriage, was by common consent an angel of sweetness and light. One is accustomed to discount two-thirds of the panegyrics lavished upon royal and eminent personages by their sycophantic contemporaries, but an exception must be made in the case of Madame. For once the words of appreciation ring true. Not beautiful, and slightly hunchbacked, which might be attributed to her consumptive tendency, she had never allowed her deformity, as so often happens, to warp her natural warmth and capacity for bestowing and attracting affection. Descriptions of her character are all the more convincing because of their similarity: she seems to have made the same impression on very different kinds of people, men and women alike. The abbé de Choisy: 'Never has France had a princess as attractive as *Henriette d'Angleterre* . . . so fascinating, so ready to please all who approached her. Her whole person seemed full of charm. You felt interested in her, you loved her without being able to help yourself. When you met her for the first time, her eyes sought your own, as if she had no other desire in the world but to please you. When she spoke, she appeared absorbed in the wish to oblige you.' A courtier: 'There is a sweetness and gentleness about her, which no one can resist. When she speaks to you, she seems to ask for your heart at once.' Mme de Motteville: 'She was so lovable in herself, that she could not fail to please . . . she wished to reign in the hearts of all good people, by the charm of her person and the real beauty of her soul.' Mme de Suze: 'Since Madame left us, joy is no longer to be seen at St Germain. Everyone here is very dull in Madame's absence, and unless she returns soon I cannot think what we shall do with ourselves. Nobody thinks of anything else but of writing to her, and the ladies of the Court are to be seen, pen in hand, at all hours of the day. She alone can bring us back the spring-time.' Lord Falconbridge: 'She has something of particular in all she says or does, that is very surprising . . . she has a very great influence in this Court, where they all adore her, as she deserves.' Lord Falconbridge's secretary: 'She is even adored by all here . . .' Bussy-Rabutin, not a man to be easily impressed: 'She had a natural disposition to do good to everyone . . . both in mind and person, the most charming princess that ever lived.' Molière: '*Cette douceur pleine de charmes.*' The Bishop of Valence:'. . . a sweetness which made her unlike all other royal personages . . . the most human creature in the world . . . she seemed to lay hold of all hearts . . . the grace of her soul seemed to animate her whole being, down to the tips of her feet . . . the inexpressible charm, *ce je ne sais quoi*, which goes straight to all hearts.' And as for Charles II, his letters are among the most touching ever penned by a brother to a sister; each one of them breathes 'that tender passion I have for my dearest Minette.'

Other marriages took place during that year. Marie Mancini had already been married off to Don Lorenzo Colonna and was safely out of the way in Italy; the eldest of Mademoiselle's half-sisters, Marguerite Louise, after a heartrending parting from her lover, Charles de Lorraine, took a most reluctant departure for Florence as the bride of Cosimo de' Medici (later Cosimo III, Grand-Duke of Tuscany). It was only to be expected that the evergreen topic of Mademoiselle's own marriage should shortly be revived, which it was in the following year, 1662, with unfortunate consequences. A project of marriage with the duc de Savoie[1] having come to naught ('there were times when I should have been quite willing to get married, other times when I never thought of it, but I was quite glad that the possibility should be discussed, so that people should see that I was not set aside'), Turenne arranged an appointment with her, and kept her waiting so long that in exasperation she went downstairs to meet him. She was not accustomed to being kept waiting, even by so important a public figure as Turenne, and might well have anticipated Louis XIV's 'J'ai failli attendre' by an even more acid 'J'ai dû attendre.' As it was, she brought him upstairs to her room, where they sat either side of the fire on a winter evening, and Turenne started off by telling her that he had always loved her as a daughter. Mademoiselle, clearly in a bad temper already, asked what he wanted of her. 'As I am abrupt, I asked what he wanted.' 'I want to see you married.' 'That is not easy, I am quite satisfied as I am.' 'I want to make you a queen, but do not interrupt; let me speak and then it will be your turn. I want to make you Queen of Portugal.' 'Fie!' she cried, adding that it was more agreeable to be herself (il fait bon être Mademoiselle en France) with five hundred thousand livres a year, asking favours of nobody, than to acquire a dolt of a paralytic husband who would be driven out of his kingdom by the Spaniards, and to seek refuge in France, her fortune devoured, to live on charity and queen it in some small town.

Really she could not be blamed. Alfonso VI of Portugal had nothing to recommend him. According to the description given by the French envoy in Lisbon he was like a little round

---

[1] Charles Emmanuel de Savoie subsequently married, instead, Mademoiselle's youngest half-sister, Françoise Madeleine, Mlle de Valois.

La Grande Mademoiselle, by Henri de Beaubrun. 1655

Philippe, duc d'Orléans (Monsieur), by Jean Nocret

barrel, gluttonous, dirty, nearly always drunk, sick after every meal, given to tugging at people's ears and tearing out their hair, and so cowardly that he slept protected by seventeen people in his room. The envoy further enriched his report as to Alfonso's physical condition, with most unappetising details best not repeated.

All the same, said Turenne, even when one is Mademoiselle with all her advantages, one is still the King's subject. He wants his own way, and when one does not agree, he growls, he scolds; he goes even further, he drives one out; one is sent from one end of the realm to the other; sometimes one is imprisoned in one's own house, sometimes sent into a convent, and then in the end one is obliged to obey instead of doing what he wanted in the first instance with a good grace. What answer had she to all that?

He got his answer: 'People like you should not threaten people like me; I know what I have to do; if the King spoke to me in the same terms as you, I should know how to reply.' This was all very proud and fine and in Mademoiselle's own best tradition; Turenne, seeing her in one of her rages, tried to pacify her; he had already assured her that the King was no party to his proposals; Mademoiselle, correctly disbelieving this assertion, but always her own worst enemy, sat down to write a letter to the King. I think that without undue unkindness we may leave her to suggest in her own words the effect this letter was likely to produce: *La lettre était assez longue.*

The conclusion was easy to foresee. The King for political reasons desired an alliance with Portugal; Mademoiselle for personal reasons did not desire it at all. Louis must have been remarkably forbearing, not to insist, or perhaps he dreaded receiving any more of those long letters; anyway, Mademoiselle was not forced into marrying a drunken sot who might have torn her hair out by the roots. She was merely ordered into exile again, back to St Fargeau, a punishment she accepted at first with calm and even pleasure. 'I lived quietly in solitude, with a free conscience of having done nothing wrong.'

All the same, incorrigibly true to herself, 'I wrote to everybody telling them I was banished because I had refused to marry the King of Portugal. This was perhaps not very prudent of me, but one does not always pause to consider, in the first flush of vexation.'

The exile did not last very long. The first severity of the interdict was lifted next year (1663) when Mademoiselle wrote to the King complaining that she would die of the insalubrious swamps of St Fargeau in spring; she had already caught a very bad cold during Lent, she said, and it had persisted into May; she could not see what she had done to deserve death—and what a death!—so might she be allowed to go to Eu?[1] Permission was granted. One may readily imagine an irritated Louis saying, 'Let my cousin de Montpensier go where she likes, so long as I hear no more of her.'

Capricious Mademoiselle, thus to switch her affection from St Fargeau to Eu, but that is often the way with people who have a passion for doing up houses: they lose interest once the work is completed and want to turn to something fresh. Work on Eu had already started before her departure; she was transforming a pavilion, and took great pleasure in watching the carpenters and painters at their labours. It is impossible to tell today what the château d'Eu looked like when it belonged to Mademoiselle, for it was heavily altered under Louis-Philippe, and was partially destroyed by fire in 1902, but it can never have had the charm of St Fargeau nor of the deep Burgundian country, for it was bleakly situated on the little River Bresle, near Le Tréport, with views of the English Channel from every window; and we know that Mademoiselle detested the sea. 'What can one write from a desert like this?' she wrote to Bussy-Rabutin, 'where one sees nobody the whole winter long, so impracticable are the roads, and the north-west wind like a wild beast?'

[1] She had bought the château d'Eu in 1657 from Mlle de Guise. An ancient fortress, it had been restored by the architect Pierre Leroy for the duc de Guise.

It was as well for her that she was allowed back to Paris in June 1664.

The King had an ulterior motive in thus recalling his obstreperous cousin. Since she refused to marry the King of Portugal, a former project should be revived, and she should marry Charles Emmanuel II, duc de Savoie, recently become a widower through the death of Mademoiselle's own half-sister, Françoise (Mlle de Valois). This time, reluctance was on the part of the bridegroom, willingness on the part of the bride. She may have felt that she was growing old; she may have felt that it was humiliating to be, as one of her biographers puts it, still *en disponibilité*; she may have sensed that people like the abbé de Choisy were beginning to speak of her as *la vieille Mademoiselle* instead of *la Grande Mademoiselle*. Who can tell? There were a great many other complications into which it would be wearisome to enter, but the long and short of it is that Mademoiselle was eager for the marriage and the duke not eager at all. Doubtless the negotiations and persuasions of Louis XIV would have ended by overcoming Charles Emmanuel's excuses and evasions, but Mademoiselle must needs interfere and, of course, succeeded only in confusing and annoying all concerned. Louis once more gave proof of a patient if rather plaintive forbearance. 'Assuredly,' he wrote to her, 'my intention is to please you in every possible way. Only I confess that you on your side would please me greatly by facilitating things a little . . .'

This was the last of the many matrimonial schemes officially proposed for Mademoiselle. She had never been one to facilitate things, not even a little. The moment was now approaching when she would start managing the affairs of her heart on her own behalf; and this moment also brings us to the end of the chapter I have called Interlude and forces me backwards in time to introduce a new character whose name has hitherto scarcely flitted across the pages of Mademoiselle's Memoirs.

CHAPTER IX

M. de Lauzun

IN July, 1666, the Court then being at Fontainebleau, the King ordered his regiment of dragoons to give a display for the amusement of the Queen and her ladies. They should stage a mock-siege of the village of Moret. Although this was not designed as an entertainment on so grand a scale as the Court was accustomed to, the scene was extremely gay in the summer weather with all the ladies spending the hot day under canvas in rainbow-coloured tents, and in the evening emerging to accompany the King on horseback while the cavalry wheeled and paraded under the command of their colonel, M. de Puyguilhem. The star of this strange young man—he was thirty-three—was already risen above the horizon. It was observed that the King, dismounting, went to pay him a visit in his tent, which was furnished with the utmost comfort and magnificence. M. de Puyguilhem, moreover, mounted the guard with his own dragoons, a privilege which should have been reserved for the King's regiment of guards. This piece of arrogance was considered rather extraordinary; but as everything that Puyguilhem did was extraordinary, and as he was known to be in favour with the King, nobody dared to offer any criticism.

Mademoiselle, who had recently left Fontainebleau in order to take the waters at Forges, very much regretted that she had not been present. She liked Puyguilhem, and thought him very good company, though she did not at that time know him at all well.

*　　*　　*

Antonin Nompar de Caumont, marquis de Puyguilhem, or
Péguilien, or Péguilin or Piguilain, as it was varyingly spelt,
had been born in May 1633 at the château of Lauzun near
Marmande in Guyenne, the third son amongst the nine children
of Gabriel de Caumont, comte de Lauzun. Far from Paris,
far from the Court, in this remote south-western corner of
France, the boy grew up in the fortified castle dominating the
village, a typical *cadet de Gascoyne*, with no advantages of
fortune in his wallet and nothing to hope for save from his
own wits and his noble birth. It might not be true that his
family descended from the kings of Scotland, as Mademoiselle
later would willingly have believed, but they could certainly
trace their ancestry back to the early thirteenth century when
a younger son had inherited the castle from his father and the
elder branch had risen to a position of authority and power
in their ancient province. It was thus fitting and quite in the
tradition that the boy Antonin should have been despatched
to Paris to seek his own way in the world, leaving the rabble
of his brothers and sisters behind him.

He was only fourteen when, on a winter's day in January,
1647, he presented himself to his father's first cousin, formerly
comte de Guiche, now duc de Gramont and a Marshal of
France. He had had a long journey and he was very poor, being
accompanied only by some kind of tutor to whom his family
could afford to pay no more than a miserable wage, a footman,
and an old Basque lackey; doubtless also he looked excessively
dirty and untidy, being notorious even in his later years for his
disregard of personal spruceness or cleanliness. The duc de
Gramont, however, received him with great kindliness; took
him to live in his own house; and allowed him to become the
companion of his four children, two boys and two girls.

After a year of life in the hôtel de Gramont, which he must
have found considerably more civilised than his rough provincial castle and which must have opened his eyes to many
possibilities of favour and advancement, if only he were shrewd
enough to seize them, he was sent to a military academy where

he received instruction in the necessary arts of horsemanship, including some trick-riding, the use of arms, history, mathematics, dancing, and the general carriage and demeanour befitting a man of the world, *un honnête homme*. An apt pupil in more ways than one, he may have taken to heart the advice given in Corneille's comedy *Le Menteur*:

> Chez les provinciaux, on prend ce qu'on rencontre
> Et là, faute de mieux, un sot passe à la montre;
> Mais il faut à Paris bien d'autres qualités;
> On ne s'éblouit point de ces fausses clartés,
> Et tant d'honnêtes gens que l'on y voit ensemble
> Font qu'on est mal reçu si l'on n'y leur ressemble.[1]

By the next summer he had become a soldier, and thereafter went straight forward along the pleasing path of distinguishing himself in the eyes of people who mattered. By the time he was twenty-four (January 1658) he had already risen from the rank of captain to that of colonel of the King's regiment of foreign dragoons; his courage and enterprise in battle had attracted the attention of Turenne; he had rendered a service to Mazarin; and he had been presented to the King. There was a difference of only four years between these two young men: the King, and the *cadet de Gascoyne*.

A year later (1659) he was chosen to accompany Mazarin in his mission as French plenipotentiary to negotiate the marriage of Louis XIV with the Spanish Infanta; and in the following year (1660) at the head of the first company of *becs de corbin*[2] he followed close in the King's suite on that pageant of a journey to St Jean de Luz. The *becs de corbin*, so-called because of their

---

[1] You take your chance with country-born people;
Amongst them, failing anything better, a stupid man may pass muster,
But Paris demands a far higher standard.
In Paris we are not dazzled by such misleading simplicities,
And in so large a gathering of *honnêtes gens* (men and women of the world),
One is ill received unless one resembles them.

[2] The *becs de corbin*, or *gentilshommes à bec de corbin*, consisted at first of only one company, instituted in 1478 by Louis XI. The second company was created in 1497 by Charles VIII.

gilded battle-axes in the shape of a raven's beak, enjoyed the
right to march two by two immediately before the King on
all ceremonial occasions; Puyguilhem, who commanded the
first company, and the marquis d'Humières, who commanded
the second company, stood on either side of the King in church
and accompanied him to the altar. It was perhaps unfortunate
that Puyguilhem should just then have elected to quarrel with
M. d'Humières, thus provoking an embarrassing unpleasant-
ness. Mademoiselle, who noted the incident, commented that
he carried it off with his usual high-handed arrogance, pro-
phetically adding that it was natural to him in all circumstances,
since he was not cut out for things on a small scale (*il n'est pas
destiné, comme il a paru, pour les petites*).

He had need of all the effrontery at his command, for he
was becoming involved in one of those Court love-affairs
which always led to complications and trouble. To do Puyguilhem justice, his passion for the lady was perfectly sincere and
went back to the days of their adolescence when they had
grown up together in the house of her father the duc de
Gramont. Charlotte de Gramont, now married against her
will to the duc de Valentinois, prince de Monaco, appears to
have reciprocated Puyguilhem's feelings, if Mme de La Fayette
is to be believed, but family ambition must be satisfied and
what was a poor country *hobereau* such as Puyguilhem compared with the ruler of an independent principality on a rocky
peninsula off the then lonely but beautiful shores of the
Mediterranean? Charlotte de Gramont's wishes were not consulted. Puyguilhem and she, nevertheless, had every opportunity
for meeting, since she had been appointed amongst the ladies-
in-waiting to that centre of attraction, the frail and doomed
figure of Henrietta of England—Madame.

This was the time of dazzling gaiety at the French Court,
whatever the little homesick Spanish Queen may have thought
of it. Her great *guardia-infante* had been taken away from her
after her marriage and they had redressed her after the French

fashion, which she did not like and in which she felt uncomfortable; reputed very much in love with her husband, she had to watch him surrounded by other women, whose lighthearted merriment offended her Spanish ideas of decorum; one watches her becoming more and more peevish as time goes on. How could she, for instance, compete with Madame, that centre of attraction, less of an alien, who seemed more of a French than an English princess? Everyone knew that the King was by no means indifferent to the charms of his new sister-in-law; in fact Mme de La Fayette observed with true French subtlety that everybody noticed them taking that particular pleasure in each other's company which ordinarily precedes the birth of passion; everyone knew likewise that the comte de Guiche was enamoured of Madame; everyone knew that young Puyguilhem loved Guiche's sister, Mme de Monaco.

Only the Grande Mademoiselle stalked alone and aloof; she did not like Madame; no scandal of any lover attached to her own name; there had been plenty of talk at various times of her proposed marriages, but even those were momentarily in abeyance.

One splendid fête has remained celebrated for its unwise magnificence: the banquet offered to the King by the Minister of Finance, Nicolas Fouquet, at his château of Vaux-le-Vicomte. Richelieu might with impunity excel Louis XIII in the ostentation of his housekeeping, but Fouquet for all his glory was not Richelieu, and Louis XIV was not Louis XIII. Fouquet had overstepped the mark. His small inherited property of Vaux had been transformed by the collaboration of the architects Louis Le Vau and André Le Nôtre into a mansion far surpassing the Louvre in splendour. Whence had he acquired all this wealth? Monsieur, always ready for mischief, whispered to the King, who was complaining that he could not afford to enlarge the Louvre, 'Sire, Your Majesty need only appoint yourself Minister of Finance for one year, and you will have enough.' It was rumoured that only the intervention of the Queen-Mother restrained Louis from having Fouquet arrested

on the spot; it was said also that Fouquet's attentions to Mlle de
La Vallière had annoyed the King.

Controlling his anger, the King politely admired the superb
gardens and fountains laid out by Le Nôtre, and the hundred
and twenty tables seating the guests at the feast prepared by the
famous chef Vatel, but underneath the royal courtesy lay a
deep resentment which was to culminate in a strange repercussion on the fortunes of Puyguilhem. He could little foresee,
then, that within ten years he and Fouquet would be whispering
to one another through a hole laboriously and surreptitiously
pierced in the wall dividing their cells in their common
prison.

Meanwhile a more immediate vexation came to trouble
Puyguilhem: Mme de Monaco could not absent herself indefinitely from her husband's principality. In the autum of 1661
she left for the south, there to console herself as best she might
for three years in her Frenchified palace, mounting and
descending the great horseshoe staircase copied from the one
she had known so well at Fontainebleau.

If Mme de La Fayette, again, is to be believed (but she is our
only authority for the statement), Puyguilhem in despair followed her coach for part of the way, disguised now as a
merchant, now as a postillion, or in any travesty which would
render him unrecognisable to her attendants. This may or may
not be true: the most ambitious man, frustrated in his passions,
may temporarily take risks a soberer judgement would reject.
The ex-favourite Fouquet had fallen from grace; his place was
empty; and Puyguilhem surely knew that it was not advisable
to remain for too long out of sight of the King. All that we
know for certain is that he was in Paris by the beginning of
1662, dressed now in the coveted jerkin of blue lined with red,
the outward sign that the wearer could count himself among
the favoured sixty who had the right to follow the King in 'all
his little journeys for pleasure' without having to ask the royal
permission. Puyguilhem had travelled far from that castle in
the valley of the Garonne. An accepted courtier, he is found

taking part in the great fête which gave its name to the place du Carrousel in June 1662, where the King appeared as a Roman emperor, Monsieur his brother as King of the Persians, the duc d'Enghien as King of India, the duc de Guise as King of America, and Condé as Emperor of the Turks.

The next two years saw Puyguilhem engaged on various official journeys in France and in Italy, and it was not until 1664 that he rejoined the Court. Mme de Monaco rejoined it too. Alas for Puyguilhem: this time the King was not slow to notice her beauty and the rumour went round that Mlle de La Vallière would soon have to look to her laurels. The Gascon in Puyguilhem overcame the courtier; he threatened Mme de Monaco with publication of her letters; Mme de Monaco, alarmed, warned the King; the King sent for Puyguilhem with the suggestion that he might go and see how his regiment of dragoons was getting on in Béarn. Suggestions from the King, if disregarded, were apt to be followed by most sinister consequences. Puyguilhem must have known this very well, but his Gascon temper overrode his caution. He lost his head—lucky for him not to have lost it incontinently on the block—swore that he would resign his commission sooner than go away, and would never again draw his sword in the King's service. It is perhaps hard for us to estimate the unheard-of insolence of such language addressed to an absolute, almost sacrosanct monarch. Disgrace had fallen for less. The King, however, who as already has been related and will be related again in the course of this history, always displayed an amused tolerance with the outbursts of his intractable subject, merely remarked that Puyguilhem was behaving most imprudently. Puyguilhem had the gift of amusing, rather than angering, the King. Perhaps it may have been a relief for that supreme autocrat to encounter, once in a way, a courtier who was not prepared to be wholly servile. A change from the court-crawlers and boot-lickers . . . Puyguilhem had time to rush off to Mme de Monaco's house, where, not finding her at home, he relieved his feelings by shattering a large Venetian mirror before he found himself marched off to the Bastille on the trumped-up charge of having allowed a Béarnais brigand to escape.

This not very onerous sojourn lasted for six months. It is on record that the prisoner, as a mark of repentance, allowed a full beard to grow 'like a Capuchin monk,' which amused the King so much when he saw him that he broke into laughter and the affair appeared to be forgiven and forgotten.

Puyguilhem had not forgotten. A lavish bribe to Mme de Monaco's maid revealed an assignation between her mistress and the King at St Germain. Puyguilhem hurried through the château to the spot where a private door gave admittance to a small room, and, concealing himself in an adjoining privy, waited until he had heard the King go in, when he emerged, locked the door with the key that Louis had left on the outside, threw the key down the privy, shut himself in, being careful to put the door on the hook, and sat listening for the arrival of Mme de Monaco. She came, cloaked, and escorted by a confidential valet, who, encountering a locked door, knocked. The King's steps were heard advancing within . . . St. Simon relates that Puyguilhem sat silently laughing at their discomfiture.

But he was not yet satisfied. Having taken this farcical revenge on his faithless mistress, he now determined to punish her in a more openly violent manner. She, with other ladies, was sitting on the floor in a room at Versailles, propping herself on her hand while they gambled for the possession of a jewel. The King stood by them watching. Puyguilhem came up, with a few of his usual bantering remarks, and then suddenly, as was his wont when he had said something especially stinging and witty, pirouetted round on his high wooden heels, stamping hard on the hand of Mme de Monaco. Screams and tears ensued; furious indignation on the part of the prince de Monaco and the duc de Gramont; extravagant apologies from Puyguilhem. We know precisely when this scene took place, May 18th, 1666, for it is fixed by Louis XIV himself, in a letter he gave himself the trouble of writing, anxious as ever to exculpate his favoured M. de Puyguilhem. It was a pure accident, he wrote to his ambassador in the Hague; Mme de Monaco had certainly been leaning on her hand, but it was hidden under her skirt; M. de Puyguilhem could not see it; he was in despair over what had happened; he would do anything to make reparation, even to throwing himself out of the window if that would please the princess.

Although we may well wonder at the audacity of Puyguilhem's behaviour under the very eyes of the King, he was not called upon to suffer any penalty. On the contrary, he seemed to advance in favour as the months and years went by. We have already seen him entertaining the King in his tent at the Fontainebleau review. We next see him adding to his reputation as a soldier, distinguishing himself at the siege of Courtrai, also at Lille where he was wounded, and drew from Mademoiselle (who had accompanied the King and Queen on this campaign, writing her letters in M. de Turenne's room at headquarters for the pleasure of dating them from an armed camp) the admiring comment that he was much spoken of. His exploits were rewarded (April 1668) with a new commission, expressly created by the King for his benefit, that of colonel-general of all the regiments of dragoons.

Puyguilhem was not satisfied. He was never satisfied. There was something in his restless nature which could never be content. He aspired to become Grand-master of the artillery, an assignment which in addition to other advantages such as a large share in the booty of any town captured by gunfire, carried with it the title of a great Officer of the Crown. It was in vain that Mme de Longueville intrigued to obtain the position for her son: the King promised it to Puyguilhem, enjoining him to keep silence until the appointment should be announced.

Alas for Puyguilhem once more. Too confident, he revealed his hopes to one of the King's gentlemen, when the indiscretion in that whispering gallery of the Court immediately reached the ears of the King. It seems probable that M. de Louvois, always hostile to Puyguilhem, lost no time in conveying the information. Be that as it may, the next time the King saw Puyguilhem, he passed him by without speaking, cut him dead, as we should say; and when, the same evening, Puyguilhem dared to ask for an explanation, he received nothing but 'a short and ambiguous reply.'

Any courtier less impetuous than the Gascon would have been astute enough to let the matter rest; the King's caprice was unpredictable, and in a Court of many false friends who could tell what poisonous influences might be at work? Puyguilhem had not yet learnt his lesson. Indignant, he went off to find Mme de Montespan, who by that time had begun to replace Mlle de La Vallière in the King's affections, and besought her intervention. Whether Mme de Montespan, as was currently reported, had ever been Puyguilhem's mistress or not, must remain an unanswered question; in any case, she readily promised him her good offices, and, appeased for the moment, he agreed to await results. When nothing happened, he determined, according to St Simon, on 'the most improbable, extraordinary, and dangerous observation-post conceivable.' In short, he hid under Mme de Montespan's bed. From this post of vantage, 'sweating great drops of rage and of a horrible self-restraint,' he listened to every word of the conversation going on over his head. He heard Mme de Montespan telling the King how his gentleman had warned Louvois, how Louvois had thought it his duty to warn the King, how Puyguilhem with his *fougues et hauteurs* would behave towards Louvois if ever he got control of the artillery, and how he, the King, would have more trouble than with all the rest of the army put together. As Mme de Montespan, adds St Simon, was mischievous, and amusing, her version lost nothing in the telling.

It was not to be expected that Puyguilhem should keep his adventure to himself. That evening, at the rehearsal of a ballet where the King, 'desirous of taking some relaxation from his constant preoccupation with the good of his State and the happiness of his subjects,' appeared in the rôle of the Sun, he posted himself at the door of Mme de Montespan and with the utmost civility offered his hand to escort her to the rehearsal. On the way, 'being careful to make her walk very slowly, he repeated in a low, gentle voice everything, word for word, that had passed between her and the King, not omitting one syllable; and thereafter, still in the same low, gentle tones called her by every infamous name, liar, baggage, hussy, *putain de chien*, assuring her that he would slash her face, and so leading her willy-nilly to the ballet where she arrived more dead than alive, only half-conscious, and as much distraught by the accuracy of his recital as by his abuse, his anger, and his threats.'

Puyguilhem was summoned next day to the Presence. In no mood to accept a scolding meekly, he drew his sword and snapped it in half, saying that he would never use it in the service of a king who could break his word at the bidding of a whore. One must respect the restraint and dignity of the Sovereign in the face of such outrageous language. Louis simply opened the window and threw out the stick he carried, 'lest,' he said, 'I should have to reproach myself for striking a gentleman.'

None the less, Puyguilhem went back to the Bastille. It would appear that Mme de Montespan, with considerable generosity, interceded on his behalf with a King only too willing to listen to excuses in the interests of his favourite. Not only was the prisoner released, but one of the highest honours was conferred upon him, that of captain of the first company of the King's guards, with all the privileges thereon attendant, including the ebony stick with the ivory pommel, the turquoise-blue uniform braided in silver, the scarlet breeches, the probability of soon becoming a Marshal of France, and, not least (for this rendered him independent of the hated Louvois) the right to accept orders only from the King.

Mademoiselle congratulated him. Their acquaintance had evidently progressed since the day when she had regretted not seeing him with his dragoons at Fontainebleau and since the days when she had admired his courage at Courtrai and Lille,

for he replied to her compliments that everything had begun
to go right for him since she had taken to holding some
conversation with him on occasion. From this time onwards
Mademoiselle began to take pleasure in his company, for she
found his talk most agreeable and his ways of expressing
himself most extraordinary.

Only a few months before he became captain of the guards,
Puyguilhem had ceased to be Puyguilhem. On the death of
his father (September 1668) he assumed the name and title by
which he is better known, of comte de Lauzun.

If the early adventures of Lauzun have thus been presented
in some detail, it was in an attempt to build up the character of
this very singular man. His career has been described as a living
novel; in that case, we may regard the years to 1670 as Part I.
Before embarking on Part II we shall do well to pause and ask
ourselves what quality of nature or personality enabled him to
carry off situations which for another courtier might well have
ended in disgrace, exile, or even the scaffold; why women
loved him to such an extent that a kind of 'amorous legend'
surrounded him; how the King so patiently tolerated his arrant
impertinences and insubordinations. Louis XIV, that renowned
stallion, that great womaniser, in no way resembled his father
and brother in a homosexual weakness for seductive youth, nor
was he by temperament indulgent towards defiance of his
authority, quite the reverse, nor had he much forbearance with
the unruly and the undisciplined. How then, to put it colloquially, did Lauzun get away with it?

He was endowed with no physical beauty to account for the
emotions which he aroused in women. To begin with, he was
tiny, 'one of the smallest men that God ever made.'[1] The tip
of his nose was red; his hair fair but scanty, going grey although
he was but thirty-six, greasy and neglected; his eyes blue but
usually inflamed. He was dirty and untidy, except when it
pleased him to take some trouble with his appearance. On the

[1] Bussy-Rabutin.

other hand, he appears to have been well-made within his miniature proportions: a neat, straight figure, fine legs, a very important asset in those days, and a charming smile. Above all, he knew how to make himself feared. When Lauzun appeared, mounted on his high heels, spat one of his lizard-tongued witticisms, impaling the victim, and followed it up by the famous pirouette and disappearance into the crowd, no one ventured to take it amiss. As the King himself observed, 'When people behave as he does, they have nothing to dread, whereas other people get very badly treated.' I don't know whether it is a French proverb or merely a French colloquialism which says, '*Il faut savoir se faire valoir.*'

Lauzun, in fact, had discovered the secret that nothing pays so well in the world he had chosen to inhabit as the ability to impose one's own idiosyncrasies upon others and to enforce acceptance of any vagary one may think fit. Whether Lauzun's undoubted eccentricity sprang entirely from his native humour, or whether it was deliberately cultivated as the foundation of a legend, must remain an open question. Exaggeration may be half of art; it can also be of value in the exploitation of personality. Certainly when Lauzun put on a dressing-gown and a cloak, with an enormous wig and a night-cap crowned by a plumed hat, and paraded up and down in front of his servants to see if they would dare to laugh, he could scarcely be following a natural instinct. Similarly with his bouts of terrible rages: he may have been born with the fiery temper of the *méridional*, but it is difficult to resist the suspicion that his outbursts were sometimes partly assumed. Moreover, he knew how to vary his method; people might feel indignant, but they could never be bored. 'As for his mood and his manner,' said Mademoiselle, 'I defy anybody to know, to describe, or to imitate them.' The marquis de la Fare might call him 'the most insolent little man ever seen for a hundred years,' but on occasion Lauzun would adopt an almost servile tone, as though he invited rebuffs, or would pretend to be simple to the point of idiocy, making senseless remarks in that low voice of his, an affectation which vastly amused the King. It has been suggested that he was a little mad; whatever truth there may be in that theory, one is forced to the conclusion that there was also something very odd about this Gascon adventurer who, starting from nothing, had writhed and blustered his way into the heart of the most cynical of Courts and of the most intractable of monarchs.

'With the sharpest ears and the eyes of a lynx, though he was always complaining that he could neither see nor hear,' wrote his brother-in-law the duc de St Simon, 'always busy with plans, often chimerical . . . always devious, artful, and scheming, with a silly air of affected simplicity which he laughed at inside himself, always making discoveries, skimming, searching, plotting, laying traps; always pursuing some intrigue, envious, spiteful, bold and audacious in every way, loving very few, impertinent to the last degree with women . . . dangerous and feared by the greatest and the most *accrédités*, who *ménagéd* him without loving him, beginning with the King himself.'

Such was the man with whom the invulnerable Mademoiselle, at the age of forty-three, fell disastrously in love.

'Love is an illness (like smallpox),' wrote Bussy-Rabutin to Mme de Scudéry; 'the later you catch it the worse you take it.' Mademoiselle herself opined that one might suddenly find a stone in the road, which would cause a stumble in the firmest step. It was now some years since she had begun to note with approval the successive stages in Lauzun's advancement, the eulogies he had earned for his courage and skill in war, and the benevolence so graciously extended to him by the King, but their paths had not very often crossed, which was curious considering that they both frequented the same Court. It is true that Mademoiselle had been away for some of the time, partly in her second exile at St Fargeau, partly in her frequent visits to Forges and Eu, true also that to begin with she was not at all on good terms with Lauzun's friend Madame, but from the date when he received her congratulations on his

appointment as captain of the King's guards they began to
meet more and more frequently in the Queen's rooms and also
in those of Madame. The early misunderstanding of the two
ladies had evidently been due to an insufficient acquantance.
'When one gets to know you,' said Henrietta, 'one loves you.'
Mademoiselle replied in similar terms, and indeed the charm of
the English girl, young enough to be Mademoiselle's daughter,
was notoriously hard to resist, nor had Mademoiselle ever been
indifferent to the seductions of her own sex. Besides, Lauzun
came two or three times a day to visit her. Mademoiselle was
not jealous, for although Madame was most lovable and
Lauzun only too prone to love, she had never heard a word of
there being anything but friendship between them. Delicate
and consumptive, Henrietta would lie fully dressed on her bed
and would send her two guests off to talk and warm themselves
by the fire. Mademoiselle, with one of her rare attempts at self-
deception, says that she willingly obeyed in order to please her.
Yet only a few pages earlier in her Memoirs she had written,
'I had some instinct about what was to happen.'

She began by attributing an uneasy state of mind to her
dissatisfaction with her unmarried state (we may note with a
smile that this discontent had never shown any signs of
existence before, and could speedily have been appeased if it
had), when, keeping her thoughts to herself and confiding in
no one, she came with her usual honesty but also with a strangely
delayed perspicacity to the conclusion that these novel ideas
could not be merely vague but must be based upon some
definite object. She could not, or says she could not, discover
who it was. She searched, she reflected, to no avail; but not for
long. After a few days, she perceived that it was M. de Lauzun
whom she loved and who had slid himself into her heart (*qui
s'était glissé dans mon cœur*).

It is easy to discern from the ensuing pages of Mademoiselle's
Memoirs the turmoil into which this realisation flung her. No
young girl could have been more agitated or less able to cope

than she who 'in all the Court of France was most of a novice in the management of love.' Shutting herself alone into her room, she gave herself up with rapture to an analysis of her feelings and plans for a rosy future about which she entertained no doubts whatsoever. Only too accurately she persuaded herself that no one had ever shown her any affection and that once in one's life one must savour the sweetness of knowing oneself beloved. He would love her even as she would love him; she would do all in her power to raise him in the eyes of the world, although his worth was greater than anything she could do for him. He must love her already, she thought, for he constantly sought her out either in the Queen's apartments, or contrived to meet her in a gallery or a courtyard, but of course the overwhelming difference between his rank and hers would debar him from taking the first step. A day when she did not see him seemed very long, and there were other days when she would scarcely speak to him and forced herself to think only of what people would say in criticism of her intention. Then the sight of him would undermine all her resolution, and she would remember some lines of Corneille about marriages being made in Heaven, and would despatch a messenger post-haste to Paris for a copy of the book:

On s'estime, on se cherche, on s'aime en un moment;
Tout ce qu'on s'entredit persuade aisément,
Et sans s'inquiéter de mille peurs frivoles
La foi semble courir au devant des paroles;
La langue en peu de mots en explique beaucoup,
Les yeux, plus éloquents, font tout voir tout d'un coup . . .[1]

Mademoiselle herself was not unlike a heroine of Corneille.

It did not take her very long to think out a number of good

---

[1] We set a value on one another, we seek each other out, we love at first sight;
All our private exchanges carry a ready conviction,
And far from troubling ourselves with a thousand unnecessary doubts
Faith runs ahead of any verbal expression.
Speech, in few words, may explain much,
But the more eloquent eyes reveal the whole truth all of a sudden.

reasons why, setting love aside for the moment, she should not unite herself in marriage to Lauzun. It may be difficult for us to apprehend fully the unprecedented nature of such a proposal, or the storm of astonishment that it would provoke in the hierarchical climate of the French Court. True, Mademoiselle's own half-sister, Mlle d'Allençon, had been allowed to marry a subject, the duc de Guise, but Mlle d'Alençon was far from being Mademoiselle, la Grande Mademoiselle, duchesse de Montpensier, and Lauzun with his modest country nobility was far from belonging to a princely house such as Guise. The King, at the time, had even been careful to explain to Mademoiselle that her sister's marriage was none of his making: he had merely given his consent to it. Mademoiselle knew very well that she would come in for a great deal of censure; but some, she thought, would praise her, and she went on to think how much obliged Lauzun would be to her, and how delectable it would be to disappoint the hopes of her heirs. This was perhaps not a very charitable notion of Mademoiselle's, but we know that she had a strong sense of possession and that the domains over which she kept so firm a control were very dear in her eyes. She did not at all relish the thought that her death might be greedily awaited. Then, she further considered, it would be very sweet to remain in her own country, where so few were above her in rank; quite sweet enough to cure her of any regret in not becoming a queen in foreign lands, whose kings were not made in the semblance of M. de Lauzun.

Fortified by all these reflections, she took her final decision one day when she had accompanied the Queen to church. She would approach him next day.

Mademoiselle, usually vague about dates, has remembered this one: it was the second of March, 1670. An account of their conversation is best given in her own words.

'I was feeling very gay. I spoke to him in passing; he also seemed very gay to me; I do not know if he could see what was in my heart. I was dying to give him a chance to tell me what his (heart) felt towards me. I could not think how to manage it. At last I heard a rumour that the King intended to give up Lorraine and wanted to marry me to Prince Charles [of Lorraine]. I said to myself, "Here is a good opportunity for M. de Lauzun to speak to me." I sent to fetch him from his room, but was told he was not there. As he was on very good terms with M. de Guitry, he was often in his room. Guitry had recently done it up in a very curious way and I had told him that I would go and see it. I left my own room saying, "The Queen is at her prayers; I shall have time to see Guitry's room." I went; he was not there. Downstairs, I went to the Queen's apartment, where I found M. de Lauzun talking to Mme de Guiche. I said to him, "I am delighted to have found you; I had sent for you; I have something important to tell you." Mme de Guiche said, "You can have him whenever you want him, but so long as I have got him I beg you to leave him with me." He said to me, "It will be over in a minute." My heart was beating, and I think his was beating too and that he guessed from my demeanour that I had nothing to say to him but something pleasing. He kept on looking at me the whole time he was talking to Mme de Guiche. At least, that is what I fancied.

'When he left her, I went to him and led him towards a window. With his proud mien, he seemed to me the emperor of all the world. I began, "You have shown me so much friendship for some time past that I now have the greatest trust in you and would not like to do anything without your advice.' He said he was greatly obliged to me for the honour I was doing him; that he was infinitely grateful; and that he wished I could see into his heart when I should perceive that I was not mistaken in the good opinion I did him the honour to hold. We paid each other the tenderest of compliments, then I resumed, "It is being said that the King wishes to marry me to the prince de Lorraine; have you heard that?" He said no, and that he was sure the King would wish only what I wished, and would not go against me. I replied, "At my age, one does not marry people off against their will. Up to now, there has always been much talk of marriages for me; I always listened, but to tell the truth I should have been in despair if they had come to anything. I love my country, where I am so great a lady that there is enough limit to my ambition, and when one is reasonable one should be satisfied and seek happiness in life: one could not be happy with a man one did not know.

If he were not [here Mademoiselle uses the untranslatable phrase *honnête homme*] one could not esteem him, and for my part I cannot love without esteem." He answered, "Those are very reasonable sentiments which deserve approbation; but you, so happy! are you dreaming of getting married?" I said, "It is true that I am happy, but it enrages me to hear the calculations of the aspirants to my estates." "Ah!" said he, "that would drive me to despair also, and nothing could give me a greater desire to marry." The Queen came in. He said to me, "I want to profit by the honour you do me in reposing your trust in me; and there is too much to be said on so important a matter, not to resume it there where we have left off."

'I thought: "This is a great step forward, and he can no longer doubt my feelings; next time, I shall learn his." I was very well pleased with myself for what I had accomplished.

'Next day, after the Queen had dined, he came to me and said, "One could write a book out of everything that has gone through my head since I have been without the honour of seeing you; I have built many castles in Spain." "So have I; but all that we have been thinking might well be true?" "Oh!" he said, "I do not believe it." "Let us speak seriously," said I, "for all this is of the greatest importance to me." He laughed, and said, "I should be very *glorieux* to be your chief counsellor; I should have a very good opinion of myself." "All the more," I replied, "when you saw that your advice was followed and not spurned, for I shall not consult anyone else. I mistrust everybody and am convinced that you alone will give me true and disinterested advice. So let us come to the point."

' "You left off," he said, "as you were saying that the idea of marriage had come to you because it grieved you to hear *So-and-so will have one part of my land, another will have another*. I think that is very right, for one must continue to live as long as one can and to have no love for those who desire one's death. For it is inconceivable that you should have thought *I will marry because I have found someone who pleases me*; there is no one in the world worthy of you. Thus I find you in an uncertain state of mind, and I pity you, but I count you fortunate in that you have found me and can unload your heart, for I see that you have long been seeking without finding someone meriting the honour of your trust. I think myself the happiest of men."

'Lauzun went on to say, "You must get yourself out of this

unquiet frame of mind. You have nothing to desire so far as grandeur goes, or wealth, or your establishment; everything smiles upon you under that heading. You are esteemed, you are honoured for your virtue and your deserts, as much as for your rank—a very agreeable thing to owe only to oneself.[1] The King treats you excellently well; he loves you; I can see that he likes being with you. What more have you to desire? If you had been a queen, an empress, you would have been extremely bored; that position would have raised you only a little higher and brought more trouble and less enjoyment, so spend all the rest of your life here with all its advantages. If you want to marry, you have it in your power to make any man your equal . . . He will lack nothing; but where is he? All this is all very well, but I fear it may be, as I said, only a castle in Spain through the impossibility of finding anybody fortunate enough to please you."

'I laughed. I think the delight with which I listened to him pleased him greatly. I said, "All this may well prove possible." Our conversation lasted a good two hours, and I think would have lasted longer had not the Queen emerged from her oratory. I was well satisfied, and I think he was too.'

The affair, however, did not progress as rapidly as Mademoiselle could have wished. Lauzun avoided her; it was she who had to seek him out. Naturally, she found every credible excuse for his negligence: it was not for him to say 'Take me'; his restraint was altogether admirable, considering the vast fortune at stake, which no other man would have risked losing through too much hesitation; and if they met only in public, constantly interrupted, it was because he knew well enough what he was about, and she dared not bid him to come to her own rooms. He even went so far as to discourage her. 'Well?' she said to him at last, her patience coming to an end, but he replied only that he had discovered a thousand objections. This remark displeased Mademoiselle, but made no real effect upon her, for she thought that he did not mean it and merely wanted to see what she would answer.

[1] The interested reader may note that Mademoiselle was constantly making this observation about herself. Lauzun was only repeating what he had heard her say.

' "You must not take offence," he said, "if I do not always agree with you: it is because I speak with sincerity and no desire to flatter you. I think you are quite right to wish to marry, because nothing is so ridiculous as a spinster of forty [Mademoiselle was forty-three] frivolously dressed, like an empty-headed girl of fifteen. She ought either to enter a convent or to dress quietly and give up going out in the world. Once in a way she might go to the opera, but only with apparent reluctance, and wait upon the Queen as the duty of her rank demanded; otherwise she should devote herself to good works and religious observances. Whereas if she were married, she could dress to please her husband and could go to parties because he would want her to live like everybody else; but this husband," he added, "will be very hard to find, and if you do find him he may have faults which will make you unhappy." '

Mademoiselle had been right in one conclusion: Lauzun knew very well what he was about.

A new project was on foot: the King with all the Court was to make a royal progress into Flanders and Lauzun was put in command of the escorting troops. Mademoiselle, on hearing this piece of news, offered her congratulations; yes, he said, he had felt sure that she would be very much pleased. She was especially glad, because she had spent Easter in Paris without him and had found the time terribly long (*je m'ennuyais furieusement*). 'Confess,' he had said to her, 'that you will be bored in Paris'—his self-assurance seems to have been growing —and she had frankly agreed. Very much in love, she listened greedily whenever his name was mentioned, and when on Easter Monday their coaches crossed in the street, 'my joy was not to be believed.' She was glad also because although she no longer sought the reason for her *ennui* she was in terror lest other people should guess it; some of the ladies had teased her, saying what a good wife she would be, how happy was the man who got her, but Mme d'Épernon said no one would ever have that happiness for Mademoiselle would never marry: to whom could she belong, she who had never been willing to belong to kings? Mme de Puysieux said, 'One does not always find happiness with kings, is that not true, great princess?' and went on to say why not marry M. de Longueville, handsome, brave, and rich, who would be most sensible of the honour done him? had not Mademoiselle's sister married M. de Guise, even though he was not head of his family as M. de Longueville was? Mme d'Épernon said why not marry her nephew, M. de Marsan? and so they continued until other people came in, putting an end to their banter, but Mademoiselle was not sorry that this suggestion of her marriage to M. de Longueville should gain currency, since it might accustom people to the intention really in her mind.

On the 28th of April (1670) the vast convoy rumbled and clattered out of Paris.[1] It is estimated that over 12,000 persons accompanied the King, including his wet-nurse and his two mistresses, Mme de Montespan and Mlle de La Vallière, now known simply as *les dames*. The entire royal family went, with all their attendant suites of ladies- and gentlemen-in-waiting, maids of honour, pages, flunkeys, retainers, and menials of all sorts and both sexes. The aristocracy, now in awed subservience to the King who had carried on with an even more autocratic hand the policy of subordination inaugurated by Richelieu, hastened to swell the cortège in proof of their devotion. It is easy to believe that this cohort, with its wagons and pack-mules, resembled a tribe of nomads on the move. The baggage of the effeminate Monsieur alone involved a great train of transport, for he could not dispense with his pretty treasures and a constant change in his apparel. Very important persons took their furniture along with them. The King, for his daily use, had his room hung with crimson damask; and for grander occasions, where he could dispose of a larger room, hangings of Gobelin tapestry, silver chandeliers, and an immense four-poster bed of green velvet embroidered in gold, too high for

---

[1] The object of this progress was to impress the inhabitants of Flanders, ceded to France by the Treaty of Aix-la-Chapelle in 1668.

the ceiling of a humble dwelling. Mademoiselle herself, a good traveller who never made a fuss except when she was frightened, once had to get the floor dug out in a peasant's house before her bed could be accommodated.

There can be no better instance of the contrast between the extravagant luxury of these royal progresses, where, when everything had been unpacked and set out, Their Majesties were 'as though in the palace of the Tuileries or very nearly,' and the extraordinary discomforts they were called upon to endure. The roads, of course, were atrocious; rivers had to be forded, because the bridges were either non-existent or broken down; part of the convoy was perpetually getting lost or failing to keep up, sometimes the travelling kitchens and commissariat, which upset the Queen, sometimes Monsieur's cargo of cosmetics, which upset Monsieur; and on this particular journey, although April had turned into May, the weather was as bad as anything on record. They were not four days out of Paris, at St Quentin, having got up at half-past five in the morning and started at seven, before the rain began to come down in torrents and so continued for days. Both Mademoiselle and Pellisson, the official chronicler, an eye-witness, have left detailed accounts. Coaches stuck in the mud; packs fell off the mules; chests and coffers floated in water; dead horses obstructed the roads; the River Sambre overflowed and flooded the marshes; M. de Crussol's coach was submerged up to the windows; M. de Bouligneux, afraid of being drowned, first climbed on to the roof of his coach and finally ordered his horses to be unharnessed, riding away on one of them and leaving his coach where it was, 'and where perhaps it still is.' Night was falling as they approached Landrecies; they had scarcely any torches, and the swollen river lay between them and the town. Word was brought of a possible ford a league away; the King mounted a horse; the Queen and Mademoiselle, in a coach together, both screamed loudly; there was a great deal of noise, which annoyed the King. The ford proving impassable, they decided to take refuge in a mean house (*une méchante maison*) in a field for the night. The Queen alighted; Mademoiselle, carrying the train of her gown, went up to the knee in swampy ground; the Queen said, 'Cousin, you are tugging me,' and Mademoiselle, 'Madame, I have fallen into a hole, wait until I can get out.' It was ten o'clock; they had only one candle, and there were only two rooms in the cottage. Mademoiselle decided to spend the night in her coach, making herself as comfortable as she could with cushions out of other coaches; she loosened her laces, put on a dressing-gown over her dress, and a night-cap on her head, but even so she could not sleep on account of the din going on in the darkness all round.

She presently distinguished the voice of Monsieur and sent to find out where he and Madame were. In reply, they invited her to visit them, so she caused herself to be carried to their coach where she found Madame in a state of collapse and Monsieur talking to M. de Villeroy, saying, 'For nothing on earth would I allow myself to be seen as I saw M. de Lauzun just now, with his hair all soaked; I never saw a more dreadful-looking man.' This, as may be imagined, did not please Mademoiselle. 'I thought to myself, I find him very much to my liking in whatever condition he is; he cares nothing whether he pleases you or not, and I believe he knows well enough that he pleases *me*.' Whereupon she went back to her coach.

She was fetched from there by a message that the King and Queen were about to dine: everybody was starving (*on mourait de faim*), and no wonder. Mademoiselle found the Queen in a very bad temper—she had always been something of a spoilt child—declaring that she would be ill if she could not sleep, and where was the pleasure in such journeys? The King tried to pacify her: mattresses were being brought. 'How horrible! What? all of us to sleep together?' 'Well,' said the King, who preserved his cheerfulness in a most engaging if unexpected manner, 'where is the harm in lying on mattresses fully dressed? I see no harm. Ask my cousin what she thinks and let us follow her advice.' Mademoiselle agreed that there could be no harm in ten or twelve ladies sleeping in the same room as the King and Monsieur.

Dinner arrived, soup so thin and meatless and lukewarm that the Queen refused to eat. The King, Mademoiselle, Monsieur, and even the delicate Madame, famished, fell upon it and ate it all up, when, seeing that there was nothing left, the Queen said peevishly, 'I wanted some, and it has all been eaten.' Mademoiselle felt inclined to laugh. Then came a mixed dish of meats, so tough that when the royal guests took a chicken by the legs between them they could scarcely pull it apart. And that, apparently, was all they had.

A fire had been lit in the other room; the Queen lay down on the mattress nearest the fire. Then came Mme de Thianges and Mme de Béthune sharing a mattress between them; then, on separate mattresses almost touching on account of the limited space, Monsieur, Madame, the King, Mademoiselle, Mlle de La Vallière, Mme de Montespan, the duchesse de Créqui, the marquise de La Vallière, and Mlle La Marck, a maid of honour to the Queen. They had all put on their night-caps and their dressing-gowns over their clothes, and had collected a few coats and other coverings. In the next room were some of the principal officers with M. de Lauzun; messengers came repeatedly, in search of him, and had to step over the corner of Mme de La Vallière's bedding on the way, until one of them catching his spur in her night-cap, the King told him to cut a hole in the outer wall to avoid passing through. This incident made everybody laugh except the Queen. (They seem to have been remarkably good-humoured under adversity.) Then Mme de Thianges suddenly said she heard cattle and donkeys in the adjoining stable, reminding her of the birth of Our Lord, and it seemed so droll to see the King practically in a stable that even the Queen laughed, which pleased the King, who had been grieved by her ill-temper. This very unusual party then went to sleep.

M. de Louvois came at four in the morning to arouse them with the news that a bridge had been repaired across the river.

The appearance of her companions was not lost upon Mademoiselle, 'One can imagine,' she says, 'what everybody looked like, the ladies pale without their rouge and from lack of sleep.' She herself, she thought, looked better than the rest, for she was naturally of a high colour. By seven o'clock she was in a room in Landrecies, the most horrible room in the world she thought, on awaking during the afternoon with leisure to examine it, and her women all grumbling against Lauzun for some delay on their road. Mademoiselle would have none of their complaints: Lauzun could do no wrong in her eyes, and when later in the day he scolded her for having betrayed her fears, thereby distressing the King, for whom she ought to have more consideration, she accepted his rebuke meekly, adding that her nervousness over the bad roads had been equalled by her anxiety for his own well-being.

Indeed, the concern of this proud woman for this unworthy little man was constant and pathetically touching. Awakened one night, she cursed the cavalry and their bugles, but on hearing Lauzun's voice amongst them she thought only that there he was, in the rain, and that she within doors was less to be pitied than he. When she saw him bareheaded talking to the King, dripping wet in the rain, she could not forbear from saying, 'Sire, command him to put his hat on; this will make him ill.' So often did she intervene, that she began to fear it would be noticed, so, having recourse to an artfulness foreign to her nature, on another occasion she approached the King in a roundabout way to ensure that Lauzun should sleep in a house and not in camp with his men. 'Sire, Your Majesty should have the kindness to order the troops into the town [of Avesnes]. All the horses will die if they are not under cover, and a day like this will do more harm than a long march in fine weather.' Mademoiselle was pleased with her little bit of cunning. 'They owed this to the care I took of M. de Lauzun.'

She naturally did not have very much opportunity for private conversation with him on this journey, though she tried to make herself agreeable to him in small ways, standing in the rain and the wind to admire a regiment of dragoons and complimenting him on their appearance. She observed also with satisfaction that he was constantly at the King's side, and that the King seemed as fond of him as she herself. Sometimes, she was able to eavesdrop: 'They were speaking together in low voices and no one could overhear what they said, but when one loves a person and thinks of nothing else, one can hear from a distance, especially when it is something which gives one pleasure.' Occasionally, however, she got him to herself, when in spite of his protests that he must return to his duties she managed to keep him talking for two or three hours. 'I was at a window [in the Queen's room], longing for him to come, when he entered with the comte d'Ayen . . . He said he never came to the Queen's rooms, and had come only by chance. 'Do you regret having come,' she asked, 'since I am glad to see you?' No, he said, but he would not be there long, for he was going away again. M. d'Ayen exclaimed, 'You must be mad to speak like that to Mademoiselle.' 'I am no flatterer, said Lauzun; 'I speak my mind. Mademoiselle begins to know me well enough to understand my make-up.' It was certainly not customary so ungraciously to address a royal princess, but Mademoiselle, far from taking offence, had evolved a theory that he did it in order to show her that there was some secret understanding between them.

The powers of self-persuasion are potent for those who wish to believe. Whatever may have been the workings of Lauzun's mind, his conduct towards Mademoiselle became more and more bizarre as the affair progressed, yet always she found some excuse or explanation. His manners might be extraordinary (*celles de M. de Lauzun à mon égard étaient extraordinaires*), but according to her they were those of a cautious man, aware of her feelings for him but afraid of putting her into embarrassment should she change, by too marked a cognizance. She interpreted them as a sign of his respect, as many a woman before and since in dealing with a laggard lover; and, being

Mademoiselle, added that he showed himself as a man who knew how to comport himself with people like her, with whom one should not hasten matters as with one's equals. This was all very well: there were times when Mademoiselle's faith must have been strained. Descending from her coach, she would have leant upon his arm; he moved away, and she nearly fell. Another day he would speak of nothing but mortality. 'You fear death,' he said, 'and yet you do not think about it. I shall make you reflect,' and for some time thereafter whenever he passed her he would mutter, 'Remember that you are mortal.' Yet he would suddenly praise her new skirt, when she exclaimed, 'What a miracle! you never seem to notice anything.'

More seriously, the huge question of marriage remained to be debated between them. The journey into Flanders had somewhat interrupted Mademoiselle's tentative advances; not altogether, for she contrived to throw several flies over him and got a bewildering variety of response. She can never have known what he was going to take into his head next. An ardent soldier, he would declare suddenly that his command bored him, that it enraged him, that it filched time which could be better employed, but when Mademoiselle hopefully asked how he would wish to employ it he refused to answer. Then he would announce his intention of leaving the world, of becoming a hermit; everyone would think him mad, but he alone would know he was not. Piteously Mademoiselle tried to draw him out: 'I confide in you, will you not confide a little in me? Shall you never contemplate marriage?' This straight question provoked a curious but rather encouraging reply; no, he said, never, he had always run away; if ever he thought of it, the only thing that counted would be the virtue of the lady for if she were guilty of the slightest fault he would have none of her, 'even if it were you, who are above everything; if I could marry you and someone said something against your good repute, or if your person was not pleasing to me, I should never be willing; I would rather marry your maid, if I loved her, and shut myself up in my house and lead an honourable life.' One's heart goes out to Mademoiselle; this was, after all, the first time he had ever alluded to the possibility, however hypothetical, of a marriage between them and had moreover given her a hint that she was not objectionable to him in her person. Humility was anything but natural to her; love and anxiety reduced her to the humblest reply. 'But I should satisfy you (*mais vous voudriez bien de moi*), for I am virtuous and nothing in me is repellent to you?' Lauzun evidently thought he had gone far enough, and, as was his wont, began to sheer off. 'Do not let us tell fairy-stories (*ne faisons point de contes de Peau d'Ane*).' She pressed him: 'Do let us come back to me; when will you allow me to come to a decision and free myself from a state of mind which you daily tell me arouses your pity?' He replied, 'You forget that the Ambassador is waiting for me.'[1]

Mademoiselle thought this conversation over before returning to the charge. They were now at le Catelet, nearing the Flemish border, when she cornered him in the Queen's room. She was quite determined, she said, to get married; she had overcome all the difficulties he had shown her; she had practically decided on the happy man, and now nothing was lacking but his, Lauzun's, approval. 'I tremble,' he said, 'at seeing you in so great haste over a matter which would require centuries of reflection.' 'Alas!' said Mademoiselle, 'when one is forty [she was in fact forty-three] and wants to commit a folly, one should not spend so much time thinking it over. My resolve is such that at our next halt I intend to speak to the King and the marriage shall take place in Flanders.' Lauzun, thoroughly alarmed, exclaimed, 'Oh, do nothing of the sort! I will not have it, I who am your chief counsellor; I object.'

It is not easy to interpret Lauzun's motives or the general trend of his policy. As Mademoiselle, on her own showing,

---

[1] He refers to the Venetian ambassador, Morosini, who was travelling with the Court.

Maria Teresa, Infanta of Spain. School of Velasquez

Maria Teresa and le Grand Dauphin, by Pierre Mignard

burnt all his letters, we have nothing to go on except his outward behaviour, recorded by her with such a wealth and honesty of detail. On the face of it, he had everything to gain by so dazzling a union; ambitious though he might be, he could scarcely have aspired higher. Yet it is evident that he played fast and loose with her, blowing now hot now cold, leading her on only to rebuff her, letting fall a word of encouragement only to follow it up with a show of indifference or a positive snub. He must have known that these tactics, possibly expedient with another woman, were quite unnecessary with Mademoiselle who in her rough, ingenuous way did everything to make her meaning clear. She was no flirt; her heart had always been notoriously intact; she was not a person ever to do things by halves, and when she at last loved it might be presumed that she would love for life. Are we to believe, then, that whatever assurance he might give her to the contrary he did in fact find her too unalluring and shrank, when it came to the point, from the thought of physical contact? or that his sense of the ridiculous showed him too clearly the contrast between himself, so small and frail, and this large princess? *Le petit homme* and *la Grande Mademoiselle*—what sort of a couple would they make as they walked together down the galleries of the Louvre or of Versailles? She could look down on the top of his head. No one knew better than Lauzun the mocking spirit of his compatriots. Was he afraid of the possessiveness of her passion? He may rightly have surmised the latent jealousy of which later on he was to have ample proof. He had always been free; women had loved him, and he had loved women. Mademoiselle, with her unconditional nature, was not cut out for a complaisant wife. All these objections may well have occupied his mind, or it may have been merely that with his love of mischief he amused himself by tormenting a poor besotted victim whom he knew to be securely hooked.

We may take our choice amongst these explanations, sure only of one thing, that Lauzun would not wantonly have risked the loss of so prodigious a prize. No personal dis-inclination, no dread of ridicule, no reluctance to forego his liberty, can have outweighed the advantages to be gained by acceptance of that generous hand. By far the most probable conjecture is that he feared the anger of the King. It was never safe to presume too far upon the royal favour; Lauzun himself had often gone further in minor ways than other men dared, but this was a major issue involving the unheard-of imperti-nence of a mere nobody, almost an adventurer, thrusting himself into the very heart of the royal family. Other men of little account had been seekers after fortune, and had risen from obscurity thanks to their wits or their sword, but not one of them had ventured to lift his eyes to a Daughter of France, the suggested bride of kings. The King could do as he chose; he might not stop to consider that his headstrong cousin had herself made the running; one brief order, and the unacceptable suitor might disappear for the rest of his days into exile or worse. Besides, Lauzun never ceased protesting his personal devotion, protestations which do carry a surprising note of sincerity, not cynically towards the Sovereign, dispenser of bounty, but also towards Louis as a man who knew not only how to make himself dreaded but beloved. It is no exaggeration to say that Louis XIV inspired an atmosphere of worship, partly due no doubt to an atavistic magic of kingship and a realisation that the splendour of France was vested in his person, but due also to a certain human element of approach-ability and ready good-humour. The beams of the *Roi Soleil* could warm as well as coruscate.

External events during the next two months (May and June 1670) came to interrupt the very unsmooth course of Made-moiselle's love. We hear no more of the marriage in Flanders which Lauzun had so strongly vetoed. For the moment, Mademoiselle retires into the wings and the centre of the stage is taken (alas, not for long) by Madame.

During the journey to Flanders, Henrietta's customary high

spirits had deserted her; she spoke little, and kept her eyes cast down, refusing sometimes to dine with the royal family but going off alone to drink her glass of milk and retiring to bed early. The King, who had renounced his earlier inclination for his sister-in-law and was now fully preoccupied with Mlle de La Vallière (recently created a duchess) and Mme de Montespan, nevertheless retained a deep affection for Henrietta and was much concerned on her behalf. Not so Monsieur, her husband, who lost no opportunity of insulting her and even went so far as to say in her presence that a fortune-teller had predicted her early death and a number of other wives for himself. (As he was entirely wrapped up in a most mischievous young man named the chevalier de Lorraine, the cause of half the trouble between him and his wife, this reference to many other wives doubtless struck his hearers as sufficiently ironical.) Henrietta must bitterly have contrasted his behaviour to her with his frivolity in company, for Monsieur, when his baggage had not gone astray, was a tremendous resource during the many mishaps of the journey, being always full of the latest gossip for the entertainment of the King's intimate circle and always ready to organise games or to summon the violins for a dance, if necessary in a barn.

To add to Henrietta's sorrows, her mother, Henrietta Maria, had died in the previous autumn (September 10th, 1669).

A patch of sunshine, however, lay ahead to brighten her dark days. Arrived at Courtrai, with the rest of the Court, she found English messengers from Charles II, inviting her to embark on an English ship at Dunkirk where the fleet lay at anchor, cross the Channel, and meet him at Dover. Across the narrow waters, then, was the prospect of a few days of happiness with her beloved brother. She had not seen him for nine years. Not that she had ever lost touch with him, for they corresponded continuously in terms so affectionate as to give the impression of letters exchanged between parted lovers ('I hope you believe I love you as much as 'tis possible ... and have nothing so near my heart as how I may find occasions to express that tender passion I have for my dearest Minette . . . I am sure I will never have a secret in my heart, that I will not willingly trust you with, and there is nothing I will endeavour more than to give you all sorts of testimonies, how truly and passionately I am yours. C.R.'). Henrietta was overjoyed, Monsieur was furious. He forbade the voyage, but had to give way as Louis XIV for reasons of his own was determined to throw brother and sister together. After her departure Monsieur expressed himself in such violent terms that Mademoiselle thought that he and Madame could never again be reconciled.

Meanwhile, Madame was on her way to England. For once the crossing appears to have been calm. At five o'clock on a May morning she came on deck within sight of the white cliffs which, after all, represented her native country. She had seen it only once, since she had left it as a two-year-old fugitive in disguise, protesting that she was no ragged little boy but a princess. Times had changed. Now, accompanied by a suite of over two hundred people and escorted by English warships, she was met by a royal barge rowing across the glittering water, bringing her brothers, Charles the King and James, Duke of York, the Duke of Monmouth and Rupert of Bavaria. Happy as the reunion was, and many as were the festivities both at Dover and Canterbury (for the visit happened to coincide with the tenth anniversary of Charles' Restoration and also with his fortieth birthday) a handful of well-informed persons were under no illusion as to its true purpose. 'The journey of this princess,' wrote M. de Pomponne, French envoy at the Hague, 'was not merely undertaken for the simple pleasure of seeing the King her brother.'

This is not the place to relate in any detail the outcome of that now historic meeting. It may suffice to say that six days after Madame's arrival the secret[1] Treaty of Dover, significantly nicknamed *le Traité de Madame*, was signed by Colbert de Croissy, French ambassador to England, on the part of the French, and on the part of the English by Lord Arlington, Lord

[1] The full contents of the Treaty were never made public until 1830.

Arundell of Wardour, Sir Thomas Clifford, later Lord Clifford
of Chudleigh, and Sir Richard Bellings—all, be it noted,
Catholics. By this treaty the King of England, on the verge of
bankruptcy, was to receive two million *livres tournois* from the
King of France in return for publicly pronouncing himself
convinced of the truth of the Catholic religion, as soon as he
judged fit to do so. France and England were to engage in a
permanent alliance, and both were to declare war on the
Dutch, the King of France choosing the moment for the
opening of hostilities. The King of France was to prosecute
the war on land, with a small contingent of English troops, the
King of England the war by sea, with a small contingent of
French ships. The King of France would supply a subsidy of
three million *livres tournois* a year for the expenses of the fleet
so long as the war should last. Should any territory be con-
quered in the United Provinces, the King of England was to
receive Walcheren, the estuary of the Scheldt, and the island
of Cadzand as his share.

Such were some of the more important clauses of this most
disgraceful and aggressive compact, which entirely contradicted
the terms of the Triple Alliance, concluded two years earlier
(1668) between England, Sweden, and the Dutch.

It must not be supposed, as many chroniclers have suggested,
that Madame was wholly responsible for arranging the agreement between Charles and Louis. That would be attributing
far too preponderant a part in the affairs of France and England,
to even so intelligent and charming a woman. The leaders of
great nations do not enter into far-reaching commitments for
sentimental reasons. Yet even such serious and wide-apart
historians as Voltaire and Sir Arthur Bryant can solemnly
write: 'Entrusted with the sole responsibility of bringing about
the union of the two Kings and the destruction of Holland,
Madame embarked at Dunkirk . . .'[1] and Sir Arthur Bryant:
'Within six days of her landing, her brother, who could deny
her nothing, least of all this on which her whole being was set,

[1] Voltaire, *Siècle de Louis XIV*.

had consented.'[1] Documentary facts make nonsense of such
assertions. Secret negotiations had for long been going on
between the two Kings and their representatives; the most that
may be claimed for Madame is that over the religious clause
she may have tipped the balance of Charles' hesitation. For the
rest, the position was simple: Charles wanted Louis' money
and Louis wanted Charles' navy.

The most remarkable tribute to Henrietta's tact and trust-
worthiness can be sought in the confidence that serious men
placed in her over so serious a matter. She was no typical
feminine intriguer such as Mme de Chevreuse or Mme de
Montbazon or Mme de Longueville, exploiting their sexual
charm to influence weak and amorous men. Over a long
period she had been admitted to the most clandestine counsels
of the two kings and had in fact acted as their unofficial go-
between and ambassador, duplicating in her sole person that
shadowy diplomatic appointment in both Courts. She had
conducted herself with exemplary discretion, and it becomes
apparent that apart from the lovable qualities of her nature
Henrietta possessed also a brain capable of earning masculine
respect. What we may question, and question very gravely, is
her political sagacity in her determination to convert to
Catholicism the King of a Protestant country. Regarded
objectively, it was a crazy scheme, but, as history has taught us,
religious convictions seldom take account of worldly expediency. The proselytiser thinks more of the next world than of
this, and from Henrietta's point of view the salvation of her
brother's soul might be worth more than the retention of his
revendicated kingdom.

There were many Englishmen at Calais, whither the French
Court repaired on the return from Dunkirk, and a strange
rumour spread about that the King of England intended to
divorce his wife on the grounds of her childlessness, send her
back to Portugal, and marry Mademoiselle. One would have

[1] *King Charles II* by Arthur Bryant, p. 211.

supposed that he might have chosen a younger woman, and Mademoiselle herself says that she was surprised. She must have been even more surprised when she discovered that the King of France took the rumour seriously. They were all together in his coach, the usual family party, she, the King, the Queen, Monsieur, and Mme de Montespan, when Monsieur began in his sly way, 'If I would, I could tell you a piece of news I heard.' The King, laughing, for he knew what a tattler his brother was, said, 'I wonder you have not yet told it.' They all looked in query at one another. 'I will lay a bet that my cousin knows it,' said the King, 'judging by her expression.' Mademoiselle, ill at ease, remained silent. 'No one has talked of anything else since yesterday evening,' said Monsieur, pursuing his teasing, and the King, taking pity on Mademoiselle, said that, although he had received no official intimation, he had heard from Colbert, his ambassador at the Court of St James, come to pay his respects at Calais, that the matter was public property in England and that even the most highly-placed persons among the English confirmed it. The Queen exclaimed, 'How horrible! What, cousin! would you be willing?' Mademoiselle still did not reply. 'Answer,' said the King; 'what have you to say to it?' Mademoiselle, thus coerced, said that the King's will was her will, and burst into floods of tears. (*Je me mis à pleurer de très bon cœur.*) Monsieur would not leave her in peace. 'For my part,' he said, 'I think it would be splendid: the King of England is so very much an *honnête homme*,' and Mme de Montespan, who was not without malice, said, 'You know each other so well; he used to be very much in love with you; it would be very suitable,' but the more they jested the more she wept, until the King, taking pity again, said, 'Tears over a rumour?'

This fright was without consequences, although it showed Mademoiselle that she was still regarded as eligible in the European marriage-market. The next proposal shocked and alarmed her considerably more. It was preceded by a renewal of the talk about her marrying M. de Longueville, which

Monsieur did not fail to bring to her ears. She would have given much to consult Lauzun, but he was away taking the baths at Porchefontaine; so she practised one of the little stratagems that love had taught her and by sending for Lauzun's friend M. de Guitry she aroused Lauzun's curiosity to the point of coming to Versailles to find out what they had been discussing. 'You had something to say to Guitry?' 'Yes.' 'What was it?' 'I have no wish to tell you.' But of course, under pressure, she did: it was about M. de Longueville, when Lauzun laughed and said, 'Well! you have found your man, and you ought to be grateful to Mme de Thianges for giving you the thing she loves best in the world and sharing him with you.'

It looks as though Lauzun had become slightly uneasy, for he reappeared that same evening after supper. 'What a wonder!' said Mademoiselle on meeting him, and one would like to believe that she spoke ironically. Here M. de Longueville strolled up for a moment, and when he had gone away again Lauzun said to Mademoiselle, 'He thinks I was looking for him, but what I really wanted was to see how you would treat him, for I begin to think you no longer trust me and that it is a fact that you are going to marry him.' Mademoiselle at that stage should have followed up her advantage and kept him on tenterhooks for a while longer, but that was not in her character: she would never learn the feminine arts. (Lauzun was more than a match for her in that respect.) 'Certainly I shall be married,' she replied, 'but not to him. I ask you to speak with me tomorrow, for I am resolved to speak to the King. I want all this to be over and done with before the first of July.'

He could not come the next day, Saturday, he said, for he must go to Paris, but he promised to return on Sunday without fail; he was as anxious as she for the matter to be settled. 'One can imagine,' she wrote, 'the state of surprise in which I was left.'

Sunday came. Mademoiselle evidently could not contain herself, for she talked to Lauzun's sister, Mme de Nogent, with whom she had recently made friends, saying, 'You will have a great surprise within the next few days; I intend to marry and shall ask the King's permission tomorrow. Guess to whom?' Mme de Nogent guessed M. de Longueville. No, said Mademoiselle, and told Mme de Nogent to note all the passers-by; if she guessed correctly, she should be told. Never was a grown woman so transparently and happily excited.

But alas for her plans. Before Lauzun could arrive, she met the comte d'Ayen seeking the King's doctor and saying, 'Madame is dying!' Mademoiselle ran to the Queen, who repeated, 'Madame is dying, and do you know what she said? That she had been poisoned.' It appeared, from the Queen's account, that Madame was at St Cloud in her normal health; drank a glass of chicory water, and almost immediately cried out that her stomach was on fire, since when she had never ceased to scream. Mademoiselle was horrified; she remembered seeing Madame on her return from England 'looking like a dead woman, dressed and rouged,' and how she had tears in her eyes on taking her leave, and how they had all said that death was painted on her face, and how right Monsieur had been when he said that she would not live for long.

Still the Queen hesitated to set off for St Cloud, and resisted even the scandalised persuasions of Mademoiselle, 'What! would you let your sister-in-law die, only a league away? What will people say?' It was not until the King arrived that she consented to enter his coach. Mademoiselle, as a good Bourbon with a great sense of family solidarity (*nous, nous sommes de bonnes gens de notre race*), could not understand the reluctance of this vindictive Spaniard.

At St Cloud, they found Madame in a pitiable condition, although the doctors kept up their assurances that she was suffering from nothing worse than a severe colic. Mademoiselle alone seems to have realised the truth as she saw the tormented woman lying on a small makeshift bed, trying to be sick, her hair in disorder, her chemise torn open to reveal the extreme emaciation of her throat and arms, her face pale and her nose pinched, so that one would have taken her for a corpse had she

not been crying out. Mademoiselle could not speak for weeping, her sorrow aggravated by the indifference of the spectators,
some of whom were talking together, others coming and
going, and some almost laughing.

It were irrelevant here to pursue the story of those last
agonised hours. Madame expired at three o'clock the following morning (June 30th, 1670) and what concerns us now is the
repercussion which her death had, indecently soon, upon the
fortunes of Mademoiselle. She knew her world: even before
Madame had for ever quitted it, she had been filled with
gloomy forebodings. Meeting Lauzun as arranged at Versailles
on the Sunday evening, for their vital discussion, she greeted
him with the words, 'This is most disconcerting for us,' and he,
instantly taking her meaning, replied with unusual frankness
that he feared all their projects might come to naught. 'Oh,
no!' said Mademoiselle, 'not that, whatever happens,' but
she must have noted that this was the first time he had ever
spoken of *our* projects; hitherto it had always been *your*, as
though he were in no way concerned except as a disinterested
adviser.

Mademoiselle spent a sleepless and unhappy night, asking
herself, 'Supposing Monsieur takes it into his head to want to
marry me, and if the King wishes it, what shall I do?' It may
seem to our way of thinking that her apprehensions were somewhat premature, but at Versailles in the seventeenth century
the question of royal marriages was one of expediency rather
than delicacy. Mademoiselle had not mistaken her people.
The shrunken body of Madame had not yet been submitted
for autopsy under the surgeon's knife before a summons came
from the King. 'Cousin,' he said, leading her aside in the
Queen's bedroom, 'the place is vacant: will you fill it?'
Mademoiselle felt herself become pale as death, but replied
only that he was the master and that in all things she must
subject her will to his. He pressed her: did the thought inspire
her with any aversion? She would not answer, when, presumably taking her silence for consent, he said that he would

see about it and would keep her informed. Desolation in her heart, she had to accompany the Queen and listen to the only topic of conversation: the death of Madame, and the certainty that Monsieur would soon console himself with a new wife; everyone looked at Mademoiselle, who said nothing.

She had a word with Lauzun that evening. 'My loss is greater than anybody's,' he said; 'I am in the depths of despair.' Mademoiselle had time only to assure him that nothing would alter her intentions.

Strange man. Next day, as they both attended Mass, he said to her, 'Well, so you are going to marry Monsieur. You must; the King wishes it. I should be very glad, for I prefer your greatness to my own happiness and fortune. I ask you to give me an audience: shall it be in your own rooms or the Queen's?'

So far as one can interpret Lauzun's motives without any guidance from his own pen, one must conclude that here was one of the occasions when he really feared the King's displeasure and saw that it would pay better to keep on good terms with the Sovereign than to make himself master of all Mademoiselle's wealth and titles. He was not now playing his cat-and-mouse game with Mademoiselle: he was playing for his own interests. Their conversations, as reported in great detail by her, make one long consistent record of discouragement always on the same theme. The King wished her to marry Monsieur; she must obey, blindly. She must consider Monsieur's position: none but the King and the Dauphin[1] ranked higher than he; and as for herself, she would have no one but the Queen above her. The King and all the Court would attend daily upon her; there would be endless balls and fêtes of every sort. (Mademoiselle here interjected that she was no longer fifteen, to be tempted by childish pleasures.) She must forget the past, he went on, even as he had forgotten everything she had ever said to him; he thought only of his delight in seeing her as Madame, and of watching from a window as

---

[1] Louis, b. November 1, 1661, d. April 14, 1711.

she passed down the street, escorted by her guards . . . Mademoiselle went away to weep alone in her room.

Lauzun neither weakened nor desisted. 'I come,' he said, 'to beg you very humbly to hold no further converse with me. Monsieur, who does not like me anyhow, will attribute all his difficulties to me. Do not speak to me in public: I shall not answer. Do not send for me or write to me. It grieves me to use you thus, but I must for love of you, and you should approve.' Mademoiselle replied to these harsh words that she was in despair, that she absolutely refused to marry Monsieur; and then tried to counter one of Lauzun's arguments by one of those considerations which strike us as so absurd, especially coming in the midst of her very genuine distress, but which to Mademoiselle and her contemporaries bulked so large in importance. She would no longer be so great a lady as she already was, she said; all she would gain would be an escort of guards and a place at the King's table; people would no longer be allowed to sit in her presence; and when she went in the King's coach she would no longer have to sit on the *strapontin*. Even this, she explained, which to her mind was the chief of the four advantages (the *strapontin* for a person of Mademoiselle's size must indeed have been an uncomfortable perch on a long journey) would last only for a few years, because when M. le Dauphin was married (he was then eight) his wife would take precedence, and so would the King's daughter[1] when she was grown up. More sensibly she added that Monsieur was younger than she (he was, by thirteen years) and that she was no better disposed than the late Madame to play second fiddle to the chevalier de Lorraine or any other favourite who might succeed him.

Nothing that she could say made any effect on Lauzun. He repeated only that she must obey the King, and that he would not speak to her any more. 'But do at least give me time,' said poor Mademoiselle, 'and say that you will speak to me when

[1] Marie-Thérèse, *b.* 1667, *d.* 1672. Two elder daughters, Anne Elisabeth and Marie Anne, had both died as babies.

this affair is broken off; I should be in despair if you would not.' 'Farewell,' he said; and she, 'Do not go away! What! I shall speak with you no more?' But he only advised her to retire to Forges, as was her custom at that time of year. Mademoiselle went away in tears, but she did obtain the King's permission to go to Forges, giving her promise that on her return she would ascertain Monsieur's wishes and would be governed by the King's dictate.

Mademoiselle's love-affair, which had started off with such impetuosity when realisation first came to her, now seemed sadly to be hanging fire. On the whole, for someone normally so clumsy, she managed the King with some skill, always asserting her readiness to comply, even going to the length of pretending an eagerness she was far from feeling (she was shrewd enough to discern that resistance would only arouse his obstinacy) and contriving in the end to put the matter on a joking footing between them. 'Well, Sire,' she would say to him, 'how is my marriage getting on?' and Louis would laugh and say she never gave it a thought. Laughter and good-humour prevailed; he would chaff her, when the Queen, puzzled, would ask what they thought they were about. We may wonder, indeed, whether some inkling of the truth had dawned upon the King, for one day he startled her by saying, 'By the way, is it true that at the time Madame died you were intending to ask my consent to your marriage?' The Queen said, 'What is the meaning of this?' and Louis laughed and said he had no idea: was it to M. de Longueville? And if not, said the Queen, to whom, then? for Mademoiselle could only marry a prince. Mademoiselle, emboldened by this friendly and intimate chatter, replied that she had it in her power to make a greater nobleman than any younger son of the house of Lorraine, whenever she pleased, and to give a more valuable servant to the King than M. de Guise; and, she added, since his Majesty had given his consent to the marriage of her sister with M. de Guise, she hoped that she might herself do as she pleased without opposition from him. These were brave words, and she must have held her breath for the explosion of wrath which might follow, but the King said, 'Most certainly; I will let you do whatever you like and shall never coerce anybody.'

It seems strange that she should not immediately have hurried off to impart this highly-significant remark to Lauzun; she herself gives no explanation for her reticence, but one may read between the lines of her Memoirs that at this time she was both hurt and annoyed at his continued avoidance of her company. Probably her natural loyalty forbade an outspoken criticism, since, although she expressly says somewhere that she wrote her Memoirs for her own eyes alone, she did have to get them transcribed from her own disorderly pages by another hand. Possibly also, such is the intricacy of the human heart, her love was too great to admit more than an implied acknowledgment of disapprobation. She was always far readier to make excuses for Lauzun than to blame. Censure of the beloved can sometimes prove too unbearably revealing. An unusual note of sarcasm, however, is apparent as she makes her way towards the Queen's apartments and meets Lauzun emerging from his room to attend the King's *lever*. 'As he saw that no one was about, he followed me, for we were going in the same direction. "You are very bold in venturing to speak to me," I said; "it is true that no one sees us." "Where are you going, so early in the day?" "You can very well see for yourself," I replied, "and now tell me something about my affairs: am I soon going to marry Monsieur?" "I believe so," he answered; "everyone says that you are set on it and urge the King daily. But ought you to be talking to me, when you have just come from Confession and are about to communicate?" "Oh, as for you, I shall talk to you whenever I like; the way you treat me leaves me with no scruples." "I don't understand," he said. "I understand very well, and I hope you will soon understand better, for I am sick of all this (*fort lasse de tout ceci*)." He said no more, but went his way and I went mine.'

Still they met from time to time in public; he would neither speak to her nor look at her. Once the ribbon of her cuff came undone; she asked him to tie it up; he replied that he was too clumsy. Mme de La Vallière had to do it.

Mademoiselle could not go on like this, it was not to be expected of a woman of her mettle. She tackled the King, and told him that although she respected Monsieur as her duty bade (which was perhaps putting it euphemistically, since she had recently been assured by M. de Beuvron, one of Monsieur's favourites, that neither he nor the chevalier de Lorraine would have any objection to their union, in fact would prefer it to a marriage with some impoverished German princess from which they would profit less) and was duly grateful for the honour the King had wished to confer on her, a thousand reasons would prevent her happiness, as His Majesty must well know, and that consequently she begged him to let her hear no more about it. The King, who on the right occasion could be a most amiable ogre, took it well, and promised to inform his brother.

Mademoiselle now saw her way opening clearly before her, and, however recalcitrant Lauzun might still be, in her blinding passion she had no intention of letting him escape. Here, again, it is impossible to resist the impression that he did not want to be finally caught and that her pursuit alarmed him more and more as it threatened to draw towards its close. It might amuse and flatter him to see Mademoiselle at his feet: he preferred her there than in his arms. Were he not, frankly, so contemptible a cad, one could almost feel some sympathy with his panic and his well-nigh comical struggles at evasion. There was no need for Mademoiselle to announce that thanks be to God the affair with Monsieur was broken off: he knew it already, in that Court which was a sounding-board for everything that happened as for a great deal that did not. After imploring Mademoiselle not to be hasty, a plea she had heard from him many times before, he ended by declaring himself so greatly troubled by all this that he felt almost inclined to beg her never to mention the subject to him again. The more he dissuaded her, the more she persisted in her demands for his advice.

Thursday . . . They were both at the Queen's after supper. She called him to her: 'I am determined to tell you who I have in mind.' He said, 'Wait until tomorrow'—anything for a reprieve. 'I cannot,' said Mademoiselle, who was superstitious, 'tomorrow will be Friday.' 'Ah, but I shall not be able to tell you my thoughts face to face.' 'If there were a writing-table,' she said, 'I would write it down. Look, I will breathe upon this mirror and will write on that.' Still he put her off, until, hearing a clock strike midnight, she said, 'It is no good now, for it is Friday.'

Mademoiselle may recount the sequel in her own words, lest her biographer be suspected of adding some imaginary detail to the reconstruction of this scene from the past:

'Next day, I wrote at the top of a sheet of paper: It is you. I sealed it, and put it in my pocket. I did not see him until supper-time. I said, "I have got the name in my pocket, but I don't want to give it you on a Friday." He said, "Give it to me; I promise to put it under the head of my bed and not to open it until midnight has struck; you may well believe that I shall not sleep and shall impatiently await the hour. I am going to Paris tomorrow [the Court was at St Germain] so I shall not be back till very late." "Very well, I will wait until Sunday."

'On Sunday, I saw him at Mass. He came after luncheon to the Queen's; he talked with me in the [Queen's] circle. When the Queen had gone away to her prayers, I stayed with him near the fire. I took out the sheet where there was only the one word which said so much; I showed it to him; I put it back into my pocket; I put it into my muff. He was urging me to give it him, saying that his heart was beating and that he knew what that meant. We spent half an hour in a rather embarrassing conversation, and, before giving it to him, I told him to write his answer as he thought best on the same sheet, and that in the evening at the Queen's we would speak together.

'They came to say that the Queen was going to the Récollets; I followed her; I prayed somewhat absent-mindedly, but I did pray with all my heart. It was a very cold day. When we came back, the Queen went to M. le Dauphin's [room] as was her habit; she went straight up to the fireplace. M. de Lauzun came after a moment and approached me. We did not dare speak to one another or even to look at each other. I went down on my knees to get warmer. He was very near me; I said, without looking at him, "I am frozen with the cold." He said, "I am even more frozen by what I have seen, but I am not fool enough to be taken in: I see clearly that you are poking fun at me." I said, "Nothing could be more serious or more resolute." We said nothing more.

'In the evening, after supper, he drew near to me two or three times, but I had not the strength to go up to him nor he to me. He gave me back my letter; I leant on him as I rose to my feet. I put the letter into my muff. The Queen went to see M. d'Anjou [her son, aged two] and meanwhile I went to read my letter in a closet belonging to the maréchale de La Motte. I cannot remember the exact words, but to put it briefly he complained that his zeal in my service should have been rewarded by so cutting a mockery, and that he could not flatter himself by thinking that I meant it seriously; therefore he could not answer otherwise, but that I should always find him submissive, so great was his devotion to my wishes. It was a very cautious letter, but through it all I could see what I wanted to see.

'Next day, Monday, we went to Versailles; in the morning, before leaving, I was near the door of the Queen's room; Charost and the comte d'Ayen came to speak to me. He [Lauzun] was near a mirror, and kept apart. I called him and said, "Really, it is very boorish of you not to come near people." He answered, "How was I to know that you had not some business with these gentlemen?" I walked up and down; the others went away; he remained. I asked him, "Are we not going to talk together at Versailles?" "How can one talk to people who make a fool of one?" I said, "It is you who are making a fool of me: you know very well that I mean it seriously."'

Still he continued to avoid her, and she could not get a word with him in private, but he could not escape her for ever, at such close quarters, she in attendance on the Queen, he on the King, and the next day at Versailles she pinned him down. 'I am surprised by your lack of alacrity; I am not like you; I am most impatient.' She sent her maids to go and look out of the window, while she and Lauzun walked up and down together for nearly three hours. It was almost his dying struggle: she had grassed her fish upon the bank. 'I am not so complacent as to credit the possibility you do me the honour to suggest, but if it amuses you to make me answer, I must obey. I will therefore speak as though I believed that which I am not willing to believe: what then! you want to marry a servant of your first cousin? Nothing on earth would make me give up my commission; I love the King so much that I would not desert him for all the honour you wish to do me . . . I am no prince; as for being a gentleman, I think I am that; but it is not good enough for you.' Mademoiselle said that she was quite satisfied: she could make him the greatest nobleman in the realm, with all the fortune and titles she could give him. Lauzun, seeing his path blocked in that direction, turned to a denigration of his own character; he was, he said, the most taciturn of men, whereas she appeared to enjoy conversation. He would shut himself up for three and four hours alone in his room, and would murder his valet if he dared to come in. In addition, his devotion to the King was so great that nothing would be left over for his wife if he had one, thus he would be an absentee husband, and not a very amusing one even when he was there. As for women, he hated them now as much as he had once loved them, and would have all the difficulty in the world in resuming the habit. As for ambition, he had none. After all that, did she still want him? 'Yes, I still want you.' 'Is there nothing in my person which displeases you? for that must be taken into consideration.' She said, 'You are joking; you have pleased people only too well in the course of your life; but what about me? Can you find anything in my face which dissatisfies you? I don't think I have any exterior defect except my teeth, which are not good; but that is a defect common to my race, and that race may be the excuse.' 'Naturally,' he said. Exasperated, she exclaimed, 'Answer me!' 'I shall only tell you about my faults, to show you that I know myself.' 'You have none.' He said that if she insisted on liking his faults, he had nothing further to say; but as he was neither mad nor self-delusive, the stronger her assurances the weaker his belief.

'I half-killed myself, trying to persuade him,' says Mademoiselle, but she was so cold that she could not continue, and her unfortunate maids who were still at the window and whose conversation had been neither so absorbing nor so heated, were visibly perished. 'Mesdemoiselles, I hope you are warm?' said Lauzun very amiably. They did not think this quip at all funny.

We are no nearer to the workings of Lauzun's mind. Did he really wish to dishearten Mademoiselle, or was he still playing for safety? In either case he had no right to say to her that at moments he allowed his happiness to overwhelm him, and then to take it back immediately. She, meanwhile, did all she could to enter into his interests; she had always known how close his company of guards was to his heart, closer than anything save the King; unfeminine she might be, but she was woman enough to lead him on into telling her about them. Here, his boyish enthusiasm betrays no insincerity. 'My company will look very fine at the March review,' he said to her; 'the four brigades must be mounted on Spanish horses, Barbs, geldings, Croatians; all the men must have new leather jerkins with sleeves bedizened in gold and silver.' 'They must all have white and green feathers, and flame-coloured ribbons,' cried Mademoiselle, 'and next year your retinue will be even finer than this, for the rugs over your mules and their housings will be covered with *fleurs de lys*. Unlike my sister, who adopted the livery of M. de Guise without putting her cognizances on it, you shall be welcome to take both my cognizances and my livery.' He rejoiced to see the interest she took in his company of guards, and said to her quite kindly, 'The King will say, My cousin cares for it as much as you do.'

Mademoiselle to the King:

'Your Majesty will be surprised by the favour I wish to ask; it is for leave to marry. Sire, by my birth and by the honour of being your first cousin I am so much above everybody else that I ought to be content as I am . . . My present lot is a happy one, but I am convinced that it could be even happier. The wish to marry is so usual, that I think no one could be blamed for holding it. It is upon M. de Lauzun that my eyes have fallen . . . I believe that God desires me to find my salvation in this state; it seems to me that the whole peace of my life depends upon it, and that without it I shall never know peace. Therefore I ask Your Majesty, as the greatest favour you could ever accord me, to grant me this consent.'[1]

---

[1] Mademoiselle kept no copy of her letter, being afraid that someone might come in while she was writing it and might suspect what she was doing. The extract given above was thus written from memory. She says, as we readily believe, that the original letter was longer and couched in even more urgent terms.

The full text, as she remembered it, is given in French in Appendix V, p. 350.

CHAPTER X

M. de Lauzun and Mademoiselle
[1670–1671]

Mme de Sévigné to M. de Coulanges, at Lyon:
Paris, Monday 15th December, 1670

I am about to tell you the most astonishing thing, the most surprising, the most marvellous, the most miraculous, the most triumphant, the most bewildering, the most unheard-of, the most singular, the most extraordinary, the most unbelievable, the most unexpected, the greatest, the smallest, the most unusual, the most common, the most dazzling, the most secret until today, the most brilliant, the most enviable; in short, a thing whose parallel is only to be found in bygone centuries, and even this comparison is not exact; a thing which we cannot credit in Paris, so how can it be credited at Lyon? a thing which makes everybody cry Mercy on us! a thing which fills Mme de Rohan and Mme de Hauterive with delight; a thing, finally, which will take place on Sunday, when those who witness it will think their eyes have tricked them; a thing which will take place on Sunday and which will perhaps not have taken place by Monday. I cannot bring myself to give it away; guess; I give you three guesses. Do you give it up? Well! then I must tell you: M. de Lauzun is going to marry, on Sunday, at the Louvre, guess who? I give you four guesses, I give you ten, I give you a hundred. Mme de Coulanges says, 'That's easy; it is Mme La Vallière—Not a bit of it, Madame.—Then it is Mlle de Retz?—Not a bit of it; how provincial you are.—Ah! you say, how silly we are, it is Mlle Colbert.—Even less likely.— Then it must assuredly be Mlle de Créqui?—No, you have not got it. So in the last resort I must tell you: M. de Lauzun is marrying on Sunday, at the Louvre, with the King's consent, Mademoiselle, Mademoiselle de ... Mademoiselle ... guess the name: he is marrying Mademoiselle, my faith! by my faith! my sworn faith! Mademoiselle, the Grande Mademoiselle, Mademoiselle daughter of the late Monsieur, granddaughter of Henri IV, Mlle d'Eu, Mlle de Dombes, Mlle de Montpensier, Mlle d'Orléans, Mademoiselle, first cousin of the King, Mademoiselle destined to the Throne, Mademoiselle the only match in France worthy of Monsieur ...[1]

The three days of December 16th, 17th and 18th (1670) were the happiest of Mademoiselle's life. She says so herself. Everything had not gone quite with that rush her impatient nature and belatedly unleashed passion desired; she had yet to learn that miracles do not happen overnight; but at last, at long last, she could walk openly with Lauzun as her accepted lover at her side. She had had to earn her happiness by a final fretting delay: the King's answer to her letter, although prompt, disappointed her; he had not expressed delight at her idea; he said he had read it with surprise, begged her to think it over and to do nothing rash; he did add that he loved her and would never go against her wishes, which, as Lauzun rather too reasonably remarked, was as much as she could expect, considering that what she proposed was a thing she ought not to do. From Lauzun, indeed, she received little support. Even when he agreed that she must personally seek out the King, he advised her to say, 'Sire, short-lived follies are the best and I have changed my mind.' 'What! do you really want me to tell him that?'

Armed only with this laggard backing, she awaited the King in the Queen's bedroom. He had been at the gaming-tables, and by two o'clock in the morning had not yet returned. The Queen had gone to bed, and can scarcely be blamed for saying that Mademoiselle must have something very important on

[1] The French text of this famous letter is given on p. 351, Appendix VI.

278

her mind to stay so late. In came the King: 'You are up very late, cousin?' 'I must speak to Your Majesty.' Mademoiselle might have shown a little more tact in her choice of the hour and the occasion: the King said he had the vapours and must lean up against something; Mademoiselle ('my heart was beating') had no intention of letting him off and embarked on a long speech about her love for M. de Lauzun, 'a thing such as I would not have believed in, once, but everything changes,' and about everything she could do for him to render him a suitor worthy of her hand. Louis must really have been remarkably good-natured, not to send her packing, at that hour of the morning, tired and unwell as he was; instead, he repeated only that he loved her, that she was old enough to know her own mind, that he begged her to reflect carefully, keeping her own counsel meanwhile since there were many people who had no love for M. de Lauzun, and that he would neither advise nor forbid the marriage. When she would have kissed his hands, he embraced her, and so they parted.

'So many things happened at that time,' says Mademoiselle, 'that I do not remember very precisely.' What she did remember, and recorded with pathetic fidelity, were the occasions when Lauzun either hurt her feelings, as for example when he sent her a message through his sister to the effect that after their marriage he would prefer to keep his own room at the Tuileries instead of moving to join her at the Luxembourg, or cheered her by a pretended jealousy of M. de Longueville. The snubs and the unkindnesses occurred most frequently, and one winces on reading such phrases as 'I went very sadly away' (*je m'en allai avec bien du chagrin*), or (for she was, of course, writing in retrospect) 'When one dwells on a subject which has greatly troubled one, one is in the same trouble as one recalls it, especially when the heart has not changed but retains the same tenderness.'

Mademoiselle was altogether too impetuous for the calculating Lauzun. She should have known better than to cry out, on seeing him unexpectedly enter M. d'Anjou's nursery, 'Oh,

here you are! you had told me I should not see you the whole
day.' He scolded her (*il me gronda*), but she said, 'It no longer
matters much: everyone will know by tomorrow.'

What she meant by that was that four of their friends, the
duc de Créqui, the duc de Montausier, the maréchal d'Albret
and the marquis de Guitry, were about to wait upon the King
as a deputation representing in some sort the entire nobility of
France, which as a body would be honoured by the bestowal of
the princess's hand upon one of their number. Here was the
vital moment, when the decision would be taken. Lauzun came
to her, and, drawing her aside into a window, told her that the
King was in council; that the four gentlemen had gone in; and
that the King had sent for Monsieur.

The duc de Montausier came out first, a bearer of good news.
The King had listened; he had said that, since Mademoiselle
wished it, he could but consent; he had spoken with great
kindness of M. de Lauzun; Monsieur had flown into a rage and
had accused his brother of having manœuvred the whole affair;
the ministers had listened in silence; but with the King's
consent the thing must be regarded as settled, only, M. de
Montausier added, his advice to them was to delay as little as
possible, in fact to get married that very night.

The Queen came; Mademoiselle knelt before her, broke the
news, and was very sourly received. 'I disapprove strongly,
cousin, and the King will never agree.' 'He does agree, madame;
the matter is decided.' Maria Teresa gave herself away completely: 'You would do far better never to marry and to keep
your fortune for my son Anjou.' Mademoiselle was deeply
shocked. She rose to her feet: 'Ah, madame, what sentiments
Your Majesty reveals! they make me feel ashamed for you and
I shall say no more.' Lauzun comforted her; he even took her
hand, telling her not to worry: the Queen and Monsieur could
not govern the King. But the Queen continued to sulk,
refusing to speak to Mademoiselle, and Montausier told them
that Monsieur had made a terrible scene (*Monsieur avait été
faire un vacarme au roi*). What neither Mademoiselle nor Lauzun

knew was that Monsieur had screamed that Mademoiselle ought to be put in a mad-house and Lauzun thrown out of the window. Their friends were evidently uneasy without liking to say so in so many words; the comte de Rochefort added his supplications to Montausier's: 'In God's name, get married today rather than tomorrow; at this peak of your happiness you have everything to fear.' He looked at them both, and said, 'I have never seen people look so happy. I wish you could see yourselves in a glass, contentment and joy are painted on your faces.' Mademoiselle said she was sure she had more cause for it than M. de Lauzun. As he remained silent, Rochefort exclaimed, 'What! such pretty things said to you, and you don't echo them?' Lauzun was in one of his curmudgeonly moods. 'My good fortune has not turned my head, so I shall neither utter foolish things nor commit them.'

In spite of Mademoiselle's declaration that these were the happiest days of her life, there must have been moments when clouds passed across the brilliance of her heaven. She asked no better than that the marriage should take place quickly and quietly, without informing anyone but the King, when they would suddenly reappear as duc et duchesse de Montpensier. Montausier and Lauzun had come early to visit her; she had had a bad night, being troubled by the vapours, and was asleep when they arrived. Unwilling that Lauzun should see her with her hair in disorder, she put on a mob-cap before allowing them to be admitted. Lauzun, lounging against a bed-post, was examining the pictures hanging in the *ruelle*. This was too much for Montausier, who lost his temper (*se mit en colère contre lui*) and upbraided him, saying, 'Are you thinking of setting up a picture-shop, instead of getting married? In your situation you have something better to do than to gaze at paintings. Come now: you have no time to lose . . . Where will you marry? at Eu? or at St Fargeau?' This startled Lauzun into exclaiming, 'Oh, no! it would be much too far. Fancy leaving the King for three whole days! It must be somewhere that enables me to return on the morrow.'

All the same he had allowed himself a slip of the tongue in answering Mme de Thianges, who wanted to take them both to a party: 'I ask you to let me off for the rest of this week; after that, we will go wherever you like.' They laughed at him for having said *we*. Mademoiselle, in high spirits—she had just cracked a joke with Mme de Thianges—was delighted. Credulous heart is easily satisfied.

'I present to you M. le duc de Montpensier, and request you in future to call him by no other name,' said Mademoiselle, bringing him to the assembled circle of Mme de Nogent, the duchesse de Gesvres, Mme de Rambures, M. de Guitry, and M. La Hillière. She was very well pleased; they had just been with her lawyers, who had called him Monseigneur; they had both seen the crescent moon on the right-hand side, which they regarded as extremely lucky. At last Mademoiselle's dream of heaping honours and possessions upon him was coming true: in addition to the Duchy of Montpensier she had given him the Principality of Dombes. The vast inheritance was rapidly passing away from the house of Bourbon to the *cadet de Gascoyne*. No wonder Monsieur picked a quarrel with M. de Montausier; no wonder the Queen, who had always coveted Mademoiselle's fortune for the sickly little duc d'Anjou, was annoyed, but the King rebuked Maria Teresa with anger and it was said that she had cried all the night long. Mademoiselle's star was certainly in the ascendant; she, also, had not been able to sleep, but for a very different reason. Whatever discussions might be going on behind the scenes between the affianced pair and their more intimate friends, however dilatory and ungracious the bridegroom, her triumph was externally complete. She found herself the centre of flattery and congratulation as the Court flocked into her rooms; she was the sensation of the hour; the excitement of Paris was intense, as Mme de Sévigné's letter alone attests. The Archbishops of Reims and Paris competed for the honour of performing the wedding ceremony; M. de Louvois came, smiling on the wrong side of his face, with three other ministers, Colbert, Le Tellier, and Lyonne; the duc de Richelieu threw himself at her feet; the maréchal de Bellefonds, kneeling, told her that every nobleman in the realm ought to kiss her footsteps; the duc de La Feuillade begged her to speak to Lauzun in his favour; the ladies swept deep curtsies; one of Lauzun's ex-lovers called her adorable; another kissed the hem of her skirt; they all kissed her hands; her rooms were thronged till the evening, when, exhausted, she ordered her coach and pretended to go out. An atmosphere of great geniality and even hilarity had prevailed (*on était fort gai et content*); Mme Tambonneau, that curiously independent figure in Parisian social life, to whom everything was permitted,[1] said to Lauzun, 'What a rascal you are! I should like to beat you.' Lauzun gaily cried out, 'Mademoiselle, come to my rescue!' He had had to submit to being thoroughly teased on the score of his past amours, which he did with not too bad a grace, though Mademoiselle exclaimed, 'Do not expect me to provide him with amusing companions who would not amuse me in the least.' Everybody laughed at her abruptness, and when they were alone he said to her, 'You told me that you would never be jealous.' 'We have said many idle things to one another, you and I; nothing could be further from my thoughts.' She wanted to keep him to supper with her, but he would not, saying, 'Supposing the affair were broken off after all? I must not presume in any way and must carry my respect to the furthest point.'

Mademoiselle could no doubt have done with a little less respect and a little more ardour.

Nevertheless, the marriage had now been all fixed and arranged to take place at noon the next day, Thursday, at

[1] This Mme Tambonneau who was rich and had a lovely house, managed to receive the best and most important persons of the Court and the town, without ever providing entertainments or giving them anything to eat. Princes of the Blood, noblemen holding the highest offices, generals, great ladies, were always to be seen there. She would not admit young people nor anyone she did not choose. She scarcely ever went out, but in her own house knew how to inspire the respect due to a queen. St Simon, *Mem.* I, II, p. 439. Edition Hachette.

Conflans, the seat of the duc de Richelieu. Mademoiselle, tremulous with anticipation, woke early, but before she could get up a visitor was announced, Mme de Sévigné, professional gossip, who made it her business to be abreast with the latest news. She found Mademoiselle in bed, writing letters; Mme de Sévigné knelt in that *ruelle* which always plays so much part in the chronicles of the time; she listened, all ears, as Mademoiselle told her of the fine gifts she had made to Lauzun and of the titles she had bestowed on him; full of tenderness, she seemed overjoyed (*transportée de joie*). 'My goodness, Mademoiselle, you do seem happy, but why on earth did you not conclude the affair promptly last Monday? Don't you know that so long a delay gives the whole kingdom time to jabber and that you are tempting God and the King by allowing so extraordinary a business to drag on for so long?' Mademoiselle agreed, 'but my homily made very little impression on her confidence.'

At ten o'clock Lauzun's sister, Mme de Nogent, arrived with the information that the marriage contract was not yet completed: the wedding could not take place that day. 'I felt as though I had been clubbed,' says Mademoiselle; 'it was like a precursor of what was to happen,' but with admirable courage and resilience—there is no mention of tears on this occasion, though Heaven knows there was cause enough for them—she replied, 'Then it must be tomorrow night [she means at midnight] for I will not marry on a Friday.'

Lauzun came, looking very untidy and slovenly, with red eyes and a terrible cold. They were alone. She told him to sit down, but he would not. Not in her presence. 'Oh, what a fuss: surely we no longer need to consider that sort of thing?' He started off on his usual tack about knowing the respect he owed her, and went on to ask her if she was sure she felt no last-moment regrets. Let her consider that by breaking off the engagement she would attract more approval than blame; even when standing before the priest she could still refrain from saying *yes*. Poor Mademoiselle. 'Please do not go on talking to me like that, but tell me whether it is you who feel regret and who no longer have any affection for me.' 'I am behaving as I ought to behave,' he replied; 'I shall only say that which I ought to say.' 'What then! do you not love me?' This piteous cry provoked merely the answer that he would tell her only as they came out of church.

She wept after he had gone away.

Worse was to come. At eight o'clock that evening word was brought to her by an orderly that the King commanded her to wait upon him presently; she was to go straight to his room by way of the *garde-robe*. 'Is he at the gaming-tables now?' she asked. 'No, he is with Mme de Montespan.' Mademoiselle turned to Mme de Nogent: 'I am full of despair; my marriage is broken.'

Once again we must let her speak for herself:

'When I reached the *garde-robe*, Rochefort came and told me to wait a moment. I could see quite well that someone whom I was not supposed to see was going into the King's room; then he (Rochefort) said, "Go in." The door shut behind me. I found the King quite alone, wrought-up, sorrowful. He said, "I am sick at heart over what I have to say to you. I have been told that people are saying that I am sacrificing you in order to make the fortune of M. de Lauzun, that this will do me harm abroad, and that I should not allow the affair to proceed further. You have every right to be angry with me; beat me, if you like. You could display no fury which I would not endure and which I should not deserve." "Ah!" I cried, "Sire, what are you saying? What cruelty! . . ." I flung myself at his feet; "Sire, better to kill me than to throw me into such a state. When I first told Your Majesty, and you had forbidden me, I would have put it out of my mind; but now that it has gone so far, to break off now, what will it look like? What is to become of me? And M. de Lauzun, Sire, where is he?" "Do not worry about him; no harm will come to him." "Ah, Sire, I have everything to fear for him and for myself, since our enemies have prevailed over the good-will you bore him."

'He went down on his knees also; he put his arms round me. We remained thus embraced for three-quarters of an hour, his cheek pressed against mine; he was weeping as wildly as I. "Ah, why did you give (me) time to think it over? Why did you not hurry?" "Alas, Sire, who would have mistrusted Your Majesty's given word? You have never broken it to anyone, and you begin with me and M. de Lauzun! I shall die, I shall be only too glad to die. I had never loved anything in all my life; I love and love passionately and genuinely the most worthy man in your kingdom. His advancement was my delight and the joy of my life. I thought I should spend what remains of it happily with him, honouring and loving you as much as he. You gave him to me; you take him away; you are tearing my heart out." I cried, "And if it does not make me love you less, it does make my grief the more bitter for coming from that which I love best in the world."

'I said everything I could think of to the King, most passionate and most laudatory for M. de Lauzun, most tender and most respectful for himself. I heard someone coughing behind the door into the Queen's room. "To whom are you sacrificing me there, Sire?" I said; "is it by any chance M. le Prince?[1] I cannot believe that after all I have done for him he would willingly be the witness of so cruel a scene, nor that Your Majesty would think very well of him for wishing to attack my life, after I had saved his, through his hatred for a man whose only fault is to depend entirely upon you. What, Sire? is M. le Prince part of the cabal of the House of Lorraine? They are at their height, and M. de Lauzun is rendering them a great service.[2] After this, what will Mlle de Guise not do against you? . . . Ah, Sire, I ask only one thing of you, which affects your greatness: to keep your word. What will they say abroad? Even if you were ashamed of the affair, if you did not realise what you were doing, if you had been persuaded to recant—great kings ought to abide by what they have done. There is far more shame in preventing me from doing a good action than in allowing it. Sire, will you not yield to my tears?"

'He raised his voice in order to be overheard. "Kings must please

[1] Condé.

[2] I cannot imagine what Mademoiselle means by this, nor how Lauzun could be rendering a service to the House of Lorraine by marrying her; unless she means that by her own marriage to a subject she was strengthening the position of her sister, whom the King somewhat reluctantly had allowed to marry Louis-Joseph de Lorraine, duc de Guise.

the public." "You are certainly making a sacrifice of yourself to them: those who are forcing you to this will deride you. I ask Your Majesty's pardon for saying so, but it is the truth." He answered, "It is late; however long you remain here, I shall not say more or otherwise." He kissed me, and led me to the door. I do not remember who I found there. I went away as quickly as I could to my dwelling, where I lamented aloud.'[1]

The three days of happiness were over with *ce malheureux jeudi*. Mademoiselle instead of setting off for her wedding spent the next twenty-four hours in a state almost of insensibility, without speaking save to ask where Lauzun was and what he was saying, and begging his friends (for she would see no one else) to look after him: *Ayez soin de lui*. She had seen him for a brief moment, when by the King's command he was brought to her bedroom by Montausier, Créqui, and Guitry. At the sight of him, her lamentations redoubled, nor did kindly messages from the King in any way appease her. 'He may say what he likes,' she said, sobbing with each word, 'I shall never be happy separated from him [Lauzun]' and turning to Lauzun she said, 'And you? you have enough strength of mind to make everybody think you indifferent. What have you to say?' Even if she did not inform us, we could guess what he had to say: if she would take his advice she would go next day to the Tuileries to thank the King for having prevented her from doing something she would have regretted all her life. 'I shall not take your advice; I shall spend the rest of my life weeping and hope only that it will not be very long. May I speak to him?' she asked the others, and, leading him into the *ruelle*, she

---

[1] Olivier d'Ormesson, in his *Journal*, confirms Mademoiselle's suspicion that the King had arranged for Condé to eavesdrop. He adds: 'Mademoiselle was very angry (*s'emporta extrêmement*) and said everything to the King that anger could suggest, abused M. Le Tellier as her enemy and M. de Lauzun's, and said a thousand things against the King himself, that he was a devil, which did not disturb the King at all; on the contrary, he comforted her, saying that he shared her distress.'

The abbé de Choisy, who was in her room when she returned to the Luxembourg, says that on her way home she was so distraught that she smashed the windows of her coach. He gives this description of her arrival: 'From the opposite end of the *salle des gardes* I saw the princess coming like a Fury, dishevelled, and her arms threatening both heaven and earth.'

said, 'What, shall I see you no more? If not I shall die.' He answered nothing, but in the midst of her misery she noted with pleasure that tears came into his eyes.

What could have happened during those three days to bring about so shattering a reversal? Louis XIV could be ruthless—what autocrat can afford to be otherwise?—but he was not wantonly or capriciously cruel. Although it may be true that he had never quite forgiven Mademoiselle for her part in the Fronde, his cousinly affection for her was sincere, even if tinged with amusement; and as for his feeling for Lauzun, we have seen ample evidence of a partiality amounting to love. Besides, it cannot have been agreeable to reflect that, as Mademoiselle had pertinently and immediately pointed out, he was breaking his word, a thing which a prince and a man of honour should not do—not, at least, in a private matter: it might be different under the exigencies of politics or public affairs. The fact is, that directly after giving his certainly somewhat equivocal consent, the King had found himself the centre of a storm of protest. The fury of Monsieur could have been foreseen; the Queen's attitude was already clear (both she and Monsieur refused to sign the marriage contract); they might be disregarded, as might the old Madame, Mademoiselle's stepmother, who from the depths of the Luxembourg dictated and signed a letter to the King; the opposition of Louvois, always at daggers drawn with Lauzun, was to be anticipated (it was rumoured that he persuaded the Archbishop of Paris to delay the publication of the banns); but when it came to the weighty intervention of Condé, and of the maréchal de Villeroy, the King's old governor who still retained some influence over him, and of Ministers of State and representatives of the Parlement, and the mounting indignation of the aristocracy, the middle-classes, and even rumbles from the proletariat,[1] then indeed it was time for the King to reconsider his decision.

[1] *Il (le peuple) était dans une dernière consternation:* Philibert Delamare, *Melanges.* Bibliothèque nationale, MS. française, 23-253.)

Aug 24.

I should thinke my selfe much
to blame if I lett this bearer see
you without a letter from me, I
know not whether the long time
we have been a sunder doth not
slacken the kindnesse you had for
me, I am sure neither that or
any thing else can alter me in
the least degree towards you,
deare sister be kinde to me, for
assure your selfe there is no person
living will strive to deserve it
more, then him that is and ever
will be most truly.
Yours

Charles II to his sister Henrietta

MADAME DE MONTESPAN

The Duke of Bucc

Madame de Montespan, by Louis de Châtillon
Stolen from an exhibition in London; present whereabouts now unknown

In order to understand this sudden tumult over a matter which may seem to us of the smallest importance—Mademoiselle was not even in the line of succession to the Throne—it is necessary to screw our minds round to a completely different conception of Monarchy, Royalty, and all that it stood for. It may be argued that the nobles, far from dissociating themselves as they did from the self-constituted delegation of Montausier, Créqui, d'Albert, and Guitry, should have welcomed the elevation of one of their number into the close, the almost sacred, circle of the royal family, all the more so that the King's avowed and most successful policy had been to continue Cardinal Richelieu's inroads on their hereditary, feudal power. Their willingness, nay, their inflexible determination to sacrifice the enormous honour offered as it were vicariously in the person of Lauzun to the whole of their Estate, must be accepted as the criterion, however astonishing, of their allegiance to the royal principle. They were pained, they were scandalised, to think that the King—the King!—should so far forget his sovereign responsibility. The *mésalliance* of a Princess of the Blood was a thing not to be tolerated by France. It might be a compliment to the aristocracy, but it was a lowering of the royal prestige.

Louis XIV had far too keen a sense of his own position as apex of the State to underrate the gravity of a general and gratuitous antagonism. Why should he wish to provoke a collision which could so easily be avoided? A wise man acknowledges the blunder which it is not too late to repair. And it was not as though some far-reaching question of foreign policy were involved, where the ruler might stubbornly pursue his own adopted course, confident in the long-sightedness of his vision; convinced, in other words, that he knew best. This was a purely domestic issue, to be settled at the cost of a woman's tears (but she would get over it[1]) and a man's disappointment (but Lauzun's loyalty was indestructible). The

---

[1] *C'est une fantaisie qui lui a prise en trois jours, et dans trois elle sera consolée.* But Louis denied that he had ever said this.

King, who was not accustomed to being criticised, would find himself reinstated in the popular approval, and all would go on as it had been before.

We may do Louis the justice of assuming that the thought of his cousin's distress was repugnant to him; he had known true love himself, once, and had known what it meant to bow to the obligations of rank when at the time of his Spanish marriage he had bidden farewell to Marie Mancini. In all his interviews with Mademoiselle he gives proof of a sincere regret, and indeed it would have been a hard-hearted man who could contemplate with indifference the sudden change in her, 'thin, hollow-cheeked, like a person who neither eats nor sleeps.' 'I am more sorry than you to see you in such a state,' he said to her; 'I know that it is I who am the cause of your tears, which are so understandable that I do not know what to say to you.' (Mademoiselle told him that he was like the monkeys, who suffocate their children in embracing them.) But—and I think this important—he had persuaded himself that he had a grievance against her, as people will readily do when they have a secret inkling that they are themselves in the wrong. It was thanks to the mischief-making of Monsieur, who accused Mademoiselle of saying to all comers that the King himself had arranged the marriage. Mademoiselle's vigorous denials made no impression; Louis preferred to believe, and perhaps genuinely did believe, that she had been guilty of the indiscretion. He might have known that Mademoiselle, whatever her faults, was at all times inconveniently truthful. Which was more than could be said of his brother Philippe.

There is a further story, perfectly credible in this Court of constant subterranean intrigue, to the effect that the old princesse de Carignan conceived the idea of getting at the King by a more devious but none the less cogent device of enlisting the aid of Mme de Montespan. The King's mistress had his ear: she should add her exhortations to those of the princes and ministers. Contemporary reports are contradictory; it is not clear whether Mme de Carignan went personally to see Mme de Montespan, or whether Mme Scarron,[1] at that time serving as governess to Mme de Montespan's children by the King, pointed out to her employer the danger she was running in espousing, as she had, the cause of M. de Lauzun. When the time came, as it surely would, for the King to regret having given his consent, what reproaches would he not heap upon her? It does not very much matter, since the result in the end was the same. Mme de Montespan saw the good sense of the argument.

It is possible that cupidity had already entered into Mme de Montespan's calculations. Her son, the little duc du Maine, was already in his cradle and Mademoiselle's fortune at some future date would be very acceptable for the royal bastard. Since Mademoiselle did, in fact, later make over some of her possessions to the duc du Maine, we may be sure that in her innocence she at that time suspected nothing of his mother's duplicity.

I have a fragile theory of my own, which I have not seen mentioned by any of Mademoiselle's other biographers, but which might account, though only partially, for the King's change of mind. The men of his family enjoyed a bad reputation for homosexuality. In his father's day, there had been the duc de Luynes; in his own generation, the amours of his brother with the chevalier de Lorraine and many others were a public scandal. Supposing it were whispered that in honouring Lauzun with his cousin's hand he was giving proof of too marked a predilection? Such a suggestion would be grotesque, of course; but Louis knew the world and its tongue. For what it may be worth, the theory does receive some support from a phrase I have italicised in the curious exculpatory letter addressed by him to his envoys abroad.[2]

Mademoiselle retained enough sense and pride to realise that the majority of the people who had crowded into her rooms with their compliments and congratulations, their

[1] Later Mme de Maintenon.
[2] See Appendix VII, p. 352-354.

obeisances and genuflexions, their adulation and wheedling, would now take an equal delight in her discomfiture (*bien des gens étaient ravis de me voir en cet état*). A few exceptions must be made: Mme de Sévigné, whom Mademoiselle had consented to receive during the first dreadful twenty-four hours, wrote a letter full of compassion to M. de Coulanges: 'I found her in her bed,' she writes; 'she wept afresh on seeing me, called me to her, embraced me, and bathed me in her tears. "Alas, do you remember what you said to me yesterday?" The sight of her weeping made me weep myself. I have been back twice; she is very wretched, and has always treated me as a person who sympathised with her troubles: she is not mistaken. On this occasion I have been aware of feelings one does not usually entertain for persons of a certain rank.' Mme de Scudéry, also, could write to Bussy-Rabutin, 'If you knew what a great passion can be in the heart of a fine person such as she, you would be surprised and full of pity. As for me, I have never had any experience of love, but I can understand that Mademoiselle is much to be pitied; she does not sleep at night, she cries all day; in short, she leads the most wretched of lives.'

Although she shut her doors to nearly everybody, it is harrowing to find her sending for Mme de Montespan in a desperate attempt to get her to intercede with the King. If Mme de Montespan had indeed played her false, and subsequent events leave no doubt of it, one wonders whether she felt any compunction on seeing Mademoiselle point to the empty place beside her in her bed, and hearing her cry out, 'He should be there! He should be there!'[1] For it was lying on her bed that Mademoiselle received the few people she either chose to admit, or could not refuse to admit, to the great amusement of Paris where the word went round that she was comporting herself like a widow. She could not refuse the Queen, who came but was at a loss to know what to say; she could not refuse Monsieur, who, sent by the King with instructions not to refer to past occurrences, talked of nothing but perfumes

[1] Mme de Caylus, *Souvenirs et correspondance*.

without getting much reply from Mademoiselle. Her step-mother and her sister both wanted to come, but she would not let them. She thought Mme d'Épernon wanted to come, but could not remember whether she said yes or no; in fact, 'during the first twenty-four hours I did not know what I was saying.' The King she could not refuse, but this visit was at least productive of one grace: he would not forbid her to see Lauzun. 'I have lost all my friends over this business,' she said to him sadly, 'they have all abandoned me.'

Paris might see nothing but the spectacle of a disappointed old maid making herself ridiculous; Mme de Sévigné, for all her sympathy, might compare the situation to a tragedy observing all the unities, only differing in that it had taken four days in the playing instead of the regulation four-and-twenty hours; but for us, privileged to read Mademoiselle's desolate words, there can be no question of her anguish. The phrases which poured from her pen long after the event prove by their spontaneity the raw vividness with which she was able to evoke and to relive the veriest detail of her experience. This is no worked-up hysteria, this is the clear ring of truth. Made-moiselle was no literary artist, and when she says that by dint of feeling too much she ended by feeling nothing (*à force de trop sentir, je ne sentais plus rien*), she is not making a telling phrase: the statement is authentic by its very simplicity. She need not have feared that her command of language was inadequate to convey her meaning: 'To understand my state,' she says, 'it is necessary to have been in it; this is one of the things one does not know how to describe.' The words burn.

Representations were made to her that she could not absent herself indefinitely from Court; Christmas was approaching, and she had now been for nearly a week withdrawn from the eyes of the King and the world. She tried to convince Lauzun that she would be showing the King a greater respect by sparing him the sight of an object which could only remind him of what he had done; but Lauzun, apprehensive of the consequences if she carried out her threat of never reappearing at Court, persuaded her after much haggling (*après avoir bien marchandé*) to show herself at the Tuileries on Christmas Eve. She began well, for when the Queen asked her how she did, she replied, 'Very well indeed,' but when they passed into the room where her fatal interview with the King had taken place, emotion overcame her and she had to retire into the recess of a window, too proud to make herself a motley to the view. Lauzun was very angry with her; he came to see her in her own rooms, where, in a state of collapse, she had had her laces loosened, and upbraided her as she continued to weep and to cry out, 'Will you not soon come back here?' 'No,' he said, 'not if you go on like this. If you want to see me, you must stop crying.' He treated her, she says, as one treats a child—a belated echo of the old grievance.

A few days later, she tried to run away from him to conceal a renewal of her tears, but he followed her saying that if she led him a life of this sort he would take care never to be where she was; he did, however, show some signs of emotion himself, so Mademoiselle, to please him, did all she could to appear cheerful, although her eyes were red and swollen 'as big as a fist.' She even tried to joke with him, when he took her to task for neglecting her appearance: people had noticed it, he said; why was she letting herself go like that? 'Because,' she said, 'I used to want to please a certain little man (I don't know whether you know him) and now people no longer want me to please him, so I no longer care.' Flippancy was no good: whenever she saw him she began to cry again. It was all very well for her to say that, so great was his power over her, she dared not cry when he looked sternly at her: she cried in and out of season. Even when dancing with the duc de Villeroy she stopped suddenly and burst into tears in the middle of the ballroom; the King got up and shielded her with his hat, saying, 'My cousin has the vapours,' while Lauzun, acutely embarrassed, disappeared into the crowd.

The only place where she could indulge herself was at the

Opera. Here, in the darkness of the Queen's *loge*, when all the lights were on the stage, she could gaze across the dim theatre at Lauzun in his box, and dream and weep for four hours without disturbance. (*Je le regardais; je pleurais tant que je voulais.*)

In the eyes of the world, Lauzun had behaved irreproachably as a courtier and a gentleman. No word of complaint or rebellion was known to have escaped him; he had bowed, as was his duty, to his master the King. For this he had been rewarded with the *Grandes entrées*, a signal honour which allowed him access to the King at all hours and in all places; with a present of five hundred thousand *livres*, and with the governorship of the Berri, carrying an income of twelve thousand *écus*. Mademoiselle congratulated him publicly, but added in a low voice that nothing the King could give him really pleased her: she would never be content until the King gave her to him. She was not well; her face was puffy and her hands swollen, but she made light of this, her doctor having assured her that she was not suffering from dropsy, condemned to die within six months, as some kind friends had reported to the King, but only from vapours of the spleen as the result of melancholy. She was far more concerned for Lauzun's health, touchingly anxious whenever a journey took him away. 'Remember to put on a skull-cap: the evening damp is mortally bad for the teeth; you are so liable to get your eyes inflamed; to catch cold . . . the air of Fontainebleau makes people's hair fall out.' That made Lauzun smile. He said that as to his reddened eyes, which she was always nagging him about, it came from sitting up too late; and as to his hair he had so little left that it was not worth bothering about.

Outwardly, she had resumed a more or less normal life, alternating between Paris, Versailles, St Germain, Forges; there was a suggestion that she should marry the Duke of York; the little duc d'Anjou died; there were the usual quarrels with Mme de Guise; in fact the year 1671 trailed away much as any other year before Lauzun had arisen like a volcano in her path. She was still mortally sad (*mon chagrin se renouvelait souvent*), but at least the King had not forbidden all commerce with Lauzun and she was able to consult him on every circumstance. His authority over her, almost the authority of a husband, gave her a mournful satisfaction; having been a law to herself for so long, she now enjoyed being ordered about by him; even when his counsels were not altogether to her liking, she had become 'so well accustomed that I could not do otherwise.' Should she write to her sister and her stepmother on the death of M. de Guise? Should she dismiss a servant? She turned to him so much and so often that he said laughingly it was a pity she had not had someone, meaning himself, to advise her at the time of the Fronde. It is evident that now, all danger of marriage past, he was willing to treat her more gently, less capriciously, on terms of a workable intimate friendship which, if it could not satisfy her, did at any rate act in some measure as balm on her wounds. It was even whispered in Paris that they were, in fact, secretly married (it had been stated in the *Gazette de Hollande*), and this rumour brought about a sort of happy complicity between them, for when their friends challenged them they would laugh (*on leur riait au nez*), and would reply only that the King knew the truth.

It is therefore the more curious, in these calm waters, that Mademoiselle should suddenly have been assailed by a horrible premonition without cause other than a few words carelessly dropped by M. d'Ayen on his return from Paris a day or two before. Mademoiselle and Lauzun were both at St Germain; she had spent the whole morning with the King, who had taken medicine; she made a habit of this, revolting as it may appear to us, because it enabled her to pass long hours in his company. She was profoundly uneasy, and told Lauzun without giving any reason that she was going back to Paris. 'What an idea!' he said; 'you came from there only yesterday; do stay.' But this time she would not listen to him. 'I don't know what ails me,' she said; 'I am a prey to such terrible sorrow that

296

I cannot remain here.' She went, weeping all the way along the road.

Lauzun's sister, Mme de Nogent, at supper in Paris that night with her and other ladies, was mysteriously called out of the room. Mme de Fiesque, returning after accompanying her, said to Mademoiselle, 'M. de Lauzun...' Mademoiselle thought he had arrived. 'Is that not like him!' she exclaimed; 'I believed him to be at St Germain,' and started off, laughing, to go and find him. Mme de Fiesque said, 'He has been arrested.'

CHAPTER XI

Lauzun at Pignerol
[1671–1681]

NO reason was ever officially given for the sudden and complete disgrace of the former favourite. The King's command was law; nothing compelled him to offer any explanation. Six years earlier, when it had suited him to get rid of Fouquet, some kind of trumped-up charge had been brought against the Minister of Finance before despatching him to a life-sentence in the fortress of Pignerol; Lauzun took the same sad road with nothing more than a suspicion as to the cause of his undoing. That suspicion, it is true, must have amounted to a certainty, but as Mademoiselle ignored it we must turn to other sources for this strange, ugly and very typical story.[1]

It will be remembered that Mme de Montespan had played an underhand part at the crisis of the marriage affair, of which both Mademoiselle and Lauzun were naturally ignorant. It would appear, however, that some inkling of the truth came to Lauzun during the following year, for, while preserving an outward show of amity, the violence of his abuse of Mme de Montespan behind her back alarmed his friends; nor did he confine himself to this measure of discretion, but spoke even within two steps of her, so that she could not fail to overhear.[2] By the close of the year, in November, if Philibert Delamare, Ségrais,[3] and St Simon are to be believed, he was in full

---

[1] Mademoiselle expressly says that she ignored the extent of Lauzun's hatred for Mme de Montespan. 'It appears from what people say that he often had differences with Mme de Montespan; I knew nothing about it and have taken no steps to find out, but I do know that they both caught fire very easily.'

[2] Mélanges, *Bibliothèque nationale*, 2325.

[3] Ségrais, *Mémoires-anecdotes*.

possession of the facts. To obtain them, he had had recourse to the traditional expedient of bribing one of her women. Now Mme de Montespan, naturally uneasy, made the mistake of bringing matters to a head by calling Lauzun into the privacy of her room and of telling him that she had done her best to secure the King's consent to his union with Mlle de Montpensier but that the King had refused . . . when Lauzun interrupted, flared up, and cried, 'You lie, *bougresse de putain:*[1] you told the King he could revoke his word for the honour of his House, as I know on good authority, for I pay my spies well.'

Mme de Montespan, after a show of reluctance, lost no time in rehearsing this interview verbatim to the King. She reminded him that this was not the first occasion when Lauzun had accurately repeated the actual words that had been exchanged between them in private. According to the princesse Palatine, she flung further tinder on to the flames of the King's indignation by asserting that it was not he, but Lauzun, who had fathered the son of Mlle de La Vallière—a wry twist, this, of one mistress making capital out of the supposed misdemeanour of another. The King exclaimed, 'Lauzun crosses me in every way'; sent for the delinquent; and ordered him to apologise within five days.[2]

A month later, Lauzun having merely presented a vindictive memorandum (instead of the required apology) to the King, found himself even further from Paris than his native Gascony. He found himself in the neighbourhood of Turin, the forbidding mass of a fortress looming on a hill above him. Around the coach trotted and jingled an escort of a hundred musketeers under the command of M. d'Artagnan.

* * *

[1] This, which most French authors would hesitate to print in full, is not an amiable term to apply to a woman.

[2] *Le roi, l'ayant appris, aurait imposé comme peine à Lauzun de donner satisfaction à la dame dans les cinq jours. Mais Lauzun, n'ayant pu s'y résoudre à cause de sa grande arrogance et orgueil, les cinq jours écoulés, le roi, se voyant désobéi et offensé, l'aurait fait arrêter.* Francesco Nerli, Papal Nuncio and Archbishop of Florence, to Cardinal Paluzzi Altieri, December 2, 1671.

What conclusion are we to come to about the mystery of Lauzun's incarceration? We can, I think, discredit Voltaire's theory that it followed on a secret marriage to Mademoiselle, which should have come to the ears of the King. If we are to pursue that line of argument, it would seem far more plausible that the King *feared* a secret marriage, with the consequent loss of all Mademoiselle's possessions to his descendants, legitimate or otherwise. After all, Mademoiselle never stopped telling him that her love was imperishable; she was far from having forgotten in three days; he knew her to be headstrong; how could he feel certain that, having failed to wear him down, she would not one fine day take the law into her own hands? The only safeguard was to keep Lauzun under lock and key. It is scarcely credible that the insults to Mme de Montespan should alone have provoked so severe a sentence, great though may be a woman's power over a passionate man; the most we may admit is that her expostulations came just at the right moment to tip the balance.

Mademoiselle had remained thunderstruck. That disastrous day of November 25th, 1671, dwelt in her mind as firmly fixed as the 18th of December, 1670: she wondered that the blow had not killed her outright. Meeting the King, who looked at her with sadness and embarrassment, as well he might, she could return his glance only with tears in her own eyes. She did not even know where Lauzun was; obliged to attend a ballet in honour of the new Madame,[1] she could think of nothing but earlier ballets with Lauzun there, and of how he was no longer there, but travelling somewhere towards an

---

[1] Monsieur had recently been married by proxy to the daughter of the Elector Palatine. When he saw her, he did not think much of her: it was very cold, she had omitted to put on a mask, and had been eating pomegranates which had stained her lips violet. Mademoiselle adds a charitable note: 'When one comes from Germany, one does not look French, but when she had breathed the air of France it was much better.' Moreover, she had made the mistake of arriving dressed in pale blue taffeta, a serious error in a Catholic country, for it was All Saints' Day—la Toussaint. Again Mademoiselle was charitable: 'Every country has its own conventions. As people wear a lot of furs in Germany, it had been thought that taffeta would look more French.'

unknown prison through the frightful cold and the snow (*un froid, une neige épouvantables*). It was not until Christmas Eve, as she lay resting in front of the fire before attending midnight Mass, that M. de Nogent brought her word that Artagnan's nephew, *le petit Artagnan*, had just returned to Paris after leaving the prisoner in good health, but at Pignerol.

Pinerolo; Pignerol. It was a grim citadel on a hillside, exposed to the cold winds of winter off the barrier of snowy peaks, and ironically enough had been captured for Louis XIII by Lauzun's own great-grandfather, the maréchal de La Force. The two rooms allotted to Lauzun were reasonably well furnished, but there were iron bars across the windows, an iron grating in the fireplace, and the King's instructions to the governor, M. de St Mars, were harsh in the extreme. Lauzun was to hold no communication with anybody, neither by speech nor writing; he was to be allowed neither paper nor ink; and for the first two months it appears that the unfortunate man had not so much as a book to occupy his time. Sullen and furious, he paced up and down his room, let his beard grow, refused to see even the servant detailed to wait upon him, burnt a large hole in the floor, and levered up some of the heavy planks with a log from his firewood. This brought an instant order from Paris: St Mars was authorised to threaten him with never being left out of sight; he was in any case to be visited frequently, and the floor underneath his bed regularly examined to forestall any attempt at escape. This constant supervision must have been particularly vexatious to Lauzun, who had always been in the habit of shutting himself up alone for hours at a time . . .

We must not linger too long over the details of an imprisonment which was to last for well-nigh ten years. Extremely well documented, thanks to the continuous exchange of letters between St Mars and Louvois, Lauzun's implacable enemy, we know much about the months and presently the years passed in successive phases not unusual in any history of captivity. First came the surly despair, accompanied by neglect of his person; then the complaints, real or imaginary, about his health; then the bouts of prayer, fasting, and piety; a sudden refusal to go to Confession at Easter, although warned that the consequence might be excommunication; then a piteous pleading for news —how was the King? how was Mme de Nogent? how was Guitry? was Mademoiselle married? 'Things which any washer-woman may know'—then a sudden return to piety, accompanied this time by a complete reversal of behaviour, docility in all things, an exaggerated courtesy towards the governor, St Mars, an apparent resignation which, one day, was to vanish in the flames and smoke of one of Lauzun's notorious explosions. For this cold yet fiery man had one sensitive spot; something which meant more to him than any woman except, perhaps, for a brief while, Mme de Monaco; a purely masculine fetich, closely involved with his devotion to the King; something more than a mere Court appointment; an irrational passion, a symbol, approaching a mystical significance: his love for his commission as captain of the King's guards. Of all women, Mademoiselle with her own martial tendencies, always happy in camp, loving the clatter, the plumes, and the bright accoutrements, could probably have come nearest to understanding it. She had always understood and flattered the soldierly side of Lauzun's nature, but Mademoiselle was not there; only the heartless man of iron, St Mars, who in all those years of reports and correspondence betrays not one impulse of sympathy with his prisoner.

Lauzun had been stripped of everything: his honour, his liberty, the warm favour of the King; his governorship of the Berri had been given away to the prince de Marsillac; there was nothing left but his company of guards, and that, despite rumours to the contrary, was still nominally his after one full year. It was not until the end of 1672 that Louvois officially notified him of the King's command. Lauzun was to be allowed paper and ink for once, to write only his resignation and to nominate his successor. Instead, he leapt at the opportunity and wrote a letter whose phrases scorch the paper even today: 'Nothing on earth could give me more pain than the order you have sent ... my life is less dear to me than my charge ... I know neither what evil has been spoken of me nor of what I am accused ... I implore His Majesty to take pity on a wretched man who would gladly seek certain death to please him ... If I am so unfortunate as no longer to serve His Majesty in the position in which I hoped to end my days, I will seize my *bâton* in one hand and the oar of a galley-slave in the other ...'

January brought the reply. Lauzun's humiliation was complete: in the presence of a notary he must sign a document declaring that he *voluntarily* resigned his commission for his Majesty to dispose of as best he chose.

This was the last straw. Touched as with a red hot iron on the one thing he really loved, Lauzun screamed that he would rather be hanged; that he was no criminal; that he had been thrown into a dungeon where he had lost his health and his eyesight; that if he gave his resignation 'like that' everyone would believe him guilty of treason to the State; he wept (*pleurant à grosses larmes*); and finally relapsed into silence lasting a whole week.[1]

We have had many hard things to say of Lauzun when, in the sunlight of the Court, he went from success to success, a brilliant officer in all the bravery of his velvets and ribbons, a dashing, slippery courtier pirouetting on his high heels, the *petit homme* as sharp and slender as a dagger. What of the emaciated, bearded, purblind man in the half-light of a dungeon, on his knees before a painting of the Virgin? The last word has not been said of Lauzun and probably never will be said. Supposing we had his private Memoirs, as we have those of Mademoiselle, or even some scribbled notebook, what revelation of doubt and disquiet might we not read therein?

[1] His charge was given to François de Montmorency, duc de Luxembourg.

They would probably prove far starker and less self-deceptive than hers. What paradox of a man pursuing lines of conduct which, had he but known it sufficiently, were obnoxious to himself?

We are constantly struck, in reading the memoirs or letters of the *Grand Siècle*, by the exteriority of these people's lives. Satisfied with the mundane and the superficial, excentric rather than eccentric, they went about their business of ambition, pleasure-seeking, love-making, even religious observances, all with the same veneer of zest but with remarkably little spiritual depth beneath. With Mademoiselle, for instance, since our concern is primarily with her, one always knows where one is and what her reaction is likely to be. She is predictable. Lauzun, on the contrary, might swerve off in any direction; he is the miscreant; he is amoral; he might turn into an Inquisitor or a saint.

It is true that he is circumscribed by the ethos of his day. He accepts the current values, abides by them, and acts accordingly. The King is the sun in heaven; Lauzun warms himself in the rays. The King is the fount of all bounty; Lauzun the candidate, the place-hunter, catches the drops in his extended beggar's bowl, his *écuelle*, shoving if necessary his best friend aside. It is not a very edifying portrait. But complex natures are not so lightly to be tabulated, indexed, filed and dismissed. It is just conceivable that Lauzun with all his faults—and they were obvious and many—may have been in the eye of God a valuable because so complicated a soul, unable to understand himself, baffled perhaps by many of the actions his outward self imposed upon his conduct and of which his deep conscience may profoundly have disapproved. How can we judge what unhappiness and guilt, scarcely self-acknowledged, may have risen to the surface during those hours of solitude locked into a cell alone with his bouts of religious fervour and his touch of madness—*son grain de folie*. When he scared Mademoiselle with reminders of mortality, he was not doing it wholly to tease. There is such a thing as being a twisted soul.

I shall probably not be believed (one seldom is, when one tells an unlikely truth), but on my honour I had formed my own estimate of Lauzun before reading La Bruyère's sketch of him under the name of *Straton*. I had pictured Lauzun as a Byronic character, if one can picture a Byron without physical beauty, without literary gifts amounting in their peculiar way to genius, without a European reputation for social and sexual glamour. I had tried to explain him to myself, and possibly to make him more acceptable to others in spite of his many faults. Imagine, therefore, my delight on coming across this passage in La Bruyère, which, I submit, might be applicable with slight adjustments to either of those two apparently disparate characters:

Straton was born under two stars, unhappy and happy in the same degree. His life was like fiction (*un roman*).

No, there was no verisimilitude in it (*il lui manque le vraisemblable*). He never had adventures; he had dreams, some of which were splendid and others ugly. What am I saying? No one could dream a way of life such as his. None but he extracted more from Fate. He has known both the extremes and the mediocre; he has shone brilliantly; he has suffered; he has led an ordinary life (*une vie commune*); nothing has passed him by.

Then, continues La Bruyère, 'he got himself respected by repeatedly telling people how clever and brave he was, and got himself accepted at the value he seriously placed upon himself. He said of himself, "I am clever, I am brave," and everybody repeated after him, "He is clever, he is brave . . ." An ambiguous character, tangled, shrouded; an enigma; an unresolved question.'

Meanwhile, during those four years, Mademoiselle had been leading very much her customary life. Although she had lost all real zest and enjoyment, she was too practical to follow her inclinations, which would have withdrawn her from the Court and its functions; having only one idea in her faithful heart, she decided that she must keep in the closest possible contact with the King. Therefore she appeared at balls and the theatre, and, more willingly, went on several royal progresses, notably to

Alsace and Lorraine, which she liked, and to the mountains of
the Vosges, which she did not like at all, partly because she was
lodged in a haunted house, partly because the peasants were so
ugly and all had goitres, partly because the food was so nasty
and tasted of dust, partly because for fear of the goitre she
dared not drink the icy water. She did, however, appreciate the
Rhine wines (though the crossing of the Rhine itself, over a
loose bridge without parapets, filled her with dismay), and she
did get the opportunity to bring in two or three of her little
nagging reminders to the King. (*Je faisais toujours ma cour avec
soin, et quand je trouvais moyen de parler de M. de Lauzun devant le
roi, ou de dire quelquechose qui l'en pouvait faire souvenir, j'étais
ravie.*) At St Nicolas, for instance, a place of pilgrimage, she
informed him of the local miracle: a prisoner of the Turks,
chained hand and foot, had made a vow to the saint, who then
delivered him. 'Sire,' she said, folding her hands as a hint that
she was praying him to perform a similar miracle, 'you must
go and see the irons of this man who obtained his liberty.' And
at Brisach, where they stayed in a sombre castle with grated
windows, she said, 'Does not Your Majesty feel suffocated? It
is enough to give anyone the vapours. For my part, anything
which suggests a prison gives them to me,' 'and I enlarged upon
the horrors of prison. He listened to me without saying a
word.'

She must have appeared to Louis as a walking reproach.

Once, and greatly to her amusement, Fate played into her
hands. They were received at Châtenoy by the chief magistrate
of the place, who many years ago had lived in Paris, and was
most eager for news of all his friends. What about M. de
Mortemart? he asked, and the children of the duc de Bouillon?
Finally he came to the inevitable question. 'And Puyguilhem,
Sire? I heard that he now goes under another name; where is
he? He was a good-looking young man, that M. de Lauzun as
he is now called.' No reply. 'Sire, do tell me about him. I was
very fond of him. It is said that many adventures have befallen
him.' They all looked at one another and began to laugh. 'Sire,

why does Your Majesty not answer, as you did about the others?
You were so very fond of him, when I was in Paris . . .'

The Memoirs of Mademoiselle during the years of Lauzun's
captivity make on the whole somewhat monotonous reading.
There was only the one thing which really monopolised her
mind, and for which she kept all her energies in reserve (*étant
aussi occupée d'une seule chose que je l'étais*). One has the impression
that she was flogging a listless and indifferent memory to recall,
often confusedly (*j'écris toutes les choses dont je me souviens, à
mesure qu'elles me viennent . . . Je m'écarte souvent des choses que
je commence* . . .) events which would once have bulked large in
interest and importance. Her sister, the Grand-duchess of
Tuscany, separates finally from her husband; the old Madame,
Mademoiselle's stepmother, dies unregretted; the King legiti-
mises his children by Mme de Montespan; La Vallière bids
farewell to the King and enters a convent; Mme de Longueville renews the suggestion that Mademoiselle should marry her
son, to which Mademoiselle replies that the desire to marry
does not come twice in a lifetime; Monsieur's daughter marries
the King of Spain; the Dauphin marries the daughter of the
Elector of Bavaria; she writes very civilly, 'which is not usual,
apparently, in Germany,' to *Her Royal Highness Mademoiselle
my cousin*; the scandalous affair of the poisons involving Mme
de Montespan, shakes the whole of Paris but not Mademoiselle,
who knows too little about it to make any comment; there is a
petite histoire de galanterie about the King and an anonymous
lady who, married to a jealous husband, wears emerald ear-
rings whenever she wishes to indicate to the King that the coast
is clear. And so it goes on. Mademoiselle mentions the various
campaigns and conquests of Louis XIV only casually and as it
were in passing; her interests were purely personal, and history
was not what she had set out to chronicle.

Those personal interests, however, were approaching a crisis
and Mademoiselle might begin to look forward to her reward

after the dreary years of patience and perseverance. So far as information about Lauzun went, she had had very little to go on. In the beginning, after that fatal night of his arrest, she had spoken with Artagnan[1] and had learnt something at first hand about the journey to Pignerol and about the state of mind of the prisoner. She had first caught sight of Artagnan on the eve of Twelfth Night, standing on guard while the musicians played before supper; she knew who he was, but was not acquainted with him; she feared to embarrass him by a summons, and confined herself to gazing at him, 'thinking how happy he was to have seen M. de Lauzun, and wondering [for he returned her gaze] whether he was saying to himself, "She envies me, to have seen him since she did." '

When, finally, she scraped acquaintance with Artagnan at Versailles by the simple device of pretending to feel faint and asking him to open a window for her, she carried away some rays of comfort to lay against her heart. Lauzun had spoken freely about her—Artagnan could answer for it, as he had travelled with him in the coach by day and had slept in his room by night—Lauzun had said how sorry Mademoiselle would be to see him in his present plight; that she had loved him greatly (*elle m'a fort aimé*), and that he did not believe she would ever change. He had said further that he dreaded (*je meurs de peur*) that they would marry her off, either to the King of England or to M. de Longueville; but, he added, he did not really dread it, for she took a resolve with so much difficulty that she was incapable of substituting another. All this was balm to Mademoiselle, intensifying, if further intensity were needed, her determination never to rest until she had obtained his release.

Having extracted all she could from Artagnan and also from M. de Maupertuis, another officer of the escort, she had to live as it were from hand to mouth on such scraps of news as

---

[1] This was the younger Artagnan, nephew of M. d'Artagnan who commanded the musketeers composing Lauzun's escort and who, incidentally, is the hero of Dumas' novel. *Le petit Artagnan*, as he was called, had also gone to Pignerol.

filtered through from Pignerol to Paris. She heard Lauzun had
been ill: this was an excuse for writing a note to the King,
asking for some relief in the prisoner's treatment. 'I made the
note as short as I could.' Knowing Mademoiselle, we may
doubt if it was as short as the King could have wished. Presently
she had an even better excuse for writing, for an event had
taken place at Pignerol which set all Paris in an uproar: Lauzun
had tried to escape, and had very nearly succeeded.

The truth was that under an apparent submission and
spasmodic returns to piety, Lauzun's mischief had not entirely
deserted him. He would consent to confess to a Capuchin priest,
but he would first pull the worthy Father's beard to make sure,
he said, that there was no deception. And of his real occupations
his jailer, St Mars, was comically ignorant. We have no means
of knowing how, or with what poor tools, Lauzun set about
his extraordinary excavations in walls and floors calculated to
yield only to the force of blast or pickaxe. We cannot know,
but we may be sure that it was not without a certain grim
humour that he embarked on the supreme Gasconnade of his
life. Liberty, yes; but also what a trick to play upon the vigilant,
unsuspecting St Mars!

It took him, we are given to believe, the best part of three
years. (If this estimate be correct, it would coincide with the
time he lost his precious commission in the King's bodyguard
and was at the height, or depth, of his despair.) He had already
had some practice. In the room overhead, served by the flue
of the same chimney, languished another prisoner, Fouquet,
the ex-Minister of Finance, who had been there in solitary
confinement ever since that ill-judged party at Vaux-le-
Vicomte. Fouquet's astonishment may be imagined when
one night a bearded and sooty figure scrambled out of his
fireplace and stood before him, a travesty of the fashionable
young courtier he remembered from the brilliant early days of
the reign—*ce pauvre Puyguilhem, qu'il avait laissé jeune et sur un
assez bon pied à la cour, pour son âge.* Lauzun was able to tell him
many things he did not know: how the King had smiled upon

him, how he had been made captain of the bodyguard, how he had come near to marrying Mademoiselle ...

St Mars remained oblivious of these nocturnal visits.

Encouraged no doubt by the success of this venture, Lauzun attacked the far more difficult problem of carving an escape hole from his own room. It follows the pattern of all frustrated escape stories: first the loosening and raising of solid floor-boards—no burning a hole in them this time, for St Mars to notice—then an investigation of the cell below, and the discovery that its window gave on to a deep ditch or dry moat surrounding the foot of the fortress. Lauzun could peer out, but he could not get out, for the window, like those of his room above, was heavily barred. We do not know how long it took him to cut through one of the bars, nor how long to secrete enough linen to twist into a rope, nor how long to excavate a tunnel through the wall of the moat, leading into a courtyard. We know only that one morning as day was dawning he let himself down for the last time—'and it was a miracle that he did not break his neck'—crawled through his tunnel, and came face to face with a servant-girl fetching wood.

He did what any sensible man would have done, short of knocking her on the head: he tried to bribe her. She replied that she was betrothed to a soldier; she would go and find him, and see if he was willing to connive at the escape. Instead, an officer appeared, shortly followed by St Mars, and the rest of the story may be guessed.

Two letters which Lauzun had left on his table, one addressed to the King and the other to Louvois, were sent on to Paris, together with a sample of his linen rope. This was handed round and much admired: 'It was most beautifully made.' Mademoiselle refrains from describing her feelings when she saw it, but perhaps our imagination can supply something of what passed through her mind.

It is not surprising to learn that this escapade brought about an increase of severity towards the prisoner. He was now allowed only enough linen at a time for his immediate needs; any new clothes he might order must have their linings examined; he was no longer allowed to receive books from Paris, lest they might conceal messages: any books he wanted must be bought by St Mars in Turin. What is far more surprising is to find that his sister, Mme de Nogent, and his younger brother, the chevalier de Lauzun, with their barrister named Isarn, were permitted to visit him a year and a half later (October 1677) in order to discuss certain family affairs and inheritances.[1] The interviews were to take place in the presence of St Mars and a police officer aptly named Loyauté; they might last two hours each, on four consecutive days; they must not be conducted in a low voice; no scrap of paper was to be passed to Lauzun; and Mlle de Montpensier was not to be mentioned on any pretext whatsoever.

It may appear strange that Mademoiselle should make scant reference to this surely revealing visit.[2] She must have seen Mme de Nogent on her return to Paris, bearer of the first personal account since the now far-off day of Artagnan and Maupertuis; and although it is true that she had begun to revise her opinion of Mme de Nogent, having come to the conclusion that she was *la plus grande comédienne du monde* and that Lauzun had been right in saying that if his sister thought he kept any money concealed in his bones she would break them, the opportunity of looking behind the iron curtain of Pignerol would certainly have been too great to be resisted. I think the explanation is that Mademoiselle interrupted the writing of her Memoirs immediately after Lauzun's attempted evasion (she breaks off in the middle of a sentence) and did not resume

[1] Lauzun's great-uncle, the duc de La Force, had died in 1675, leaving Lauzun as his *héritier substitué*, and in 1677 Lauzun's eldest brother Jacques had also died, leaving Lauzun as head of the family.

[2] All she says is that Mme de Nogent had been to Pignerol, stopping on the way at Turin to see Mme de Savoie and to ask for her intercession on Lauzun's behalf. Mademoiselle adds that Mme de Nogent had made herself ridiculous in a way that displeased her.

There was a coldness between them at that time, owing to a disobliging letter written by Mme de Nogent about Mademoiselle, which came into Mademoiselle's hands.

them till thirteen or fourteen years later, at which time by her own admission her memory had become confused and unreliable. It is therefore to the narrative of the barrister Isarn that we owe the graphic sketch of the scene in the room of M. de St Mars.

They had not been able to see Lauzun at once; he was suffering from one of the heavy colds Mademoiselle had always dreaded for him; but he now came in, leaning on St Mars' arm, bent almost double, staggering from weakness, dazzled by the unaccustomed daylight, his face half-hidden by his long beard, his eyes *remplis de tristesse et de langueur*. They offered him a chair by the fire, but, coughing, he turned it round to sit with his back against the painful light. Mme de Nogent wept; no one spoke; it fell to Isarn to break the silence with a dry legal exposition of the business that had brought them there. Lauzun made very few complaints; he told them not to worry about his health; if he looked ill, it was merely because of the cold and damp in his prison, where everything, even the bread, grew mouldy within twenty-four hours; he had no hope of ever leaving it; he would be quite content if only the King would deign to retain him in his charge of captain of the *gardes*; he trusted in the mercy of God and the King. He apologised for not understanding everything that Isarn had said, but having been shut away for six years and not having seen anybody or heard any news since 1671 (he did not even know whether his mother was dead or alive), his wits and his intellect had become too atrophied. Here he took out his handkerchief and buried his face in it; Mme de Nogent fainted.

For some reason unknown to us a considerable relaxation followed. Was it because Mme de Nogent, if she was really the *comédienne* Mademoiselle believed her to be, made the most of her harrowing experience in reporting it to the King? Whatever the cause, fresh orders were despatched to Pignerol: Lauzun and Fouquet were to be allowed to meet and walk together on the ramparts, with the sole condition that their

conversation should not be in private (this must have amused
Lauzun, thinking of his nocturnal expeditions up the chimney
flue); the shutters over Lauzun's windows were to be taken
down; the iron gratings might be opened during the day;
Lauzun and Fouquet might meet freely at any hour and
wander wherever they chose within the citadel (only under an
armed escort, with orders to shoot Lauzun if necessary); they
might eat their meals with the governor, even if guests were
present; they might write letters, of course under censorship;
they might receive and read the public *gazettes*. Lauzun learnt
by means of these news-sheets that his early love, Mme de
Monaco, had died.

These successive mitigations were not without bringing their
troubles. The old devil in Lauzun was not quite dead, and when
Mme Fouquet arrived on a visit with her daughter he could not
resist making love to the girl. This ended the companionship
between the two prisoners. Perhaps Lauzun did not mind so
very much; he may have got bored with Fouquet; he who had
always loved horses now had four horses to ride; his brother
came to stay at Pignerol, and so did Le Nôtre; he was allowed
a seal wherewith to close his letters (not knowing that St Mars
had a duplicate). The prospects of liberation might seem as far
away as ever, but at least he was not too badly off, and above
all he had been allowed to see his friend Barrailh.

This Barrailh, described as a *gentilhomme gascon*, originally an
officer in Lauzun's company, had long been Lauzun's and
Mademoiselle's devoted ally. They were fond of him for
himself, not only for the services he could render them, and
he needed indeed to be a man of remarkable tact, situated as he
was between those two firebrands. Mademoiselle pays tribute
to him with her usual frankness: 'When I lost my temper, he
would put everything right (*il raccommodait tout*); never was
there so faithful a friend as he, or one who knew so well how
to manage so ungovernable a person as I.' And when even
Mademoiselle's faith and loyalty wavered, as they sometimes

did, she could turn to him for reassurance. 'One wearies of everything, especially when one does not see the beloved, and when people come and say, "He never loved you; as soon as he was promised wealth and honours, he left you in the lurch (*il vous a plantée là*); the day the King broke off your marriage, he spent the whole evening calmly gambling; he had no thought of you.' People never stopped saying these things to me, so often that he not being there to defend himself, I don't know if my heart could have put up a fight against myself daily on his behalf, receiving no support from anybody, but Barrailh came to its help.'

To Mademoiselle, divorced for over eight long years from all communication with Lauzun, the visit of Barrailh to Pignerol meant everything. It meant not only that she now had a go-between whom she could trust, but also that the time had come when this true friend could be of very practical as well as moral help. Contact was established, and after the visit (February 1680) affairs began to enter on a new phase and to move rapidly towards the desired end. It was true that all Barrailh's conversations with Lauzun had taken place in the presence of St Mars, but what St Mars did not notice was that Lauzun had slipped a piece of paper into the folds of the fire-screen, and that Barrailh had similarly returned an answer.

We do not know what they had written, but we do know that Lauzun agreed to a scheme which had germinated in the crafty head of Mme de Montespan. Through the agency of Barrailh, he sent word to Mademoiselle that, so far as he was concerned, she could transfer some of her property to Mme de Montespan's son the duc du Maine,[1] on the understanding that her reward should be Lauzun's release from captivity.

The negotiations were long and complicated. They began with hints repeatedly dropped to Mademoiselle by Mme de Montespan to the effect that she should think over what she could best do to please the King and obtain the wish nearest to

---

[1] Louis-Auguste de Bourbon, duc du Maine, *b.* 1670, *d.* 1736. Married Anne Bénédicte, grand-daughter of le Grand Condé.

her heart. Mademoiselle did think it over. She remembered
Pertuis, a friend of Lauzun's, once saying to her, 'But you led
them to believe that M. du Maine would be your heir!' She
had noticed also that trouble was taken to keep M. du Maine
on the best possible terms with her; this was not difficult, for
she had always loved children, and she had a special affection
for the pretty little lame boy who had already had so much to
suffer in his short life. On the several occasions when he was
taken away to undergo some useless though painful cure (*après
lui avoir fait des maux extrêmes*) he would write her letters
which we may be sure she answered. Mademoiselle might be
naïve, but she was quite capable of putting two and two
together, and it was not long before she sent Barrailh to Mme
de Montespan with her proposals. They were explicit: she
would make M. du Maine her heir, provided the King would
send for M. de Lauzun and consent to their marriage.

It would be wearisome to follow in detail the path by which
Mademoiselle was first despoiled of her property and then
finally tricked. She was at the mercy of people far cleverer than
she. Mme de Montespan thanked her and flattered her in all
ways: 'I thought she was acting in good faith,' writes Mademoiselle. '. . . I took nothing but pleasure in her company; for
although her conversation is always delightful, it [the pleasure]
increased daily through the pains she was at to please me and to
say everything which could be most agreeable to me.' M. du
Maine was brought to see her; they had decided that, although
only ten years old, he could be trusted with a secret; he
thanked her very prettily. And one evening, after they had
been gambling for jewels at the Dauphin's, M. du Maine was
sent bearing a little gold cup studded with diamonds which
Mademoiselle had coveted as an ornament to put on her
dressing-table. 'All these attentions delighted me; when one is
dealing with an obstinate person, it is easy enough to keep her
contented and to make her fall deeper and deeper into the trap
one is laying for her (*de la faire donner de plus en plus dans les
panneaux qu'on lui tend*).'

M. du Maine, dutifully carrying out his mother's instructions, was probably less impressed by the promise of vast but
vague domains which he had never seen, than by the concrete
present his aunt, Mme de Thianges, had given him: a doll's
house as big as a cow-shed, all gilded, and populated by wax
models of himself, Mme de Thianges, Mme de La Fayette, the
duc de La Rochefoucauld, M. Bossuet who was tutor to M. du
Maine's own half-brother the Dauphin, and the two poets
M. Boileau and M. de La Fontaine.

Still Mademoiselle could get no definite promise from the
King; expressions of gratitude and vague assurances of goodwill were all that she could extract from him. Lauzun's name
was never mentioned. Questioned, Mme de Montespan recommended patience; an adept at the art of not committing herself
(*elle est beaucoup plus habile que moi . . . elle prenait bien plus de
mesures pour aller à ses fins que moi aux miennes*), she said first
one thing and then the other: she was sorry to say the King
would never consent to the marriage—what about the letter
he had written to all his ambassadors abroad?—and then she
would add that time might change all things. Mademoiselle did
not know where she stood. Mme de Montespan began gently
to press her: supposing she were to carry out her intentions and
then see what would happen? perhaps the King was as anxious
as she for the release of M. de Lauzun? perhaps presented with a
fait accompli he would say, 'My cousin has behaved towards me
in such a way that I have nothing to refuse her.' Mademoiselle, bewildered by all these contradictions and advice, had her suspicions.
'Supposing,' she said to Barrailh, 'after I have made my gifts, they
deceive me and do not let him go free?' She could not sleep
at night, for turning all these things over and over in her head.

Mme de Montespan, having prepared the ground, now
came a little further forward into the open with the suggestion
that Mademoiselle should make a donation of the principality
of Dombes and the *comté* of Eu[1] to the duc du Maine. Made-

---

[1] Mademoiselle had made over the *comté* of Eu to Lauzun while he was at Pignerol;
this explains why his consent was necessary. See p. 314.

moiselle, who had not bargained for an immediate transfer, exclaimed that she had only meant to leave her gifts by will; that her health was much too good for her to think of death; that she had given her word and that was enough. Matters again seemed to be at a standstill. But now, after much coming and going (*après bien des allées, des venues*), fair words began to be succeeded by threats. If Barrailh could not bring things to a head, he would be thrown into the Bastille . . . This frightened Mademoiselle into giving way, and in the presence of Mme de Montespan, Colbert, Barrailh, and a notary, the deeds were duly signed and executed. (February 1681.)

Colbert went to tell the King. Mme de Montespan, after expressing a thousand thanks, said to Mademoiselle that she could not resist telling her that she was about to become the happiest person on earth, to the discomfiture of all her enemies; the King would think only of how to manifest his gratitude, and a great deal more to the same effect. Mademoiselle listened, drinking it all in like incense (*cet encens me montait fort à la tête*), but her intoxication was shortlived, for on returning to her room she dropped, and presumably broke, her hand-glass of thick rock-crystal. 'I am frightened to death,' she said to Barrailh, 'lest it should augur my regret for what I have just been doing.'

She very soon had good cause to respect her superstition. It had entailed a real sacrifice to give away Dombes and Eu, for, as we know, she had a very deep-seated love for her properties and a very strong sense of possession; in fact, there was nothing in the world she loved better, with the overwhelming exception of Lauzun. Her readiness to make him master of all her dear estates had shown the measure of her love for him; the next best thing she could do was to barter them against his liberty. Eu, where she had spent so much of her time; Dombes, where as a sovereign princess she had been so warmly received! It now began to appear as though her generosity had been in vain.

Mme de Montespan implied by her urgency in seeking Mademoiselle's company for a walk—they were at St Germain —that she had something of good portent to announce. 'You were in no hurry to come,' she said, 'and I was in a great hurry that you should. The King has instructed me to tell you that M. de Lauzun is coming out of Pignerol and going to Bourbon.' What!' said Mademoiselle, 'will he not come straight here, after all that I have done?' and she began to cry, whereupon Mme de Montespan in evident irritation said, 'It is really very difficult to satisfy you: when you have got one thing, you want another.'

Joined by Barrailh, they went out into the garden, where Mme de Montespan continued, 'The King has told me to tell you that you are never to dream of marrying M. de Lauzun.' At this, Mademoiselle cried more than ever, and protested that her gifts had been made solely on that condition. 'I never promised you anything,' said Mme de Montespan, but Mademoiselle thought that she would have done better to speak the hard truth instead of flattering her with false hopes over a thing she so ardently desired and which she was now told to be impossible. Mademoiselle doubtless said a great deal more, and expressed her views at considerable length, for she walked Mme de Montespan up and down for hours—and Mme de Montespan was no walker. It is nice to think that Mademoiselle sometimes had her revenge.

After all this wail of misery and frustration, it is a relief to turn to the one thing in which Mademoiselle had been able to find some solace. It must be admitted that she was in many ways a hearty and unashamed materialist, glad to be rich, glad to indulge her taste for houses and for all pretty things. She patted herself on the back for the improvements she had made at the château d'Eu, and as for St Fargeau had she not redeemed it from the ruin she found and transformed it into the Baroque splendour it still is? It was not merely that she gave her orders and then left them to be carried out; she showed a personal

interest, exercised a constant supervision, and was perhaps
more determined to have her own way than can always have
been agreeable to her architects.

The château d'Eu was convenient for taking the waters at
Forges. St Fargeau had its charm, but it was a long way off and
Mademoiselle had no real taste for prolonged rustication. All
her life, she tells us, she had wanted a house near Paris, but
although she was always on the look-out and had been to
inspect many, she invariably found something wrong, either
in the position or in the building. But now, as though God
were willing to show her a little kindness in the midst of her
tribulations, she heard of a property for sale two leagues from
Paris, near the village of Choisy, on the Seine. There was no
house, but there were two little bits of woodland, and in short
the whole situation caught her fancy. Having bought it for
40,000 francs, she took Le Nôtre there, with a prepared design
of a house on only one storey. Le Nôtre—such is the way of
architects—immediately said that all the woodland must be cut
down. Mademoiselle did not like this idea, but there was worse
in store. In her excitement (*fort entêtée de ma maison*) she went
off to describe it to the King, who listened to all she had to
relate, and then tactlessly said that Le Nôtre thought she had
chosen an atrocious site (*la plus vilaine du monde*) whence one
could see the river only as through a dormer-window.

Mademoiselle incontinently sacked Le Nôtre (*je le plantai là*),
and engaged a less eminent architect, Gabriel,[1] who was more
willing to carry out her ideas. There is a note of defiance when
she says she got things done according to her own taste. (*Je fis
accommoder ma maison et mon jardin à ma mode*.) It was to be very
much *ma* maison and *mon* jardin, and *à ma* mode. All the same,
it would seem that Le Nôtre may have been right, for Mademoiselle's honesty forces her into a half-admission: the river
could sometimes be seen from the windows, but 'not at every
time of year.' Making the best of it, she explains that as she was

---

[1] Father of the more celebrated Jacques Gabriel and grandfather of Jacques Gabriel's
son Ange-Jacques, both of whom were associated with the building of Versailles.

building her house for the summer months only, she arranged for the river to be seen when the water was at its lowest; she could see it from her bed, and the boats passing.

It sounds very much as though Mademoiselle's swan had turned out to be a goose.

But what did that matter? She was inordinately pleased with it, and consecrates pages to its description. If she had chosen to read a book on architecture, she says, she could have written a very beautiful account, but that would have been an affectation she did not approve of. The house was small, but with an air of grandeur—*multum in parvo*. There were pavilions and terraces, flanked by the two little coppices she had saved from Le Nôtre; an orangery and a kitchen-garden; alleyways, by which she probably means pleached walks; fountains as many as necessary, 'but if I wanted more, I should have them.' One regret: Monsieur had told her that one could not give the name of *parc* to less than a hundred *arpents*, and the whole property including the house and courtyards did not run to more than that.

Indoors, there was a billiard-room, a gallery, and a chapel beautifully painted by La Fosse. The gallery was not painted, partly because it would have taken too long and partly because it would have smelt. (One can read between the lines that Mademoiselle was impatient to move in.) There was also a little room, decorated with small paintings of the King's conquests, by Van der Meulen, and in the dining-room hung so many portraits, of which Mademoiselle rapturously gives a complete catalogue, that either the portraits must have been very small, or the room very large, or the walls terribly over-crowded. The portraits included her grandfather, Henri IV, her grandmother Marie de' Medici, Louis XIII, Anne of Austria, her aunts the queens of Spain and England, and their husbands, her aunt and sister the duchesses of Savoy, a princess of Savoy, the duchess of Parma, the Infanta Isabella, Mademoiselle's mother and stepmother, her other grandparents M. de Montpensier and his wife Catherine de Joyeuse; the princesse Palatine; and the princes Henri, Henri-Jules, Armand, and Louis de Bourbon—le Grand Condé. Above the fireplace hung the portrait of Mademoiselle herself, holding the portrait of her father inset, in an oval frame. Every picture bore the name of the sitter, to instruct anyone so ill-informed as not to know it (*une ignorance assez crasse*).

The billiard-room contained other portraits, all equally distinguished; they included the little duc du Maine, fully armed, under a tent, with a battalion of Swiss guards of which he was colonel; and his brother the comte de Toulouse, aged two, Grand Admiral of France, suitably depicted as a tiny sea-god sitting on a shell on the waves. One wonders how he was ever persuaded to sit for his portrait, for Mademoiselle, describing him, says that although beautiful as an angel he was rather shy (*un peu farouche*), not being accustomed to seeing many people, and insisted always on being carried by his valet, saying, 'Picard, don't desert me.'

Mademoiselle evidently thought that she had dwelt too long on the charms of Choisy: 'It will be apparent, from all the details I have gone into, that I love Choisy; it is my own work; I made it entirely myself,' very much as she had said about St Fargeau. She was childishly delighted when the King gave her a boat, 'very pretty, painted, gilded, furnished in crimson damask with gold fringes.' In this she could go to Paris by water, and dine on board.

CHAPTER XII

The End
[1681 – 1693]

LAUZUN left Pignerol on April 22nd, 1681, ten years
and four months after he had entered it. Spring in Italy,
very different from that dismal December journey
through snow and gales. Still, in this season of hope, he was
not yet quite a free man: he travelled under the guard of M. de
Maupertuis and an escort of twelve musketeers. Nominally, it
was still as a prisoner who by the King's grace had been transferred from one place to another, that he arrived at Bourbon
ostensibly for the purpose of taking the waters.

Barrailh had proved himself invaluable in all the negotiations
preceding this prelude to release. He it was who had returned
a second time to Pignerol, taking with him a doctor prepared
to certify that Lauzun's state of health necessitated a cure. He
it was who had pleaded with both Mme de Montespan and the
King; he who had frequently pacified Mademoiselle; he, finally,
who with great ingenuity managed to establish a regular and
secret correspondence with Lauzun. It lasted from May to
November 1681, and it kept Lauzun informed of all events
touching his interests in Paris.

Maupertuis had received orders to keep a very strict watch
over his charge, orders which he carried out to the last scruple.
The letters therefore had to be conveyed backwards and
forwards with every possible precaution, Barrailh's by the
hand of some trusted messenger (sometimes Lauzun's brother)
who in turn delivered them to an equally trustworthy confederate wherever Lauzun happened to be at the moment.

Lauzun's replies were sent under cover to M. Firmini, harness-maker, rue du Chantre, or to M. Bernard, master-tailor, rue St Honoré, addressed not to Barrailh himself (which might have aroused the suspicions of those two good tradesmen) but to his brother, the abbé. For greater safety, they were in code: *Bien beau* or *Beau* meant the King; *Qualité* or *votre jeune avocat*, Mme de Montespan; *Petit*, Colbert; *Vertu*, Louvois; *Esté*, Lauzun; *La Vie*, or *votre avocat* or *votre ancien avocat*, Mademoiselle.[1] All this had been perfectly organised and was never discovered, but, risky and complicated as it may sound, this clandestine interchange of letters was by no means the most serious trouble with which the unfortunate Barrailh had to contend.

The most serious trouble was Mademoiselle herself. The years had not modified either her impatience, her temper, or her indiscretion. Moreover, she had now become—and not without reason—passionately suspicious of Lauzun. Jealousy drove her to mean and sorry actions foreign to her nature; thus, intercepting a letter, *pleine de tendresse*, addressed by Lauzun to the maréchale d'Humières who had recently returned to Paris from Bourbon, she learnt that a thousand times a day he kissed a book the maréchale had given him, as his only consolation now that he no longer saw her. It was quite in vain that Barrailh, on Mademoiselle's instructions, had advised Lauzun to live very quietly at Bourbon, to pay no visits, and to indulge in no activities which might suggest that the plea of ill-health had been but a pretext. Only the wildest optimism on Barrailh's part, and the most wishful thinking on Mademoiselle's, could have led either of them to believe that Lauzun would pay any attention to their recommendations. He had been shut away for ten years. The social world of conversation, news, and agreeable women was once more open to him.

Mademoiselle's anger took the inevitable form of turning upon Barrailh. There was no one else she could bully.

---

[1] The letters, which Lauzun showed to St Simon, have been preserved and are the property of the duc de La Force.

Barrailh, afraid that something in his correspondence with
Lauzun might displease her and that by her impetuosity she
might upset, to her own detriment, all his careful plans, saw to
it that she read only what he intended her to read. Sometimes
he was driven to writing two separate letters, one of them to be
shown to Mademoiselle, the other to be despatched to Lauzun.
His precautions were not unnecessary, for he knew she set her
spies on him and even, on occasion, had him followed, and
once kidnapped his servant. This he could bear, and could
circumvent; what really tried his patience was her personal
maltreatment of him. She would not believe that he was not
double-crossing her. She accused him of not caring whether
Lauzun married her or not, 'and nothing that I can say or do
restores her confidence.' Both by her tongue and her fists she
made his life a misery; he had to run away and hide, before he
could console himself and recover. When she insulted him, he
could protest his innocence; when she beat him, he could not
retaliate; but when she got to the point of threatening him
with a knife, he thought it prudent to keep out of her way for
a whole fortnight. 'I hope,' he wrote to Lauzun, 'that you will
never find yourself in a position requiring such patience as I
have to practise. If so, you would think Pignerol bliss in
comparison.' Barrailh's plaints proceeded from a sensitive and
wounded heart. His sufferings, he wrote, equalled or surpassed
those of the martyrs. Only God could know what he had to put
up with, and he prayed to God to give him strength. When
Mademoiselle had taken something into her head, he wrote,
there was no stopping her. He believed that God himself, if He
came back to earth, would succeed no better. She had accused
him, Barrailh, of wanting to despoil her of her property and of
wanting Lauzun to marry Mlle de Noailles; she had called him
a swindler ...

One is reminded of what the faithful, long-suffering
Préfontaine had had to put up with.

Poor Barrailh's task of pacifying Mademoiselle was not made
any easier by his own mistrust of Lauzun. There had already

been Mme d'Humières; there was now Mlle de La Motte, advertising all over Paris that she was *au mieux* with Lauzun who, according to her, incessantly made fun of Mademoiselle. Barrailh, after assuring Mademoiselle that there could be no truth in these stories, wrote off to Lauzun that although he believed them to be nothing but calumny there could be no baser ingratitude, if true, before God and man, after Mademoiselle's 'ten years of perseverance at a time when you were, as you still are, abandoned by the whole of France,' and especially just then, when the princess was proposing to confer a considerable benefit upon him.

This brings us to the real business which Barrailh was trying to transact on behalf of two principals who threw every possible spanner into his works. He had no personal interest, and in all this tale of intrigue, cupidity, ingratitude, double-dealing and cynicism, there can be no purer example of selfless and sorely-tried devotion. No wonder that he often told Mademoiselle he should retire from the world as soon as M. de Lauzun had obtained his full release.

To put it briefly, he had two things to negotiate. The first was to induce Mademoiselle to declare publicly the donations she had signed in favour of the duc du Maine (this was at the request of Mme de Montespan and the King); the second was to persuade Lauzun to renounce all claim to the principality of Dombes and the *comté* of Eu (see page 314) which now formed part of the donation to the duc du Maine, and to compensate him in return for this renunciation with other gifts in kind.

Mademoiselle was most unwilling to agree to the first request. She had, after all, made the secret donation only on condition that Lauzun should be set free and that they should be allowed to marry: and, once Mme de Montespan and the King had secured her property, she found that she had been duped. Now, she was being asked to commit herself even more irrevocably, with no definite promise except the return of Lauzun. It was true that Mme de Montespan had once suggested a clandestine marriage, when the King would pretend not to know; he would never consent openly, nor would he ever allow Lauzun to be called M. de Montpensier, but he would confer a dukedom on him if Mademoiselle liked. This proposal made Mademoiselle very angry; what! she said, should he live with her as her husband, unacknowledged? what would people say and think of her? One can scarcely blame her for her reluctance to play once more into their hands. As she remarked to Colbert, she considered herself as a person to whom everything was owed, but for whom nothing was done. She was right, but it did not make matters any easier for Barrailh.

On the second point, both Lauzun and Mademoiselle were far more amenable. Lauzun had already indicated his willingness to abandon his claims (see page 314) and Mademoiselle, much as she disliked the idea of parting with any of her possessions to other people, had always shown herself most touchingly generous where Lauzun was concerned. It was now agreed, with the King's approval, that he should receive the Duchy of Châtellerault, the *vicomté* of Brosses, and the Barony of Thiers in Auvergne, carrying an income of 22,000 *livres* plus 10,000 *livres* on the *gabelles* of Languedoc, 32,000 *livres* in all.

One is surprised—or is one?—to find that Lauzun was not satisfied. He told Mme de Montespan, with whom he had had a meeting at Bourbon,[1] that Mademoiselle must be coerced into giving him 100,000 francs; this was repeated to Mademoiselle, who also heard that he declared he found it difficult to accept so beggarly an offer. Ungraciousness could hardly go further; but Mademoiselle, although the entry in her Memoirs shows clearly enough that she was hurt, returned good for evil by sending him a golden goblet.

This part of the bargaining seemed to be settled, when a snag arose from an unexpected quarter. The English ambas-

---

[1] She had gone to Bourbon to see her daughter, Mlle de Tours, aged seven, who was taking the waters there. The child died.

sador weighed in with a protest that the Duchy of Châtellerault was not at the disposal of Mademoiselle nor even of the King of France, having been granted in 1548 to James Hamilton, Earl of Arran, who had negotiated the marriage of Mary Queen of Scots to the then Dauphin François II.[1] Barrailh strongly suspected that Mlle de La Motte had had a hand in this upset, since the ambassador haunted the house in the rue St Honoré where she habitually lived with Mme de la Sablière, that *petite femme de la ville* who has achieved a small immortality in the world of letters as the Egeria of La Fontaine. In some consternation, the Duchy of St Fargeau was hastily substituted for that of Châtellerault, and the deeds were duly signed at the end of October 1681. Lauzun was no better pleased, but when Mademoiselle at last gave way and consented to acknowledge publicly her gifts to the duc du Maine, Lauzun was at least set free.

The rest of the story is perhaps the saddest of all, for it has neither a tragic nor a happy ending. The great romance simply peters out in a series of sordid wrangles, due partly to Mademoiselle's jealousy but chiefly to the insufferable hectoring that Lauzun inflicted upon her. So long as he remained on the Loire at Amboise (for he had not yet obtained permission to return to Paris) she had nothing worse to put up with than reports of his 'gallant ways' with the local ladies, especially the beautiful marquise d'Alluye, wife of the governor of Amboise, but when the King finally relented (March 1682) to the extent of allowing him back to Paris though not to the Court, Mademoiselle soon discovered that ten years of prison had done nothing to soften his temper. Their first meeting was quite propitious; true, she was shocked by his appearance, wearing a dreadful wig and his old doublet all in holes and too short, besides being twelve years out of fashion—for these doublets or *justaucorps à brevet*

---

[1] As a matter of fact, the ambassador was mistaken. The duchy had been confiscated by Charles IX in 1567. It was revived in 1864 and bestowed on William Alexander, 12th Duke of Hamilton, by Napoleon III.

were accorded only as a great privilege under the King's warrant and their style was changed every year—but at least he came civilly to greet her, throwing himself at her feet and saying that he owed everything to her and that she was the source of all his good. Mademoiselle was so much surprised that she made no answer.

These professions of gratitude were short-lived. A few days later he joined her at Choisy, came into her room as she was having her hair done, and rated her for tying it with coloured ribbons at her age. At first he was kind enough to express approbation of Choisy, and it is apparent that she proudly showed him all over it, for on his return to Paris that evening he flung himself into a chair exclaiming, 'I am half-dead! if Mademoiselle made me walk up and down every day as she has today, I *should* die.' Their friends were careful to report the remark to Mademoiselle.

He then started reproaching her for having spent so much money on Choisy. He remembered a rope of pearls. Where was it, he asked? She had sold it to pay for building Choisy. 'What a useless building!' he exclaimed; 'all you needed here was a little house where you could come and eat a fricassée of chicken, not a house to sleep in. All these terraces cost a fortune, and what good are they? . . . I have good reason to complain. You would have made better use of the money by giving it to me.' Mademoiselle replied patiently that she had given him quite enough to satisfy him, and had given more to buy him back into forgiveness.

Still he continued to storm at her and to say the meanest things about her behind her back. She offered him four diamonds valued at a thousand *pistoles* to be mounted as cuff-links; he showed them to his friends. 'Everyone thought them very poor (*fort vilains*) and not worth the value set on them. I have found some fine ones, but I should need another two hundred *pistoles*.' Mademoiselle refused. The next thing she heard was that he had taken her diamonds and sold them, telling their friends it was in order to live on the proceeds, 'for

I had not a *sou*.' Yet he was gambling heavily, and whenever he lost he came growling and complaining to Mademoiselle.

There was worse than all this. He had not long been back in Paris, in fact not a week, before she discovered that he was telling her quite unnecessary lies. He would take his leave of her, pretending that he was tired and must go home; then she would find out that he had gone somewhere else. She began to see through him, even when he arrived with all the appearance of good humour because he wanted some favour of her. '*Faisant le miquelot*' she calls it, meaning that he was behaving hypocritically. 'How are you today? Last night you went to bed after leaving M. Colbert, or so Barrailh brought me word from you.' 'Certainly; I was in bed by nine.' 'Then you must have got up again to go and see Mme de Langlée? for you were there at ten.' 'What a fib!' (*Quel conte!*) 'Tell her not to tell such fibs, then, for she and Mme de Valentinois came to see me and described how tired you were and how delighted that I should be going away today.' He seemed embarrassed, says Mademoiselle, but she would not let him off. 'I resumed the conversation. "You went to see M. Colbert; did that tire you?" ' Lauzun asked how much longer she intended to keep up these pleasantries. 'As long as I like; I have every right to say anything I choose to you, and you are under every obligation to listen.' Mademoiselle was entirely justified, and one is glad to observe her showing something of her natural spirit towards the little man for whom she had done so much and for whom one fears she still preserved some rags of love, but their renewed relationship promised little for their future. It was not a good basis for a possible coming-together after all their tribulations, in their advancing years. She comes out with one of her abruptly sad little reflections: 'I see that in this world people make fun of people who do good: they are boring (*l'on s'ennuie avec eux*).'

Lauzun's underhand deceptions were matched by his external manners. Mademoiselle, as of old, was often baffled. 'Sometimes he reproached and scolded, sometimes he begged graciously; never a quarter of an hour the same.' Mme de Montespan took him to task: 'What *do* you mean, and what seizes you? You would never have got out [of prison] without Mademoiselle, and without her you would have been completely forgotten.' Far from showing gratitude, his reproaches and his demands increased to such an extent that some biographers have seen in his behaviour a proof that they had, in fact, been secretly married before Lauzun ever went to Pignerol. No man, they argue, could treat a woman so cavalierly were she not his wife—which does not speak very well for some people's idea of marriage—least of all a royal princess at a time when such things held an exaggerated importance. He made it clear, for instance, that in his opinion all her affairs ought to be under his control, adducing the surely rather odd example of the chevalier de Lorraine, who controlled everything for Monsieur. When she needed money, she ought to come and ask him for it. This suggestion outraged the independent Mademoiselle: 'What, me, come and ask you for money?'[1]

He was irrepressible. The common talk, he said, was of how badly she treated him and how little attention she paid to him; she ought to have got a house ready for him, and a coach with six horses for his sole use; instead of which he had to hire a carriage, being unwilling to have one of his own until he became a duke and could blazon a ducal coat of arms; and as for a house to live in, he had been obliged to buy one on the Ile Notre-Dame, so as not to live like a beggar, whereas she ought to have provided him with a beautifully appointed *appartement* and a well-furnished table to which he could invite his friends to dinner . . .

As the house on the Ile Notre-Dame (now the Ile St Louis) was the magnificent hôtel de Lauzun, 17 Quai d'Anjou, still to be seen, and as he had presumably paid for it with a grant of four hundred thousand *livres* from the King, it is difficult to see that Lauzun had much cause for financial complaint. As for

[1] See Appendix XIX, p. 357: Did Lauzun ever marry Mademoiselle?

his grievances against Mademoiselle, he seems to have over-looked entirely the thirty-two thousand *livres* of annual income she had given him.

One is really tempted to think that Lauzun at moments was a little mad. His contemporaries thought so too. St Simon called him an inconsistent man, not in harmony with himself, and whose humour and fantasies had on several occasions cost him the attainment of high fortune. Colbert said, 'He is making everything worse for himself; he does not know what he is doing; he talks to me in a way that will do him harm if he talks in the same terms to other people.' Even his own mother got wind of his conduct and wrote him a severe letter:

'Mademoiselle is greatly embarrassed by all the talk, she casts down her eyes and says not a word. She must wish she had never set eyes on you, if all she hears is talk about your ingratitude towards her.'

It is obvious that Lauzun was deeply embittered by the King's refusal to receive him except for one brief interview immediately after his return. He had doubtless seen himself as the pardoned prodigal, taken back into favour with everything forgiven and forgotten, instead of which he found himself in an entirely false position, living in Paris but not of it, free to go anywhere except where he most wanted to go—to Versailles. His grievances ate into his strange soul, with Mademoiselle as the indicated victim. One can readily understand the sense of obligation being intolerable to a man of his temperament.

For a time she took it all fairly patiently. A comprehensible pride came to shore her up against the disillusionment that was gradually creeping over her. 'I began to know his moods and to grow weary of them, but I was determined to take up the challenge, and was unwilling, after having done so much for him, to let him go without having achieved my aim, that is to say to make him a duke and to get him back to Court.' This is the language of obstinacy rather than of love. Although she would not listen to Colbert, who warned her that before long she might be inciting the King to send Lauzun away with as much urgency as she had previously shown in asking for his recall, she was reaching the end of her endurance and their relationship was rapidly degenerating into a series of scenes, now violent, now grotesque. Yet they did not seem able to leave one another alone. In Paris they met almost daily, and he also came frequently to Choisy; at first, hating the country (*je m'ennuie à la campagne*), he had managed to avoid staying with her at Eu, untruthfully telling her that the King had forbidden it—but she found him out, and made him come, having, poor Mademoiselle, arranged a room for him just above her own, with a flight of Cupids painted across the ceiling. The visit was not a success. Perhaps the Cupids turned his thoughts in the wrong direction. With reckless bad taste he amused himself by exploiting the charms of the Norman peasant-girls; of course it came to Mademoiselle's ears; she fell upon him, scratched him, beat him (to which he replied in kind), and would have turned him out but for the intervention of Mme de Fiesque, who somewhat inexplicably reappears in the story.[1] The mountebank in Lauzun rose to the occasion. Crawling on all fours down the length of the gallery at Eu, he reached Mademoiselle who was awaiting him at the other end, and, lying at her feet, asked her forgiveness. I suspect that in their separate ways they both rather enjoyed this most undignified exhibition, and I am quite sure that Mme de Fiesque did, and that her relation of it lost nothing in the telling.

Such a state of affairs, half-farcical, half-tragic, could not continue indefinitely. The unexpected death of the Queen, Maria Teresa (July 30, 1683) brought them together temporarily in a shock they could both understand. But the end was in sight. For the last time in this history, Mademoiselle shall recount their dialogue in her own words:

'M. de Lauzun came to see me; I went up to him cheerfully

[1] Perhaps not so inexplicably after all. St Simon says that although she and Mademoiselle spent half their time quarrelling, they could not get on without one another.

(*d'un air riant*) and said, "You must go off to Lauzun or to St Fargeau, for as you cannot accompany the King[1] you would look ridiculous staying on in Paris, and I should be sorry to think people blamed me for the ban against you." He said, "I am going (*je m'en vais*), and I bid you farewell for the last time in my life, never to see you again." I answered, "Your life would have been far happier if I had never seen you, but better late than never (*il vaut mieux tard que jamais*)." "You ruined my career," he said; "you cut my throat; it is owing to you that I cannot get on terms with the King; you have prevented it." "Oh! as for that, it is untrue, the King would tell you the truth of it." He got into a rage (*il s'emporta beaucoup*) but I kept calm (*je demeurai dans un grand sang-froid*). I said, "Well, good-bye,' and went away into my little room. I stayed in it for some time, then I came out, and found him still there with my ladies. "Do you not want to play?" they said (presumably they were at the gaming-table). I went up to him: I said, "This is too much; stick to your resolution; get out (*allez-vous-en*)." '

He went, and they never saw each other again.

He made some attempts to keep in touch with her. Why? He could hope for nothing more from her; she had already despoiled herself of her most valuable possessions as the price of his freedom. He can have had no affection for her; he probably actively disliked her by now, even if (as I surmise) he had not disliked her all along. He could say in a tone of exasperation to his old enemy Louvois, 'As for Mademoiselle, I am under an obligation to her, but if I had had my way she would never have meddled in my affairs and in future she will meddle no longer.' Even Louvois was shocked at this way of speaking of a woman who had given him such practical as well as emotional proof of devotion over so many years. Yet Lauzun seemed unable or unwilling to cut entirely adrift. It was now Mademoiselle's turn to reject his advances. 'He sent a gentleman to bring me his compliments; I believe he wrote to me, but I returned no answer. He had bought a lot of Chinese merchandise, and sent a lot of it to Choisy; very pretty, but I would

[1] The King had left Versailles to rejoin the army on April 22nd, 1684.

not accept it.' There follows a very human touch. 'I could not resist going to look at it.'

Knowing Mademoiselle's taste for embellishing her houses, the rejection of Lauzun's *marchandises de la Chine, fort jolies,* must have represented almost as great a sacrifice as her refusal to respond to the advances of the little man on whom she had once irrevocably bestowed her heart.

Mademoiselle was growing old. Not old according to our ideas of 1959 when people live happily on into the seventies, eighties and even nineties. She was not quite sixty-six when she died—at the same age as her present biographer writing these lines with sorrow, love, and regret at parting. There is very little left to record of Mademoiselle. An elderly princess, frustrated in love, but still dashing to parties at Versailles, does not present a very attractive or dignified figure. Yet there is another picture of her—the picture of her wandering through the Norman countryside, talking to the village girls about their loves and marriages, and coming back to her château of Eu, saying, with tears in her eyes, how far happier she would have been in a cottage.

I wonder . . . Would she really have been happier? I doubt it. She did love being Mademoiselle. *Il fait bon être Mademoiselle en France.*

On March 15th, 1693, she fell ill. It appears to have been a disease or stoppage of the bladder, but I feel that Mademoiselle with her pride would prefer us not enquire into so personal a detail. Let us hope only that she did not suffer too greatly. I could not bear to think of her in pain, even 266 years ago.

Lauzun asked to see her. On her death-bed she refused. A last flash of pride and self respect.

On Sunday, April 5th, 1693, she died, in her palace of Luxembourg.

But that was not the last of Mademoiselle. She still had a surprise in store for those who attended her funeral—a most unexpected surprise, not engineered by Mademoiselle herself. An element of buffoonery had accompanied the whole of her career; the affection the Parisians bore her was largely due to regarding her as something of a lovable clown. Often in the course of this history I have let contemporaries speak for themselves, lest I might be suspected of exaggeration. So at this very end St Simon shall describe the final scene:

'She lay in state, her body invigilated for several days, two hours at a time, by a duchess or a princess and by two ladies of quality, all wearing the *mante*[1] . . . A most ridiculous thing then happened. (*Il y arriva une aventure fort ridicule.*) In mid-ceremony, the urn containing the entrails exploded with a frightful noise and an insufferable stink. (*Un bruit épouvantable et une puanteur intolérable.*) Instantly, some of the ladies were swooning with horror, others taking flight. The heralds, and the monks of St Bernard in the act of singing psalms, all made for the doors, together with the crowd who pushed even harder than they did. The chaos was extreme. It was all because the entrails had been badly embalmed, and, fermenting, had caused all the commotion (*fracas*).

'Still,' St Simon adds, 'everything was put right, the stench was dispersed' (*tout fût parfumé et rétabli*); and the fright they had had provided them with just another jest at the expense of Mademoiselle. "*Cette frayeur servit de risée.*" '

[1] i.e. a long veil of black crêpe, hanging from the head down to the feet, secured at the arms and waist, and ending in a long train on the ground.

Epilogue

LAUZUN survived Mademoiselle by thirty years. This history would not be complete without a brief account of how he employed his energies, when it will be seen that his adventures neither ceased with his middle age nor did his character modify its capacity for violence and mischief. He had always had a liking for the unexpected; now, at the age of fifty-two, he went off to England to offer his services to James II at the time of the Duke of Monmouth's rebellion (1685).

Back in Paris, he found the Court still forbidden to him, his friends giving him the cold shoulder, and Mademoiselle adamant in her refusal to receive him. Another and a better pretext than Monmouth's abortive attempt took him again to England in 1688, shortly after the arrival of William of Orange at Torbay with a Dutch army, when an errand very much to Lauzun's taste was committed to his charge. Thanks to various documents which have been preserved,[1] we see Lauzun in secret confabulation with James II and an Italian named Riva, concerting a plan of escape for the Queen (Mary of Modena) and the little five-months-old Prince of Wales. It was decided that the Queen and her son should leave Whitehall by a garden gate where a coach would be awaiting her, and, escorted by Lauzun, should make their way to Horseferry and so by boat to Lambeth where another coach-and-six would be in readiness. From there the Queen would proceed to Dover, the infant prince to Portsmouth.

This plan had to be slightly altered, owing to the rumours

---

[1] In the Este archives at Modena; in the *Archives des Affaires-étrangères* in Paris; in the *Bibliothèque nationale.*

which were running round London; Gravesend was substituted for the more distant ports, and in the end the Queen and her baby took flight together. The scene in Whitehall is vivid; Riva arriving by a private staircase, disguised as a sailor; the Queen weeping, throwing herself into the King's arms, saying that she preferred to remain and die with him; the King gravely entrusting his wife and son to Lauzun, 'to bring them at all hazards into France.' It was two o'clock in the morning, on a wild December night; safely past the sentries, the little party of six—the Queen, the Prince of Wales, Lauzun, Riva, and two nurses—crowded into a small boat at Horseferry and, after a stormy passage in a gale of wind and torrents of rain, reached Lambeth on the opposite bank. The Queen, not daring to show herself, waited in the rain, huddling for shelter under the wall of a church. Once in the coach, which they had not been at all sure of finding, they set off pursued by cries of 'Let's go and see, it may be a coach-full of Papists.'

With relief, for the poor Queen was half-dead with fright, they found at Gravesend a yacht which had been bespoken for the service of 'an Italian lady.' It was very rough, and at one moment near the mouth of the Thames the captain decided to cast anchor for fear of being driven ashore by the wind on the coast of France. Even so, they nearly ran aground on a sandbank when finally they arrived at Calais, two days after leaving London. The Queen, sinking into an armchair, declared that not for three months had she enjoyed such a feeling of rest and safety.

It recalls the escape of Henrietta Maria, years earlier. History does, monotonously, repeat itself.

The adventure did more for Lauzun than to satisfy his sense of the romantic. It was pleasing enough to plot the flight of a Queen and an Heir-Apparent; it was even more pleasing to find therein a means of restoring himself into the good graces of his own Sovereign. Lauzun was quite sufficiently shrewd to see the opportunity and to take it. In an urgent letter which he despatched to the King he informed him that he had that morning happily conducted the Queen of England and the Prince of Wales to Versailles, having given his word on oath to the King of England to deliver them only into the hands of the King of France; but that being unfortunately precluded from His Majesty's presence, he now awaited his Majesty's dispensation from his oath and instructions as to how to hand over his charges. Louis XIV, for once driven into a corner, was perhaps not sorry for an excuse to welcome back a courtier in whose company he had always found entertainment. All should be forgotten; he trusted that Lauzun also would forget the past; he was 'full of impatience' to see him again. The King wrote this letter with his own hand, and said, as he sealed it, 'M. de Lauzun has not seen my writing for a long time though once he was familiar with it; I think this letter will please him.'

It did please him. Once again Lauzun had triumphed. As Mme de Sévigné wrote, 'He had found the road to Versailles by passing through London.'

Honours poured on him. James II made him a Knight of the Garter. He was given rooms in the palace of Versailles, and a room at Marly. The *grandes entrées*, of which he had been deprived, were restored to him, 'the rarest and most conspicuous of favours,' meaning that he now had the right to enter unannounced into the King's private apartments, even should his Majesty be still in bed. This was a privilege accorded only to the King's children, the Princes of the Blood, the Great Chamberlain, certain functionaries in close personal attendance on the King, and such chosen courtiers as the King might select.

The year 1690 saw Lauzun again crossing the Channel, not to England but to Ireland, not in secret this time, but as the representative of the French King, in command of the French troops sent to the assistance of James II in his ill-fated Irish campaign. Lauzun was not happy; he managed to make friends with Tyrconnel, but the arrival of a French army on Irish soil aroused the resentment of the English; the Irish authorities were incompetent, and left seven hundred sacks of good French flour to rot in the rain; everything, as Lauzun wrote to Louvois, was in chaos, like in Genesis before the creation of the world. There is no need to follow Lauzun's movements in any detail, though we may pause for a moment in amusement before the incongruous figure of *le petit homme* taking part in the siege of Limerick and at the battle of the Boyne.

He returned to France as 'our very dear and well-beloved Antonin Nompar de Caumont,' henceforth to be known as duc de Lauzun.

He was now a man of sixty, but far from coming to an end of the odd things which in this life were always happening to him. Two years after the death of Mademoiselle, when he went into mourning, conducted himself like a widower, and hung portraits of Mademoiselle all over his walls, he took it into his head to marry a girl of fourteen.[1] Surprise at Court. To the King's jokes and laughter, Lauzun replied politely that he was only too happy to get married, as it was the first time since his return from Ireland that his Majesty had been pleased to laugh with him. The *Mercure Galant*, after flattering the bride, remarked that it would say nothing about the bridegroom since everyone was aware of 'the dazzling tapestry of events' that his life had woven. Mme de Sévigné hurried to her writing-table: M. de Coulanges must immediately be informed. 'The marriage of M. de Lauzun,' she wrote, 'has surprised us all, I should never have guessed at it that day when I wrote you another letter to Lyon,' adding, somewhat complacently but not without justification, since it has survived as one of the most famous letters ever written, 'Mme de Coulanges still remembers it.'

It was not to be expected that the marriage should turn out well, either from the point of view of the husband or the wife.

[1] Geneviève de Durfort-Lorge, known as Mlle de Quintin, younger sister of the duchesse de St Simon.

Lauzun was now called upon to endure the tortures of jealousy which, years ago, he had callously inflicted on Mademoiselle. We may consider that it served him right, especially as it appears that his docile young duchess gave him no real cause for disquiet. He behaved towards her with the unreasonable tyranny to be expected of him, forbidding her to hold any communication with her mother, her father, or any of her relations except Mme de St Simon, and engaging two maids to attend her with the injunction never to let her out of their sight. On the other hand, he treated her handsomely in all material ways. He lodged her in great splendour in Paris and at Passy and encouraged her, as was natural, to take part in all the fêtes of the Court. Somewhat left out of current affairs, and having lost much of the King's old affection, he busied himself in his old age (he is now eighty) by building on to his house when he would terrify the masons by descending on them sword in hand. He amused himself also by playing practical jokes of the unkindest nature on any gullible victim; for example, on observing the maréchal de Marsin making his way down a crowded staircase at Versailles, Lauzun went up to meet him and respectfully offered him his hand. Marsin, who is described as a fulsome little chatterbox, in some surprise ignored the extended hand, when Lauzun exclaimed, 'Oh, M. le maréchal, I beg your pardon, I mistook you for a lady.' Such jokes were perhaps not very funny, but it is evident that people were still frightened of the thin little old mannikin and of what he might say or do next.

His health was astonishing; at the age of eighty he was to be seen riding a half-broken colt in the Bois de Boulogne; he paid a visit to his old home at Lauzun; he ate and drank whatever he liked, and we know from St Simon that it was a good deal, 'everything, without any precautions,' fruit and cakes, beer, cider, and lemonade always ready to hand on a table, from which he would help himself, 'walking up and down, eating and drinking, every day after dinner.' His temper remained as uncontrollable as ever, but with advancing age the inevitable pathetic note creeps in, sad moods overwhelm him, he confesses to Mme de Maintenon that sometimes he crawls under his bed and hides there, 'not very comfortably, madame.' Did he then remember another bed under which he had once hidden, in the days of his youth when everything lay before and not behind him?

St Simon noticed also that his memory was becoming impaired, an exasperating eventuality for the greatest contemporary gossip. Think! St Simon had available, in his brother-in-law, a man who had lived in intimacy with Louis XIV, who had seen the whole of that great reign, who had seen the *Grand Siècle* in all its glory, who could remember Mazarin, Fouquet, Colbert, Louvois, Condé, Turenne, Racine, Molière, Mme de Montespan, Mme de Maintenon, who had seen Versailles rising from the ground—and that brother-in-law incapable of telling him the stories he so greedily desired. St Simon extracted such scraps as he could. 'A thousand times,' he wrote, 'have I regretted his total inability to write down anything that he had seen or done. It should have been a treasure of the most curious anecdotes, but he lacked both continuity and diligence. A further misery: he would begin to narrate . . . then he would leave the central character and would take up another person, and then another, and then a third, so that after the manner of romances such as the *Thousand and One Nights* he would string a dozen stories together at the same time, which made one lose one's foothold. They chased each other without one of them ever coming to an end.' Louis XIV was gone, Louis XV was on the throne, a more exquisite elegance was coming in with the eighteenth century, something of the massive solidity was evaporating, the legs of furniture began gracefully to curve, the heavy Buhl went out of fashion, women's clothes became lighter and more elegant; little pink roses began to appear poked into powdered wigs; rosy young goddesses began to float about on fleecy clouds. A lighter frivolity, acceptable to the French taste, forecast the merry days of Mme de Pompadour. All that St Simon could recapture from Lauzun was a flavour of a forgotten dignity, the 'civility of the old Court, distinguished and discriminating, which we no longer know.'

It was in October 1723 that Lauzun at the age of ninety left his house in Paris for the last time and made his way on foot to the neighbouring monastery of the Petits-Augustins. Here he installed himself in a room overlooking the kitchen-garden and furnished with chairs, tables, clocks, tapestries, and a bed upholstered in crimson damask, all of which he had had carried round from his own hôtel. Here, suffering atrociously from cancer of the mouth, he awaited the end with a courage and a composure which cannot but command our admiration.

He would receive practically no one. His wife could visit him at any time, through a communicating door between the hôtel de Lauzun and the monastery; his brothers-in-law and his nephews were admitted occasionally, but out of consideration for their feelings he would send them away again very quickly. Not a word of complaint escaped him; his patience and docility were exemplary; nothing lugubrious or dolorous was allowed to appear; he, who had never been noted for his personal cleanliness was now irreproachably kempt; he had lost all interest in the doings of the world, speaking little for speech had become too painful, but always with perfect politeness masking his indifference. With a return to the religious convictions he had once evinced at Pignerol, he now preferred the conversation of priests and the holy books they read aloud to him. It was thus that the poor *cadet de Gascoyne*, on the 19th of November, 1723, ended his long life as duc de Lauzun, K.G.

Appendices

APPENDIX I

THE BAPTISM OF ROYAL CHILDREN

THE confusion here can probably best be resolved by differentiating between *baptism* and *christening*. The O.E.D. definition of baptism is, 'The action or ceremony of baptising, immersion of a person in water, or application of water by pouring or sprinkling, symbolical of moral or spiritual purification or regeneration, and, as a Christian ordinance, betokening initiation into the Church . . . Baptismal name: the personal or "Christian" name given at baptism.'

To christen, on the other hand, although it also means 'to make Christian . . . to admit or initiate into the Christian church by baptism,' more specifically implies the bestowal of the personal or Christian name, as it were a complement conveniently combined with the ceremony of baptism. In other words, a person could be baptised without the bestowal of a name, whereas he could not be christened without being baptised.

The inclusion of the name thus not being of the essence of baptism, it became customary in the royal house of France to practise *private* baptism at birth, or shortly after, deferring the bestowal of a name until a later and more public occasion. Thus, Louis XIII and two of his sisters received no name until they were aged six, five, and one respectively. A brother of theirs died nameless at the age of four. Louis XIV received no name until he was nearly five, la Grande Mademoiselle not until she was nearly ten.

The royal bastards did not enjoy the same privilege—if as a privilege it should be regarded—but were baptised by name in the first instance like ordinary infants.

A word further should be said about this ceremony of private baptism. In French it is called *ondoiement* (verb, *ondoyer*), an expression which has a special theological liturgical meaning. It indicates, in fact, that only the essential ceremony has been carried out, i.e. the pouring or sprinkling of water with the simultaneous utterance of the words: 'I baptise thee in the name of the Father and of the Son and of the Holy Ghost.' This ceremony may be performed by anybody, but only if the child is in imminent danger of death. Failing this emergency, it was forbidden by the Church's Canon Law, *except* in France where a long-standing custom (which seems to have begun by royal precedent) permitted *ondoiement* even where the infant was not in danger of death. I presume that in these cases of non-emergency the ceremony had to be carried out by a priest, and not by any relation or friend who happened to be at hand.

I am much indebted for some of the foregoing information to the Rev. Father James Walsh, S.J.

APPENDIX II

THE DESIGNATIONS *MONSIEUR, MADAME, MADEMOISELLE*, ETC.

THERE can be no better guide to this matter than the arch-snob the duc de St Simon. What a pity that two centuries should have separated him from Marcel Proust: they were made for one another; what letters they might have exchanged!

Here, very much abbreviated, is what St Simon has to say about these colloquial courtesy titles:

'Gaston, brother of Louis XIII, was the first Son of France truly and continuously to be called, for short, Monsieur ... a name consecrated to the brother of the King. He retained it until his death, when it was taken by the duc d'Anjou' (brother of Louis XIV).

St Simon goes on to explain (not very clearly) the appellations *Madame, Madame la Princesse, Madame la Duchesse, Madame la Comtesse*. What I think he really means, but omits to say, is that the wife of Monsieur was known as Madame, the wife of Condé (M. le Prince) as Mme la Princesse, the wife of the duc d'Enghien as Mme la Duchesse, the wife of the comte de Soissons as Mme la Comtesse. This need not detain us. What we want to know is why Mademoiselle was called Mademoiselle, and, above all, why she was called la Grande Mademoiselle.

'This distinctive name (*ce nom singulier*),' says St Simon, 'was of even more modern origin (than the name Monsieur). So long as she remained the only daughter of Monsieur, during eighteen years, she was never known as anything but Mademoiselle. Then, rightly or wrongly, she wanted to mark the difference between herself and her half-sisters of the second marriage, and insisted on being known as Mademoiselle . . . and thus this unique new name became accepted and she remained Mademoiselle all her life.'

The reason she became known as *la Grande* Mademoiselle is a bit more complicated. It was not due to her excessive stature, although St Simon does remark in this connexion that 'her height was in fact very considerable' (*fort haute*). It was due to the fact that the younger Monsieur, Philippe d'Anjou, when after Gaston's death he had become duc d'Orléans, wished his eldest daughter to be known as Mademoiselle. This never quite caught on, but in order to avoid any possible misunderstanding the appellation *la Grande* Mademoiselle did creep in. It is thus incorrect to translate it as the Great Mademoiselle; the Elder would be nearer the mark, though no doubt her stature also contributed something to the popular acceptance of the name.

APPENDIX III

MADEMOISELLE AT THE BASTILLE

AT the risk of spoiling a good story, on which every schoolchild in France has been brought up, historical exactitude compels us to look a little further into the recorded facts. Was Mademoiselle actually present at the firing of the cannon? Reading her Memoirs carefully, it would appear not. She says clearly that, after pacing for a long time round the towers, she had the direction of the guns altered: *je fis changer le canon*, and that she caused others to be placed *du côté de l'eau et du côté du faubourg pour défendre le bastion*. She then surveyed the heights of Charonne and the royal army below, sent her page to inform Condé, and *went back to the house* where she had spent most of the day. There is no word of her having been on the towers when the guns were let off. On the contrary, she says, 'They fired three or four volleys, as I had ordered *when I came away*.' (Incidentally, in a letter written by her next day, now in the *Bibliothèque nationale*, she says twenty volleys.)

On the other hand, practically all contemporary writers and memorialists believed that she stood by the gunners. This is in entire contradiction with her own account, and, even though she was writing from memory, she cannot possibly have been mistaken on so dramatic a point. She would have been far more inclined to say that she herself had pushed in the first ramrod.

Cardinal de Retz' account is slightly ambiguous. 'She entered the Bastille, where Louvière, out of respect, did not dare to oppose her; she caused the cannons to be fired on the troops of the maréchal de la Ferté, which were advancing upon the flank of M. le Prince's (troops). After that (*ensuite*), she harangued the garrison of the Porte St Antoine.' This would seem to suggest that Retz believed her to have remained on the towers of the Bastille during the shooting.

Later on, it is true, she went so far as to deny that she had given the order. 'She told me,' writes Mme de Motteville, 'that it had not been done at her command.' I think we may disregard this statement; Mademoiselle was only trying to attenuate or repudiate an action which had drawn upon her the reproaches of the Court. Mme de Motteville adds that both the King and the Queen-Regent believed Mademoiselle to have given the order.

Whatever the truth may be, it remains clear that the guns of the Bastille fired on the King's troops by her instructions and no one else's. Nor must it be forgotten that she carried with her a note from her father to M. de la Louvière, governor of the Bastille:

'From Monseigneur, Son of France, uncle of the King, duc d'Orléans. It is commanded that M. de la Louvière shall in every possible way favour His Royal Highness's troops and shall fire upon those [he means the King's] which shall come into sight of the château [the Bastille]'
Written at Paris, 2nd of July, 1652.
Gaston.

Omer Talon certainly implies that the original if not the immediate responsibility lies with Gaston. 'That which was done at the Bastille,' he says, 'is the crime of only one man, over whom the Hôtel de Ville has no power.'

APPENDIX IV

ST. FARGEAU

THE history of St Fargeau goes back to about A.D. 980 when it appears to have been founded by Héribert Bishop of Auxerre, a natural son of Hugues Capet, elective King of France towards the end of the tenth century. It was then a hunting-box, in wild country rich in game, but might also have served as a defence-post in troublesome times.

Jacques Coeur, that wealthy citizen of Bourges who financed Charles VII of France in his wars against the English, bought St Fargeau in 1450, and one of the towers is still known as *la tour de Jacques Coeur*.

It seems improbable, however, that Jacques Coeur could have had time to do much building at St Fargeau, since his arrest (1451) and disgrace occurred within eighteen months of the purchase.

It is far more probable that Antoine de Chabannes, comte de Dammartin, who acquired St Fargeau after an interval of legal dispute with the heirs of Jacques Coeur, was responsible for much of the reconstruction and that his son Jean carried on the work. It is through the family of Chabannes that St Fargeau eventually came into the possession of la Grande Mademoiselle, as follows: Jean de Chabannes married Suzanne de Bourbon, comtesse de Roussillon. Their daughter Antoinette de Chabannes married René d'Anjou, baron de Mezières. Their son Nicolas d'Anjou, marquis de Mezières, created comte de St Fargeau by letters patent of François I^{ier}, 1541, married Gabrielle de Mareuil. Their daughter and sole heiress, Renée d'Anjou, comtesse de St Fargeau, married François de Bourbon, duc de Montpensier, in whose favour Henri III advanced St Fargeau to the dignity of a duchy. Their son, Henri de Bourbon, duc de Montpensier, married (1597) Henriette Catherine de Joyeuse. Their daughter, Marie de Bourbon, duchesse de Montpensier, married Gaston d'Orléans. Their daughter was la Grande Mademoiselle.

She, as we have seen, made a gift of St Fargeau to Lauzun in 1681. Long after her death in 1693 Lauzun sold it (1714) to one Antoine Crozat who resold it a year later to Michel Robert Le Peletier des Forts. From him and his wife it has descended to the present co-proprietors, M. M. Roger, Alexandre, and Henri Anisson du Perron and their sister the marquise d'Ormesson.

St Fargeau has suffered badly from fire, once in 1752 and again in 1850. Nothing can be seen of Mademoiselle's rooms, or of her picture gallery, or of her *salle des gardes* or of the apartments once occupied by Mmes de Fiesque and Frontenac. Fortunately, the exterior with its six great circular towers and the fine semi-circular staircase remain intact and may be contemplated today by any pilgrim willing to go a few kilometres off the main road into the depths of la Puisaye.

APPENDIX V

MADEMOISELLE'S LETTER TO THE KING

'VOTRE Majesté sera surprise de la permission que je veux lui demander d'approuver que je me marie. Je me trouve, Sire, par ma naissance et par l'honneur que j'ai d'être votre cousine-germaine, tellement au dessus de tout le monde, qu'il me semble que je n'ai rien à désirer que ce que je suis. Lorsqu'on se marie à des étrangers, on ne connaît ni l'humeur ni le mérite des gens avec qui on doit passer sa vie; ainsi, il est difficile de se pouvoir promettre une condition hereuse; la mienne l'est beaucoup, Sire, par l'honneur que j'ai d'être auprès de votre Majesté; celle que je veux prendre ne m'en éloignera point. J'aurai donc celui de lui dire qu'il est si ordinaire d'être marié, que je crois qu'on ne saurait blâmer les gens qui le veulent être. C'est, Sire, sur M. de Lauzun que j'ai jeté les yeux; son mérite et l'attachement qu'il a pour votre Majesté sont ce qui m'a plu davantage, et ce qui a le plus contribué à ce choix. Votre Majesté se souviendra combien j'ai désapprouvé le mariage de ma soeur, et n'aura pas sans doute oublié tout ce que l'ambition m'a fait dire mal à propos là-dessus; je la supplie très-humblement d'oublier tout ce que cette passion m'a fait dire et imaginer; et si elle pense que ce soit une autre passion qui me fait parler à présent d'une manière différente, je la supplie de croire qu'elle est fondée sur la raison, puisqu'il y à long-temps que j'examine ce que je veux faire, et je n'en fais la proposition à votre Majesté qu'après avoir trouvé que Dieu me veut faire faire [*sic*] mon salut dans cet état; il me paraît que le repos de ma vie en dépend. Je demande à votre Majesté, comme la plus grande grâce qu'elle me puisse jamais faire, de m'accorder cette permission: l'honneur que M. de Lauzun a d'être capitaine des gardes de son corps ne le rend pas indigne de moi. M. le prince de Condé, qui fût tué à la bataille de Jarnac,[1] était colonel de l'infanterie, devant que cette charge fût en office de la couronne; il y a encore, Sire, bien d'autres exemples, sans parler de celui des femmes. Madame la princesse de la Roche-sur-Yon, femme d'un prince du sang, cadet de la branche de ma mère, était dame d'honneur de la reine; et moi, Sire, je tiendrais à grand honneur d'être surintendante de la maison de la reine, et je ne sais si votre Majesté n'a pas sû que, lorsque madame la comtesse de Soissons pensa mourir, j'avais projeté de la supplier de trouver bon que je l'achetasse, en cas que madame la princesse de Carignan ne la prit pas. Je dis tout ceci à votre Majesté pour lui marquer que plus on a de grandeurs, plus on est digne d'être un de vos domestiques, et comme toutes les charges de votre maison honorent ceux qui les ont, je suis bien aise que M. de Lauzun en ait une.'

Voilà à peu près comme était ma lettre, hors qu'elle était plus longue, et qu'elle avait des termes plus pressants.

APPENDIX VI

MME DE SÉVIGNÉ TO M. DE COULANGES

Á Paris, lundi 15 decembre, 1670.

JE m'en vais vous mander la chose la plus étonnante, la plus surprenante, la plus merveilleuse, la plus miraculeuse, la plus triomphante, la plus étourdissante, la plus inouie, la plus singulière, la plus extraordinaire, la plus incroyable, la plus imprévue, la plus grande, la plus petite, la plus rare, la plus commune, la plus éclatante, la plus secrète jusqu'à aujourd'hui, la plus brillante, la plus digne d'envie; enfin une chose dont on ne trouve qu'un exemple dans les siècles passés, encore cet exemple n'est-il pas juste; une chose que nous ne

---

[1] Louis I, killed at Jarnac, 1569.

saurions croire à Paris, comment la pourrait-on croire à Lyon, une chose qui fait crier miséricorde à tout le monde; une chose qui comble de joie Mme de Rohan et Mme de Hauterive; une chose enfin qui se fera dimanche, où ceux qui la verront croiront avoir la berlue; une chose qui se fera dimanche, et qui sera peut-être pas faite lundi. Je ne puis me résoudre à la dire, devinez-la, je vous la donne en trois; jetez-vous votre langue aux chiens? Hé bien! il faut donc vous la dire: M. de Lauzun épouse dimanche au Louvre, devinez qui? je vous le donne en quatre, je vous le donne en dix, je vous le donne en cent. Mme de Coulanges dit: Voila qui est bien difficile à deviner! c'est Mme La Vallière. Point du tout, madame. C'est donc Mlle de Retz? Point du tout: vous êtes bien provinciale. Ah! vraiment nous sommes bien bêtes, dites-vous; c'est Mlle Colbert. Encore moins. C'est assurément Mlle de Créqui. Vous n'y êtes pas. Il faut donc à la fin vous le dire: il épouse dimanche, au Louvre, avec la permission du roi, mademoiselle, mademoiselle de . . . mademoiselle, devinez le nom: il épouse *Mademoiselle*, ma foi! par ma foi! ma foi jurée! *Mademoiselle*, la grande *Mademoiselle*, fille de feu Monsieur, *Mademoiselle*, petite-fille de Henri IV, Mlle d'Eu, Mlle de Dombes, Mlle de Montpensier, Mlle d'Orléans, *Mademoiselle*, cousine germaine du roi, *Mademoiselle*, destinée au trône, *Mademoiselle*, le seul parti de France qui fût digne de *Monsieur*. . . .

APPENDIX VII

The following circular letter, addressed by Louis XIV on Friday, 19th December, 1670, to all his representatives at the courts of foreign powers, is at the Bibliothèque de l'Arsenal, MSS. *Conrart*, Vol. XI, p. 949.

As the events of the past five or six days, brought about by the intention of my cousin de Montpensier to marry the comte de Lauzun, one of the captains of my bodyguard, will doubtless cause a great sensation everywhere, and as my own conduct may be maliciously interpreted and blamed by ill-informed persons, I have thought it my duty to apprise all my ministers serving me abroad. About ten or twelve days ago, my cousin, as yet lacking the temerity to speak to me herself on a subject which she knew would cause me the greatest surprise, wrote me a long letter announcing the resolve which (she said) she had taken concerning this marriage, imploring me by every reason she could think of to give my consent, begging me at the same time to have the goodness not to mention it to her, when I happened to meet her with the Queen, until it pleased me to agree. My answer, in a note I sent her, was to ask her to think better of it and especially to be on her guard against acting precipitately in an affair of this kind, which might immediately be followed by a prolonged repentance. I refrained from saying anything more, hoping verbally and with all the valid considerations that I should put to her, to bring her through gentle usage to a change in her sentiments. She continued nevertheless, by renewed notes and by all other means which came into her head, to urge me for the consent she requested, as the only thing (she said) would constitute the happiness and peace of her life, even as my refusal would render her the unhappiest woman on earth. As she began to perceive that she was not making as much progress as she would have liked in her pursuit, she contrived to enlist the interest of the highest nobility in my realm; she and the comte de Lauzun delegated four persons of the said nobility, namely the ducs de Créqui and Montausier, the maréchal d'Albret and the marquis de Guitry, master of the Wardrobe, to represent to me that if, having consented to the marriage of my cousin de Guise (Mademoiselle's sister), without making any difficulties, but with pleasure, I now resisted this other marriage which my cousin so ardently desired, I should be showing the whole world the great discrimination I made between the younger sons of a ruling house (he refers here to the house of Lorraine) and the officers of my Crown, a distinction which did not obtain in Spain, where, on the contrary, the native nobility was preferred above all foreign princes, and that this discrimination would inevitably mortify the entire nobility of my Kingdom. They alleged further that several instances were in their favour, not only of Princesses of the Blood Royal who had honoured gentlemen by marrying them, but even Dowager Queens of France. To conclude, the insistence of these four persons was so pressing and their reasoning so persuasive on the grounds of not giving offence to the French nobility, that I finally gave way to the extent of giving a tacit consent to this marriage, shrugging my shoulders in surprise at my cousin's anger (*emportement*), and saying only that she was forty-five and could do as she liked. From that moment onwards, the affair was regarded as settled; all preparations were begun; the whole Court went to pay its respects to my cousin and its congratulations to M. de Lauzun.

'The following day, it was reported to me that my cousin had told several people that she was undertaking this marriage at my wish. I sent for her, and being unwilling to speak to her except in the presence of witnesses, namely the duc de Montausier, and M.M. Le Tellier, de Lyonne, de Louvois, not finding any others ready to hand, she forcibly denied ever having spoken in such terms, assuring me that on the contrary she had always testified and would always testify to all and sundry that I had left nothing undone to drive her project from her mind and to persuade her to alter her resolve. But as yesterday I heard from divers sources that most people were entertaining an opinion most injurious to me, and that all the resistance I had put up in this affair was only make-believe and play-acting, and that *in fact I had been only too glad to procure so great a favour for the comte de Lauzun, whom everybody believes me to love and highly esteem*, as is true, I decided, seeing that my pride was in question, to break off this marriage without further consideration either for the gratification of the princess or the comte, on whom I can and intend to confer other favours. I sent for my cousin, and declared that I would not stand for this marriage, nor would I consent to her union with any prince among my subjects, but that with the sole exception of the comte de Lauzun she might choose whomsoever she liked from the qualified nobility of France, when I myself would lead her to the altar.

'It is superfluous to describe the chagrin with which she received the news, how many tears and sobs, throwing herself on her knees as though I had driven a hundred daggers into her heart; she tried to move me, I resisted every attempt; and after she had gone I called in the duc de Créqui, the marquis de Guitry, the duc de Montausier, the maréchal d'Albret not being available, and declared my intention of speaking to the comte de Lauzun, as I presently did, and may say that he received the intimation with all the constancy and submission that I could desire.

APPENDIX VIII

THE DEATH OF ANNE OF AUSTRIA

IT is difficult for us to reverse our minds into a realisation of what people had to suffer. The good old times were not so good as all that, even for Kings and Queens.

I reproduce here, without comment, a much abbreviated account given by Mme de Motteville of the last weeks of the life of Anne of Austria. Rumours of cancer had been current for some time, and it was nearly two years since she had courageously said to Mademoiselle, 'I no longer keep it a secret.'

Anne, profoundly religious, had wished to die at her favourite convent of the Val-de-Grâce, and caused herself to be transported there in a carrying-chair of black velvet, followed by her officers bearing cordials and vinegar lest she should collapse on the way. The chair must have been boxed in, for Mme de Motteville describes it as 'a sort of tomb.' Arrived at the convent, she went to bed after telling the Abbess that she was content now for God to dispose of her according to His will. But the unfortunate princess was not long allowed to remain there in peace. Her doctors began complaining that the convent was inconveniently distant (it was in the rue St Jacques); it was impossible, they said, to attend her in a place where the doors could not be opened without a lot of fuss (*ne pouvaient s'ouvrir qu'avec de grandes cérémonies*); it was a long way for the King and other members of the royal family to come on frequent visits; she must, in short, be brought back to the Louvre. Even her first woman of the bedchamber, Mme de Beauvais, not relishing this semi-banishment from the heart of Paris to a doubtless austere and uncomfortable residence (*elle cria fortement contre cette demeure*), added her mite of protest: it was impossible to obtain so much as a fresh egg.

The Queen-Mother was carried back to the Louvre.

'Her cancer, far from having hardened, was open on all sides, and her breast was full of holes. . . . They doubled the applications of lime-water (*eau de chaux*) when her pain also doubled. Her pain was so extreme and excessive that one night she admitted feeling near to despair. But only once did she cry out that she could bear it no

355

longer. The comtesse de Flex having represented to her that she must suffer with Jesus Christ on the Cross, the Queen-Mother, a prey to this terrible suffering, replied in these admirable terms, "Ah! madame, do not speak to me; I feel that I am losing my reason, and in my present state I fear I might not be able to accept your words with sufficient respect." '

There were ups and downs. Sometimes she seemed better, her pulse stronger, her fever abated, then, whenever she seemed a little more able to endure the remedies of the medicine-men, Dr Alliot resumed his treatment. 'They mortified the flesh, and then cut it in slices with a razor. It was a surprising operation, performed every morning and evening in the presence of the whole royal family, of the surgeons, and of everyone who had the honour of serving the princess familiarly.

'No doubt it distressed her to expose part of her body to the gaze of so many persons, although the monstrous cancer on her breast still permitted a degree of admiration; but as by then she knew how to judge things of this world at their true worth, she no longer regarded what had been an object of pride with any feelings other than a holy horror and anger, inspiring her with the wish to sacrifice herself to Divine justice. She watched them cutting her flesh with exemplary patience and meekness, often remarking that people usually putrefied only after death, but that God had ordained that she should putrefy while still alive.

'All this time, she suffered greatly, but her sufferings increased to excess when Dr Alliot's treatment touched the living flesh. . . . Pain forced tears from her eyes. "Do not suppose that I am weeping," she said; "these tears that you see are only produced by pain; you know that I am not given to weeping," ' Another time she said to Mme de Motteville who was kneeling beside her bed, 'I suffer; there is no part of my body which does not pain me; God wills it, and I will it also, yes, with all my heart.' She could even laugh. La Molina came to see her and exclaimed that she looked very red. 'Y como, Molina! en verdad que tengo muy buena calentura (I should say so, Molina! I have a high fever). It was only at night, when the curtains of her bed had been drawn, that they sometimes heard her moaning to herself; never by day.

The devoted Mme de Motteville could not bear to see her hands, which had always been celebrated for their beauty, becoming swollen like the rest of her body. Anne looked down at them, and Mme de Motteville heard her say in a low voice, as though to herself, 'My hand is swollen; da! it is time to go.' Her shoulders and back became ulcerated; Mme de Motteville informed the doctors, who promised a remedy, but applied none. Yet, distressed by the terrible smell which emanated from her sores, she insisted on having her bed made, which was not easy as she had become so weak and heavy. She could still think of others; had Mme de Motteville dined? she asked. No? Then she must go at once and eat with la Molina.

This was almost the last time she spoke to her faithful friend. Having received the last sacraments, she opened her eyes once more and recognised the King. '*Ah! voilà le roi!*' After contemplating him for a moment, 'Go, my son; go and dine.' To Maria Teresa she spoke in their native Spanish. '*Hija mia, vayase*' (My daughter, go away).

She died in the early hours of the morning, January 20, 1666.

APPENDIX IX

DID LAUZUN EVER MARRY MADEMOISELLE?

THIS question will never be answered unless some definite documentary evidence turns up in affirmation. Negative evidence to the contrary would be of no value. The question is of small importance; only, one would like to know.

The problem divides itself into two parts: did a secret marriage ever take place, and if so at what stage in their relationship?

I have no fresh theory of my own to adduce, so can only tabulate such facts and assumptions as we have to go on.

In favour of a marriage:

(1) Lauzun's own behaviour towards her after his return from Pignerol. This has already been touched on, and the reader is referred to p. 330.

(2) His behaviour immediately after her death:

He went into very deep mourning, like a widower, appearing openly at Court in that guise, and surrounded himself with her portraits. St Simon who, after all, became his brother-in-law, says that Lauzun always allowed it to be understood that they had married.

(3) A letter from Barrailh, dated September 28, 1681, which the duc de La Force regards as decisive and which is certainly significant:

Mademoiselle, afraid lest Mme de Montespan should suspect her of wishing to live secretly in sin with Lauzun, and not believing that I [Barrailh] had reported her desire to marry him, had an explanation with Mme de Montespan in my presence. Mme de Montespan said, 'When you have married Lauzun incognito, as you wish to do, the King will put his hand over his eyes and will not seek to learn if Lauzun goes to your room at midnight and leaves it only at dawn.'

(4) The abbé Anquetil (see *infra*) says that in 1744 he was shown a private staircase communicating between Mademoiselle's room and Lauzun's, at Eu. It certainly seems unlikely that Mademoiselle, with her sense of propriety, would have permitted such an arrangement without the legitimate justification to her own conscience.

The date of the supposed marriage.

Barrailh's letter of September 1681 naturally leads the duc de La Force to place the date some time after Lauzun's return from Pignerol.

There is one curious story which should be put on record, however valueless it may be. The abbé Anquetil, a very indifferent historian, relates[1] that in 1744 he met at Le Tréport a tall old lady of seventy to seventy-five years of age, who bore a resemblance to the portraits of la Grande Mademoiselle still hanging in the nearby château of Eu. This lady was in receipt of an annual pension of 1,500 francs, regularly paid from some unknown source. The local people believed her to be Mademoiselle's daughter, and she herself shared the belief.

Supposing this gaunt female to have been between seventy and seventy-five in 1744, she must have been born somewhere around 1671. This date, as attentive readers of this book may realise, corresponds with the highest and most hopeful peak of Mademoiselle's romantic passion for Lauzun. There were those three days, December 16, 17 and 18, 1670, when she really believed that their marriage had been accepted by the King and that it might be

[1] *Louis XIV, sa cour et le Régent*, Louis Pierre Anquetil, Paris, 1789.

celebrated at any moment. During those three days, she had every reason for considering herself officially affianced to Lauzun. She was then happily convinced that within the next forty-eight hours they would be made man and wife. It is conceivable, I think, that during those three days of apparent security Mademoiselle may have capitulated to Lauzun's suggestions and to her own belatedly aroused passions. St Simon states categorically that he was her lover. How can one tell? All that we know is that she loved him and was not of a nature to refuse even what she must have regarded as the supreme gift: her virginity. It would be consistent also with the whole twisted teasing character of Lauzun. At one moment he might reject and snub the infatuated Mademoiselle; at another moment, as the fancy took him, he might suddenly tempt her into his bed or creep into hers. As I said, how can one tell? These private relationships are known only to the two people concerned. One can never know the truth, and one does not want to. One does not pry through keyholes.

It would be strange indeed, but not unimaginable, that a tall spinster passing the time of day with the greengrocer of Le Tréport in 1744 was the daughter of Lauzun and Mlle de Montpensier.

I should like to believe this.

APPENDIX X

THE HALF-SISTERS OF MADEMOISELLE

LITTLE has been said in the foregoing pages about the three daughters of Gaston d'Orléans' second marriage with Marguerite de Lorraine, so a note about them may not come amiss. Only one of them seems to stand out as anything like a definite character.

This was the eldest, Marguerite Louise, known as Mlle d'Orléans (July 28, 1645, d. 1721). At the age of sixteen she was married by proxy (April 19, 1661) at the Louvre to Cosimo de' Medici, who became Grand-Duke of Tuscany on the death of his father in 1670. She went off to Florence with death at her heart for she was in love with Charles de Lorraine. At the very last moment she tried to evade the foreign ambassadors who were presenting themselves to offer their compliments and congratulations. She broke into

Mademoiselle's stables in search of a horse; Mademoiselle's grooms, acting on instructions, informed her that all the horses were lame; she would not listen, and Mademoiselle had to go down in person to make her dismount. 'I took her by the hand to lead her back, asking her what the Papal Nuncio and the Venetian ambassador would think if she failed to keep the appointment she herself had fixed with them.' Mademoiselle had in fact considerable difficulty in getting her sister out of France. She accompanied her as far as St Fargeau on the road to Marseille where she was to take ship for Leghorn; Marguerite Louise gave the maximum of trouble, disappearing all one day until two o'clock in the morning so that they thought she had run away, and insisting on sleeping in Mademoiselle's bed, 'which surprised and annoyed me very much as I like to be comfortable and am not accustomed to sleeping with anybody. Luckily she went to sleep first, which was fortunate for me as she began to dream and got me by the throat, when I believe she would have strangled me if I had been asleep myself. I was so much afraid this might happen a second time, that I never went to sleep all night.'

This pause at St Fargeau was not made any easier by the unexpected arrival of Charles de Lorraine. Mademoiselle was not sorry to hand her sister over to the escort awaiting her at Cosne, yet her kind heart was touched. 'She cried terribly (*elle faisait des cris épouvantables*), and aroused everyone's pity, even to tears.'

When the reluctant bride finally arrived in Florence, she was so miserable and set her face against it to such an extent that she refused to learn Italian and wrote despairing letters to Louis XIV begging to be allowed to take refuge in a convent sooner than remain in Italy. A touching story is related that two silver coins in the Archæological Museum of Florence 'were discovered to be hollow and to be in reality boxes, and in one of these was a miniature of Charles of Lorraine in his youth, believed to have been concealed in this manner by Marguerite Louise so that she might wear it without detection.'

It all reads like historical fiction of the cheapest type, even to the accounts of Marguerite Louise shutting herself up in the Medici villa of Poggio a Caiano threatening to throw a missal at her husband's head if he should come to seek her out, and to the accounts of Cosimo relegating her to a palace at Pisa, when she started to arrange her escape in connivance with a band of the local gipsies. Dumas could have imagined nothing more wildly romantic.

It was not to be expected that this unhappy union would long endure. Marguerite Louise finally struggled herself free—'You make the unhappiness of my life and I make the unhappiness of yours,' she had written to Cosimo—and in June 1674 she reappeared in Paris where nobody was particularly pleased to see her. The Florentines, on the other hand, were relieved at having got rid of her. To them she had been a source of shame and trouble; to the French she had become that unforgivable thing, a bore. From being a high-spirited if bizarre and unpredictable person, they now found that she talked too much and not amusingly, telling incessant stories about her servants and her horses, their names and where she had acquired them, 'in short, all the recitals of a horse-coper or a rustic Madam going to the fair, and dressed accordingly.'

This sad little biography ends in a convent at Montmartre, but anyone wishing to pursue the record may find in the long corridor uniting the Uffizi with the Pitti palace in Florence (the corridor that runs above the Ponte Vecchio) portraits of the sixteen noble Florentine damsels assigned as maids-of-honour to the Grand-Duchess.[1]

Mademoiselle's second sister, Elisabeth, Mlle d'Alençon (*b.* December 26, 1646, *d.* 1696), was equally unfortunate in many ways. Her appearance was unprepossessing. *Fort laide* is Condé's comment on her 'and, to add to her charms, furiously marked by smallpox.' Condé did not think M. de Savoie would ever bring himself to marry her, in which opinion he was justified, for she was given instead to Louis Joseph de Lorraine, duc de Guise, a frail delicate boy not yet seventeen, so thoroughly under the thumb of his aunt, Mlle de Guise, that he dared do nothing without her permission, neither eat dishes she had not ordered, nor speak to his wife, nor go to St Germain without his aunt who then slept next

---

[1] Colonel C. F. Young, in *The Medici*, p. 381, Vol. II, 1909, says there are twenty-five, but the Florentine inventory of 1890 mentions only sixteen, of which the names of ten are recorded.

At the moment of writing (1958) the portraits are temporarily put away during repairs to the Ponte Vecchio, but will be replaced when the reconstruction work is finished, in two or three years' time.

For this information I am indebted to Professor Anna-Maria Crinò, of the Università degli Studi di Firenze.

door to the conjugal bedroom. Mademoiselle, with her sense of seemliness, was always afraid that he might call her *ma bonne tante* in public. Even their wedding had been celebrated in that curiously hugger-mugger way that so often attended the movements of royal personages, in other words there were no hassocks for the bride and bridegroom to kneel on, and the best that could be produced at a moment's notice were the cushions belonging to Mme de Montespan's dogs.

The third sister, Françoise Madeleine, Mlle de Valois (*b.* October 13, 1648, *d.* January 14, 1664), seems to have been the one that Mademoiselle preferred, or at any rate about whom she was least catty. '*Pour la petite de Valois, elle était fort jolie.*' Mademoiselle even liked to think that they both resembled their father, and would willingly have adopted this child who called her '*petite maman.*' It was not to be, and Mlle de Valois was no more fortunate in her life than her two sisters. Married before she was fifteen in March 1663 to Charles Emmanuel de Savoie, she died within the year (January 14, 1664). Shortly after her death, M. de Savoie married Mlle de Nemours, in spite of having turned her into ridicule to the great amusement of his whole Court by describing how he had made a hole in the ceiling and watched her making-up her face.

Biographical Notes

ALENÇON, Mlle d', Elisabeth d'Orléans, b. Dec. 26, 1646, d. Mar. 17, 1696; daughter of Gaston d'Orléans q.v. and Marguerite de Lorraine q.v.; second of la Grande Mademoiselle's half-sisters; m. May 15, 1667, Louis Joseph de Lorraine, duc de Guise q.v.

ANJOU, Philippe duc d', b. Sept. 21, 1640, d. June 9, 1701; son of Louis XIII q.v. and Anne of Austria q.v.; only brother of Louis XIV; known as Monsieur after the accession of Louis XIV in 1643; became duc d'Orléans after the death of his uncle Gaston d'Orléans q.v. in 1660; m. (1) Henrietta of England q.v. (Madame) Mar. 31, 1661; m. (2) Elizabeth Charlotte of Bavaria, Nov. 16, 1671.

ANNE of Austria, Queen of France, b. 1601; d. Jan. 20, 1666; daughter of Philip III, King of Spain and Marguerite d'Autriche; m. Nov. 1615 Louis XIII, King of France q.v.; mother of Louis XIV and Philippe d'Anjou q.v.; known as Queen-Regent during the minority of Louis XIV (1643 to 1651) and as Queen-Mother after his marriage in June 1660.

BARRAILH, Henri de, b. (?), d. 1705; one of Lauzun's officers; Lieutenant to the Governor of the Bastille in 1662; m. secretly, 1677, Mlle de La Motte.

BAVARIA, Rupert of, b. Dec. 17, 1619, d. Nov. 29, 1782; son of Frederick V, Elector Palatine and Elizabeth, daughter of James I, of England; d. unmarried.

BEAUFORT, François, duc de, b. 1616, d. 1669; son of César, duc de Vendôme; d. unmarried.

BOUILLON, Léonore-Catherine-Fébronie de Berg, duchesse de, m. Frédéric Maurice de La Tour d'Auvergne, duc de Bouillon, 1605–1652, brother of Turenne q.v.

CHARLES I, King of England, b. Nov. 19, 1600, executed Jan. 30, 1649; son of James I and Anne of Denmark; succeeded his father, Mar. 27, 1625; m. May 11, 1625, Henrietta Maria q.v.

CHARLES II, King of England, b. May 29, 1630, d. Feb. 6, 1685; son of Charles I q.v. and Henrietta Maria q.v.; m. Catherine of Braganza, Infanta of Portugal, May 20, 1662; restored to the Throne, 1660.

CHEVREUSE, Marie Aimée de Rohan, *b.* Dec. 1600, *d.* Aug. 12, 1679; daughter of Hercule de Rohan, duc de Montbazon and Madeleine de Lenoncourt; *m.* (1) Charles d'Albert, duc de Luynes *q.v.* in 1617; (2) Claude de Lorraine, prince de Joinville and duc de Chevreuse, 1622.

CHRISTINA, Queen of Sweden, *b.* Dec. 8, 1626, *d.* Apr. 26, 1689; daughter of Gustavus Adolphus and Maria Eleanora of Brandenburg; succeeded him as Queen of Sweden, Nov. 6, 1632; abdicated voluntarily 1654; *d.* unmarried.

CINQ-MARS, Henri Coffier d'Effiat, marquis de, *b.* 1620, executed Sept. 12, 1642; known as M. le Grand (*M. le Grand Ecuyer de France*); son of Antoine d'Effiat, Comptroller of the Treasury under Richelieu.

COLBERT, Jean-Baptiste, marquis de Seignelay, *b.* 1619, *d.* Sept. 6, 1683; son of a merchant of Reims; *Intendant des Finances* and Minister of Marine under Louis XIV.

CONDÉ, Claire-Clémence de Maillé-Brézé, princesse de (Madame la Princesse), *b.* 1629, *d.* Apr. 18, 1694; daughter of Urbain de Maillé-Brézé and Nicole du Plessis-Richelieu; niece of Cardinal Richelieu *q.v.*; *m.* le Grand Condé (then duc d'Enghien), Feb. 11, 1641.

CONDÉ, Louis II de Bourbon, prince de, *b.* Sept. 8, 1621, *d.* Dec. 11, 1686; *premier prince du sang*; son of Henri de Bourbon, prince de Condé, and Charlotte Marguerite de Montmorency; le Grand Condé, commonly known as M. le Prince. The Condés descended from a younger son of Louis IX (St Louis).

CONTI, Armand de Bourbon, prince de, *b.* Oct. 11, 1629, *d.* Feb. 21, 1666; younger brother of le Grand Condé and Madame de Longueville; *m.* Anne Martinozzi, a niece of Cardinal Mazarin.

CORNEILLE, Pierre, *b.* June 6, 1606; *d.* Oct. 1, 1684.

ELISABETH de France, Queen of Spain, *b.* Nov. 22, 1602, *d.* Oct. 4 or 5, 1644; daughter of Henri IV, King of France *q.v.* and Marie de' Medici *q.v.*; *m.* Philip IV, King of Spain, 1615; mother of Maria Teresa *q.v.* who married Louis XIV, King of France *q.v.*

ENGHIEN, duc d' (*see* Condé, le Grand); le Grand Condé was known by this title until his father's death in Dec. 1646, and was then referred to as M. le Duc.

ESTRÉES, Gabrielle d', *b.* 1573, *d.* 1599; daughter of Antoine d'Estrées and Françoise Babon de la Bourdaisière; mistress of Henri IV, King of France; mother of César, duc de Vendôme, Alexandre, chevalier de Vendôme and Catherine Henriette; *m.* Charles de Lorraine.

FIESQUE, Gilonne Marie Julie d'Harcourt Beuvron, comtesse de, *b.* 1619, *d.* 1699; daughter of Jacques II, marquis de Beuvron; *m.* (1) Louis de Brovilly, marquis de Piennes, *d.* 1640; (2) Charles-Léon de Fiesque, comte de Lavagne.

FOUQUET, Nicolas, *b.* 1615, *d.* 1680; *Surintendent des Finances* under Louis XIV; arrested in 1661 and sent as a prisoner to Pignerol, where he died.

FRONTENAC, Anne de la Grange-Trianon, comtesse de; lady-in-waiting to Mademoiselle; *m.* the comte de Frontenac *q.v.*

FRONTENAC, Louis de Buade, comte de Palluau et de Frontenac, *b.* 1620, *d.* 1698; *m.* Anne de la Grange-Trianon, comtesse de Frontenac *q.v.*; Governor of Quebec, where he died.

GRAMONT, Antoine, duc de, *maréchal de France*, *b.* 1604, *d.* 1678; *m.* (1) Charlotte de Biron, *d.* 1635; (2) Anne de Mornay, *d.* 1646; (3) Isabelle de Clermont-Gallerande.

GUICHE, Antoine Charles de Gramont, comte de, *b.* 1645, *d.* 1720; eldest son of Antoine, duc de Gramont, whom he succeeded in 1678; *m.* 1658, Marguerite Louise Suzanne de Béthune, daughter of Maximillien, duc de Sully and Charlotte Séguier.

GUISE, Henriette Catherine de Joyeuse, duchesse de, *b.* 1585, *d.* Feb. 25, 1656; daughter of Anne, duc de Joyeuse and Marguerite de Lorraine-Vaudemont; *m.* (1) Henri de Bourbon, duc de Montpensier; (2) Charles de Lorraine, duc de Guise; grandmother of la Grande Mademoiselle.

GUISE, Louis Joseph de Lorraine, duc de, *b.* 1650, *d.* 1671; *m.* Elisabeth d'Orléans, Mlle d'Alençon.

HARO, don Luis de, *b.* 1599, *d.* Nov. 26, 1661; Spanish diplomat and Prime Minister under Philip IV; negotiated the peace of the Pyrenees with Mazarin, 1659.

HAUTEFORT, Marie de, *b.* 1616, *d.* 1691; dame d'atour to Anne of Austria; *m.* the maréchal de Schomberg, 1646; mistress of Louis XIII.

HENRI IV, King of France, *b.* Dec. 14, 1553, assassinated, May 14, 1610; son of Antoine de Bourbon, duc de Vendôme, and Jeanne d'Albret, Queen of Navarre, who *d.* 1572 when Henri became King of Navarre; succeeded Henri III as King of France, Aug. 1589; *m.* (1) Marguerite de Valois (*see* Margot, la reine); (2) Marie de' Medici *q.v.*

HENRIETTA (Henriette d'Angleterre), *b.* June 16, 1644, *d.* June 30, 1670; daughter of Charles I and Henrietta Maria; *m.* Philippe, duc d'Anjou *q.v.*, brother of Louis XIV, Mar. 30, 1661; known as Madame.

HENRIETTA MARIA, Queen of England, *b.* Nov. 25, 1609, *d.* Sept. 10, 1669; daughter of Henri IV of France and Marie de' Medici; sister of Louis XIII and Gaston d'Orléans and aunt of Mademoiselle; *m.* May 11, 1625, Charles I, King of England *q.v.*

LA ROCHEFOUCAULD, François, duc de, *b.* 1613, *d.* 1680; author of the Maximes.

LA SABLIÈRE, Mme de, *b.* 1636, *d.* Jan. 8, 1693; *m.* Antoine de Rambouillet, sieur de la Sablière; had a *salon*; La Fontaine lived in her house for some years.

LAUZUN, Antonin Nompar de Caumont, duc de, *b.* May, 1633, *d.* Nov. 19, 1723; son of Gabriel de Caumont, comte de Lauzun, a nobleman of Guyenne, and Charlotte de Caumont La Force, daughter of the marquis de Castelnau, later duc de La Force; *m.* May 21, 1695, Geneviève de Durfort, younger daughter of the maréchal de Lorge.

LA VALLIÈRE, Louise Françoise de la Baume le Blanc, duchesse de, *b.* 1644, *d.* 1710; daughter of Laurent de la Baume le Blanc; mistress of Louis XIV, who created her a duchess, 1677; never married; retired into a Carmelite convent.

LE NÔTRE, André, *b.* 1613, *d.* 1700; architect.

LONGUEVILLE, Anne Geneviève de Bourbon, duchesse de, *b.* Aug. 28, 1619, *d.* Apr. 15, 1679; daughter of Henri II de Bourbon, prince de Condé and Charlotte de Montmorency; sister of le Grand Condé and the prince de Conti; *m.* 1642, Henri, duc de Longueville, *d.* 1663. The ducs de Longueville were descended from Dunois, known as the Bastard of Orléans.

LONGUEVILLE, Mlle de (*see* Nemours, duchesse de).

LORRAINE, Charles IV, duc de, *b.* 1604, *d.* 1675; brother of Marguerite, second wife of Gaston d'Orléans.

LORRAINE, Marguerite de, *b.* 1613, *d.* Apr. 3, 1672; *m.* Jan. 31, 1632, Gaston d'Orléans; known as Madame; stepmother of la Grande Mademoiselle.

Louis XIII, King of France, *b.* Sept. 27, 1601, *d.* May 14, 1643; son of Henri IV and Marie de' Medici *q.v.*; succeeded his father May 14, 1610; *m.* Anne of Austria *q.v.* Nov. 25, 1615.

Louis XIV, King of France, *b.* Sept. 5, 1638, *d.* 1715; son of Louis XIII *q.v.* and Anne of Austria *q.v.*; succeeded his father May 14, 1643; *m.* Maria Teresa, Infanta of Spain *q.v.*, June 9, 1660; *m.* secretly Mme de Maintenon *q.v.* (?) 1683.

Louvois, François Michel Le Tellier, marquis de, *b.* Jan. 18, 1641, *d.* July 16, 1691; son of Michel Le Tellier, Minister of War, who died 1666; succeeded his father as Minister of War, 1666.

Lully, Jean-Baptiste (Lulli, Giovanni Battista), *b.* in Florence 1633(?), *d.* 1687; director of the Court orchestra, 1652; Court composer, 1653.

Luynes, Charles d'Albert, duc de, *b.* Aug. 5, 1578, *d.* Dec. 14, 1621; Grand Falconer of France; favourite of Louis XIII; *m.* 1617, Marie de Rohan (*see* Chevreuse, duchesse de).

Madame, *see* Henrietta (Henriette d'Angleterre), wife of Philippe, duc d'Anjou *q.v.*

Madame, *see* Lorraine, Marguerite de.

Maine, duc du, Louis Auguste, *b.* Mar. 31, 1670, *d.* 1736; illegitimate son of Louis XIV and Mme de Montespan; *m.* Anne Bénédicte, grand-daughter of le Grand Condé.

Maintenon, Françoise d'Aubigné, marquise de, *b.* Nov. 28, 1635, *d.* Apr. 16, 1719; daughter of Constant d'Aubigné and Jeanne de Cardilhac; *m.* 1652 Paul Scarron who died, 1660; governess to the children of Louis XIV and Mme de Montespan *q.v.*; *m.* secretly, probably in 1683, Louis XIV.

Malherbe, François de, *b.* 1555, *d.* 1628; poet.

Mancini, Laura duchesse de Mercœur, *b.* 1636, *d.* 1657; niece of Cardinal Mazarin; *m.* 1651, the duc de Mercœur.

Mancini, Marie, princess Colonna, *b.* 1640, *d.* (?)1715; niece of Cardinal Mazarin; beloved in youth by Louis XIV; *m.* 1662, Lorenzo Onofrio, prince Colonna.

Mancini, Olympe, *see* Soissons, comtesse de.

Margot, la reine; Marguerite de Valois, *b.* 1553, *d.* 1615; daughter of Henri II, King of France and Catherine de' Medici; *m.* Henri IV, King of France, who repudiated her in 1599; author of poems and memoirs.

Maria Teresa (Marie-Thérèse), Queen of France, *b.* Sept. 20, 1638, *d.* July 30, 1683; daughter of Philip IV, King of Spain, and Elisabeth de France *q.v.*; *m.* Louis XIV, King of France *q.v.*, June 9, 1660.

MAYERNE, Sir Theodore Turquet de, *b.* Sept. 1573, *d.* Mar. 22, 1655; appointed physician to Charles I on his accession.

MAZARIN, Cardinal (Giulio Mazarini), *b.* July 14, 1602, *d.* Mar. 9, 1661; son of Pietro Mazarini, a solicitor, and Ortensia Buffatini; Vice-legate at Avignon 1634; Papal Nuncio in Paris 1634–1636; naturalised French in 1639; made a cardinal, Dec. 1641.

MEDICI, Cosimo III de', Grand-duke of Tuscany, *b.* 1642, *d.* 1723; son of Ferdinand II and Vittoria della Rovere; succeeded his father in 1670; *m.* Apr. 19, 1661, Marguerite Louise d'Orléans, half-sister of la Grande Mademoiselle.

MEDICI, Marie de', Queen of France, *b.* 1573, *d.* 1642; daughter of Francesco I, Grand-duke of Tuscany, and Joanna of Austria; *m.* Henri IV, King of France *q.v.*, Dec. 9, 1600; mother of Louis XIII *q.v.*, Gaston d'Orléans *q.v.*, Elisabeth, Queen of Spain *q.v.*, Henrietta Maria, Queen of England *q.v.* and Christine, duchesse de Savoie *q.v.*; grandmother of la Grande Mademoiselle.

MONACO, Charlotte de Gramont, princesse de, *b.* 1639, *d.* June 1678; daughter of the duc de Gramont *q.v.*; *m.* Mar. 30, 1660, Louis I de Grimaldi, prince de Monaco.

MONTBAZON, Marie d'Avaujour de Bretagne, duchesse de; *b.* 1612, *d.* 1657; daughter of Charles, comte de Vertus, and (?) de la Varenne-Fouquet; second wife of Hercule de Rohan, duc de Montbazon and consequently stepmother of the duchesse de Chevreuse *q.v.*

MONTESPAN, Françoise-Athénaïs de Rochechouart, marquise de, *b.* 1641, *d.* May 27, 1707; daughter of Gabriel de Rochechouart, duc de Mortemart; *m.* 1663, Louis Henri de Pardaillon de Gondrin, marquis de Montespan; mistress of Louis XIV.

MONTPENSIER, Marie de Bourbon, duchesse de, *b.* Oct. 15, 1605, *d.* June 4, 1627; known as Madame; daughter of Henri de Bourbon, duc de Montpensier, and Henriette Catherine de Joyeuse; married as his first wife Gaston d'Orléans *q.v.*; mother of la Grande Mademoiselle

MOTTEVILLE, Françoise Bertaut, Mme de, *b.* 1621, *d.* Dec. 1689; daughter of Pierre Bertaut, a gentleman of the King's (Louis

XIII) and of a half-Spanish mother, attached to Anne of Austria; niece of Jean Bertaut, 1552–1611, Bishop of Seez and a poet; *m.* 1639, Nicolas Langlois de Motteville, then aged 90, who died two years later; devoted friend and *dame d'honneur* of Anne of Austria; author of *Mémoires.*

NEMOURS, Henri de Savoie, duc de, *b.* 1624, *d.* 1652; *m.* 1643, Elisabeth de Vendôme, sister of the duc de Beaufort *q.v.*, who killed Nemours in a duel.

NEMOURS, Elisabeth, duchesse de, *b.* (?), *d.* May 19, 1664; daughter of César, duc de Vendôme *q.v.*; *m.* 1643, Henri de Savoie, duc de Nemours *q.v.*

NEMOURS, Marie, duchesse de, author of the *Mémoires de la duchesse de Nemours; b.* 1625, *d.* June 16, 1707; daughter of Henri, duc de Longueville, 1595–1663, and Louise de Bourbon-Soissons, his first wife (his second wife was le Grand Condé's sister); *m.* 1657, Henri II de Savoie, duc de Nemours.

NOGENT, Diane Charlotte, marquise de, *b.* (?), *d.* Nov. 4, 1720; daughter of Gabriel de Caumont, comte de Lauzun and Charlotte de Caumont La Force; sister of Lauzun; *m.* (?) Bautru, marquis de Nogent, of a family from Angers.

ORANGE, Mary Stuart, princess of, *b.* Nov. 4, 1631, *d.* Dec. 24, 1660; daughter of Charles I *q.v.* and Henrietta Maria *q.v.*; *m.* William of Nassau, who *d.* Nov. 1650.

ORLÉANS, Gaston Jean-Baptiste, duc d', known as Monsieur, *b.* Apr. 25, 1608, *d.* February 2, 1660; son of Henri IV *q.v.* and Marie de' Medici *q.v.*; brother of Louis XIII *q.v.*; father of la Grande Mademoiselle; *m.* (1) Marie de Bourbon-Montpensier *q.v.*; (2) Marguerite de Lorraine *q.v.*

ORLÉANS, Marguerite Louise d' (Mlle d'Orléans), *b.* July 28, 1645, *d.* Sept. 1721; daughter of Gaston, duc d'Orléans *q.v.* and Marguerite de Lorraine *q.v.*; the eldest of la Grande Mademoiselle's half-sisters; *m.* April 19, 1661, Cosimo III de' Medici, Grand-duke of Tuscany *q.v.*

ORLÉANS, Philippe, duc d', *see* Anjou, Philippe duc d'.

PALATINE, Anne de Gonzague, princesse, *b.* 1616, *d.* July 6, 1684; daughter of Charles de Gonzague, duc de Nevers and Duke of Mantua, *d.* 1637, and of Catherine de Lorraine; *m.* Edouard, son of Frederick V, Duke of Bavaria; their daughter, Anne, *m.* Henri de Bourbon, duc d'Enghien, son of le Grand Condé.

PHILIP IV, King of Spain, *b.* Apr. 8, 1605, *d.* 1665; brother of Anne of Austria; *m.* Elisabeth de France *q.v.*

PORTE, de La, Pierre, *b.* 1603, *d.* Sept. 13, 1680; attached to the service of Anne of Austria; *1er gentilhomme de la chambre de Louis XIV; m.* Françoise Cottignon de Chauvri.

PUYGUILHEM, PEGUILIEN or PIGUILAIN, *see* Lauzun, duc de.

RAMBOUILLET, Catherine de Vivonne, marquise de, *b.* 1588, *d.* Dec. 2, 1665; daughter of Jean de Vivonne, marquis de Pisani, and Giulia Savelli; *m.* Charles d'Argennes, marquis de Rambouillet.

RETZ, Jean François Paul de Gondi, Cardinal de, *b.* Sept. 20, 1613, *d.* Aug. 24, 1679; son of Philippe-Emmanuel de Gondi and Marguerite de Lilly; became a cardinal in Feb. 1652.

RICHELIEU, Armand Jean du Plessis, Cardinal de, *b.* Sept. 9, 1585, *d.* Dec. 4, 1642; son of François du Plessis, *d.* 1590, and Suzanne de La Porte, *d.* 1616.

ST GEORGES, Jeanne de Harlay, marquise de, *b.* (?), *d.* Feb. 24, 1643; daughter of Mme de Montglat, governess to Louis XIII; governess to la Grande Mademoiselle.

ST SIMON, Louis de Rouvroy, duc de, *b.* Jan. 16, 1675, *d.* Mar. 2, 1755; son of Claude, duc de St Simon, and Charlotte de L'Aubespine; *m.* Apr. 8, 1695, Gabrielle de Durfort, elder daughter of the maréchal de Lorge; he was thus a brother-in-law of Lauzun *q.v.*

SAVOIE, Charles Emmanuel, duc de, *b.* 1634, *d.* June 12, 1675; second son of Victor Amédée I, duc de Savoie, and Christine, daughter of Henri IV and Marie de' Medici; *m.* (1) Françoise Madeleine, Mlle de Valois; (2) Marie Jeanne-Baptiste, daughter of Charles Amédée de Savoie, duc de Nemours, and Elizabeth de Vendôme *q.v.*

SAVOIE, Christine, duchesse de (Madame Royale), *b.* Feb. 11, 1606, *d.* Dec. 27, 1663; daughter of Henri IV and Marie de' Medici; *m.* Feb. 10, 1619, Victor Amédée, 1er, duc de Savoie.

SAVOIE, Françoise Madeleine (Mlle de Valois) duchesse de, *b.* Oct. 13, 1648, *d.* Jan. 14, 1664; daughter of Gaston d'Orléans *q.v.* and Marguerite de Lorraine *q.v.*; half-sister of la Grande Mademoiselle; *m.* March 4, 1663, Charles Emmanuel II, duc de Savoie.

SÉGRAIS, Jean Regnauld or Renaud, sieur de, *b.* Aug. 22, 1624, *d.* 1701;

BIOGRAPHICAL NOTES

entered the service of Mademoiselle in 1648 and accompanied her to St Fargeau; man of letters and a member of the French Academy; may possibly have collaborated with Mme de La Fayette in her novel *La Princesse de Clèves*.

SÉGUIER, Pierre, created duc de Villemor by Anne of Austria, *b*. 1588, *d*. 1672; Chancellor of France; foundation member of the Académie Française.

SÉVIGNÉ, Marie de Rabutin-Chantal, marquise de, *b*. 1626, *d*. 1696.

SOISSONS, Olympe Mancini, comtesse de, *b*. 1639, *d*. 1708; niece of Cardinal Mazarin; *m*. 1657, Eugène Maurice de Carrie-Corignan, *d*. 1673, for whom the title comte de Soissons was revived; mother of Prince Eugène.

TARENTE, Amélie de Hesse-Cassel, princesse de; *m*. Henri Charles de la Trémouille, prince de Tarente.

TARENTAISE, La, was a province in the Duchy of Savoy.

THIANGES, Gabrielle de Mortemart, marquise de, *b*. (?), *d*. (?); elder sister of Mme de Montespan *q.v.*; *m*. 1655, Claude de Damas, marquis de Thianges.

TURENNE, Henri de la Tour d'Auvergne, vicomte de, *maréchal de France, b*. Sept. 11, 1611, killed in battle July 27, 1675; second son of Henri, duc de Bouillon, and Elizabeth, daughter of William the Silent, Prince of Orange; *m*. a daughter of the maréchal de La Force.

TUSCANY, Cosimo III, Grand-duke of, *see* Medici.

TUSCANY, Grand-duchess of, *see* Orléans, Marguerite Louise.

VALOIS, Mlle de, Françoise Madeleine, *see* Savoie, duchesse de.

VENDÔME, César, duc de, 1594–1665; illegitimate son of Henri IV and Gabrielle d'Estrées.

Index

Alluye, marquise d', 327

Alfonso VI King of Portugal, 224–5

Anne of Austria (Anne d'Autriche), present at marriage of Gaston d'Orléans, 14; implicated in plot against Richelieu, 16; accused of intrigues with Spain, 35; the Val-de-Grâce affair, 36–8; her pregnancy, 44; birth of Louis XIV, 49; becomes Queen-Regent, 63; her popularity, 63–4; she appoints Cardinal Mazarin as Prime Minister, 65; welcomes Charles Prince of Wales, 75; suspected liaison with Mazarin, 80 *n*, 91; angry with Mademoiselle, 81–2; removes her children to St Germain, 91; goes to Bordeaux, 98–9; receives Condé, Conti and Longueville, 101; misleads Mademoiselle, 104; tries to control Louis XIV, 106; returns to Paris, 138; receives Mademoiselle back into favour, 193–6; encourages Louis XIV's marriage, 208; snubs Mademoiselle, 214; reconciled with Mademoiselle, 193–194; her last illness and death, 355–7. Character: *la bonne reine*, 35, 63; gentle and indolent, 100. Appearance, 35–6

Arlington, Lord, signatory to the Treaty of Dover, 260

Artagnan, M. d', escorts Lauzun to Pignerol, 299; meets Mademoiselle, 308

Arundell of Wardour, Lord, signatory to the Treaty of Dover, 261

Austria, Don John of, 205, 206

Avenant, Sir William D', staying in Paris, 73

Barrailh, Henri de, at Pignerol, 313; he corresponds with Lauzun, 314, 322–25

Bavaria, Rupert of: see Rupert of Bavaria

Beaufort, duc de, playfellow of Mademoiselle, 32; plots against Mazarin, 66; imprisoned at Vincennes, 66; his popularity, 93; attempted assassination of, 99; meets Mademoiselle on her way to Orléans, 110; meets her at the Hôtel de Ville, 121–2; kills the duc de Nemours, 124; banished from Paris, 139; gives advice to Gaston d'Orléans, 142

Bellegarde, duc de, admires Mademoiselle as a baby, 20

Bellings, Sir Richard, signatory to the Treaty of Dover, 261

Berkeley, Sir John, left in charge of Princess Henrietta, 72

Blancmesnil, Roger Potier, seigneur de, arrested by Mazarin, 89

Blois, château de, 32

Bois-le-Vicomte, a property of Mademoiselle's, 105, 149

Bouillon, duchesse de, sets up a salon in the Hôtel de Ville, 94–5

Boultz, M. le, at St Fargeau, 190

Bouthillier, Mme, 148; receives Mademoiselle at Pont, 157; offers further hospitality, 158

Brancas, comte de, gentleman-in-waiting to Anne of Austria, 29; put in command of Mademoiselle's regiment, 127

Bréauté, marquise de, accompanies Mademoiselle to Orléans, 110, 112

Broussel, Pierre, arrested by Mazarin, 89; liberated, 90

Bryant, Sir Arthur, quoted, 261
Bussy-Rabutin, Roger de, quoted, 56, 223, 241

Carignan, princesse de, 290
Chabot, Henri, marries Marguerite de Rohan for love, 78; resentment of her family, 78
Chalais, Henri de Talleyrand, marquis de, involved in plot against Richelieu, 15; turns King's Evidence, 16; conspires again, 17; arrested and tried for high treason, 18; executed, 18
Chambord, château de, described by Mademoiselle, 32
Charles I, King of England, writes to Sir Theodore de Mayerne, 72; execution of, 82 n
Charles II, King of England, arrives at Fontainebleau, 75; greeted by the French royal family, 75; described by Mademoiselle, 75; accompanies Mademoiselle to a party, 76; at a party at the Palais-Royal, 77; his second visit to Paris, 82-5; proposed marriage with Mademoiselle, 82; returns to Paris after battle of Worcester, 106; friendship with Mademoiselle, 106; rejected by Mademoiselle, 106-7; his Restoration, 221; affection for his sister, 223, 259-60; meets her at Dover, 260
Charny, chevalier de, Mademoiselle's half-brother, 166, 181
Châtillon, duchesse de, known as Bablon to Charles II, 85; engaged in political intrigues during the Fronde, 98; exile from Paris, 139
Chavigny, comte de, persuades Gaston to send Mademoiselle to the Hôtel de Ville, 116; references to, 130, 137 n
Chenonceaux, château de, described by Mademoiselle, 33

Chevreuse, Marie de Rohan, duchesse de, her influence over Chalais, 15, 17; involved in plot against Richelieu, 17; exiled (1626), 18; involved in the Val-de-Grâce affair, 38; escapes in disguise to Spain, 38; returns to France, 64; plots against Mazarin, 66; engaged in political intrigues during the Fronde, 97
Choisy, Mme de, gives a party for Mademoiselle, 76; used as a go-between by the princesse Palatine, 105; frightened by Mademoiselle's reckless behaviour, 143-4
Choisy, Mademoiselle's house at, 319-21
Christina of Sweden, meets Mademoiselle, 183-8
Cinq-Mars, Henri d'Effiat, marquis de, relations with Louis XIII, 57-8; he conspires against Richelieu, 58; is arrested and executed, 58
Clifford, Sir Thomas (Lord Clifford of Chudleigh), signatory to the Treaty of Dover, 261
Colbert de Croissy, French ambassador to Charles II, signatory to the Treaty of Dover, 260; meets Louis XIV at Calais, 263
Comminges, M. de, (French ambassador in London), in Paris, 84
Condé, Henri de Bourbon, prince de, involved in plot against Richelieu, 15; his curious behaviour, 68
Condé, family, 68-71
Condé, Louis de Bourbon, prince de, (Le Grand Condé), his victory at Rocroi, 64; his overbearing character, 69; emotional nature, 78-9; on the Fronde, 86; does not wish to overthrow the Monarchy, 87; his victory at Lens, 89; lays siege to Paris, 92; his insolence to Mazarin, 96-7; imprisoned at Vincennes, 97; released from

prison, 101; returns to Paris, 101; received by Anne of Austria, 101–2; reconciled with Mademoiselle, 102; his marriage to Mademoiselle suggested, 103; fails to check Mazarin's troops, 108; wins battle of Bléneau, 114; captures St Denis, 115; loses it again, 115; retires to Charenton, 115; is attacked near Montmartre, 115; meets Mademoiselle near the Bastille, 118; fighting in the faubourg St Antoine, 118–9; master in Paris, 123; makes a fool of Mademoiselle, 126–7; leaves Paris, 138–9; defeated at the battle of the Dunes, 206; reconciled with the Court, 214; eavesdrops on Mademoiselle, 286–7 nn

Condé, princesse de, (Madame la Princesse), made to look a fool at parties, 30–1; puts Bordeaux into a state of siege, 98; falls dangerously ill, 102, 130; recovers, 103, 131

Conti, Armand de Bourbon, prince de, physically malformed, 69; under the domination of Mme de Longueville, 70; sides with the Parlement, 93; imprisoned at Vincennes, 97; released from prison, 101; returns to Paris, 101; Mademoiselle kind to him, 102

Corneille, Pierre, at the hôtel de Rambouillet, 26

Cours-la-reine, laid out by Marie de' Medici, 53; described by Mlle de Scudéry, 53

Cowley, Abraham, assistant secretary to Henrietta Maria, 74

Crashaw, Richard, living in Paris in poverty, 74; taken into the service of Henrietta Maria, 74

Créqui, duc de, 280, 287

Cromwell, Oliver, Henrietta Maria calls him ce scelerat, 75

Dalkeith, Anne Villiers, Lady, left in charge of Princess Henrietta, 72; takes Princess Henrietta to France, 74–5

Denham, Sir John, in attendance upon Henrietta Maria, 74

Dover, Treaty of, 260–2

Elisabeth de France, Queen of Spain, her death, 80

Enghien, duc d': see Condé, le Grand

Enghien, duc d' (son of le Grand Condé), his strange delusions, 68–9

Épernon, duc d', involved in plot against Richelieu, 15

Épernon, Mlle d', friendship with Mademoiselle, 79; enters a convent, 79

Essex, Robert Devereux, 3rd Earl of, writes a harsh letter to Henrietta Maria, 72

Eu, château d', bought by Mademoiselle, 199; her work there, 226

Ferdinand, Cardinal-Archbishop of Toledo, jestingly suggested as a husband for Mademoiselle, 78

Ferdinand III, Emperor, Mademoiselle considers marrying him, 81

Fiesque, comte de, begs Gaston to come to Orléans, 110; sent by Condé to appeal to Gaston and to Mademoiselle, 115–6

Fiesque, Mme de (the elder), succeeds Mme de St Georges as governess to Mademoiselle, 60; annoys Mademoiselle, 61; is locked into her room by Mademoiselle, 62; arrives at St Fargeau, 167

Fiesque, comtesse de (the younger), accompanies Mademoiselle to Orléans, 110; at St Fargeau, 166; friendship with Mme de Frontenac, 167; at St Fargeau, 179, 180,

189; leaves Mademoiselle, 192; announces Lauzun's arrest, 297

Fontevrault, abbey of, visited by Mademoiselle, 33

Fouquet, Nicolas, his fête at Vaux-le-Vicomte, 232-3; his disgrace, 233; Pignerol, 309

Fronde, the Parliamentary, its tragicomic character, 86; differs from the Civil War in England, 86; a feud between Crown and Parlement, 88; the journée des barricades, 90; origin of the name Fronde, 90

Fronde of the princes, Chapter V passim

Frontenac, comte de, at St Fargeau, 189-90 n

Frontenac, comtesse de, accompanies Mademoiselle to Orléans, 110; to St Fargeau, 152 n, 153, 159; frightened at night, 160; at St Fargeau, 179, 180, 189

Gabriel, Mademoiselle's architect at Choisy, 319

Gazette de France, founded, 43 n; quoted, 43

Gondi, Paul de: see Retz, Cardinal de,

Goulas, Nicolas (gentleman-in-waiting to Gaston d'Orléans), thinks Mademoiselle ugly as a baby, 20; receives a letter from her, 26; she mistrusts him, 176 n

Gramont, duc de, envoy to Madrid, 217; takes Lauzun into his household, 229

Guémené, princesse de, her influence over the duc de Lorraine, 115

Guiche, comte de, at the hôtel Rambouillet, 27; loves Henrietta (Madame), 232

Guilloire, replaces Préfontaine, 203-4; Mademoiselle's opinion of him, 204

Guise, duchesse de (grandmother of Mademoiselle), Mademoiselle's attitude towards her, 23; deceives Mademoiselle, 175; cuts her out of her will, 180; her death, 180-1

Guitaut, sieur de, wounded during the Fronde, 117

Guitry, marquis de, a friend of Lauzun, 245, 264, 280, 287

Halluin, duchesse d', involved in a quarrel at marriage of Gaston d'Orléans, 14

Haro, Don Luis de, meets Mazarin at Bidassoa, 213; stands proxy for Louis XIV, 219

Hautefort, Marie de, Louis XIII in love with her, 44-5; their hunting parties, 44

Henri IV, his son's affection for him, 45; severity towards his son, 46, 47 n

Henrietta, Princess (Henriette d'Angleterre, Madame), birth at Exeter, 72; is left in England as a baby, 72; is taken to France in disguise, 74-5; rejoins her mother, 75; marries Philippe d'Orléans, 222; description of her, 222, 223, 242; on the journey to Flanders, 251, 252, 259; goes to Dover, 259; her part in the Treaty of Dover, 260-2; her death, 265-6

Henrietta Maria, Queen of England, her marriage with Charles I, 72; she gives birth to a daughter, 72; her letter to Charles I, 72 n; she escapes to France, 72-3; her return to Paris, 73; welcomed by the French royal family, 73; given lodgings and an allowance, 73; her little Court in Paris, 73; her increasing poverty, 74-5; she schemes to marry Mademoiselle to Charles II, 75-6; the scheme revived, 181-2; death of, 259

Hérouard, Jean (physician to Louis XIII), quoted, 29, 45-6

Hocquincourt, maréchal d', in command of Mazarin's German troops, 108; devastates the Blaisois, 109

Hôpital, maréchal de l', at the Hôtel de Ville with Mademoiselle, 117; escapes through a window, 122

Huxley, Aldous, quoted, 207

Les Importants, party formed against Cardinal Mazarin, 66

La Bruyère, Jean de, quoted, 305

La Fayette, Louise de, loved by Louis XIII, 47

La Fayette, Mme de, quoted, 232, 233

La Guérinière, maître d'hôtel to Mademoiselle, 152 n; at St Fargeau, 159, 160; on Mademoiselle, 175

La Motte, Mlle de, 325, 327

La Porte, Pierre, acts as a go-between for Anne of Austria, 38

La Rochefoucauld, duc de, his devotion to Mme de Longueville, 69–70; wounded during the Fronde, 117; banished from Paris, 139

La Sablière, Mme de, 327

Lauzun, comte de, his early life, 228–31; his career, 229–39; at Court, 231; love for Mme de Monaco, 231–6; hides under Mme de Montespan's bed, 237–8; at the Bastille, 238; his character, 239, 240; personal appearance, 239–40; Mademoiselle falls in love with him, 241–8; in command of troops in Flanders, 248, 253–4; erratic behaviour, 254–8 passim; marriage with Mademoiselle proposed, 277–85; the marriage forbidden, 285–93; his arrest, 297; in prison at Pignerol, 298–305; strangeness of his character, 303–5; his attempts to escape, 309–10; visited by Mme de Nogent, 311–

12; released from Pignerol, 322; corresponds with Barrailh, 322–5; he goes to Bourbon, 322–3; dissatisfied with Mademoiselle's generosity, 326–7; he returns to Paris, 327; his unkindness to Mademoiselle, 328–33; buys the hôtel de Lauzun, 330; Mademoiselle parts from him, 333; he tries to keep in touch with her, 333–4; his life after her death, 336–42

La Vallière, Louise de, with the Court in Flanders, 237, 249, 252

Le Nôtre, André, employed at Vaux-le-Vicomte, 232–3; at Pignerol, 313; consulted by Mademoiselle, 319

Le Vau, François, employed at St Fargeau, 165

Le Vau, Louis, architect of Vaux-le-Vicomte, 165, 232

Lit de justice, 87, 88

Longueville, duc de, involved in plot against Richelieu, 15; sides with the Parlement, 93; imprisoned at Vincennes, 97; released from prison, 101; returns to Paris, 101

Longueville, Anne Geneviève de Bourbon, duchesse de, quarrels with Mme de Montbazon, 66; description of her manner and appearance, 69; devotion to her of the duc de Rochefoucauld, 69–70; and of her brothers, 69–70; sets up a salon in the Hôtel de Ville, 94–5; escapes to Dieppe, 97; banished from Paris, 139

Longueville, Mlle de (see also Nemours, duchesse de), friendship with Mademoiselle, 43–4; her character, 52

Lorraine, duc de, arrives in Paris, 115; unpopularity of his troops, 115

Lorraine, the duchy of, 39

Lorraine, Charles de, in Paris, 126; Mademoiselle's weakness for him, 131–4; his high spirits, 133–4

Lorraine, Marguerite de (Madame), marries Gaston d'Orléans, 25; her adventures, 67; rejoins Gaston at Meudon, 67; is thought uncouth by Mademoiselle, 67; goes to live in Paris, 67; her son the duc de Valois dies, 124–5; shows her good sense, 140–1; described by a monk, 155

Louis XIII, present at marriage of Gaston d'Orléans, 14; loves Marie de Hautefort, 44–5; Marie de Hautefort replaced by Cinq-Mars, 57; his death, 62. Character: his reluctance before the act of love, 36 n, 47; dislikes being a king, 45; his life as a child, 45–7; complications of his sex-life, 47; relations with Richelieu, 48. His homosexuality: Charles de Luynes, 47; Cinq-Mars, 57–8

Louis XIV, birth of, 49; succeeds his father, 63; presented to the Parlement, 63; begins to assert himself, 106; his resentment of Mazarin, 122; returns to Paris, 138; meets Mademoiselle at Sedan, 196–8; serious illness, 206–8; marriage to Maria Teresa, 216–19; takes control on death of Mazarin, 220–1; forbids Mademoiselle's marriage, 285–7; his reasons for forbidding it, 288–91

Louvois, marquis de, hostility towards Lauzun, 236–7, 288

Lulli, Giovanni Battista, in Mademoiselle's household, 169

Luxembourg, palais, or palais d' Orléans, given by Marie de' Medici to Gaston d'Orléans, 67

Luynes, Charles, duc de, influence over Louis XIII, 36

Madame: see Lorraine, Marguerite

de: see Henrietta, Princess (Henriette d'Angleterre)

MADEMOISELLE, la Grande (Anne Marie Louise d'Orléans, duchesse de Montpensier), birth, 19; installed in the Tuileries, 20; her titles, 20; 'Daughter of France', 20–1; her household, 21–2; her upbringing, 22–3, 26; her dislike of Richelieu, 24–5; her childhood friends, 26; her poor education, 28; meets her father on his return to France, 30; happy in his company, 30; he devises entertainments for her, 31; they travel in Touraine together, 31–2; she visits the abbey of Fontevrault, 33; and the village of Richelieu, 33; goes to visit Louis XIII and Anne of Austria at Chantilly, 37; much upset by the Val-de-Grâce affair, 37; visits the King and Queen at St Germain, 43; gives a ball in Paris, 43; friendship with Mlle de Longueville, 43–4; goes to stay at St Germain, 44; birth of Louis XIV, she decides to marry him, 49; is sent for and scolded by Richelieu, 50–1; her dislike of the Condés, 52; is given Mme de Fiesque as governess, 60; resents her attempts at control, 61–2; accompanies her father to Meudon, 67; is much disappointed by her stepmother, 67; her comment on Henrietta Maria, 73; her comment on Charles II, 75; party given for her by Mme de Choisy, 76; accompanied there by Charles II, 76; attends a great party at the Palais-Royal, 76–7; why had she not yet married? 77–80; her views on love and marriage, 78; her desire for a crown, 80; she contemplates marrying Ferdinand III, 81; has unpleasant scene with Anne of Austria and Mazarin, 81–

82; if she had married Charles II, 82; she discusses it with Lord Jermyn, 83; she turns against the idea, 84; her dislike of Condé, 89; she attends a Te Deum in Notre Dame, 89; her first reactions to the Fronde, 89; accompanies the royal family to St Germain, 91; is better off there than they are, 92; returns to Paris, 95; dances with Louis XIV at the Hôtel de Ville, 95; gets smallpox, 96; accompanies the Court to Bordeaux, 98–9; reconciliation with Condé, 102; her marriage to Condé suggested, 103; she still thinks of marrying Louis XIV, 103–6; friendship with Charles II, 106; he asks her to marry him, 106; she reproves and rejects him, 106–7; gives a party at mi-carême, 109; she goes to Orléans, 110; her adventures at Orléans, 111–14; she returns to Paris, 114; goes to the Hôtel de Ville, 116–17; horrified by seeing wounded men, 117–18; enters a house near the Bastille, 118; meets Condé there, 118; goes to the Bastille, 118–19: (see also Appendix III, pp. 347, 348); spends a sleepless night, 119; adopts the symbol of the straw, 120; returns to the Hôtel de Ville, 121; explores the burnt-out rooms with the duc de Beaufort, 121–122; the death of her little half-brother, 124–6; she is persuaded to equip a regiment, 127–9; made fun of by Condé and Charles de Lorraine, 127; renewed suggestion of marrying Condé, 130–1; her weakness for Charles de Lorraine, 131–4; her expedition to the princes' army, 134–7; her sorrow at the departure of Condé and Lorraine, 138; begins to worry about her fate, 144; no help from her father, 144–7; she seeks refuge in the houses of her friends, 147; is persuaded to leave Paris, 150; sets out for St Fargeau, 152; stays with Mme Bouthillier, 153; meeting with a monk, 154–7; her journey to St Fargeau, 157; corresponds with Condé, 157; arrives at St Fargeau, 159–60; refuses to stay there, 160; stays at Dannery, 160; returns to St Fargeau, 161; her life there, 164–9; she begins writing her Memoirs, 169–72; her style, grammar and spelling, 170–1; troubles with her father, 174–7, 180; dismissal of Préfontaine, 177–8; she entertains Henrietta Maria, 181–2; meets Christina of Sweden, 183–8; troubles with Mmes de Fiesque and Frontenac, 189; tries to replace Préfontaine, 190; amused by M. de Frontenac, 190; and by Mme de Thianges, 191–2; reconciliation with the Court, 193; she travels to Sedan, 193; meets Anne of Austria, 193–4; meets Louis XIV and the duc d'Anjou, 195–8; buys Eu, 199; at Champigny, 199–201; writes her own portrait, 201–2; replaces Préfontaine, 203–4; considers marrying Philippe d'Orléans, 204–5; her opinion of him, 206; accompanies the Court to Lyon, 208; visits Dombes, 209–10; teased by Mazarin, 210; accompanies the Court to Provence, 211; at St Fargeau, 211; in Paris, 211–13; accompanies the Court to Provence again, 213; death of her father, 215–16; at St Jean de Luz, 216–19; refuses to marry the King of Portugal, 224–5; banished to St Fargeau, 225–6; starts repairs at Eu, 226; is growing old, 227; begins to like Lauzun, 239; falls in love, 241; accompanies the

Court to Flanders, 248; the journey described, 249–53; new marriage projects, 262–4; death of Henrietta, 266; should Mademoiselle marry Monsieur? 266–9; continued love for Lauzun, 269–75; she writes to the King, 276; happy for three days, 278–85; the marriage forbidden, 285–7; her despair, 287, 292–5; she tries to resume normal life, 295–6; arrest of Lauzun, 297; her distress, 300; she learns that he is at Pignerol, 301; her life during his imprisonment, 305–7; she signs away Dombes and Eu, 316–17; tricked by Mme de Montespan, 318; she buys an estate at Choisy, 319–21; her jealousy of Lauzun, 323; abuses Barrailh, 323–5; finds herself duped, 325–6; return of Lauzun to Paris, 327; his ingratitude towards Mademoiselle, 328–33; she parts with him for ever, 333; her last illness and death, 334–5. Character: dislikes being treated as a child, 61; her views on love and marriage, 78; her friendships with women, 79; her readiness to acknowledge her mistakes, 89; warm-hearted, 104, 125; her gullibility, 105; her intractibility, 167–8, 173, 178, 227; indifference to public affairs, 172–3; her lack of intellect, 174; probably a bore, 196, 214; her temper, 199, 224–5; describes herself, 201–2. Appearance: her complexion, 77, 79, 96; uncouth and hoydenish, 79, 85. Relations with her father: early affection for him, 24; happy time with him in Touraine, 30–3; her suspicions of his treatment of M. de Puylaurens, 34–5; her suspicions of his treatment of Cinq-Mars, 57–8; her pride in his success at Gravelines, 67; gradual

mistrust of him, 150, 175–7; 203; hurt by him, 144–5

Maillé-Brézé, Claire-Clémence de: see Condé, princesse de (Madame la Princesse)

Maine, duc du, 314–16

Maintenon, Mme de, 291

Malherbe, François de, at the hôtel de Rambouillet, 26–8

Mancini, Laura, sought in marriage by the duc de Mercœur, 97

Mancini, Marie, loved by Louis XIV, 208, 211, 216–17; marriage of, 223

Mancini, Olympe, 186

Margot, la reine (Marguerite de Valois), 26 n

Maria Teresa, Infanta of Spain, her marriage with Louis XIV, 216–19; at the French Court, 231–2; on the journey to Flanders, 250–2; behaviour over Henrietta's death, 265; opposes Mademoiselle's marriage to Lauzun, 280, 282; her death, 332

Maupertuis, M. de, escorts Lauzun to Pignerol, 308; escorts Lauzun away from Pignerol, 322

Mayerne, Sir Theodore Turquet de, appeal made to him by Charles I, 72

Mazarin, Cardinal, appointed prime minister by Anne of Austria, 65; description of his manner and appearance, 65; estimate of his abilities, 65–6; blamed for the poverty of Henrietta Maria, 74; unpopularity of, 88, 90–1; his known cowardice, 97; effigies hung in Paris, 99; escapes from Paris, 100; banished from France, 101; rejoins the Court at Poitiers, 108; accompanied by 4,000 Germans, 108; edict of banishment renewed, 108; a price set on his head, 108; he requests Orléans to open its gates, 109; he removes himself to Bouillon, 138; reconciliation with Mademoiselle, 198; gives a party, 205; friendly to Mademoiselle, 212; signs the Peace of the Pyrenees, 213; his death, 220–1

Medici, Marie de', present at marriage of Gaston d'Orléans, 14; exiled, 24 |subsequent life and death, 24 *n*; her treatment of Louis XIII as a child, 46; lays out the Cours-la-Reine, 53

Meilleraye, maréchal de la, incapacitated by gout at Bordeaux, 99

Ménage, Gilles, at the hôtel de Rambouillet, 26–7

Mercœur, duc de, plays with Mademoiselle as a child, 32; plots against Cardinal Mazarin, 66; seeks Mazarin's niece Laura Mancini in marriage, 97

Mercure de France, 43 *n*; annual publication quoted, 73

Molière, quoted, 27, 54, 223

Molina, la, description of, 218

Monaco, princesse de, her affair with Lauzun, 231–6; he hears of her death, 313

Monaldeschi, marquis of, assassinated, 187

Monmouth, James, Duke of, 85

Monsieur: see Orléans, Gaston, duc d': see Orléans, Philippe, duc d'

Montausier, duc de, 280–1, 287

Montbazon, Mme de, quarrels with Mme de Longueville, 66; engages in intrigues during the Fronde, 98; banished from Paris, 139

Montespan, Mme de, and Lauzun, 237–8; with the Court in Flanders, 249, 252; over Mademoiselle's marriage, 290–2, 298–9; intrigues to get Mademoiselle's property, 314–18; reproaches Lauzun, 330

Montglat, Mme de, governess to Louis XIII, 22, 46–7; her severity, 47 *n*

Montpensier, Anne Marie Louise d'Orléans, duchesse de: see MADEMOISELLE

Montpensier, Marie de Bourbon, duchesse de, marries Gaston d'Orléans, 13–14; their wedding night, 18–19; gives birth to a daughter (la Grande Mademoiselle), 19; death, 19

Morosini, Venetian ambassador, quoted, 101

Motteville, Mme de, her Memoirs quoted, 48, 57, 66, 70, 73, 74, 98, 103, 217–18, 223

Nemours, duc de, his frivolity in war, 109; meets Mademoiselle on her way to Orléans, 110; he warns Mademoiselle, 114; killed in a duel, 124

Nemours, duchesse de (see also Longueville, Mlle de), her character, 52; comment on Mme de Longueville and Conti, 70

Nogent, Mme de, 264–5; 284–5, 297; visits Lauzun at Pignerol, 311–12; Mademoiselle's opinion of, 311

Orange, Princess of, entertained by Mademoiselle, 181–2

Orléans, Anne Marie Louise d': see MADEMOISELLE

Orléans, city of, desires to remain neutral during the Fronde, 109; refuses admittance to Mademoiselle, 111; Mademoiselle in authority at, 112

Orléans, Gaston, duc d', marries Marie de Bourbon, 13–14; involved in plot against Richelieu, 15; betrays his accomplices, 16, 17, 18; receives a reward, 17; takes refuge with the duc de Lorraine, 24; marries Marguerite de Lorraine, 25; renounces and denounces his friends, 30; returns to France, 30; sends for Mademoiselle, 30–5; betrays Cinq-Mars, 58; meets his wife at Meudon, 67; returns with her to Paris, 67; is put in command of the French army in Flanders, 67; lieutenant-general during the Fronde, 99; storms at Anne of Austria and Mazarin, 100; allies himself with the princes, 108; cannot decide to go to Orléans, 110; watches Mademoiselle leave for Orléans, 110; writes letter of approval to Mademoiselle, 113; refuses to go to the Hôtel de Ville, 116; sends Mademoiselle in his place, 116; refuses a second time, 120–1; allows Mademoiselle to go in his place, 121; he deceives Mademoiselle, 175; his death, 215 Character: his nocturnal escapades, 20; his gaiety, 24; his duplicity, 58, 175; his evasiveness, 99; his irascibility, 100; his irresponsibility, 116, 120, 140–2

Orléans, Marguerite Louise d', marries Cosimo de' Medici, 223–4

Orléans, Philippe, duc d' (Monsieur), his birth, 64 n (duc d'Anjou); with Louis XIV in boyhood, 194–5; meets Mademoiselle at Sedan, 197; his character, 198, 205–6, 222; marries Henrietta, 222; his conduct in Flanders, 249–59; his anger with Henrietta, 260

Ornano, maréchal d', tutor to Gaston d'Orléans, 15; involved in plot against Richelieu, 15; imprisoned at Vincennes, 16

Palais-Royal, once the Palais-Cardinal or hôtel de Richelieu, 52; bequeathed by Richelieu to Louis XIII, 52 n

Palatine, la princesse, engaged in political intrigues during the Fronde, 98; Cardinal Retz's opinion of her, 98; her adventures and gallantries, 105; intrigues to make Mademoiselle Queen of France, 105; quoted, 299

Paris (see also Cours-la-Reine; jardin de Renard), description of under Louis XIII, 28–9; maisons des baigneurs, 56

Parlement, the French, as compared with the English Parliament, 41–2

Peace, Party of, 115, 122, 137

Philip IV, King of Spain, 218, 219

Préfontaine, discusses the Condé marriage with Mademoiselle, 103; accompanies Mademoiselle to Orléans, 110; his worries over Mademoiselle, 147–50; accompanies her to St Fargeau, 152 n; gives Mademoiselle good advice, 158; his coach attacked, 158; annoyed with her, 159, 167; transcribes her Memoirs, 171; dismissed by Gaston, 177–8

Puyguilhem: see Lauzun, comte de

Puylaurens, M. de, a friend of Gaston d'Orléans, liked by Mademoiselle as a child, 34; she suspects her father of betraying him, 35

Rambouillet, hôtel de, la chambre bleue, 26

Rambouillet, marquise de, her salon, 26–8

Renard, jardin de, 53

Renaudot, Dr Théophraste, founds the Gazette de France, 43 n

Retz, Paul de Gondi, Cardinal de, describes Richelieu's character, 50; opinion of Condé, 64; opinion of Conti and Mme de Longueville, 70; his own character and appearance, 94; quoted, 94–5; imprisoned at Vincennes, 139; his interview with Gaston d'Orléans, 139–42

Retz, maréchale de, 26 n

Riche, madame, a vendor of ribbons, 121

Richelieu, Cardinal, solemnises marriage of Gaston d'Orléans, 13–14; his internal policy against the territorial aristocracy, 40; relations with Louis XIII, 48; his ill-health, 48–9; his character described by Cardinal de Retz, 50; he scolds Mademoiselle, 50–1; as a host at the Palais-Cardinal, 52; his sufferings and death, 59–60

Richelieu, the village, described by Mademoiselle, 33

Rivière, abbé de la, gives unwise counsel to Mademoiselle, 81

Roche-Giffard, wounded during the Fronde, 118

Roger, Louison (mistress of Gaston d'Orléans), Mademoiselle meets her at Tours, 34; goes into a convent, 166 n

Rohan, duc de, suspected of having betrayed Angers, 109; accompanies Mademoiselle to Orléans, 110; persuades Gaston to send Mademoiselle to the Hôtel de Ville, 116; banished from Paris, 139

Rohan, duchesse de, involved in a quarrel at the marriage of Gaston d'Orléans, 14

Rohan, Marguerite de, marries Henri Chabot for love, 78; resentment of her family, 78

ruelle, la, did Mme de Rambouillet innovate it and did Malherbe name it? 27, 28 n

Rupert of Bavaria, acts as interpreter between Mademoiselle and Charles II, 76

to Mademoiselle, 21; her antecedents and character, 22–3; her lack of intellectual interests, 26–8; her intimacy with Anne of Austria, 37; her death, 60

St Mars, an emissary from Condé, 157

St Mars, governor of Pignerol, his severity towards Lauzun, 301–2

St Simon, duc de, quoted, 241, 335, 340–2

Saujon, gives unwise counsel to Mademoiselle, 81; is imprisoned in the Bastille, 81

Sauvat, Mlle, sous-gouvernante to Mademoiselle, 21

Savoie, Marguerite de, proposed as a bride for Louis XIV, 208–9

Savoie, the duchy of, 39

Scudéry, Mlle de, quoted, 53, 56, 200

Ségrais, Jean Renaud, his opinion of Mademoiselle, 167–8

Séguier, Pierre, Chancellor of France, interrogates Anne of Austria at the Val-de-Grâce, 36; announces that she has been appointed Regent, 63

Sentinelli, assassinates Monaldeschi, 187

Sévigné, Mme de, her letter about Mademoiselle's marriage, 277–8; visits Mademoiselle, 284, 292; quoted, 293

Simonne, Dame, member of Mademoiselle's household, 21

Soissons, comte de, involved in plot against Richelieu, 15; suggestion that he should marry Mademoiselle, 51, 77

Suckling, Sir John, his description of Paris, 28

St Fargeau, 159, 161–2, 164–5

St Fiacre, 49

St Georges, Jeanne de Harlay, marquise de, appointed governess

Talon, Omer, Advocate-General, his speech at a lit de justice, 87–8

Tambonneau, Mme, 283, n

Tarente, princesse de, with Mademoiselle at Champigny, 200

Thianges, Mme de, at St Fargeau, 191–2; in Flanders, 252

Trémouille, Mlle de la, with Mademoiselle at Champigny, 200

Toulouse, comte de, 321

Turenne, maréchal de, defeats frondeurs at Étampes, 114–15; fights against Condé in the faubourg St Antoine, 118–19; defeats Condé at the battle of the Dunes, 206; has a scene with Mademoiselle, 224–5

Val-de-Grâce, convent, The Val-de-Grâce affair: see Anne of Austria

Valois, duc de, his illness and death, 124–6

Vandy, Mlle de, at St Fargeau, 189, 192

Vatel, chef, 233

Vendôme, Cesar, duc de, involved in plot against Richelieu, 15; imprisoned, 16; plots against Cardinal Mazarin, 66

Vendôme, Mlle de, plays with Mademoiselle as a child, 32

Versailles, hunting-box acquired by Louis XIII, 48

Vigeau, Marthe du, 79

Villeroy, maréchal de, 119, 288, 294

Voiture, Vincent, at the hôtel de Rambouillet, 27

Voltaire, quoted, 172, 217, 261, 300

Wales, Prince of: see Charles II, King of England

Waller, Edmund, staying in Paris, 73

Walter, Lucy, mother of James, Duke of Monmouth, 85

Westphalia, Peace of, 90